GLORIOUS CONTENTMENT

GLORIOUS

CONTENTMENT

★ ★ ★ ★ ★ ★

THE GRAND ARMY

OF THE REPUBLIC,

1 8 6 5 – 1 9 0 0

★ ★ ★ ★ ★ ★

STUART McCONNELL

The University of North Carolina Press

Chapel Hill and London

The paper in this book meets the guidelines for permanence
and durability of the Committee on Production Guidelines for
Book Longevity of the Council on Library Resources.

96   95   94   93   92   5   4   3   2   1

Library of Congress Cataloging-in-Publication Data
McConnell, Stuart Charles.
   Glorious contentment : the Grand Army of the Republic,
1865–1900 / by Stuart McConnell.
       p.   cm.
   Includes bibliographical references and index.
   ISBN 0-8078-2025-3 (cloth : alk. paper)
   1. Grand Army of the Republic—History—19th century.
2. United States—History—Civil War, 1861–1865—Veterans.
I. Title.
E462.1.A7M34   1992
973.7'4—dc20   91-50793
                                                         CIP

Portions of chapter 3 appeared earlier, in somewhat different
form, as "Who Joined the Grand Army?: Three Case Studies
in the Construction of Union Veteranhood, 1866–1900," in
*Toward a Social History of the American Civil War:
Exploratory Essays,* ed. Maris A. Vinovskis, pp. 139–70 (New
York: Cambridge University Press, 1990), and are reproduced
here by permission of Cambridge University Press.

For my parents

CONTENTS

ILLUSTRATIONS

PREFACE

This is not a Civil War book, or at least it did not start out as one. I came to the study of the Grand Army of the Republic (GAR) indirectly, through the back channel of community history and through a fascination with the culture of the United States in the Gilded Age. Yet the more deeply I delved into the day-to-day life of the GAR, the largest of all Union veterans' orders, the more I realized how closely connected were the youthful soldiering experiences of these men and the brand of nationalism they came to espouse by the 1890s. Thus, while I originally set out to write about the postwar years, the war experience kept creeping into the narrative in ways I had not anticipated.

It now seems to me that this unexpected development was no accident. The Civil War experience hung over the postwar North in a thousand different ways, which the habitual separation of Civil War scholarship from Gilded Age scholarship has served only to obscure. The standard history of the war, for example, closes with Appomattox, with perhaps some hazy foreshadowings of the Reconstruction South or of subsequent Northern industrialization. The typical Gilded Age study opens by alluding briefly to the great changes brought by the war, then moves on to its real subject (the year 1877, generally considered the last year of Reconstruction, is a favorite starting point). Such a periodization does not allow us to see something that would have been very clear to a Victorian American: the late nineteenth century was a postwar era.

Since we now live in a postwar era of our own, it is perhaps not surprising that scholars have recently begun to tamper with the boundary between wartime and peacetime. Eric Foner's *Reconstruction,* for instance, begins not in 1865 but in 1863, with Lincoln's Emancipation Proclamation. The war narratives of Gerald Linderman and Reid Mitchell both, in different ways, explore the battle experiences of Civil War soldiers by first examining the assumptions that they brought to combat. Gaines Foster's *Ghosts of the Confederacy* is almost entirely concerned with the uses to which Southerners put remembrances of the war. And most of the essays in a recent Civil War social history collection focus less on the fighting than on the war's implications for postwar society.[1]

The essential trend of this scholarship, it seems to me, has been away from questions of what caused the Civil War (a problem that, under the guise of the "avoidable tragedy" argument, preoccupied historians before the 1960s) and toward examinations of the war's effects. Battle narratives based on soldiers' diaries rather than on official war records have almost inevitably shifted the focus of discussion from exegeses of battles to questions of the war's meaning for the ordinary foot soldiers who fought it, and ultimately to a discussion of its long-term effects on those men. By the same token, studies of wartime municipal politics or charity practices are clearly studies of civilians, not of warriors.

Some of the new postwar emphasis, if that is indeed what it is, obviously can be attributed to the growth of social history as an intellectual outlook over the last two decades or so. Social historians in all areas of study have been inclined to focus on ordinary people rather than on leaders, on processes rather than on events, on the subtle connections between historical eras rather than on the radical discontinuities between them. From the standpoint of the social historian, Appomattox may well appear less final than it does to a

conventional military historian.

Aside from changes in methodology, however, we should not discount the influence of another factor in recent historical writing, namely the shadow of the Vietnam War. If the Civil War now appears exceptional for the idealism that both sets of combatants expressed, perhaps it is because the motives of warriors have come to seem more confused and ambivalent. If the experiences of ordinary foot soldiers now seem more important than the campaign plans of generals, it may be because much of the pain of Vietnam has been expressed through the memoirs and novels of its veterans. And if we have finally come to see the Civil War and the Gilded Age as intimately connected, perhaps it is because we now live in a post-Vietnam culture, a culture that I suspect recent events in the Persian Gulf have done little to change.

In the Grand Army of the Republic, we see an earlier group of veterans trying to cope with issues that are as relevant now as they were in 1865: the extent of society's obligation to the poor and injured, the place of war memories in peacetime, the meaning of the "nation" and of the individual's relation to it. By the turn of the century, the GAR had staked out its position on these issues. Although the order continued in existence until its last member died in 1956, it was clearly in decline (both numerically and politically) by the late 1890s. After 1900, the date at which this narrative draws to a close, the GAR served largely as an organization for the promotion of patriotism and the commemoration of Memorial Day.

In its heyday, however, the GAR was a powerful organization whose political might has led most subsequent historians to identify it primarily as a pension lobby or a bloody-shirt Republican club. Both activities, especially the pension agitation, provoked much comment in the 1880s and 1890s and have long been documented beyond any serious doubt. True, some writers have found GAR leaders and posts in support of Democratic policies, and in the absence of concrete data on how veterans actually voted, it has proved fairly easy to reach the unspectacular conclusion that veterans voted for candidates of both political parties who favored their interests. But most studies have ended by corroborating Mary Dearing's early thesis that the Grand Army's political sympathies were Republican from the outset, and unless the views of its national leaders were wildly out of touch with those of the membership there seems little reason to question her judgment (though in this partisan preference the Grand Army was only typical of the Gilded Age electorate at large).[2]

But the partisan politics of the GAR are only part of the story and, particularly after Grant's reelection in 1872, not the most important part. True, some issues of interest to GAR members during that period—pensions, veteran preference in hiring, censorship of school textbooks—can hardly be called apolitical. Yet the overt involvement of the order in electoral politics—endorsing candidates, participating as posts in marches and other campaign events, denouncing political opponents—did not long survive Grant's first term. Instead, the GAR after 1872 wore several masks: fraternal lodge, charitable society, special-interest lobby, patriotic group, political club.

For some veterans, Grand Army membership undoubtedly did mean pensions and partisanship, but it meant other things as well. It would be more accurate to say that Republican voting was only one of a cluster of behaviors in which GAR members engaged, all of which were intimately connected. The meaning of Grand Army "veteran-hood" to members is evident in all of these behaviors, not just in the narrowly partisan activities of founders such as John A. Logan and Richard Oglesby. And even in politics, an analysis of the GAR world-view elucidates at least as much of what members meant by voting Republican as does an analysis that simply writes off the GAR as a cynical interest group. We need to ask, in other words, how Union veterans came to see themselves as constituting an interest.

Thus, while I have not ignored the GAR's obvious Republican partisanship, I have not attempted to duplicate Dearing's exhaustive analysis of elections. Instead, I have tried to cast my net widely, to recapture the social and cultural meaning of Grand Army membership. From partisan origins in 1866, I will argue, the GAR soon foundered and by 1872 was virtually moribund. It revived in the late 1870s as a fraternal order, and by 1890 it had become a powerful lobby for pensions, "correct" history, and a particular brand of American nationalism. I hope I have done justice to the complexity of the Union veterans' worldview, the bundle of attitudes that I have here called their cosmology of Union. At the same time, I have tried to suggest ways in which the Grand Army experience illuminates certain aspects of Gilded Age society outside the post room door. Thus in chapters 2 through 4, I focus on the veterans who belonged to the GAR and on what that membership meant to them. In chapters 5 through 7, I expand the analysis to consider the Union veterans' relations with the noncombatants they called "civilians."

This, then, is as much a book about Gilded Age Americans as it is a book about Union Army veterans. The GAR's pension campaigns of the 1880s, for example, argued for a significant new public attitude toward charity. At the same time, the ways in which the Union veterans remembered the Civil War both shaped and were shaped by a late Victorian culture that emphasized sentiment and high morality. Finally, the aging Grand Army members of the 1890s provided a preservationist model of the American nation that many white, middle-class Northerners found congenial as they faced the serious social upheavals of that decade. The nineteenth-century history of the GAR is a study in microcosm of a nation trying to hold fast to an older image of itself in the face of massive social change.

Any project as lengthy and far-flung as this one involves the aid of many people, only some of whom I can hope to acknowledge here.

My most important debt is to my parents, who gave support to this endeavor from the outset, and especially to my father, who first interested me in history. John Higham was an ideal graduate adviser, offering criticism when needed and not when not. His suggestions, even when I did not take them, made me think harder about the GAR and about American culture in general, and his encouragement has been unflagging. I also would like to thank Ronald Walters for his good advice on revisions, both when he served as a member of my dissertation committee and since that time.

My Claremont colleagues Hal Barron and Lynn Dumenil read the entire book manuscript. I hope that Hal will see some of his influence in the reworked versions of chapters 2 and 3, while Lynn has provided aid at so many points that it is difficult to know where to begin thanking her (perhaps a secret fraternal hailing sign will do). Donald Brenneis, Jeff Charles, David Glassberg, Pieter Judson, Patrick Miller, William Offutt, and Daniel Segal all read chapters of the manuscript and offered useful suggestions. Pieter in particular has been a wonderful partner in those long-winded hallway and office discussions that are the real substance of academic life. Daniel Horowitz provided timely advice during the publication phase. I want to acknowledge the help of all of these colleagues without necessarily implicating them in the finished product. Pitzer College generously provided summer research support in 1988 and 1989.

At the University of North Carolina Press, I would like to thank Ron Maner, Jan McInroy, and especially Lewis Bateman, who probably will long remember the phoenixlike circumstances of the original manuscript's arrival. Much of chapter 3 has appeared previously, in somewhat different form, as "Who Joined the Grand Army?: Three Case Studies in the Construction of Union Veteranhood, 1866–1900," in *Toward a Social History of the American Civil War: Exploratory Essays*, edited by Maris A. Vinovskis. It appears with the permission of Cambridge University Press.

My work on Post 2 of Philadelphia would not have been possible without Bud and Margaret Atkinson, the keepers of the flame at the Philadelphia Camp, Sons of Union Veterans of the Civil War. Not only did they provide access to the collection at the camp's GAR Memorial Hall, they also put me up at their home on more than one research trip to Philadelphia and helped locate photographs. A local history grant from the Pennsylvania Historical and Museum Commission funded portions of my research in 1985; at the PHMC, I would like to thank Carl Oblinger and Matthew Magda, as well as the PHMC Archives and Pennsylvania State Library staffs in Harrisburg.

In Massachusetts, my primary debts are to Mr. A. Dean Sargent of Rockland and Mr. Ken Oakley of Randolph, who were able to locate the records of Post 13 and arrange for me to use them. Captain Frank Tucker of the Massachusetts State House police detail, a former Sons of Union Veterans officer, arranged for me to use the GAR records housed in the Memorial Room of the State House. In addition I would like to thank James Fahey of the Massachusetts War Records Research Military Division, the staffs of the Rockland and Brockton public libraries, Robert Nevins of Brockton, Ken Parsigian, and Shay Mayer.

In Wisconsin, I cannot say enough good things about Richard Zeitlin, Lynn Wolf, and the rest of the staff of the GAR Memorial Hall in Madison. In addition to assisting me with their own collection, they pointed out sources not known to me, made large numbers of photocopies, and were instrumental in contacting archives elsewhere in the state. In Chippewa Falls, I am grateful for the aid of Dolores Beaudette of the Chippewa County Historical Society. Also of assistance were the Chippewa Falls and Eau Claire public libraries, the State Historical Society of Wisconsin in Madison, its area research center at Eau Claire, Katharine Knoepfler, and Kate Offutt.

I would also like to thank David Blight, Jan Graf, Alan Lessoff, Ane Lintvedt, Ted Ownby, Douglas Schoettle, and Michael Sewell, as well as the staffs of the following libraries: the Library of Congress, especially Mary Ison of the Prints and Photographs Division; the Special

Collections Division of the Chicago Public Library; the Oregon State Library, Salem; and the Minnesota Historical Society Research Center, St. Paul, especially Ruth Ellen Bauer.

Finally, the only debt I can never repay is to my greatest creditor, Rebecca, who puts up with a lot.

GLORIOUS CONTENTMENT

CHAPTER 1 PARADE

It was unusually beautiful in the city of Washington on the afternoon of May 23, 1865, when the victorious armies of the Union began assembling to pass in grand review before their commanding officers. Although some of the men had been in federal service for as little as two weeks, others had served through four years of war, and all were itching to return home. Some had not been able to wait and had simply left their regiments upon the cessation of hostilities; they would be classified as deserters and not officially pardoned until eight years later. Others had been mustered out years earlier and now waited at home with the rest of the civilian population. But about 150,000 were still in their ranks for one last great show, and now they lined the side streets near the Capitol, unwieldy agglomerations of blue uniforms gradually being herded into place for the parade up Pennsylvania Avenue.

The officers doing the herding positioned troops for maximum theatrical effect—the normal distance between units was shortened, brass artillery pieces were polished and grouped together, thinned companies were redeployed "for the sake of uniformity," in the words of General George Meade's parade order.[1] Colonel Charles Wainwright of the First New York Light Artillery, an especially fastidious officer, borrowed another officer's sash for the parade and announced to his disappointed troops that "only the most soldierly in appearance" would be chosen to march in the review. "I regretted more than ever not having a trained corps of buglers," Wainwright lamented afterward, "but as I had none I directed them not to play at all."[2] Elsewhere, the Twentieth Maine Volunteers snapped up new issues of clothing and white parade gloves, while the Hundredth Indiana Volunteers, recently arrived from the South, worked to remove years' accumulation of mud from their boots and uniforms.[3]

By 9:00 A.M. every unit was to be organized into ranks and marched to its proper spot off the avenue, ready to wheel into the grand procession as it passed. Some regiments began forming as early as 2:00 A.M., since a later start would have meant that part of the twenty-five-mile column would not have been able to pass the presidential reviewing stand near the White House and reach camps in Maryland and Virginia before nightfall. The thrust of the parade orders was that the column be kept moving. Regiments were not to slow down before the reviewing stand, only mounted officers were to salute, and "ruffles" for the dipping of colors were not to interfere with the continuity of the march music.[4]

Even with such restrictions, the Grand Review eventually would take two days—six hours Tuesday for the Army of the Potomac, six hours Wednesday for the Western armies. Despite the length of the procession, however, the huge crowds lining the avenue never seemed to weary of the passing spectacle. People had begun pouring into the city on Sunday, packing the express trains from New York to the point that they ran hours late and offered only standing room. On Tuesday the crowds began to assemble two hours before the beginning of the parade and filled every available viewing spot. Business in the city was entirely suspended. At the old Penitentiary, even the trial of the Lincoln assassination conspirators was adjourned for two days. "Stands, staging, boxes, tables, chairs, vehicles, lamp-posts, indeed everything that promised a look-out, was crowded to suffocation with eager people," reported the *New York Tribune*.[5] People waved handkerchiefs and flags, cheered favorite regiments, and covered General Custer's horse with so many flowers that the animal panicked and was reined back into the ranks only with difficulty. On Wednesday thousands of spectators overflowed the section of the avenue that was to have been reserved for dignitaries holding grandstand tickets.[6]

The outpouring of enthusiasm for the returning troops was, of course, little different in origin from that which had greeted victorious armies of other wars. But in the American experience up to 1865, nothing like the Grand Review had been seen. The sheer size of the armies involved was new, as was their concentration in a single city. Had all the men under arms at the close of previous American wars been gathered in one place for parade, the assembled host would have been smaller than the one brought together at Washington, a force that itself represented only about 10 percent of the federal troops engaged for some period in the fighting. But in fact soldiers of the earlier wars had assembled for no such final reviews. They had come home in regiments or as individuals, not as armies; generals such as Washington and Scott had said farewell to their officers, but not to their troops en masse. The massing for parade of all the troops in service at the end of a war was unprecedented, and it gave the spectators at Washington some sense of the size of the force about which they had been reading in the newspapers for four years. "The Army of the Potomac is our old acquaintance," commented the *New York Times*, "but the Armies of Georgia and Tennessee few people here had ever seen."[7] Indeed, it must have given many of the men in the ranks the same sense. It was their first opportunity to view the enormity of the organization of which they had been a part.

Lacking an American precedent, newspaper editors resorted to comparing the review with those of Napoleon's armies or those of the Russian troops in Paris in 1814. But there was a difference: This was the volunteer army of a republic. Presumably it represented the armed nation in a way that no imperial or mercenary army could, "fighting men in fighting trim, not plumed nor polished, nor set on hobby-horses, but in the worn paraphernalia of battle, with their engines of death all rusty with mud." These troops, said the *Philadelphia Public Ledger*, "in their plain and unpretending uniforms, may not present so dazzling a show, but 200,000 armed men, attended with all the paraphernalia of war and moving as if by one common impulse can give a better idea of the forces employed in war than any written description."[8] Colonel Stephen Minot Weld, marching with the Fifty-sixth Massachusetts Volunteers, found the scene "splendid. It really seemed as if the statue of the Goddess of Liberty were alive and looking down on us with triumph and pleasure." Lucy Webb Hayes, watching from the congressional grandstand, hoped that foreign dignitaries watching the parade would be impressed with the power of the United States. Captain Allen Geer of the Twentieth Illinois, after viewing the parade and touring the fortifications around the capital city, concluded that "Washington could not now be taken by an invading army of the combined world." And in a refrain that would find favor among Union veterans for the rest of the century, the *Philadelphia North American* asserted that only under democratic institutions could such a mass of armed men be trusted in a capital city. "Is this not," its editor asked, "as great a tribute to free government as was ever paid?"[9]

As the several divisions fell in behind the cavalry and proceeded up the avenue from the Capitol grounds, spectators were struck by the sight of a steady, undulating wave of men streaming toward the White House in tight, regular ranks, sixty abreast. "When I reached the Treasury-building, and looked back, the sight was simply magnificent. The column was compact, and the glittering muskets looked like a solid mass of steel, moving with the regularity of a pendulum," General Sherman remembered later.[10] "It was a glorious sight to look from the Capitol up Pennsylvania avenue," commented the *Philadelphia Inquirer.* "The centre was a moving mass of glistening steel, reflecting the bright rays of the sun, while ever and anon was a tattered banner, or a war-torn guidon, or a bright battle flag. On either hand, forming as it were a living frame work, were the people." An Associated Press reporter thought the mass of uniformed men presented "a grand appearance. . . . Looking up the broad Pennsylvania avenue, there was continuous moving line as far as the eye could reach of National, State, division, brigade, regiment and other flags."[11] All observers routinely complimented the uniform appearance and marching style of the troops. The unprecedented spectacle of thousands of soldiers from all parts of the country—or, to be more precise, all parts of the North—marching as one well-oiled machine was breathtaking. It was more than a collection of local militias; it was, as more than one newspaper put it, "the grand national pageant." The Grand Review was the visual embodiment of a reunified nation.

*Infantry unit nearing the Treasury Building during the Grand Review. Note
the large gap between the unit in the foreground and the one in the background, with spectators walking in between them. Newspaper engravings of
the review tended to eliminate the distances between regiments and to
tighten their ranks. (Library of Congress)*

Yet within the prescribed, orderly form of the march at Washington, several important anomalies belied the predominant image of a
unified nation in arms. In the first place, the adherence to military
parade formalities—that is, to order, discipline, and subordination—
was at best uneven. The tweaking of military formalities was particularly evident in the second day's march of the Western armies,
units that had already acquired the nickname of "Sherman's bummers" or "Sherman's foragers" as a result of the Georgia campaign.

Straggling along with these regiments was a gaggle of mules and pack horses loaded with plunder from the army's sweep through the Confederacy. To the saddles of some of the animals had been strapped pet chickens, billy goats, and even half a dozen raccoons, "which crawled over the dinner kettles and plunder as though they were at home."[12] Captured slaves were paraded alongside some regiments. The soldiers themselves wore uniforms that were "a cross between the regulation blue and the Southern gray," while "their guns were of all designs, from the Springfield rifle, to a cavalry carbine, which each man carried as he pleased."[13] It was as if the privileged private militia companies of the antebellum period and their working-class burlesquers had somehow ended up in the same parade.[14]

As these regiments passed the reviewing stand, many soldiers, disregarding orders to the contrary, began to cheer; when the last units began to move up the avenue, the shouting became general. More serious was the failure of some units to keep up the pace of the parade, which created gaps between corps of as much as half an hour, allowing the crowd to rush into the avenue. "At every interval in the line of march," wrote an appalled reporter for the *Inquirer,* "thousands crowded around the reviewing stand, and only left when the cavalry threatened to ride over them." Between the Ninth and Fifth Corps of the Army of the Potomac, a huge throng broke through the guard near the reviewing stand of President Andrew Johnson "and cheered until he bowed before them." Similar cheers were raised for General Ulysses Grant and Secretary of War Edwin Stanton before guards succeeded in pushing the crowd back so the parade could continue. As the supply trains following the last regiments were moving past the stand late Wednesday afternoon, the crowd again spilled into the street, making it difficult for the wagons to keep up with the troops.[15]

The austere Colonel Wainwright, who had remained in Washington an extra day to see Sherman's army parade, was willing to grant the Western soldiers' "magnificent physique." As a proper soldier, however, he was appalled to find that the pack mules and slaves "interested most of the spectators more than anything else" and moreover that many considered the slovenly Westerners (including the "slouchy" General Logan) better marchers than his own meticulously organized Army of the Potomac. Puzzled, he asked one onlooker—a Miss Woolsey, the daughter of an officer with whom he shared a reviewing box—why she liked Sherman's army better. "She said the Army of the Potomac marched past just like its commander

(Meade), looking neither to the right nor the left, and only intent on

passing the reviewing officer properly," Wainwright reported, "while Sherman's officers and men were bowing on all sides and not half so stiff. I told her she had just paid the greatest compliment to the Army of the Potomac I had heard."[16]

Enlisted men such as Sergeant Theodore Upson and Private Theodore Gerrish were more in sympathy with Miss Woolsey than with Colonel Wainwright. Upson, who had arrived for the parade several days ahead of his Indiana regiment, found the Eastern officers anything but displeased with the Western "bummers." Rather, they were fascinated and demanded to hear tall tales of his exploits. As for the Westerners' marching, "our boys fell into the long swinging step, evry man in perfect time, our guns at a Right Shoulder Shift, and it seemed to me that the men had never marched so well before." The look in their eyes was not insubordination but rather "what one might call a *glory look*." Gerrish, like Wainwright and other Army of the Potomac veterans, noted the "ragged, dirty, and independently demoralized" appearance of Upson and the rest of Sherman's troops. But having been forced to wear dress gloves and maintain closed ranks on Tuesday, "much to our disgust," Gerrish and his comrades of the Twentieth Maine found something appealing in the informality of the "bummers" on Wednesday. "The men chatted, laughed and cheered, just as they pleased, all along the route of the march," he observed. "Our men enjoyed this all very much, and many of them muttered, 'Sherman is the man after all.' "[17]

The Grand Review, in other words, sent a decidedly mixed message about rank and order. To Miss Woolsey, Theodore Gerrish, and others like them, the discipline and uniformity exhibited by the Eastern regiments were suspect qualities. The spontaneity of Sherman's men made them seem more like a crowd of independent "civilians" than an organization of disciplined "soldiers," more like coequals and less like conquerors. The message of the "bummers" was that of a return to peacetime and an end to the antidemocratic features of army life—rank, discipline, subordination. For those who had worried about the militarism of the war years, the familiar appearance of the troops came as a relief. "The man of destiny on horseback was thought to be far more likely at the close of the war to enter the National capital and cross the threshold of the Executive Mansion than a peaceful army from quiet review," commented the *Boston Post*. "Behold all these dangers ended in this magnificent spectacle of peace."[18]

Colonel Wainwright was less sanguine. Following his interview with Miss Woolsey, Wainwright was forced to the reluctant conclusion that her dislike for precision and formality was typical of his countrymen. "No doubt this was one of the main causes of the greater admiration for the Western army," he noted ruefully that evening. "We are not a military people."[19] For Wainwright's type of veteran, in 1865 and in later years, there was more to fear from the disorderly crowds lining Pennsylvania Avenue than from the orderly troops marching along it.

A second defect in the Grand Review's picture of national order, despite its awesome size and scope, was its exclusiveness. For one thing, it obviously included no partisans of the Confederate cause, who needed somehow to be returned to the national body politic. A Union victory parade was hardly the place for such reintegration. Still, the Southern question simmered just below the surface even on the Pennsylvania Avenue reviewing stand, where Sherman refused to shake hands with Stanton because of their differences over the politically charged surrender terms Sherman had offered Confederate general Joseph Johnston's army in North Carolina the previous month.[20] The problem of sectional reintegration would continue to vex the Northerners. Among the Union veterans, in years to come, it would arise over such issues as Confederate monuments, Blue-Gray reunions, and the content of United States history textbooks.

More surprising was the exclusion from the parade of the black Union regiments, some of which had fought a good deal longer than the white units on parade. A number of observers commented on their absence, the *Inquirer* concluding that "by some process it was so arranged that none should be here. . . . They can afford to wait. Their time will yet come."[21] The few blacks in the review marched as parts of "pick and shovel" brigades or were included as comic relief. Two large black soldiers with Sherman's army, for example, were displayed "riding on very small mules, their feet nearly touching the ground." Captured slaves were described as "odd looking 'contrabands' dressed in all the colors that ever adorned Joseph's coat." In the rear of the First Pennsylvania, one such captive, mounted on a solitary Confederate mule, "created much laughter, in which the President and others joined heartily" as he was carried past the reviewing stand.[22] Neither the black former slave nor the free black soldier was to be the hero of this national pageant; instead, each was relegated a secondary, rather uneasy position within it. The exclusion

The reviewing stand for the Grand Review. President Andrew Johnson is visible in the front row, third from the left of the post marking the center of the stand. General William T. Sherman, who, while on the stand, publicly declined to shake the hand of Secretary of War Edwin Stanton, is just to the right of the same post. (Library of Congress)

of blacks from the celebration was a clear message about the sort of Union the white veterans felt they had preserved.

The others who watched from the sidewalks—women, children, men who had never enlisted—were obvious enough exclusions under the circumstances. But in May 1865 the question of the Union veteran's future relationship to them and to other "civilians" was still an open one. Was he still the privileged savior of the nation, to be honored in perpetuity by those who had not taken up arms? If so, then the privileged were a peculiarly narrow group: white, male, largely rural in origin, and mostly (considering the makeup of the armies) of British, Irish, or German extraction. Or was he to disappear quietly into the society from which he had emerged in 1861, a world of local and state allegiances in which "the grand national pageant" would be just a fond memory? Might he become again a simple "civilian," with no more claim on the national government than his neighbor?

The Grand Review offered no clear answers to these questions, but an important clue lay in the inscription on an enormous and much-discussed banner that hung from the Capitol on the day of the parade: "The only national debt we can never pay is the debt we owe the victorious Union Soldiers." The words were prophetic. Although the veterans would not press their special claim to national privilege for almost fifteen years, that claim, in the form of pension demands, would become one of the hottest political issues of the late nineteenth century. In 1865 the writing was already on the nation's most prominent wall. To the perceptive eye, so was the response of the future "civilian" opposition: "I could not help wondering," mused Charles Wainwright after viewing the Capitol banner during Tuesday's march, "whether, having made up their minds that they *can never* pay the debt, they will not think it useless to try."[23]

Disorder and exclusion detracted from the facade of national unity, but a third force was also a factor—that of localism. True, the national state was stronger in 1865 than it had ever been. During the war the central government had instituted a temporary income tax, issued $450 million in greenbacks, and organized the country's first military draft, while millions of Northerners had served in the army or in such national organizations as the United States Sanitary Commission. Yet recent studies have shown how fundamentally limited the national state remained in spite of wartime pressures and how localistic was the frame of reference of the Northerners who staffed the new organizations. Though they fought to save the Union, they also fought to save Portland, or Indianapolis, or Jacksonville.[24]

Both in Washington and in the country at large, civilians stressed the heroics of state regiments rather than those of the federal armies as a whole. The *Philadelphia Inquirer*, for example, said of the Washington review that "every Pennsylvanian here has felt his heart swell with pride, for no other State could boast of as many officers and men in the ranks of the laurel-crowned host." Along the parade route, especially between Fifteenth and Seventeenth streets, individual states had set up their own sections of grandstand, hung with such mottoes as "Massachusetts Greets the Country's Defenders" and "Connecticut Greets all who Bravely Fought, and Weeps for those who Fell." The more important welcome, said the *Boston Post*, was yet to come, in the veterans' home cities and towns: "Their reception at home will touch their hearts more tenderly than any they have participated in yet, for here they will look into eyes that have been watching long for them, and catch the sound of voices whose familiarity has been invaded by an absence of years."[25]

For most soldiers it was a matter of two or three weeks between the Grand Review and the "tender receptions" of home: a tedious

wait in camp outside the District of Columbia, a train ride to the
dispersal point, a formal discharge, a solitary ride home. In many
cases the veteran's return was not marked by public ceremonies at
all, and even the celebrations that did take place usually generated
limited public interest and emphasized images of localism at least as
much as those of Union. Sergeant Upson remembered his regiment's
welcome thusly: "When we reached Indianapolis the women of the
City had a good breakfast ready for us. Govermer [*sic*] Morton made
us a grand good speech of welcome and gave us some excellent advice
which I hope we shall all take to heart. We went to our old Quarters
in Camp Morton. A few days later we were mustered out of the
Service of the United States. Each received an Honerable [*sic*] Discharge and again we were private citizens."[26]

In smaller and more distant cities, the soldiers were welcomed
back with even less fanfare. In the northern Wisconsin settlement of
Eau Claire, for example, no notice at all had been taken of the
national march at Washington, possibly because so few local volunteers were involved in it. When most of the local veterans seemed to
have returned home, one Eau Claire editor proposed a picnic for
them, but nothing came of it. Another local editor suggested that
every county in Wisconsin spend $2,000 on a war monument, but the
Eau Claire Free Press declared that spending on such "a ghostly pile"
would be wasteful.[27] Instead, the townspeople—many of whom, in
such unsettled territory, were strangers to the returning veterans—
watched the discharged soldiers slip back into town in ones and twos.
They were, the *Free Press* editor said, "quiet, unobtrusive men. . . .
They are, 'tis true, stern looking men, and pass along our streets, with
a gloomy melancholy, particularly the disciplined soldiers, claiming
no immunity, asking no applause, and seemingly unconscious of the
great service they have rendered." The main public tribute to the Eau
Claire returnees was a dinner and an address on "Union," given as
part of a grander-than-usual Fourth of July celebration.[28]

In Boston, the major civic event was a procession on June 1, a fast
day in memory of Abraham Lincoln. In this parade the veterans were
one unit among many as they joined the police, fire companies, and
civic societies in a somber march designed more to express a sense of
public loss than to celebrate a victory. Although Massachusetts veterans were arriving in town by the carload, they were dispersing just
as quickly. "Almost silently they pass through our streets," noted the
editor of the *Boston Post*. The city of Boston contented itself with a

banquet for the Thirty-third Massachusetts at Faneuil Hall, the mayor explaining that the veterans "after surprising their enemies by means and deeds unknown in the annals of war . . . had to-day by their arrival unannounced surprised their friends, who could not therefore give them the reception they would have been glad to have given."[29]

To be sure, some cities, New York and Philadelphia among them, staged major welcomes for the returning regiments. But like the procession in Boston, the events were more civic than national. The June 10 review of the troops in Philadelphia, where a rainstorm was enough to keep many spectators away, was typical. Respectable bodies of troops from six regiments were on hand for the parade down Broad Street, along with smaller detachments from other units. Still, the showing of veterans was not as large as it might have been, since most of these soldiers, unlike the troops at Washington, had been mustered out of service and were under no compulsion to turn out for a long march on a wet afternoon. The 116th Pennsylvania Volunteers, for instance, paraded only 65 of the 123 men who had returned from the war. "Many of the men resided in the country and had left for their homes," commented the *Inquirer*.[30] Some local boosters were worried lest the relatively small turnout mislead other communities as to the strength of Philadelphia's patriotism. "Our people will be disappointed in not being able to extend their grateful welcomes to a larger number of their brave defenders," fretted the *Philadelphia Public Ledger*, "and the strangers who happen to witness the reception will form a very erroneous idea of what Philadelphia has done in the way of furnishing men for the war."[31]

The regiments that did parade in Philadelphia exemplified the local and personal way in which volunteers had been recruited. Usually regiments had been formed by men living in a particular locality, occasionally by men of a single nationality or those engaged in a single profession. Thus in the Philadelphia parade marched the Corn Exchange Regiment, recruited from the men working in that institution. There was the Scott Legion, composed of men who had fought in the Mexican War; there were the predominantly Irish 116th Pennsylvania Volunteers and the stately 114th Pennsylvania Zouaves, "one of the best drilled regiments in the service, and many of its officers are scions of our first families." But most regiments on parade were distinguished chiefly by their identification with the city of Philadelphia. The parade was led not by General George Meade but by delegations of firemen from each of the city's brigades, a brass

band, and the long-established First City Troop, "commanded by
their smiling cornet, Congressman Randall."[32]

Even when national figures were lauded, it was from the local point of view. General Meade, a member of a well-to-do Philadelphia family, was the primary beneficiary of such treatment. Meade, said the *Public Ledger,* was "second to no other general than Grant." Although the newspaper conceded a place for Generals Sherman, Thomas, and Sheridan, it contended that "no well-informed man, who bears fully in mind the remoter history of the war, as well as its more recent passages, can say that Meade is not at least the *equal* of either [*sic*]." As for Meade's most memorable victory, the *Philadelphia Evening Bulletin* wrote: "Gettysburg was a Pennsylvania battle; it saved Pennsylvania from devastation, and Harrisburg and Philadelphia from capture, pillage and perhaps destruction."[33] Despite the national scope of the war, public identification with the victors was primarily local.

When all was said and done, however, the soldiers on parade would remember the national spectacle of the Grand Review, not the distractions of disorder, sectionalism, or localism. To Sergeant Rice Bull of New York, it was "a proud day for all of us, and the Review was a fitting ending of our long service"; to Sergeant John Bloodgood of Pennsylvania, the review was "an occasion long to be remembered"; to Private Gerrish of Maine, "when we fell into line that morning we were as fine a looking [*sic*] body of troops as were ever mustered upon the continent." The night after the review, soldiers from two divisions went so far as to reenact the review spontaneously in camp, using candles from the quartermaster: "There was scarcely a commissioned officer present," recalled Robert Tilney, a clerk in the Fifth Corps adjutant's office. "The drum corps and bands turned out with the columns *en masse,* and the men marched to the cadenced step and in as perfect an order as if on review. . . . I would go a long way to see such a sight again." Years later, more than one veteran would list the Grand Review among the most significant events of his war career.[34]

Nonveterans, too, would recall the Grand Review fondly when they thought of the war. For thirty years after the Washington event, every major soldiers' reunion, or "encampment," made some attempt to recreate the pageantry of that day, and it was a rare reunion parade that did not elicit from some observer an explicit comparison with the Washington review of 1865. A reporter at the national veterans' encampment at Boston in 1890, for example, called a parade there "the greatest military pageant that has taken place in America since the grand parade in Washington after the close of the War of the Rebellion." A similar procession at Washington in 1892 provoked Vice President Levi P. Morton to comment: "Your march to-day and to-morrow will recall to you, as it will to us, the great review when Grant ranged himself by the side of the President of the United States, when Meade saluted for the veterans of the East, and Sherman for those of the West, and when the light that fell upon the dome of the Capitol was flashed back by the sword of Sheridan."[35] Indeed, when Bret Harte came to contemplate the soldiers who had not survived the war, the Grand Review was his chosen metaphor:

> And so all night marched the nation's dead,
> With never a banner above them spread,
> Nor a badge, nor a motto brandished;
> No mark—save the bare uncovered head
> Of the silent bronze Reviewer;
> With never an arch save the vaulted sky;
> With never a flower save those that lie
> On the distant graves—for love could buy
> No gift that was purer or truer.[36]

In short, the Grand Review offered a startling and unprecedented vision of national unity, albeit a less than perfect one. In each regiment, in each town, in the life of each soldier, the standardization and homogenization of the Union Army experience collided with stubborn and important centrifugal tendencies in American society. Order versus disorder, nationalism versus localism, the self-discipline of the Army of the Potomac versus the self-expression of the "bummers"—all were themes destined to be played out over the next thirty years across the American North.

For the Union veteran, the tensions between these forces would persist well beyond the muster-out, as he labored to adjust to "civilian" society. To be a "veteran" in the wake of the Grand Review was to be identified with words like *nation, army, rank, order,* and *discipline.* Yet in civilian life, there were other pulls on the ex-soldier's allegiance. "Veteran" was only one role among many. A former soldier might easily think of himself primarily as "Westerner," "Philadelphian," "farmer," "Protestant," "father," "Irishman," or any of a thousand other potential identities before he thought of himself as a "veteran." To define what it meant to be a Union veteran, and to

explain that identity to nonveterans, would be the task of the largest
and most influential of the new ex-soldiers' organizations, the Grand Army of the Republic (GAR).

The meaning of membership for the veterans who joined the GAR will be the first concern here. Between the order's birth in 1866 and its apogee in the 1890s, its members developed a cosmology with something to say about the most mundane details of everyday life: what a veteran wore, what he drank (or did not drink), with whom he associated (and with whom he did not), which holidays he celebrated, whose hardware store he patronized. It was also a cosmology of nation, of Union, and it prescribed duties for nonveterans as well: liberal pensions, "loyal" textbooks, reverence for the flag. The various strands of the GAR worldview illuminate its concept of "nation" during a period in which the meaning of that term was still in lively dispute.

The implication is by no means that the GAR's version of the nation was the only one propounded during the Gilded Age or that everyone subscribed to it. By the 1890s many civilians and more than a few veterans viewed it as dated, distasteful, exclusionary, or even dangerous. But in most cases the dissenters were reacting in terms of an argument already molded by years of Grand Army agitation. While they approached the issue of national identity from more parochial concerns (a desire to increase tariff revenues, for example, or a need to ease local poor-relief burdens), the very origins of the GAR were bound up with the concept of "nation." The veterans, everyone agreed, had saved the Union. And although the Grand Army was hardly the only organization to issue pronouncements on the nature of the Union, it wrestled early with the issue and was in a uniquely advantageous position to do so.

Just as important, in the thirty-five years between the Grand Review and the turn of the century, the order built the political muscle to make itself heard. With a membership larger than that of all other Union veterans' groups combined, with a post in almost every Northern town, with the aura of the Union victory still glowing behind it, the GAR was perhaps the single most powerful political lobby of the age. By 1900 the electorate had chosen only one postwar president who was not a GAR member, and Union Army pensions were consuming one federal tax dollar of every three.

But this story is not only, or even predominantly, one about veterans. For if the ex-soldiers had to struggle to construct the idea of "veteran," the society they rejoined had to reckon with the impact of a war that had involved nearly every citizen, killing more than 600,000 of them (360,000 Union soldiers, 258,000 Confederates). In the North, at least 2 million men out of a total population of 22 million had served at some time in the Union armies. In the South, 750,000 out of a total nonslave population of about 5.5 million had served. These figures represented 8.9 percent of the total population of the United States in 1860; the survivors of both armies tabulated by the Census Bureau in 1890 still represented 2.3 percent of the population at that late date. It was hard to find an American of the Civil War generation who did not know someone who had been killed or wounded in the fighting.[37]

The experience of the war touched all spheres of culture. In literature, Ambrose Bierce, Henry James and other writers spun stories that recalled the war, while armies of penny-a-line journalists specialized in "tales of camp and battle" for general circulation magazines and newspapers. Noted generals were commissioned to write best-selling memoirs or analyses of particular battles. In music, the period produced a flood of sentimental odes and transcriptions of war songs meant for singing in the parlor. In architecture, it saw the construction of public monuments ranging in size from modest stones in small-town cemeteries to mammoth markers such as the arch in Brooklyn's Grand Army Plaza and the 265-foot Soldiers' and Sailors' Monument in Indianapolis. In politics, Republicans continued to wave the "bloody shirt" until well into the 1890s, a practice more easily comprehended when one realizes that even in 1890, one of every ten eligible voters was a Civil War veteran.[38]

More pervasive than any of the cultural productions was the day-to-day participation by hundreds of thousands of veterans and civilians in an ongoing conversation about the implications of the war for postwar society. Sometimes their discourse was political, as in arguments over the appropriate level of pension expenditures. Sometimes it took the form of symbolic acts: the military parade, the Memorial Day service, the monument dedication, the nostalgic Civil War "campfire" entertainment. And sometimes, especially in the 1890s, it was more diatribe than discourse, as the veterans tried to prescribe an older vision of the nation for an impatient and burgeoning industrial state. Through all of these devices, the men who had fought the war on the Union side first explained to themselves what it meant to be veterans, then tried to tell civilians what it meant to belong to the nation the war had preserved.

The parade at war's end presented the veterans as indistinguishable units in a national mass, over which was laid the hurrah of

national approval. In the mythology woven around the parade later, the veterans stood for the ideal self of the nation—orderly, self-sacrificing, uniform. Yet the Grand Review also showed veterans in another aspect: casual, disorderly "citizen-soldiers," tied as closely to the localities from which they had been recruited as to the federal government. As they broke camp for the last time in early June at dozens of dispersal points across the North, they took with them the new experience of federal military service. They also took with them a welter of older, particularistic attachments to region, race, religion, class, ethnic group—and, even more basically, to self—that the national pageantry of the Grand Review could camouflage but not erase.

CHAPTER **2** RANK

Once the parades were over, the ex-soldiers tried to settle back into what they hoped would be peaceful civilian lives. At first the task was complicated not only by the economic strains typical of most postwar periods—destroyed property, high unemployment, inflation—but by a political situation that threatened at any minute to break into renewed fighting. In March 1867, a Congress dominated by Radical Republicans passed the Tenure of Office Act in order to curb the patronage powers of President Andrew Johnson and block his conservative Reconstruction policy. When Johnson attempted to remove Secretary of War Edwin Stanton without congressional consent in August, Radicals moved to impeach the president. All through the winter of 1867–68 the country was on

edge, with rumors of coups and countercoups flitting through the
national capital.

The Union veterans played a small role in the impeachment drama. At the height of the crisis, some Radical members of Congress surreptitiously armed small groups of veterans as a precaution against the intrigues of Johnson. Meanwhile, former soldiers from across the North telegraphed their willingness to return to Washington to prevent their recent enemies from, as they saw it, stealing with the ballot what they had lost with the bullet. It is no wonder that some civilians expressed fears of a veteran "Praetorian guard" or that when the Grand Army organized in these years, it organized as a secret society.[1]

With Johnson's acquittal by the Senate in May 1968, and Ulysses Grant's sweeping victory in the fall presidential election, the crisis passed. Politics returned to its normal channel, and before long the country ceased to regard the former Union soldiers as significantly different from the rest of the citizenry. For the veterans themselves, however, the transition from wartime to peacetime did not end so neatly. After years on the sea of battle, it took time to find their social, political, and cultural land legs. In the spring and summer of 1865 they had been mustered out of the army, a national organization predicated on discipline, hierarchy, and the use of force. Now they were expected to become part of a localistic civilian world that professed individualism, democracy, and peace.

The contrast should not be overdrawn, since the distinction between military and civilian forms of order was hardly clear-cut. Many Union regiments, for example, had been locally recruited and had insisted on electing their own officers. Moreover, while soldiers had lived the ranked life, they also had undergone a leveling process in which every man wore a uniform and operated under a more or less uniform code of behavior. Though the army had been distinguished by a formal hierarchy, it also had created "the boys in blue," an undifferentiated identity to which all veterans, regardless of rank, could subscribe. At the same time, the nominally egalitarian civil society of the postwar years had hierarchies of its own that marked an individual almost as clearly as if he had been issued a military rank.

Still, the Union veterans of 1865, like their Confederate counterparts, had lived for several years under a form of social organization essentially different from that which they had left and to which they returned. Insofar as they had absorbed military forms, they had absorbed a model of order at variance with that of civil society. In organizing themselves as "veterans," the men of the Union Army first needed to decide whether any aspects of the military model were worth preserving, perhaps even worth imposing upon those who had remained at home.

At first, nothing military seemed likely to survive demobilization. The regular army quickly dwindled to a tiny fraction of the size it had attained by Appomattox, while in popular accounts the Union volunteers were characterized chiefly by the speed with which they discarded the sword in favor of the plow.[2] General John Alexander Logan, as able a practitioner of Victorian spread-eagle oratory as existed among the veterans, compared the peaceful state of the disbanded Northern soldiery favorably with the state of postwar republican Rome. "No outbreak, no revolution, no disaster of any magnitude has followed the segregation of these million warriors," he told a gathering of veterans in 1869. "They sought their homes with joyful hearts and tuneful voices. There were no tears of mourning over the cast-off trappings and habiliments of strife. The hand grown cunning in the use of arms applied itself to the axe, the hammer, the loom and spade."[3] While some civilians continued to denounce military rule in the South as "despotism," others expressed thanks that the war had produced no man on horseback more menacing than Ulysses Grant.[4]

The Northern soldiers themselves showed little inclination to dwell on the war. The average Union veteran of 1865 was a former farmer, mechanic, or laborer approximately twenty-six years of age—not old, certainly, but not so young as to have been without either a steady occupation before the war or an immediate need for one afterward.[5] The war had provided a paycheck, but also an interruption. As these men settled back into their hometowns or moved west to new places, the associations of wartime faded. Many of the earliest Union veterans' organizations remained limited to ex-officers, while the more broadly based Grand Army of the Republic experienced a precipitous drop in membership in the 1870s, reaching a low of 26,899 in 1876. Major newspapers catering to veterans were not founded until the late 1870s or early 1880s; the few in existence in the immediate postwar years (such as the *Soldier's Friend* of New York and the *Great Republic* of Washington, D.C.) disappeared. And among prominent veterans, the most notable characteristic of war memoirs in the 1870s was their absence. Especially when compared with the experience of ex-Confederates or with the bitter disillusionment and massive social upheavals that followed later demobilizations (notably after World War I), the return of Union veterans to civil life was smooth.[6]

One reason for the relatively easy transition seems obvious: The dislocations of the war were largely glossed over by the exalted place that the event occupied in Northern postwar culture. As Thomas Leonard aptly puts it, "The value seemed so much greater than the price. . . . Different images expressed the pervasive sentiment that the war had unlocked American energies and produced a glorious period of national growth. Smoking factory chimneys, rails across the continent, free settlers in the West—that was the popular iconography."[7] If there was disillusionment in the North, it remained well below the surface, which argues against the facile assumptions that all wars are assimilated into postwar culture in the same way or that returning veterans always face the same adjustments. Among Northerners at least, the Civil War was unlike World War I or the Vietnam conflict in that it seemed to have achieved the declared aims of the national leaders.

The war's place in the popular estimation as a successful crusade allowed Union veterans to assume the role of savior, and they did not hesitate to do so. "I say the Army and Navy maintained our liberty; they have done more . . . they preserved for humanity the Republican form of government; they elevated the country to a high dignity," General Daniel Sickles told a GAR banquet at Albany in 1879. "With all due reverence we make the comparison," reported one committee to the 1885 national encampment, "when we claim the loyalty of the comrade of the Grand Army should be as unsullied as was the purity and piety of the Christian martyrs."[8] By the end of the century such rhetoric would wear thin for many listeners, but in the North of the 1870s it went largely unchallenged.

Another reason for the apparent ease of the transition may have been that individual combatants tended to understand the war as an accretion of local actions by small units of known individuals: the fight in the Peach Orchard at Gettysburg, the Bloody Angle at Spotsylvania, the Cornfield at Antietam. When added up, these actions might be understood as parts of broad strategies, but they were also comprehensible as individual struggles with meanings of their own. One device of remembrance that became popular in the 1890s, the "personal war sketch," allowed each veteran to give his own service record and to recount the war from his own standpoint—actions participated in, wounds received, striking incidents observed. The narratives were then collected and preserved in ornate bindings.[9] When discussing the war with each other—"Fighting Them Over," as one newspaper column devoted to such reminiscences was titled— the veterans also tended to the particular. "H. O. Martin, Battery A, 1st Ohio L.A., Akron, Ohio, referring to the question of Comrade Doyle, Fleming, Mo., says he thinks it was his battery that Gen. Thomas had in the works on the hill above the bridge at Peach Tree Creek," begins one such exchange. "The battery belonged to New- ton's Second Division, Fourth Corps. It did very effective work during the engagement."[10] Unlike the trench-bound, continuously bom- barded soldiers of World War I, who experienced the war as some- thing impersonal and meaningless with a life of its own, the Union veterans were able to grasp their own positions in the overall drama.[11] Because the war was understood through the actions of small units, usually recruited from the same locality, it represented less than a complete break from the experience of peacetime.

The discarding of the sword is, however, never an easy matter. As Eric Leed reminds us, soldiers in war undergo a passage with marked similarities to what Victor Turner and other anthropologists have called "liminality": the formal separation of an individual from his accustomed place in society, the ritual fixing of the individual as a "passenger" between settled states or conditions, followed by post- liminal or incorporation rites welcoming the individual back into the group.[12] In the intermediate stage of this process, the liminal state, the individual undergoes experiences ordinarily denied him in the group. In the case of war, the most important of such experiences is freedom from ordinary social restraints on killing, though others may also be involved—the temporary submergence of the individual sol- dier in the mass, for example.

During the liminal passage the veteran may also be able to view "normal" society and its institutions as an outsider or a stranger might, in ways not possible for those remaining within it. Knowledge is gained not through any manipulation of language but through immersion in a dramatic event with its own structure; the experience is not integrative but disjunctive, producing a discontinuous sense of self.[13] Perhaps that is why veterans' war diaries such as those of Theodore Gerrish and Theodore Upson ended with muster-out day. The dramatic event they narrated was seen to have reached its conclusion.

Unlike liminality, however, the passage through the world of war typically does not end neatly with rites of return. If such ceremonies

take place at all, they are brief, sporadic, and incomplete (the victory
parade at Washington comes to mind), leaving the warrior only partially reintegrated into civil society.[14] The incomplete readoption of
returning veterans at war's end has been known to lead to disorienta-
tion among ex-soldiers and often to violence directed against civilians who have not shared the prolonged liminality of war. In politics it
has sometimes led to withdrawal from what are seen as strange and
petty "civilian" quibbles or, more ominously, to movements for independent "soldiers' parties."

Incidents of violence by soldiers did occur in the wake of the rapid
demobilization of 1865. In Washington, soldiers not yet mustered out
were reported to have attacked "disreputable houses and tippling
houses, occupied by both colored and white persons, indiscrimi-
nately attacking the inmates, driving them away, breaking up their
furniture, helping themselves to liquors and edibles and committing
various outrages. The rioters showed particular animosity against
colored persons, who were severely beat and robbed." Violence also
was directed at citizens in New York, and in Madison, Wisconsin,
where veterans enraged by the failure of the city to pay them bonus
money attempted to set fire to the town.[15]

Again, such actions were mild in comparison with the carnage that
has followed twentieth-century wars. In post-World War I Britain,
for example, rioting between soldiers and civilians involved thousands of troops and killed at least one hundred people, while in the
United States the race and class warfare of the summer of 1919 was
notoriously bloody.[16] Even though the alienation of veterans from
civilians in 1865 was not as severe as it might have been, the ex-
soldiers remained, to varying degrees, estranged from those who had
not enlisted. They had shared a world in which the values of peacetime society had been stood on end. Violence had been justified,
social distinctions leveled, individual preference submerged in discipline and order, death experienced as a daily occurrence. Then they
had come back to a society that by and large expected them to pick up
where they had left off, as if the strange passage of war had not been a
reality.

The question facing ex-soldier and civilian alike after the Grand
Review was whether wartime values had any applicability to peacetime society. To put it another way, the issue was what the war had
meant, which components of the military experience were to be
integrated with the existing structures of meaning among civilians
and which were to be smothered or forgotten. In a more conventional

liminal passage the problem does not arise, since the warrior finds a culturally defined place waiting for him. The experience of war is not smuggled back into peacetime but remains truly a foreign country, a netherworld, a place with a boundary fixed by ritual. It does not imply social or cultural change. For the veteran reentering the fluid society that was Victorian America, however, the question was very much alive. Probably no ex-soldier in 1865 could have said with any certainty what the diffuse military experience of a million Northern veterans "meant" for the postwar nation. But all would have agreed that it meant something.

The missing element at war's end was an explanatory myth: a story about the place of the Union veteran in the newly restored Union and, at a deeper level, a story about the new Union itself. In 1865 the story of the war was scattered across the country in a million personal narratives. By 1880 it would come together in the powerful explanatory myths of the Union veterans' organizations, most prominently in those of the Grand Army of the Republic. Through a close look at all aspects of life in this large and influential order—recruitment of members, ritualized behavior, political activity, shared beliefs—one can trace the historical construction of a Union veteran cosmology in the three decades following the GAR's birth in 1866. First, however, it is necessary to look at how the veterans created their organization, deciding as they did so what to keep and what to discard from their military experience.

Mythical Origins

The legendary version of the founding of the Grand Army of the Republic goes something like this: In 1866 a gentle former Union Army surgeon, Dr. Benjamin Franklin Stephenson, and several of his former comrades in arms were pining for the camaraderie of camp. Envisioning a broad brotherhood of veterans, Stephenson created the GAR as a fraternal organization suffused with brotherly love and dedicated to the relief of fellow veterans. When he formed the first local post, at Decatur, Illinois, in April of that year, he found ready support. A second post was formed at Springfield, Illinois, fledgling soldiers' organizations in other northwestern states adopted the GAR ritual and constitution, Eastern soldiers joined following a September mass meeting at Pittsburgh, and late in the year the first GAR convention, or "national encampment," met at

Indianapolis. Although the order was usurped by conniving Republican politicians in the 1870s and suffered severe reverses, it subsequently recovered and went on to a long career of civic usefulness,
celebrating Memorial Day, promoting benevolence, and "inculcating
patriotism."[17] This charming narrative is captured by the modest
national GAR monument in Washington, on which kindly Dr. Stephenson gazes down upon tableaux representing the order's three
founding principles: Fraternity (a soldier receiving succor on the
battlefield), Charity (a widow and orphans), and Loyalty (a soldier
and a sailor with flag).

The real story is more complicated, and much more interesting.
Mary Dearing's definitive early research established that whatever
Stephenson may have said about it publicly, he undoubtedly envisioned his new veterans' group as a tool to further the political
ambitions of two Illinois Republicans, General John A. Logan and
Governor Richard Oglesby. These two men, firmly on the Radical side
of the gathering storm over Reconstruction policy, were the political
movers behind an organization to which Stephenson's professions of
benevolence and charity lent a nonpolitical veneer. Actually, it seems
likely that Stephenson conceived of the GAR as *both* a charitable and
a political organization, there being no necessary incompatibility
between the two, but the political side of the order was not proclaimed publicly. In any case, the new order worked effectively for
the Grant-Colfax ticket during the campaign of 1868.[18]

To soldier-politicians like Logan, Oglesby, and Norton P. Chipman,
the ambitious Republican politico who served as Logan's "adjutant
general" (secretary) in 1868–69, the GAR was a voting machine,
which they fondly hoped to ride to political prominence. Logan, who
was elected to the top Grand Army office of "commander-in-chief" in
1868–69, had been active in national politics even while serving as a
major general during the war. Eventually he would serve the Republicans in both houses of Congress, comanage Andrew Johnson's impeachment trial, and run for vice president with James G. Blaine
in 1884. Chipman, a Washington patent and pension attorney, was
equally active in Radical Republican politics. A mingler in the capital
city's business circles, Chipman would go on from the GAR to hold
important positions (including secretary and representative to Congress) in the District of Columbia territorial government under the
favor of successive Republican administrations. Other early Grand
Army officers had similar ambitions.[19]

For such men, the maintenance of a tight national organization was

General John Alexander Logan, prime mover behind the early Grand Army of the Republic, comanager of Andrew Johnson's impeachment in the House, and Republican vice presidential candidate in 1884. (Library of Congress)

vital; accordingly, they set out to whip the GAR into fighting shape. "Previous military experience has taught the value of consolidated effort," Logan told the members in one of his first general orders as commander-in-chief. "Discipline lies at the foundation of all enterprises which look for their success to the cooperation of individuals, scattered over large territory. Orders must be promptly obeyed and the rules and regulations strictly enforced if we are to hope for any good to result from our efforts."[20] He appointed special "assistant inspectors general" responsible to him alone, spies from headquarters who could provide "valuable information" that would enable officers to pressure subordinates for reports, reorganize posts whose rosters had fallen into disrepair, and disband posts that were beyond hope. Logan asked for complete rosters of all local Grand Army posts and their officers, information that, he said, "would be of great service at these headquarters." Although he phrased his order in terms of administrative efficiency, the partisan political motive behind Logan's national name-gathering was apparent to everyone. "Anybody," wrote former Indiana department adjutant Oliver Wilson in 1905, "can read between these lines the purpose."[21] As a crony of Indiana's Radical war governor, Oliver P. Morton, Wilson certainly knew whereof he wrote.

On paper, the organization that Logan and Chipman hoped to streamline looked much like the army they had just left. Stephenson had created an organization with three levels: post, department (the Union Army's term for its administrative divisions), and national. The post was the basic unit of the order. No veteran could be a member of the GAR except as a member of a post, and almost all posts represented a specific town or city. To move between posts required a "transfer"; to leave the GAR required an "honorable discharge"; to absent oneself from meetings required a "leave of absence." The meeting place, or post room, was set up as a model army camp. Its doors were "outposts" manned by "sentries" who challenged visitors to give the secret password. Inside, the post commander and his staff, perched on chairs atop raised platforms, issued the orders that kept the post running. Offenses against decorum were punished by formal "courts-martial."

Each post commander reported to a department commander, whose jurisdiction covered an entire state (in the South and West sometimes more than one state). The annual department encampment, composed partly of elected delegates and partly of past officers, chose department officers and set policy for the year. The department commander, advised by an elected cabinet or "council of administration," ran the department between encampments by issuing "general orders." He and his subordinates reported to counterparts at the national level, who issued orders of their own and reported to the national encampment—the sovereign body of the order, which, like the department encampment, was made up partly of elected delegates and partly of honorary ones. If the national officers had their way, they would soon head an organization of self-governing but disciplined camps, formed into uniform departments and ready to march as one national army.

What such an army could accomplish when properly drilled was already apparent to these political officers from their experience in marshaling the massive "soldier vote" for Lincoln in 1864 and Grant in 1868. Military discipline meant success at the polls. But the military model of order was attractive to others as well. During the war, even Ralph Waldo Emerson had made the discovery that "war organizes," while other Northern intellectuals had rethought their ideas about force and discipline. Later, Edward Bellamy would predicate his famous utopia on an "industrial army," while Oliver Wendell Holmes would glorify the soldier who "throw[s] away his life in obedience to a blindly accepted duty, in a cause which he little understands, in a plan of campaign of which he has no notion, under tactics of which he does not see the use."[22] It is impossible to say whether many of the Grand Army's early recruits shared such sentiments, but they could hardly have overlooked the new order's quasi-military orientation. If the army was only one model for postwar society, it was a model that the GAR organizational structure explicitly prescribed.

Logan and Chipman's task of energizing that structure proved to be a formidable one, however, for just as the Grand Review of 1865 gave a misleading impression of national unity, the Grand Army of 1868 offered a deceptive picture of organizational coherence. When Adjutant Chipman took over at "national headquarters" in 1868, he discovered that he had inherited a mess from the bungling management of Dr. Stephenson and the first GAR commander-in-chief, General Stephen Hurlbut. "The records which came into my hands furnish no evidence of there having been reciprocal relations kept up between the Posts and Departments and National Headquarters," an appalled Chipman reported to the 1869 national encampment at Cincinnati. "Indeed, it would appear that Posts and Departments must have organized largely upon their own responsibility, and many of them appear not to have made any reports or returns to headquarters during the administration of General Hurlbut."[23]

The problem went beyond administration, particularly in the West and outside the cities. From most Western states Chipman considered himself lucky to get reports at all, and even those he did receive were almost useless. In Illinois, for instance, the department commander wrote "that he has established headquarters at Chicago, and has entered vigorously upon the work of reorganization; has kept a clerk constantly employed in opening communications with the Posts, and has expended considerable money in that direction; but with all his efforts, he writes that he has been unable to obtain returns from more than six Posts in the State, and yet there is, perhaps, no doubt of the existence of over three hundred Posts." Similarly, Kansas was presumed to contain "about fifty Posts, but no returns or reports have ever been made, and I can find nowhere any official information as to the strength of the organization in that Department." Neither Kansas nor Illinois had paid any dues to national headquarters, but in that they were not alone—Iowa, Indiana, Missouri, and Louisiana were similarly delinquent and Wisconsin partially so. The nonpayment of dues left the order so far in debt by 1870 that it could not even afford to pay an inspecting officer to find out what was going on in the nonreporting posts.[24]

The major reason for the decay of national headquarters was that since the national election of 1868, most post activities had been local or, at most, statewide in scope. Robert Beath, serving in 1869 as adjutant of the Pennsylvania department, discovered one case "of a Post meeting regularly, well attended and doing good work, yet had never made a report, and was of course without direct information of any kind from Headquarters." In another case a post quartermaster collected dues but embezzled them rather than forwarding them to his superiors.[25] In Philadelphia's Post 2, the two original committees were formed to provide relief of needy members and procure jobs for those out of work, both charitable activities that allowed concerted action with other Philadelphia posts but hardly required a national organization.[26]

While some posts did make use of the Confederate-cannon-metal membership badge, initiation ritual books, and other supplies required by national headquarters, many did not. Badges and stationery could be procured or produced locally, often at a lower cost than those ordered from national headquarters, while the initiation ritual was changed so frequently that to keep current copies on hand required yearly purchases.[27] Local practice of the ritual seems to have varied somewhat in any case, which was probably one reason the national encampments of the 1860s were presented annually with several proposals to change it.[28] Finally, aside from charity, the main function of the local post was as a social meeting place, a fact that Chipman acknowledged when he suggested that "the Posts which contribute most to the relief of comrades and their widows and orphans, and which arrange entertainments among themselves for the purpose of rendering the Post meetings attractive are the ones the most prosperous in every respect."[29] National affairs impinged upon such activities only slightly if at all.

The localism of the posts left their representatives gathered at the national encampment of 1868 with widely different ideas of what they had been doing. "The convention found itself in anything but a proper condition for intelligent action," Chipman lamented at the 1869 national encampment in Cincinnati. "There had been no inter-communication among the different Departments, no correspon-dence with headquarters, and no general interchange of opinions, theories, and ideas, but each delegate had apparently come with his own more or less crude ideas. Neither the Commander-in-Chief nor the Adjutant General laid before the convention any suggestions as to the result of their experience." Chipman could only guess at the number of posts in most states, much less the number of members. "It is greatly to be regretted," he told the delegates at Cincinnati, "that amid all this rapid growth of our Order, and the enthusiasm with which it seems to have spread, that there should appear no-where any record of its progress."[30]

Despite the grandiose vision of Stephenson and the more prag-matic machinations of Logan and Chipman, then, the early Grand Army was marked by a diffuse agenda and a high degree of local indifference to the national organization. Logan's centralizing re-forms might eventually have changed the situation; certainly the national officers of 1868–69 hoped so. Before the reforms could have any noticeable effect, however, an attempt by other GAR officers to create a different sort of order—one modeled on the Gilded Age fraternal lodge—nearly killed the fledgling Grand Army. The failure of their early attempt to civilianize the GAR through the introduction of "grades" or "degrees" reveals much about the veterans' postwar attitudes toward rank and about the sort of social order its members sought.

Egalitarianism and the Grade System, 1869–1871

Graded ranks for the GAR were the brainchild of several Eastern officers, led by James Shaw of Rhode Island and J. Waldo Denny of Boston. Approved by the same 1869 national en-campment that heard Adjutant Chipman's laments about administra-

tive chaos, the GAR grades were based on the Masonic system of
degrees. Under the Masonic system, a new recruit entered at the
lowest degree and was promoted by a vote of his fellows to suc-
cessively higher degrees over time, each promotion being accompanied by a special ritual and a series of allegorical performances
intended to illustrate the meaning of Masonry. The basic Masonic
degrees were Entered Apprentice, Fellow Craft, and Master Mason.
In the GAR scheme, the degrees were to be Recruit, Soldier, and
Veteran.[31]

A Recruit was to remain at that grade for two months, without the
privilege of voting in meetings. He was then able to become a Soldier,
provided he was recommended in writing by two other members and
received a two-thirds vote of his post. After six months, he could
become a Veteran under the same promotion rules. It was only at this
point that he was eligible for post, department, or national office.
Each grade carried with it a dues surtax, a badge, a secret grip and
password, and an initiation ritual.

When a member was initiated as a Recruit, he received a lecture on
the virtues of "fraternity" and an explanation of the allegorical symbols used in the initiation. His blindfolding outside the post room
door, for example, "was significant of the fact that you were yet
ignorant of the secrets of this Grand Army. Let it remind you also of
the dark nights when you groped your way in front of the enemy's
lines; and, still more, of those dark days in the history of the war,
when, though many faltered, the soldiers of our country stood bravely
waiting for the light which was to come." On advancing to the grade of
Soldier, a member heard a homily on "charity"; on becoming a Veteran, he was instructed in "loyalty."[32]

Degrees or grades were standard fare in Gilded Age fraternal
orders, and advocates of GAR grades felt that the device would
attract members who otherwise might gravitate to rival fraternal
bodies. Grades provided social distinction in a formally egalitarian
society, while fostering a quasi-military solidarity that young men
found attractive. The Improved Order of Red Men, for example, had
created a highly successful new "Adoption Degree" in 1868 that drew
thousands of new members in the 1870s. Other orders were thriving
under similar systems. The grade system aimed to change the GAR
from a political club into a fraternal order.[33]

Grades also promised to aid Logan and Chipman's GAR reorganization in two ways. First, the probationary period before a member
could hold office meant that officers under the grade system were

likely to be men with a long-term interest in the organization. Second, since all members were required to be remustered using the new system, it offered an opportunity to identify the active members of the order and cut the dead wood. The grade system, said its proponents, "will greatly promote the interest and efficiency of the GAR."[34]

Despite its similarity to the successful plans of other orders, however, the GAR grade system was an unmitigated disaster. Instead of pruning the disinterested, the order ended up slashing its membership wholesale, as the veterans either declined to be remustered under the new forms or ignored them entirely. In Pennsylvania, at least fifty posts disbanded for failure to comply, despite department commander Oliver C. Bosbyshell's suggestion that members already remustered wait on the delinquents personally to give them application forms.[35] In Bosbyshell's own post, recruits were occasionally promoted through all the ranks in a single evening, while back dues piled up until they had to be remitted (forgiven).[36] At the national level, William T. Collins, the adjutant-general who succeeded Chipman, said the three-grade system "has been the cause of much complaint," while Inspector-General F. A. Starring felt that the ritual would have been better performed had the change never been made. "I find from personal observation that there is great diversity of ways of doing the work and confusion of the different grades, the effect of which is a loss of interest in the order, and a general tendency to apathy and indifference," Starring reported. " . . . I find that but few of the posts in our Department have committed the work of the several grades or even worked them, their time being principally taken up with advancing old members to the grade of Veteran."[37] Most old members declined to be remustered, even after the probationary period between the first and third degrees was shortened from eight months to six weeks.

In 1871 the national encampment admitted its error and abolished the system. But the damage already had been done. Grand Army membership had entered a steep decline, from which it would not recover until the end of the decade. By 1875 the departments of Delaware, Indiana, Iowa, Kansas, Maryland, Michigan, Minnesota, Missouri, and New Mexico were defunct, and those of California, Illinois, Nebraska, Ohio, and Wisconsin nearly so—the Ohio department in 1875 numbered only eight posts, the Wisconsin department, only four. The order continued to hang on in New England and the middle states, but even there the total number of posts and members declined until 1876, when the entire organization numbered only 26,899 members.[38] The system's impact on membership left Logan's concurrent attempt to centralize the order a mixed success—consolidation was achieved only by liquidating posts and sometimes entire departments.

The grade system, however, cannot be viewed as the sole cause of the Grand Army's membership decline in the 1870s. Other and more fundamental forces were at work, not the least of which was the general desire to forget war that is common to most postbellum periods. The partisan character of the early GAR most likely had already deterred potential recruits who were not sympathetic to Radical Republicanism, even though the same national encampment that created the degree system also ruled that no "comrade," as the members called each other, was to use the order "for partisan purposes, and no discussion of partisan questions shall be permitted at any meeting of the Grand Army of the Republic, and no nominations for political offices shall be made."[39] The depression following the Panic of 1873 undoubtedly prevented some members from keeping up their dues, while the unsettled state of the young veterans (the great majority were still under thirty years of age) also took its toll. But the proximate cause of a great many desertions was the unwelcome new system of degrees.

The primary problem with the grade system was this: members of the GAR already *had* ranks. To begin with, they had rank in the Union Army, which played no small part in determining rank in the GAR. In the wake of demobilization, veterans of both Civil War armies flaunted whatever rank they could plausibly lay claim to—military rank, brevet rank, militia rank—and inspired such stock Gilded Age fictional characters as Mark Twain's Colonel Beriah Sellers and Albion Tourgée's Colonel Ezekiel Vaughn. The country was notoriously flooded with "officers" of all varieties. John Espy of St. Paul, Minnesota, for example, had been a private in the war but served as a staff officer in the Pennsylvania national guard in the 1870s; "it was by reason of this service that the title of 'Major' was accorded me by which I am generally known," he said. "The outside public are already talking and saying that there are nothing but generals and colonels and captains and majors in the Grand Army," complained John Vanderslice of Philadelphia's Post 2 in opposing an 1883 proposal to add rank straps to some GAR badges. A *New York Times* reporter made the same caustic observation at an 1879 New Jersey GAR encampment.[40]

To veterans who took such pride in their military titles, grades represented the intrusion of irrelevant civilian distinctions on what was basically a military body. Oliver Wilson, a vocal opponent of the 1869 system, recalled in a retrospective screed of 1905 some of the sarcastic comments of veterans on learning of the new cornucopia of ranks, rituals and badges. "One wanted a 'thousand commissions—pink satin—to distribute to the poor,'" Wilson remarked. Another wrote: "'Can't raise money enough to buy a "leave of absence" to come up to headquarters to see you about it.'" A third drew the contrast between his military and GAR experiences bluntly: "'We'll see Grant about it.'"[41]

Second, and more important, the Union veterans of the immediate postwar years continued to set themselves above "civilians" as a class by virtue of their military service: all of them held the rank of "veteran." The veterans' prickliness on this point can be seen most readily in the way they screened potential members. Applicants were first required to produce honorable discharges; then, as in other fraternal orders, they were "investigated" by several members and voted upon by the whole post, with a single negative vote constituting cause for rejection. Even with such restrictions, some posts declined to muster applicants whose military terms, in the post's view, had not been long enough. And GAR members wrangled constantly over what types of military service qualified a man as having been "subject to the orders of U.S. General Officers" and thus eligible for membership. Was state militia service enough? Did being a revenue marine officer count? Between 1866 and 1900 the GAR's chief judicial officer, the judge advocate-general, would hear more cases involving questions of eligibility than any other type of dispute—71 cases out of 378.[42]

Both in the GAR's formative years and in the decades to come, the Union veterans further distinguished their order from those of civilians by constant reference to military usage. Ruling in an 1873 dispute over the appointment of a GAR court-martial, for example, Judge Advocate-General W. Douglas decided that since army regulations gave the detailing officer power to appoint anyone he liked to the panel, the GAR commander must have the same power. When Philadelphia's Post 2 presented a ragged appearance on parade in 1876, member John H. R. Storey "moved that hereafter when the Post turn out, it follow the U.S. Reg. that forming in line comrades fall in according to height of shoulder, and that the Commander act as Capt., S.V. and J.V. as 1st and 2nd Lts." Faced with a conflict over appointed officers at the national encampment of 1881, Commander-in-Chief Louis Wagner noted: "Even in the army these positions are filled by assignment from higher authority, and not by appointment from the Colonel or the General." Even when it was clearly inappropriate, the military model served as a point of reference for GAR officers. In 1889, for instance, the judge advocate-general ruled that if a member tried by a GAR court-martial wanted legal representation, the attorney had to be a GAR member; otherwise, the secret passwords, grips, and ritual might be revealed. "I am aware that in the United States Army the right of the accused to appear by such counsel as he may choose is recognized," he wrote. "But the conditions are entirely different. The Grand Army of the Republic is a secret organization, while the United States Army is not." The military model was the relevant one, even when departures from it were required. Even correspondence between GAR officers was to be carried on "in accordance with military usage."[43]

Those outside the Grand Army acknowledged its semimilitary nature as well. Some newspapers carried news of the order alongside reports on the militia and the regular armed forces. When Baltimore staged a civic procession in 1880 to commemorate the city's founding, the local and visiting GAR posts paraded on the day reserved for military, police, fire, and other uniformed societies, not on the day designated for fraternal orders, and they marched between the military and the police units. In a similar parade in Philadelphia marking the centennial of the Constitution in 1887, the posts marched with the military units. The practice was enough the norm that when the GAR posts were placed well behind the militia in President Garfield's funeral procession in 1881, they complained. "We were soldiers when it meant something," wrote one disgruntled member to a national veteran newspaper.[44]

By introducing civilian considerations to such a quasi-military order, the grade system of 1869–71 threatened to blur the distinctiveness of the one rank the ex-soldiers valued most—that of veteran. In the words of the crusty Oliver Wilson, "the morbid, 'goody-goody' in the Order, for sentimental degree work" had produced a change "from what the comradeship of the field offered, to the sentiment of the lodgeroom." Even the original GAR initiation ritual had been "cumbersome," Wilson charged, and the degree system only added a ritualistic ceremony that had been no part of the veterans' lives in the army. The veterans, he said, "were not in a frame of mind to accept any formula, or subscribe to any doctrine or rule that prescribed other methods for preserving the fellowship of army life than those formed in the field and trench, in bivouac and battle. If such ties of friendship could not muster the 'boys' at a 'camp-fire,' a ceremony that never entered into any part of the soldier's life could not do so."[45]

Finally, the grade system offended not just those veterans attached to Union Army rank or veteran distinctiveness but also those who looked back at the war as a leveling experience. As an often-cited sentimental ode put it:

> There are bonds of all sorts in this world of ours,
> Fetters of friendship and ties of flowers,
> And true lovers' knots, I wean;
> The boy and the girl are bound by a kiss,
> But there is never a bond, old friend, like this—
> We have drunk from the same canteen[46]

The verse was a plea for egalitarianism, not for distinction by rank. A term in the Union Army, Adjutant Collins noted in 1871, "is held by many of our old comrades-in-arms to be a sufficient qualification for admission to full membership without being required to serve six or nine weeks in a subordinate position."[47] Even Robert Beath, a prominent Philadelphia member and in-house GAR historian who was otherwise a defender of fraternal ceremony, was ready to admit that the introduction of grades had been a mistake. "Having been mustered into the United States service upon a simple obligation, members now strongly objected to such complicated manoeuvers as were required in passing from one grade to the other in the Grand Army," he wrote in his 1889 *History of the Grand Army of the Republic*, "and recruits, full of enthusiasm when they joined, were disgusted at having to wait two months before having a vote."[48]

To true levelers like Wilson, not just the grades but all the order's ranks and quasi-military usages were pernicious. "Distinction by reason of rank disappeared with the muster-out," he wrote, "and at no time was the line drawn between the two [officers and privates] as representing a difference or grade of soldiers in such fraternity; the only passport to fraternity was an honorable discharge."[49] True fraternity, he argued, implied the absence of hierarchy, a complaint that he generalized into an indictment of the official GAR brand of fraternity promoted by such men as Robert Beath.

Wilson also ridiculed the Grand Army's pretensions to military usage and discipline. Calling the orders Logan had issued in his effort to consolidate the Grand Army "silly, bombastic," he asserted that what the early members sought was not a return to military discipline but a return to the camaraderie of camp. "The idea," he exclaimed,

"that a comrade in this organization, founded only on comradeship
and good-fellowship, would be required to have a 'leave of absence'
from his Post, or a 'transfer', or a 'discharge'! That there should be
'an inspector' to report the material, mental, physical, and presumably sanitary condition of his Post! That there would be Post 'descriptive books,' lest he should—desert, probably, and wander off to some
other camp of veterans and fraternize, because, mayhaps, some old
'coffee cooler' was there who had 'drunk from the same canteen'
with him!"[50]

Though Wilson, like many other early officers, was more concerned with the effect of the GAR's decline on Radical Republicanism
than on the order itself, his attack on hierarchy and discipline cut to
the heart of the impossible handicap created by graded ranks. By
offering distinctions based on purely civilian considerations, the system alienated those members to whom the GAR represented military achievement. By offering distinctions at all, it offended those
who viewed all veterans as equal. In short, the grade system failed
because it attempted the difficult stunt of minimizing both the military distinctions of Union Army service and the egalitarian basis of
Grand Army membership.

The chastening experience of the 1870s led ever afterward to a
certain disavowal of GAR rank on the part of those who held it, or
who had held it. "From Commander-in-Chief to Outside Sentinel of a
Post the grand title of 'Comrade' fits always and is always proper,"
said Pennsylvania department commander James F. Morrison in
1899. "Your Department Commander has been addressed as General, Colonel, Major and Captain, respectively, while the highest
military rank he ever held was that of corporal."[51] There was the case
of "Corporal" James Tanner, a legless veteran who rose to GAR
prominence (and to the position of Pension Commissioner in 1889)
by parading his low rank. And when Commander-in-Chief John L.
Kountz called on General William T. Sherman—seated, significantly,
with the rest of the delegates rather than onstage with the other
notables—for a few remarks at the 1884 national encampment in
Minneapolis, the following notable exchange took place:

Comrade Sherman—Is that an order or a request?
The Commander-in-Chief—That is an order. [Laughter.][52]

The scene was funny to the delegates because Kountz obviously was
Sherman's superior only in the most nominal sense—that of GAR

rank. Other notables could and did turn down such "orders" (though in this case Sherman used the opportunity to make some remarks on the virtue of following orders). In most cases, GAR leaders were living dangerously if they tried to make their Grand Army rank count as something more than an honorary designation.

A Promise of Order

What, then, remained of Union Army regimen in the Grand Army after 1871? Despite all its quasi-military forms, the GAR's basic organizational structure did not differ much from that of any other late-nineteenth-century fraternal organization or, for that matter, from the form of a corporation: at each level, the commander was roughly the equivalent of a president; the "quartermaster," the treasurer; the adjutant, the secretary; and so forth. Other fraternal organizations, from the Masons down to the Concatenated Order of Hoo-Hoo, had their own grand masters, imperial wizards, grand viziers, and exalted heads. Whereas the Masonic "conclave" emphasized the tools of the building trades, the GAR post employed the imagery of a military camp: sentinels stood guard at their "outposts" while within, a commander, assisted by his staff, issued orders to the men under his command; "inspectors" traveled from unit to unit for formal reviews, reporting to their department superiors; members joined by being "mustered in" and received "transfers" or "honorable discharges" in order to change posts. In all of this it is easy to see simply a parody of military forms or, as the contemptuous Oliver Wilson put it, "play soldiers."[53]

But the GAR was not just one more fraternal organization among the hundreds that sprouted during the Gilded Age. Unlike the Masons, few of whom had ever been masons, or the Improved Order of Red Men, none of whom had ever been red men, the Grand Army existed only because all of its members had at one time been members of a real army with real ranks engaged in real combat. Made up of men to whom the war had been a central experience of youth, the GAR aimed first to "preserve and strengthen those kind and fraternal feelings which bind together the soldiers, sailors and marines who united to suppress the late Rebellion."[54] Its military forms, vicarious when viewed against the individual member's postwar civilian status, were not so when viewed in the context of his life history. At one time, he had been a soldier. Whatever the degree of playacting involved in the GAR's ceremonies, they were rooted in the war experiences of its members. Its model camps, ranks, and orders could be measured against real-life counterparts in the memory of each veteran.

It is also worth remembering that the national organization, the managerial hierarchy, and the discipline fostered by the Union Army and mimicked by the Grand Army were still relative novelties in the civilian world of 1871. Although some volunteers, notably those employed by the railroads, had worked in large, bureaucratically managed corporations before the war, most soldiers encountered organizational life for the first time when they joined the army. That they did not especially enjoy this encounter is illustrated by the difficulties experienced by both Civil War armies in enforcing discipline.[55] Yet by 1865 the average veteran had undergone an apprenticeship in regimentation that his civilian counterpart had largely been spared.

Whether these veterans were better organization men as a result of their army experiences is an interesting, though to date largely unstudied, question. Some historians have hinted at such a connection, though their focus usually is on other subjects. Drew Gilpin Faust, for example, has suggested that evangelical religion in the Confederate Army helped discipline enlisted men for work in an industrial economy. Similarly, George Fredrickson argued many years ago that the war caused Northern reformers to appreciate the value of organization. And economic historians, while chiefly preoccupied by the question of whether the Civil War helped or hindered industrialization, have pointed to the link between military training and railroad management (though here most would probably agree with Alfred Chandler that such influence was at best "indirect").[56] The problem has always been one of disentangling the trend toward order and organization in the Gilded Age generally, evidenced by the rapid growth of civilian fraternal orders, from the veterans' specific military experience.

Although the history of the GAR offers no conclusive answer to this riddle, its members did try to replicate certain aspects of military discipline. In decisions about Grand Army eligibility, the formal dividing line between members and nonmembers was submission to federal officers' orders, rather than active combat service. Not to have lived the experience of rank, not to have been subordinate, was to be ineligible for GAR membership. The tendency of Grand Army officers to refer to military models in interpreting their own rules has also been mentioned. Perhaps a more subtle indication, however, is the importance that GAR members attached to order and the use they made of the quasi-military "court-martial" to enforce it.

From the GAR's inception, questions of orderliness permeated the organization, though not always in ways that are easily conveyed. Members rarely spoke in favor of "order" as such, though during crises, such as the railroad strikes of 1877, they might offer their services, as did Philadelphia's Post 2, "in defense of law and order" or applaud leaders such as Commander-in-Chief William Warner when he called the Grand Army "the great conservative element of the Nation . . . recognizing the dignity of labor but having no sympathy with anarchy or communism."[57] Rather, the love of order was apparent in a certain propensity for rule-making and rule-following. Between the Grand Army's elaborate written rules and its judge advocate-general's opinions, no situation arose that could not be referred to some formal regulation.

Recourse to the judge advocate-general was remarkably frequent. Between 1869 and 1892 that officer gave opinions in 378 cases; in an average year he issued 14 opinions and settled many other cases by referring to existing rules or previous decisions. Some disputes submitted for solution were extremely petty. In 1872, for instance, the judge advocate-general was called upon to decide whether all members were required to wear the same hat during ritual opening ceremonies. Doggedly noting that the framers of the ritual seemed to have contemplated the standard use of the army forage cap, Judge Advocate-General W. W. Douglas conceded that the question of the hat was "rather a question of taste or propriety than law." But he concluded: "If the object of wearing the forage cap is to give uniformity to the line, and as much of a military appearance as possible, I think that the object would be nearer attained by not wearing different styles of head-coverings when the forage cap is not supplied."[58] On other occasions, judges advocate-general ruled on whether the names of charter members were to remain on a charter after the post was reorganized (they were) and whether supplemental reports were to be considered full reports (they were not).[59] These were hardly major problems.

Other cases, however, concerned questions of national importance: reconciliation with the South, racism, pensions. On several occasions the judge advocate-general upheld an absolute ban on admitting ex-Confederates to the order, even those who said they had deserted to join the Union Army. Rulings in 1890 and 1891 upheld the rights of blacks to sit in the same department encamp-

ment with whites in the South, though the judgments said nothing
about sitting in the same post. A decision in 1887 upheld one post's
denunciation of a Grover Cleveland pension veto; another in 1888
undercut a post's attempt to instruct its delegates on a pension vote in
the department encampment.[60]

Some members even sought GAR rulings on what were essentially
civil cases. In 1882 a veteran who had lost a civil court judgment in a
dispute over property with another veteran tried to haul his opponent before a GAR court-martial on charges of perjury, a case that
the judge advocate-general said had "no reference whatever to the
Grand Army of the Republic; and if the crime of perjury has been
committed and a Comrade has been injured thereby, the proper
place to take the case is to a criminal court." Similar rulings were
issued in an 1887 incident in which one member had caused another
to be court-martialed for cheating him in a business deal and in an
1892 case in which one member charged another with slander. After
the latter decision, Judge Advocate-General Joseph O'Neall pleaded
with the members to exercise restraint in using the GAR's judicial
system. "If every comrade making false statements of or concerning
other comrades should be court-martialed," he wrote, "the membership would find constant employment serving upon courts-martial."[61]

Courts-martial were in fact the underpinning of GAR law. For a
commander's "orders" or a judge advocate-general's "decisions" to
mean anything, they had to be backed by sanctions, and the court-
martial provided them. The *Rules and Regulations* recognized five
offenses punishable by court-martial: disloyalty to the United States;
disobedience to orders; commission of "a scandalous offense against
the laws of the land"; "conduct unbecoming a soldier and a gentleman"; and "conduct prejudicial to good order and discipline." Whenever one member made such a charge against another, the commanding officer was to appoint nine members to a court-martial panel.
There they were to "be governed in their mode of proceeding and
rule of evidence by the Revised United States Army Regulations and
established military usage."[62] If convicted, the offender could face a
"dishonorable discharge"—that is, expulsion from the order.

Courts-martial were uncommon—the three local posts examined
most closely here convicted only one member by court-martial among
them, while the thirty-six posts of Philadelphia averaged slightly
more than two convictions each between 1875 and 1900. Moreover,
the details of courts-martial are not plentiful; the charges made and

the finding of the panel usually constitute the available information. The record is sufficient, however, to indicate the types of offenses against order of which the GAR took cognizance and the penalties it inflicted. In each case, the extremely formal nature of the court-martial proceeding undoubtedly sent members who attended as strong a message about discipline and order as did any finding or sentence of the panel itself.[63]

For the GAR, as for the Masons during the same period, morals and temperance offenses led the list, with public drunkenness (usually classed as "conduct unbecoming a soldier and a gentleman") probably the most common cause of court-martial.[64] Also common were business offenses, such as embezzlement and flight from creditors. In Post 2 of Philadelphia, for example, E. G. Lippert was investigated on the charge of another that he had "left the City under discreditable circumstances." And in a Minnesota case, Comrade Edwin J. Walsh, a salesman, combined defalcation with intemperance by spending road money from his employer on a drinking spree in Duluth.[65]

Other charges varied widely. In Brockton, Massachusetts, Fletcher Webster Post 13 convicted Ephriam Tinkham, a charter member and junk dealer, of refusing to return a sword claimed by the post and served him with a dishonorable discharge in 1877 for "disobedience of orders."[66] In Illinois a veteran was prosecuted for exposing himself at a public fair. In Pennsylvania a post commander was brought to task for setting aside the rules whenever it suited him and telling those who objected that "he, Comrade Wm. Wilson, was commander of the post and did not wish to be dictated to." In the Dakota territory, a serviceman was convicted of using the excuse of mustering a new GAR post at Deadwood to desert the army.[67]

In those cases and dozens of others like them, the GAR court-martial could try "offenses" of which civil courts took no notice. A comrade denied redress by civil authority might seek it from the order; another, feeling himself wronged in a way not actionable in civil law—being deceived in a business transaction, for instance—might try to apply the more stringent standards of GAR "law." To the largely native white middle-class male membership of the GAR, which sometimes felt the turbulence of the late nineteenth century as a decay of social order, the support of the GAR judicial process was not an inconsiderable benefit. For such men, even the unpredictable GAR procedure was sometimes preferable to the anarchy of the Gilded Age marketplace, particularly the urban marketplace. Grand Army "justice," in short, offered a model of order to a society that,

from the perspective of the average member, had precious little of it.
Like the other popular fraternal orders of the period, the GAR offered not perfect order but the promise of order—a promise that, in
the case of the GAR, had tangible roots in the experience of rank and
discipline in wartime.

It was a promise that in many instances ran headlong into the
disorderly egalitarianism of civilian life. The original GAR rules, for
example, called for courts-martial to rely on "established military
usage," thus presuming a familiarity with army regulations that most
members did not possess. That difficulty, combined with the open-
ended categories of offenses (what, after all, was "conduct prejudicial to good order and discipline"?) led to a rash of courts-martial on
petty charges and to procedural mayhem. In 1874, a post published
its sentence of court-martial in a local newspaper, a practice that the
judge advocate-general said was "wrong. . . . I do not think we have
any right to divulge to the world any information concerning a man's
character which we have obtained by means of his membership in
the Grand Army."[68] Another post failed to furnish a copy of the
charges to the accused; when he showed up late at the meeting after
he had been found "guilty," he "alleged that the proceedings against
him were characterized by malice and unfairness." In another case a
post commander asserted that he had "pardoned" a member whom
the post had convicted; in yet another, the post commander suspended a member from the post before he was tried.[69] Some posts
court-martialed members for failing to pay their dues.[70]

"Military usage" aside, the GAR faced a second problem in adapt-
ing army discipline to civilian life: its major offices (and, at the post
level, many of its minor ones) were elective. Balloting made officers
more responsible to the men they nominally "commanded" than to
their superiors. A post officer subject to yearly elections was not
likely to call many courts-martial or to insist on more discipline than
his comrades were willing to endure. And, if he wanted to gain office
above the post level he was required to engage in a brand of politicking very similar to the questionable practices of Gilded Age civilian
campaigns.

In 1890, for example, Webster Post of Brockton told its delegates to
"use all honorable means" to elect one S. M. Weale as department
commander despite the *Grand Army Record*'s charges that at the
previous year's encampment Weale's "unprincipled partisans . . .
interviewed many country delegates before the Encampment and
endeavored by innuendoes to poison their minds against the other

two candidates."[71] In the same year, T. L. Taylor of San Francisco
wrote to solicit support for his candidate from the Minnesota department adjutant. "I said if [the candidate's character was] satisfactory I
would use my influence with the delegates to the encampment," that
officer told his superior, "and as I had much to say in selecting the
committee for appointing the delegates, of course they would be my
friends."[72] But when James Tanner of New York was unsuccessful in
his bid for the office of commander-in-chief at San Francisco in 1886,
the *Record* attributed it to "the dirty business of his delegation on the
floor of the encampment," while the contest at Minneapolis in 1884
led another veteran newspaper to decry "the introduction of disgraceful personal detraction and vilification into the canvass for
Commander-in-Chief."[73] It was unfortunate, wrote veteran Cyrus
Bates of Cohasset, Massachusetts, that some officers had to "wire-
pull, and move heaven and earth to get some office, simply so they
may use it as a stepping stone to some fat berth."[74]

Periodic canvassing wrangles aside, the elective system undercut
the authority of Grand Army officers even in day-to-day matters. If
a commander wanted to run a peaceful post, he had to expect a
certain amount of insubordination. "You cannot apply *strict military*
rules to the Grand Army of the Republic," wrote Judge Advocate-
General James Carnahan in an opinion of 1883. "This is an organization for mutual aid and for the *benefit* of the Comrades in the nature
of other benevolent and charitable organizations, and if you apply the
strict military rules that governed in the army you impair the objects
of the Order."[75] In an 1891 case resulting from a contentious post
election, the judge advocate-general held that even personal abuse
by opponents did not necessarily constitute an offense against discipline. "To hold that a Comrade whose friends or faction have been
beaten at an election must not vent and ease his feelings of disappointment by a reasonable amount of abuse of his successful opponents, somewhat as is usually done after our public elections, would
seem to be an unreasonable abridgment of the time-honored privileges of American citizens," he ruled. "Grumbling, mixed with abuse
and suggestions of fraud, affords the customary and indeed the only
relief and satisfaction left to the defeated in such cases."[76]

Under such circumstances, the rules of GAR law were gradually
softened in the years following the demise of the grade system. In
1872, for example, "dispensations" from headquarters for irregular
musters (that is, initiations that failed to follow the rules) were of-

ficially condoned. Other easements soon followed: the elimination of
courts-martial in cases of delinquent dues (1872); permission for
unlimited applications (1879) and withdrawals of applications already made (1886); provision for appeals resulting from the refusal
of superior officers to sanction new posts (1887) and from court-
martial sentences (1895).[77]

The net effect of the changes was to make it easier to join the GAR,
less constricting to belong, and harder to be expelled. Along with
aggressive recruiting on the part of national officers, the relaxation of
the rules would lead to a boom in membership in the 1880s. But it
also loosened the control of "headquarters" over its outposts. As late
as 1887 the inspector general could still complain that "with few
exceptions among Departments, little attention is given to orders
from National Headquarters," and department adjutants still spent
much time harassing local adjutants for reports ("I asked for information for roster in G.O. No. 9 and received responses from three
posts," reads a typical lament from Minnesota in 1890. "Sometimes
three or four letters are necessary to procure an item of information").[78] To members like William Tyler of Wakefield, Massachusetts, who wrote the *Grand Army Record* in 1897 to ask "Is the
National Encampment of the Grand Army of the Republic of Any
Possible Use to the Comrades?," the center of life in the order even at
that late date remained in the posts. "The Grand Army will live in
history as associated with the grand work of the Posts," he wrote.
"The National Encampment will be remembered only for its parade
and display."[79]

The erosion of military forms in the GAR was a mild defeat for
national officers such as John Logan and Robert Beath. In 1895, when
appeals were finally allowed with regard to courts-martial, Beath
noted (with some regret, one senses): "The various rulings—in accordance with United States army practice, that there can be no appeal
from the decision of a reviewing officer—are thereby annulled and
an appeal can now be taken in such cases."[80] Beath—prosperous
Philadelphia insurance man, army colonel, codifier of GAR law in the
Grand Army Blue Books—was indulging in the wishful thinking of a
man who yearned for more order than the GAR could provide. Given
the equality of standing among the GAR membership, given its voluntary nature, given the democratic way it chose officers, it is hard to
see how the GAR could ever have operated "in accordance with
United States army practice." At most, it could combine the forms of

military unit and voluntary fraternal order. The Grand Army of the Republic, in short, was part army and part republic, but in pure form it was neither.

Still, the extent to which even working-class and rural posts attempted to preserve military forms is impressive. Officers, even if they achieved office through "dirty business," expected their orders to be obeyed, as in fact they usually were, if the low incidence of courts-martial is any guide. Judges advocate-general still considered a remarkable volume of cases—remarkable when one considers that GAR "judicial" decisions carried no more weight than the members cared to give them. And life in the post room itself was circumscribed by rituals and rules that stressed order above all else. Even under the eased rules of later years, one did not join the Grand Army of the Republic in order to express oneself.

Citizen-Soldiers

If the GAR did not behave much like an army, it did bear an important resemblance to another military institution of the nineteenth century: the militia. Indeed, it could be argued that the average Grand Army post resembled nothing so much as a militia company that had already fought its battles. The difference was that militias and independent companies were organized around the possibility—however remote—of war, while GAR officers had to justify their "orders" and discipline on some other basis. Still, the structure of the GAR was in many ways a continuation of the militia experience. Many members, in fact, had begun their military careers in such units.

The prewar military companies, as students of the subject have pointed out, were social organizations with guns. Electing their officers, sometimes armed only with sticks or axes, meeting for irregular "musters" that served mostly as excuses for drinking, the militias were targets of much humorous abuse. In literary accounts, militiamen paraded in ridiculous costumes, broke camp to drink with passing strangers, declared that "they would never *vote* for another captain who wished to be so unreasonably strict" as to impose forty-five minutes of drill.[81] By 1850 most state militias were defunct or existed only on paper. Militia service, Marcus Cunliffe has concluded, "became a joke, a bore, a nuisance to the majority of citizens."[82] The "volunteer companies" that replaced the militias were somewhat more serious—they formed the core of the volunteer force gathered

at the outset of the Civil War—but spent much of their time in
showing off gaudy uniforms and paying social visits to companies in
neighboring towns. Their elections were a means of acknowledging
social distinction; many had exclusive membership policies. The volunteer companies, Cunliffe writes, "were clubs, conferring status and
identity. On parade, or dining together and applauding florid toasts,
they were liberated from domestic and commercial preoccupations,
and transformed by magnificent costume."[83] To middle-class young
men, they offered attractions supplied in later years by college societies and athletics—special dress and gestures, the opportunity for
spectacle, athletic activity, rivalry.

This activity was interrupted by the Civil War, during which the
volunteers were pressed into service under federal commanders. But
with the muster-out in 1865, the militias returned to a half social, half
military status. By 1878 the *New York Times* was again pointing to the
decay of the militias and the archaic statutes that justified them.
Ambrose Bierce joked about the militia's response to the governor
who insisted they have real guns rather than wooden ones with which
to practice (" 'Thank you, thank you,' cried the warriors, effusively.
'We will take good care of them, and in the event of war return them
to the arsenal' "). And even on the eve of the Spanish-American War,
the typical National Guard unit remained a local institution existing
largely for recreational purposes, holding drills and encampments
that were virtual picnics.[84]

Many of the tensions in the GAR organizational structure—the
difficulty with elected officers' giving orders, the wire-pulling to
achieve ranks that were in fact largely ceremonial, the problem of
discipline—were mirrored in the militias and independent companies of the postwar era. GAR posts and volunteer militias also
engaged in similar activities, sometimes jointly. Posts often invited
militia companies to social events or marched with them on parade;
occasionally they held joint encampments. At the New Jersey department encampments of 1878, 1881, and 1883, the veterans engaged in
"sham battles" with regiments of the New Jersey National Guard.[85]
Some posts sponsored independent drilling companies—Philadelphia's Post 2, for example, fielded the splendidly uniformed and
armed Post 2 Guard, while working-class Webster Post of Brockton,
Massachusetts, had a more modest marching unit. And on rare occasions, GAR posts were called into active service alongside the militias. Several Pennsylvania posts helped put down the railroad strikes

of 1877, and the national commander informed the encampment that he had offered the services of others. The Post 2 Guard even volunteered its aging members for the Spanish-American War, while a post in rural Chippewa Falls, Wisconsin, offered to help recruit younger men.[86] Such active duty was extremely uncommon, but it helps explain why newspaper editors sometimes referred to the GAR as a "semi-military body." Of course, the Grand Army spent more time in speeches, toasts, parades, drills, and elections than in fighting—but until 1898 so did the militias.

Perhaps the best way to illustrate the continuing appeal of rank and order to Grand Army members in the postwar years, despite the counterattractions of democracy, is to suggest one final similarity between antebellum militias and GAR posts—a similarity that masks an important difference. In both militia company and GAR post, burlesques of military order were sources of occasional entertainment. In musters before the Civil War, when the militia laws had become a bad joke, working-class citizen-soldiers often gave indications that they took discipline less than seriously. Participants might appear on parade carrying broomsticks and wearing cabbage leaves as helmets, waving ridiculous banners with proclamations such as "We'll fight till we run, and we'll run till we die." Sometimes they passed resolutions parodying militia regulations or wore costumes ridiculing those of upper-class volunteer units. The parodies were at once symbolic representations of class conflict and lampoons of a militia system that no longer worked.[87]

The GAR also had its burlesques of military order, the favorite targets being parades and courts-martial. At the 1882 Pennsylvania encampment at Gettysburg, members of two Philadelphia posts acted as the "Lambs and Razors," a reference to the practice of foraging in Sherman's army on the wartime march through Georgia. The Lambs parodied not only the military parade but also the pompous oratory that usually accompanied the raising of war monuments. "After a burlesque parade, in which such orders as 'lay down,' 'turn over,' 'git up' and others were obeyed," reported the *Pittsburgh Telegraph*, "they marched forward in a body, and proceeded to plant the mountain, a huge sack filled with straw, and bearing the inscription: 'Sacred to the memory of the Boss Ram, who fell at or near this spot, on the fourth day's fight, immortally wounded by a malt shot.' " The proceedings were capped by brief remarks from the Boss Ram's "widow"— one of the members dressed in women's clothes—who announced: "I am his real widow of a marriageable age. Patriotism and gluttony were prominent in his character. He will long be mourned by his

entire son." Two years later the Lambs, dressed in military uniforms,
disrupted the parade at the Bellefonte summer encampment by ca-
vorting along with it, carrying dead chickens and a pig in a bag, which
"Lamb" Harry Taylor "tried to initiate in the order by ramming it into
the mouth of a cannon."[88] The parades of the Lambs were parodies of
GAR dress parades, but they also poked fun at military order in
general. The group's barnyard props, as well as its name, called to
mind the casual march of "Sherman's bummers" at the tail end of the
Grand Review of 1865—comic relief from too much regimentation.

Another target of GAR satirists was the court-martial. In 1889,
Commander William Hoyt of Chippewa Falls's James Comerford
Post 68 fined his adjutant "six mince pies" for being late to the
meeting and assigned two guards to escort him to the kitchen. When
one of the guards "skipped out and neglected his duty in not helping
convey the pies," it was suggested that he be fined three gallons of
beer. But the members had their revenge three weeks later when
they convened a "drum head court martial" to "try" Hoyt. The
charges: "conduct unbecoming the Commander" in "allowing loud
and boisterous talk and walking around the post room"; "usurpation
of authority" for authorizing the burial of pauper soldiers without the
post's approval; "conduct prejudicial to good order and discipline"
for his fine of the adjutant; and "incompetency and lack of military
authority" for delegating work to subordinates. The fine: four pies
and one peck of apples. Similarly, Brockton's Webster Post launched
an 1893 investigation of "charges" against a prominent member, Fred
Hanson; the investigators' report, given at a subsequent inspection
dinner, was "full of Wit, Pathos and Eloquence and caused much fun
by its reference to Local affairs." In some instances a post even staged
a mock court-martial or trial as part of a formal entertainment. At an
1873 campfire held to entertain visiting Post 19, Philadelphia's Post 2
brought mock articles of impeachment against Comrade D. Newlin
Fell, a circuit court judge, as part of the program. In 1891 the Brockton post put on a mock trial at a public theater, netting more than
$200 for its treasury.[89] The mock courts-martial emphasized in a
humorous vein the point that real courts-martial drove home to
officers who did not take the hint: Grand Army military trappings
were not to be taken too seriously.

Unlike the burlesques of the militias, however, those of the GAR
were not challenges to the legitimacy of the military forms; they were
only reminders that the quasi-military hierarchy and imposed order

rested at base on the consent of the members. Like the militia parodies before them, the burlesques emphasized the egalitarian, fundamentally civilian nature of membership. Even D. Newlin Fell—judge, department encampment delegate, longtime Post 2 trustee—had to acknowledge ceremonially that he was no better than the body of clerks and mechanics in the post. Thus the parodies subtly helped to undermine whatever coercive authority the officers and hierarchy might have been able to summon. But unlike the prewar militia burlesques, the GAR shows were not spontaneous; they were set up intentionally as entertainments, as performances. They were lampoons from within, created by members who had no serious quarrel with the Grand Army. Like the "order" given Comrade Sherman, they were in every way in-house jokes.

An organization that stages parodies of its own institutions is an organization in which substantial agreement on the legitimacy of those institutions already exists. Real parades and real courts-martial were deadly serious affairs. If the burlesques drove home the point that no one was forced to obey GAR rules, the day-to-day functioning of the order demonstrated that many obeyed them anyway. Buried in most of the rulings of the GAR officers was an undercurrent that said to the disputants, in effect: Even though we can't force you to do anything, and even though you can leave whenever you want, you really ought to know better than that. Admitting that members could wear the GAR badge to political meetings if they wished, Commander-in-Chief Robert Beath nevertheless thought the practice "in bad taste"; conceding that a comrade who ran a business could use the letters *GAR* on his sign, the judge advocate-general still hoped he would not do so; ruling that the GAR could not expel a man for a wrong committed outside his relation to the order, the judge advocate-general pointed out that, nevertheless, other members did not have to associate with him.[90] Compliance with Grand Army discipline was not based, as it is in a truly military body, on coercion. It was based on mutual acknowledgment of what constituted proper and improper behavior among veterans.

The courts-martial indicate the types of behavior considered inappropriate: drunkenness (especially in public), bad faith in business dealings, and other "conduct prejudicial to good order and discipline." By the same token, the behaviors most commonly prescribed for veterans were "orderliness" and "discipline." "I believe that the key to the soldiers' success will be found in the school of discipline and training from which they graduated twenty-seven years ago,"

Commander-in-Chief John Palmer told the national encampment of

1892. "Each was obedient to authority, mindful of duty, brave in disaster, loyal to law and order; in a word bristling with those qualities which lie at the foundation of all success."[91] Similarly, General Sherman recalled the virtues of army discipline for the national encampment delegates of 1884. "In the Grand Army of the Republic I don't say you should do that, but you should approximate that," Sherman told the assembled veterans. "Give to your officers your absolute confidence. Let your Commander-in-Chief be commander-in-chief. Let your Adjutant-General be adjutant-general, and hold him responsible. When you receive his orders, obey them as military orders, and you will be a better citizen therefor."[92] Because the veterans lived in a republican society, the orderliness appropriate to them was not strict army discipline, but it was something "approximating" it. Veterans were to exercise self-control, obey rules, respect superiors—and they were to do these things voluntarily.

The GAR's stress on order was not a necessary consequence of the members' war experience. Many other messages could have been drawn from service in the Union Army—war is hell, might makes right, perhaps even the radical disillusionment so often remarked upon by students of World War I veterans. That the Northern ex-soldiers seized the theme of order speaks volumes not only about the GAR but about the late Victorian culture in which it and the hundreds of other voluntary fraternal orders existed. Their emphasis on self-control, uncongenial to the twentieth-century mind, was inseparable from the general Victorian preoccupation with order in the self and in society at a time when both were under increasing pressure.

In the long run, of course, it proved impossible for men who had returned to civilian life to impose military forms upon themselves voluntarily. The failure of grades, the relaxation of GAR "law," the continued electioneering for ceremonial office, all pointed toward an order more fraternal than hierarchical, one in which camaraderie was more important than distinction of rank. Gradually the memory of wartime regimentation would fade into a hazy nostalgia for the fraternity of camp life. By the 1890s, officers would express the wish that the GAR enroll every living veteran, while the order's burial rolls often included Union veterans who had never belonged to the GAR; all were considered parts of the same body, even though they had not gone through the formality of joining.

The fading of rank in the Grand Army represented the leaving behind of the Union Army's stress on hierarchy and discipline and the assimilation into civilian society of the Union veterans. In the thousands of GAR posts that would spring up across the North as the order revived in the late 1870s and 1880s, the currents of democracy and local particularism ran strong. At the same time, the resilience of rank as an ideal showed the ex-soldiers' consciousness of themselves as a unique group within the postwar civilian world. Among these men, the title of "veteran" was more important than any distinctions of rank they might draw among themselves.

CHAPTER **3** ROSTER

In the years following the abject failure of the grade system, one might have expected the Grand Army to be characterized by inclusiveness and egalitarianism. All honorably discharged Union veterans were still eligible to join, and as of 1871 every man mustered was to be a voting member of equal standing. Certainly democratic rhetoric prevailed among GAR officers. Inside the post room, said Commander-in-Chief William Warner in 1889, "the general and the private, the merchant prince and the clerk, the millionaire and the laborer, sit side by side as comrades, bound each to the other, by ties the tenderest yet the most enduring of any in this world, outside of the family circle."[1]

In practice, posts developed subtle patterns of inclusion and exclusion, of hierarchy and equality, as different as the various communities in which they were situated. They were also fortunate if they enrolled as many as half the eligible local veterans. In Chippewa Falls, Wisconsin, for example, the local GAR post mustered only 42 percent of the surviving Union veterans in Chippewa County in 1885 and 34 percent in 1895. The lone post in Brockton, Massachusetts, had 45 percent of that city's veterans on its rolls in 1890, while the 36 posts of Philadelphia included only 43 percent of the city's 20,349 Union veterans in 1890. Nationally, the GAR membership included only about one-third of the surviving veterans found by the special census of 1890—351,244 out of 1,034,073.[2]

What sorts of men joined the GAR, and what was life like in the local post room? Obviously it is not possible to examine in detail each of the 6,928 GAR posts that ultimately dotted the Northern landscape. But an analysis of the memberships of 3 representative posts (with an aggregate membership over thirty-five years of 2,225), supplemented by selected data from other posts, will give a good idea of what kinds of people were involved in the GAR between 1866 and 1900.[3] In the comparisons that follow, Post 2 of Philadelphia could stand for any of the large, urban, commercial posts that headed the GAR column in major Northern cities. Fletcher Webster Post 13 of Brockton, Massachusetts, typifies the hundreds of mid-sized industrial city posts concentrated mostly in the Northeast. And James Comerford Post 68 of Chippewa Falls, Wisconsin, is only one of thousands of "country posts," small organizations located in out-of-the-way county seats, typically in the Midwest or the West.

The differences among the three posts illustrate the diversity of local life in the Grand Army. At the same time, continuities among their memberships and officeholding patterns give important clues to the underlying meaning of Grand Army veteranhood. For Union veterans, GAR membership reflected both the persistent localism of Gilded Age life and the nascent nationalism of the Union Army experience. A close look at the memberships of the Brockton, Chippewa Falls, and Philadelphia posts in the years 1866 to 1900 will give an idea of the sorts of men who participated in the rituals, political campaigns, and charity drives detailed in subsequent chapters.

To begin with, the urban context in which a post operated influenced the kinds of men it recruited. Many of the earliest posts were located in major cities. In Pennsylvania, for example, six of the first eight posts (Post 2 among them) were in Philadelphia, the other two in Pittsburgh. Of the nineteen formed in the first month, twelve were in Philadelphia. Several of the early Philadelphia posts actually were formed by charter members of Post 2 who had withdrawn from the older post in order to found the new ones.[4] These posts followed the emerging pattern of residential segregation in the American metropolis of the late nineteenth century, concentrating their recruiting in single wards of the city or among particular groups: Post 6 was based in Germantown, Post 55 in Frankford; Post 363 admitted only former cavalrymen, while Post 400 admitted only ex-sailors; Posts 27, 80, and 103 were all black, while others were predominantly German. A similar arrangement held sway in New York City, where different posts catered to Germans and Irishmen, ex-musicians and ex-sailors, printers and journalists.[5] By contrast, "leading" Philadelphia posts, such as Post 2, George G. Meade Post 1, and Ulysses S. Grant Post 5, had citywide bases that spanned geographic, if not class and ethnic, distance.

Every major Northern city had its leading GAR posts, known for their substantial citywide charity funds, local political power, and especially the social prominence of their memberships. In New York, the leaders were Lafayette and Hamilton posts; in San Francisco, Thomas Post; in Boston, Dahlgren and Kinsley posts; in Milwaukee, Wolcott Post; in St. Louis, Ransom Post; in Lynn, Massachusetts, Lander Post; in Baltimore, Wilson Post.[6] These elite posts spent large sums for the relief of indigent veterans, tendered receptions and armed escorts to visiting military dignitaries, provided the largest delegations from their departments to national encampments held in faraway cities, and represented the order locally in civic pageants such as parades. In Philadelphia, for example, Meade Post 1 boasted Ulysses Grant as a member and arranged a ceremonial banquet for him on his return from Europe in 1879. Post 2 could claim General James Selfridge as a member and hosted such distinguished visitors to post meetings as General Philip Sheridan, Michigan governor (and later secretary of war) Russell Alger, and ex-president Rutherford B. Hayes.[7]

The dominance of these leading urban posts within the GAR was widely recognized. Between 1866 and 1888, for example, Post 2 provided five national GAR officers, three state commanders, and every year at least one other state officer or national delegate. When GAR national encampments were held at Philadelphia in 1876 and 1899, the Post 2 hall was the scene of informal campfire entertainments for the visitors, while at the national encampments of 1876, 1877, and 1878, Post 2 officers were invited to demonstrate the secret "unwritten work" of the order (the initiation ritual, accompanied by images of the war projected with a stereopticon) to the delegates.[8] When the members of Post 2 attended out-of-town national encampments, they were recognized as, in the words of the *Springfield Republican*, "apparently men of affairs." The *Providence Morning Star*, on viewing the elaborately uniformed and armed Post 2 Guard on parade in that city in 1877, reported that the post "consists of the wealthiest and most influential citizens of Philadelphia. Among the members are more than a score of colonels and about a dozen generals."[9] The Providence correspondent's tabulation of colonels and generals was somewhat exaggerated, possibly because of the ex-officers' habit of referring to themselves by their brevet ranks; also, at a national encampment he was seeing only those members who could afford the journey to Providence. But for the most part his perception was correct: like other elite posts, Post 2 was not an organization for veterans of small means.

The exclusivity of the elite posts did not mean, as one might think, that they blackballed more applicants than other posts did. If anything, they blackballed fewer. Between 1866 and 1900, Post 2, for example, rejected only 37 applicants for membership (8 of whom were later elected after reapplying), while admitting 1,367—about the same rate of rejection as that in Chippewa Falls (8 rejections, 318 members) and lower than that in Brockton (20 rejections, 540 members).[10] Philadelphia's other leading posts, Meade Post 1 and Grant Post 5, reported even fewer rejections, and the service-exclusive Cavalry Post 363 listed none at all. In fact, the most prolific blackballers seem to have been posts in small industrial cities such as Williamsport (27 rejections), Reading (26), Allentown (18), York (20), and Lock Haven (20).[11] In such cities, which usually housed only one or two posts, the absence of an alternative may have made a veteran more likely to apply even though his chances of acceptance were not good. In larger cities he could more easily find a post that would take him on the first try.

The Post 2 Guard marching in the national encampment parade in Boston, 1890. Leading urban posts spent much time and energy drilling for such affairs, where their positions near the head of the parade line reinforced their high status within the order. (Courtesy Philadelphia Camp, Sons of Union Veterans of the Civil War)

Instead of blackballing applicants, the leading posts maintained their exclusivity by charging unusually high initiation ("muster") fees or by imposing other requirements that working-class veterans could rarely meet. In 1876, for example, Post 2 began charging a stiff $10 muster fee, which, remarked the *Philadelphia Sunday Transcript*, "has a tendency to keep aspirants for GAR honors away." Chicago's Columbia Post 706 limited its membership to 100, charged a prohibitive $15 muster fee, and required members to attend meetings, drills, and parades dressed in expensive uniforms. In New York, George Washington Post 103 limited its membership to 103 members of the Army and Navy Club and held its monthly meetings at Delmonico's.[12] Few veterans were rejected by such posts because few applied.

The result in the case of Post 2 was an organization that drew its membership largely from the commercial and professional upper middle class of Philadelphia. Among its charter members were Robert Beath—then a clerk, soon to be an insurance executive—who withdrew before long to found Post 5, physician Samuel B. Wylie

Mitchell, lawyer Joshua T. Owen, insurance agent Robert Bodine, banker Louis Wagner, and merchant Frank Crawford.[13] High-status white-collar individuals—manufacturers, judges, stock brokers, clergymen, physicians, hotel keepers, lawyers—eventually made up 19 percent of the post membership, a proportion more than double that of white-collar members in the posts in Brockton and Chippewa Falls and well above that of most other posts in Pennsylvania (table 1).[14] Another 17 percent of the post consisted of merchants and proprietors, some of them small businessmen—druggists, grocers, clothiers, butchers, lumber dealers, tobacconists—and others of them undoubtedly quite well off.[15]

Despite the high initiation fee, a significant number of low-status white-collar and semiprofessional workers also found their way into Post 2. Mostly salesmen, clerks, and bookkeepers, they accounted for 32 percent of the membership, almost as much as the merchants, proprietors, and high-status white-collar individuals put together.[16] Skilled workers made up another 26 percent of the post membership, a figure that may seem impressive in view of the high cost of membership but that in fact is quite low compared with other urban posts in Pennsylvania and even in Philadelphia. At Danville, for example, 42 percent of the members of Post 22 were skilled workers; at Pottsville, 40 percent; at Reading, 35 percent. In Philadelphia, the number of skilled workers ranged from 38 percent of the membership of Post 21 to 55 percent of Post 94. Relative to total membership, no post in Philadelphia had as few skilled workers as Post 2.[17] For semiskilled and unskilled laborers, the high fees acted as an almost absolute bar; together, these two groups made up less than 5 percent of the membership.

One attraction of GAR membership for the affluent members of such a post was obvious: it offered them a chance to reassert the dominance they enjoyed in civilian life. To some extent they did so. Between 1866 and 1900, for example, high-status white-collar individuals, representing 19 percent of the Post 2 membership, filled 24 percent of the post's elective offices and accounted for five of its thirty commanders. They dominated the financially important post board of trustees, accounting for at least six, and probably eight, of its eleven members before 1900.[18] Merchants, 17 percent of the membership, accounted for 30 percent (nine of thirty) of the post commanders and two of the other five trustees. On the other hand, the low-status white-collar group held 29 of percent the offices, provided ten of the thirty post commanders, and served on major committees

Occupation	Post 2, Philadelphia (N = 1,367)	Webster Post, Brockton (N = 540)	Comerford Post, Chippewa Falls (N = 318)
High-status white-collar	250 (19%)	38 (9%)	26 (9%)
Proprietors	223 (17)	45 (11)	25 (9)
Low-status white-collar, semiprofessional	428 (32)	35 (8)	24 (9)
Skilled workers	344 (26)	95 (23)	37 (13)
Semiskilled and service workers	52 (4)	174 (42)	14 (5)
Unskilled and menial laborers	6 (0.4)	10 (2)	65 (23)
Active-duty military	25 (2)	0 (0)	1 (0.4)
Farmers	11 (0.8)	18 (4)	89 (32)
Unknown	28	125	37

Source: See notes 2 and 3, this chapter.

Note: All percentages are expressed as a percentage of members whose occupations are known. For an explanation of the categories, see note 14, this chapter.

frequently, though they tended to serve once or twice, rather than year after year, as did some of the more prominent members. Nor were they any more likely to be rejected as applicants—over thirty-two years, Post 2 blackballed four clerks, two painters, and one park guard, but also four physicians, three manufacturers, and nine merchants.[19] While merchants and professional men often filled the highest offices, in other words, the clerks and salesmen who largely made up the post were not without influence.

A more subtle way in which Post 2 membership promised to aid merchant and professional members was through the possibilities it opened for clientage. Without a sponsor, or proposer, a recruit could not even apply for membership. Once he did apply, he relied on his sponsor to shepherd his application through the admissions process. In 1887, for example, Post 2's Frank Taylor wrote the post adjutant to make sure the members of the investigating committee were not planning any lengthy probe of his friend William Ball; he was assured that they "would *investigate* him in the ante-room, on that evening." If the application looked likely to fail, the proposer usually was

The meeting room of Post 2 as it appeared in 1880. In the center is the altar; at the rear, between the two cannons, is the "station" of the post commander. In 1876 the post hall was the site of the small GAR national encampment. (Courtesy Philadelphia Camp, Sons of Union Veterans of the Civil War)

allowed to withdraw it, sparing his client the embarrassment of a blackball; the withdrawn application could be resubmitted after objections to the recruit were overcome by "friendly discussion." If the vote was favorable, the sponsor guided the recruit to the altar during the muster-in ceremony; in the original 1869 initiation ritual, he also held the new member's hand during the taking of the membership oath.[20]

Throughout the process, the sponsor stood surety for the character of the recruit, but the clientage relationship benefited the sponsor as well. By proposing a host of successful candidates, he built a network of supporters within the post, which would be useful to him if he sought post office. More important, clientage reinforced whatever links proposer and proposed had in private dealings; it was of particular value to merchants who sponsored their clerks, salesmen who sponsored their customers, and manufacturers who sponsored their employees. The would-be recruit was dependent on his sponsor, a position that the GAR initiation ritual reinforced through images emphasizing individual helplessness and filial piety.[21]

Although any member could sponsor a new recruit, in practice Post 2's major proposers were proprietors of businesses. Leading sponsor John H. R. Storey was a teacher, but fifteen of the twenty-six men he sponsored between 1877 and 1887 were dropped members seeking reinstatement. The leading proposers of new members were clay

pipe salesman Frank Lynch (twenty-one clients) and hardware merchant Matthew Hall (twenty). Of the other eleven members who
sponsored more than ten applicants, six were merchants or proprietors; one, a real estate broker; one, a salesman; one, a machinist; and
two, clerks. In all, more than 40 percent of the applicants between
1877 and 1887 were proposed by businessmen.[22]

The benefits of clientage may have been one reason so many middling salesmen, clerks, and skilled workers were willing to pay
the high Post 2 muster fee. Among skilled workers, for example, the
most common employments were in the building trades—carpen-
ters, plumbers, painters, plasterers, paperhangers, roofers, masons,
stonecutters. Building and contracting during this period relied on
personal contacts to a greater degree than other businesses did, and
GAR membership offered an opportunity to cross paths with potential customers at every post meeting. Unlike manufacturing, construction work was neither continuous nor performed at a single site.
Contractors had to line up suppliers and laborers, coordinate different projects, and above all, watch the market for opportunities—
when one job was finished, the contractor had to find another one.
From the point of view of the construction worker, the sporadic
nature of the business meant he had to be on the lookout for employment almost constantly. The post meeting provided an arena in which
such deals could be cut by men who "drank from the same canteen."
Similar contacts awaited salesmen, who could thumb through the
published Post 2 Business Directory on meeting nights in Philadelphia and use their Post 2 membership as a prestigious calling card at
posts in other cities when on business there.[23]

By contrast, the potential for clientage in GAR posts such as
Fletcher Webster Post 13 of Brockton, Massachusetts, was virtually
nil. A heavily industrialized city of 13,608 (in 1880) located 23 miles
south of Boston, Brockton could claim both a dry ordinance and a
strong labor movement that not infrequently elected socialist city
officials. It was also the site of a dozen major shoe factories and twice
as many smaller concerns, as well as every conceivable business
supplementary to the shoe trade—manufacturers produced shoe
tools, shoe boxes, shoe counters, shoe trees, shoe polish, and a bliz-
zard of related items. The shoe manufacturers of the city had hit early
upon the idea of turning out a cheap, uniform product and advertising
it under the catchall term "the Brockton Shoe," and ever afterward a
shoe was the city's image to the world at large. When members of

Post 2 adopted a post badge, it was an expensive piece of jewelry; when members of Post 13 created a modest badge in 1890, it was in the form of a shoe.[24]

The occupational structure of Brockton's lone GAR post differed sharply from that of Post 2, with businessmen and manufacturers heavily outnumbered by shoe workers.[25] Proprietors and merchants made up only 11 percent of the members whose occupations are known, while high-status white-collar individuals made up only 9 percent. As in Post 2, most of the merchants were small businessmen, but of the thirty-eight high-status white-collar members, seventeen were manufacturers, at least twelve of them in the shoe industry. For the most part, these members were not, as in Philadelphia, translocal worthies with extensive business interests elsewhere. Some prominent members of the post, such as shoe manufacturer James Packard and stove dealer E. Z. Stevens, did have extensive business interests elsewhere, but they lived in Brockton, as did all but nineteen of the other members. "Many of the [shoe] manufacturers had grown up in town, commencing their experience by working at the bench for day wages," boasted the Brockton Board of Trade, "and if not natives of Brockton, as many of them were, they had commenced their business careers within its bounds and learned to regard it as their chosen home for life."[26]

Webster Post also contained few of the clerks, bookkeepers, and salesmen who loomed so large in Post 2; these low-status white-collar workers constituted only 8 percent of the Brockton post. What Webster Post did have in abundance was skilled blue-collar workers and especially semiskilled shoe factory workers.[27] Of the ten charter members of the post whose occupations are known, four were shoe factory workers and two were skilled workers, one of them a maker of shoe tools. The predominance of blue-collar workers among the founders of the post continued in later years, when skilled workers made up 23 percent of the membership and semiskilled and service workers—overwhelmingly shoe factory employees—made up 42 percent. Between them, these two classes of workers constituted almost two-thirds of the members whose occupations are identifiable.

Such a working-class membership could not support a high muster fee or dues, and the Webster Post charges of $3.50 and $3.00, respectively, in 1881, were low compared with those of Post 2. But even that amount worked a hardship on the shoemakers in the post, resulting in a high number of suspensions. Although the number of individuals suspended or dropped at least once was only slightly higher than in

Post 2 (39 percent, compared with 36 percent), suspensions were
considerably more frequent, since the same members tended to fall
into arrears over and over again, periodically lapsing and settling up.
An extreme example was shoe stitcher George Sturtevant, who was
suspended six times between 1877 and 1893 before finally being
dropped from membership in 1894. Another shoemaker, George
Handy, was suspended and reinstated four times in four years before
being dropped in 1880. Ten percent of Webster Post membership
was suspended more than once; less than 3 percent of Post 2 members fell in this category. Yet even those who had chronic problems
keeping up their dues made more of an effort to pay up in Webster
Post than in Post 2. In Webster Post, about half of the members
suspended for the first time settled their arrearages; in Post 2, less
than one-third did so.[28]

It was important for a Brockton member to make his dues payments; otherwise, he would miss the post's frequent social events,
primarily dinners and dances, which were an inexpensive form of
entertainment as well as a fraternal good time. More important, only
members in good standing could rely on the post to pay funeral
expenses and provide the GAR's semimilitary funeral service in case
of death. While the same was true of Post 2, few Philadelphia members seem to have insisted on the GAR service. The death of a
member in Post 2 usually was marked by symbolic actions—leaving a
chair empty in the post room or a page blank in the minutes, draping
the post charter in crepe. For the struggling members of Webster
Post, however, the funeral benefit was probably a major reason to
join the order.[29]

The Brockton shoe workers, like the Philadelphia clerks, tended to
choose high-status individuals for post offices, but not at the expense
of denying themselves a significant number of positions. High-status
white-collar members, representing 9 percent of the membership,
filled 16 percent of the offices between 1876 and 1893. Semiskilled
and service workers, conversely, represented 42 percent of the membership and filled 34 percent of the offices. Thus, while the shoe
workers filled fewer than their share of post offices, they still accounted for more than a third of the total. More important, the
positions in which they served were not minor. Seven of the eighteen
post commanders were from the semiskilled group, as were two of
the seven trustees. In fact, the post was commanded by a shoe worker
more often than by a merchant or a professional man. While many of
the high-status officers were clergymen serving as post chaplains

or physicians serving as post surgeons, the working-class members tended to fill the secondary leadership positions—senior vice commander, junior vice commander—that eventually led to the commander's chair. The pattern of leadership was the reverse of that in Post 2: instead of a merchant commander with a staff of clerks, Webster Post usually found itself with a blue-collar commander and a staff of business and professional men.

The lone attempt to change the prevailing pattern was made in 1886, when the members elected a new man from Oregon, civil engineer Alfred F. Sears, as post commander. Sears would have been a natural for office in Post 2, having served as a major in the First New York Engineers. But he found that his profession did not leave him time to devote to the office, and after three months he resigned the commandery; a year later he transferred out of the post. Chastened, the members reverted to form and elected a previous commander, shoe leather cutter George Grant.[30] In most subsequent years, this post of shoe workers was run by shoe workers.

A third variant of local post life can be seen in the occupational structure of James Comerford Post 68. Though not quite agricultural enough to qualify as what GAR officers called a "country post," it was hardly as urban as the Philadelphia and Brockton organizations. Located in the northwest Wisconsin city of Chippewa Falls, it drew members not only from the town of 8,670 residents (in 1890) but also from the farm and sawmill hamlets that dotted heavily rural Chippewa County. The dense forests of the area and the navigable Chippewa River had made Chippewa Falls a major lumber entrepôt by the 1880s; before the war, however, it had been little more than an oversize logging camp. When the county was organized in 1855 it had only 600 residents; at the outbreak of the war it still had only about 2,500.[31]

Comerford Post, named for a prisoner of war whose widow still lived in the area, was founded much later than either Post 2 or Webster Post. Both of the Eastern posts had organized more or less spontaneously in the first year of the GAR's existence, Post 2 in late 1866 and Webster Post in early 1867. The Chippewa Falls post was not formed until 1883, a product of the national order's renaissance in the West during the late 1870s and early 1880s. As with most posts organized during that period, Comerford Post was the deliberate creation of national and department GAR officers who were seeking to increase membership. Wisconsin department commander Philip Cheek presided personally at the post's formative meeting.[32]

The late-forming Western posts usually were made up of veterans who had joined the large westward migration of soldiers after the war. In one of the leading posts of Chicago, for example, only 30 percent of the members were veterans of Illinois regiments.[33] So many veterans resettled in the "Great Soldier State" of Kansas that for a time it had more GAR members per capita than any other state. By 1892 Nebraska would have enough veterans to make a bid for Lincoln to host the national encampment. And throughout the West the place names of new towns such as Soldiers Grove, Wisconsin, attested to the movement. Comerford Post was no exception to the rule—of the 153 post members known to have been born in the United States, only 19 had been born in Wisconsin and only 1 in Chippewa County.

Although the post included some low-status white-collar employees (9 percent of those whose occupations are known), skilled workers (13 percent), and semiskilled workers (5 percent), they were not numerous compared with the makeup of posts in other small Wisconsin cities.[34] Most Comerford Post members were farmers and workers in the nearby lumber camps. The farmers, 32 percent of the membership, were scattered from one end of the county to the other. Only occasionally able to make it to town for meetings, they were not usually among the most prominent of post members. The unskilled workers, almost all lumbermen, accounted for 23 percent of the membership. These out-dwelling farmers and transient lumbermen made up the majority of a post in which suspensions, as in Brockton, were common despite the low dues ($2 per year in 1883). Unlike Webster Post, however, Comerford Post often had to suspend members permanently when they simply moved on, as in 1888 when three members were dropped, "having left the country."[35]

The unsettled nature of the county gave Comerford Post an extremely high turnover rate. After the founding of the post in 1883 there was a rush of new members—71 percent of the total membership joined between 1883 and 1890. The post experienced its peak membership of 215 members in 1884, only a year after it was founded.[36] But almost at once the new recruits began falling away. Some (8 percent) did not last two years; substantially more (37 percent) did not last five. Although new members continued to sign up, membership declined almost without interruption for the rest of the century because so many of the members were in arrears or had been dropped from the rolls. More than half the membership (52 percent) was suspended or dropped at one time or another, and of these, very few (about one in seven) were ever reinstated—a steep rate of loss that more than offset the extraordinary gain in the first few years.

What kept this transient post together was a small but stable elite of the type that characterized many other Western towns in the nineteenth century.[37] Not much is known about some of Comerford Post's fifty charter members, a number of whom ceased to participate in the post shortly after its formation. But the characteristics of the officers elected at the initial meeting are clear enough: They were the town aristocracy. Post commander William Hoyt was a lawyer, soon to be a county judge; Senior Vice Commander John J. Jenkins was a judge, soon to be a state representative; Junior Vice Commander W. S. Munroe was a manufacturer. Among the lesser officers, Surgeon Alex McBean was a doctor; Officer of the Day Joseph Hesketh ran a hardware store; Officer of the Guard William W. Crandall was county register of deeds; Adjutant Thomas J. Kiley was principal of a school; and Sergeant Major Frank Clough owned a general store. These local worthies ran the post at its inception; they, and others like them, would continue to run it most of the time afterward.

An examination of the line of post commanders tells the story simply. Hoyt himself was post commander four times between 1883 and 1899; William H. Howieson, a sawmill builder,[38] headed the post four other years. The other nine members who served one term each in the commander's chair included a merchant, an editor, a pension attorney, a bookkeeper, a lumber inspector, a painter, a lumberman, a deputy sheriff, and one man whose occupation is not known. Of the eight members who served at least five times in lesser offices, three were merchants; one, a banker and real estate dealer; one, a hotel keeper; one, the publisher of the *Chippewa Herald*; one, a lumber clerk; and one, a carpenter. In sum, the leadership of Comerford Post was tightly held among a small group of well-off members over a period of seventeen years. With a membership that spanned the county, the post was run from the town.

The townspeople among the membership dominated the officers' ranks despite the fact that high-status individuals were not numerous in the post membership. Merchants and high-status white-collar members (mostly lawyers and doctors) each represented 9 percent of those with known occupations. Members from these classes were bound to hold post offices if they remained members long enough. Of the fifty-one high-status or merchant members, thirty-two served in offices or on major committees. As in Post 2, they were also the

leading sponsors of clients. Aside from two adjutants who routinely
signed as "proposers" on applications from recruits who had not found sponsors, the leading proposers of new members were Judge Hoyt and merchant Hesketh (twenty-eight clients each), sawmill builder Howieson (nineteen), merchant Clough (eleven), and hotel keeper Barney Himmelsbach (seven).[39] While the membership as a whole was fluid, with an average of thirteen members joining and sixteen departing or dying each year, these men stayed put and commanded. In fact, there were really two Comerford Posts: the mass of hastily recruited loggers and farmers who made up the bulk of the membership at any given point and the smaller group of longtime residents who led it.

Occupationally, then, the posts at Philadelphia, Brockton, and Chippewa Falls were quite distinct. And since military rank and social status often went together, the Civil War careers of the post members told similarly divergent stories (table 2).[40] On the average, the veterans who joined Post 2 had served longer, suffered more wounds, and attained higher rank than members of Webster and Comerford posts. Better than eight in ten had served in the Union armies for more than a year, many of them (about six of every ten) for three years or more. By comparison, 64 percent of Webster Post members and 71 percent of Comerford Post members had served for longer than a year.

The reason for the longer average service term among Post 2 members was the post's practice of quietly rejecting men who had served short terms. Of the seventeen rejectees from Post 2 for whom terms of service are known, thirteen had served for less than a year and ten for less than six months. In 1885, each of three "hundred days men" (a disparaging term for those who had served briefly and relatively painlessly in the early months of the war) was rejected three times, despite the pleas of their sponsors that nothing in the GAR rules prohibited short-term veterans from joining. Such blackballing was not consistent and had subsided by the 1890s, but it was enough to keep many short-service veterans out of the post. Though direct evidence is lacking, similar reluctance to muster short-service men also seems to have existed in other posts—four of the six rejectees from Comerford Post, for example, also had served less than one year. In any case, the service terms of Webster and Comerford post members were slightly longer than those of non-GAR members in their respective communities.[41]

The blackballing of short-service men may help explain why Post 2

Table 2. Military Terms of Service and Ranks of GAR Members, Philadelphia, Brockton, and Chippewa Falls, 1867–1900

Term and rank	Post 2, Philadelphia (N = 1,367)	Webster Post, Brockton (N = 540)	Comerford Post, Chippewa Falls (N = 318)
Term of Service			
More than one year	1,088 (81%)	298 (64%)	197 (71%)
90 days to one year	201 (15)	149 (32)	75 (27)
30 to 90 days	47 (3)	14 (3)	3 (1)
Less than 30 days	11 (0.8)	2 (0.4)	1 (0.4)
Unknown	20	77	42
Rank			
Commissioned officer	193 (14%)	9 (2%)	12 (4%)
Noncomm. officer	465 (34)	77 (16)	55 (17)
Surgeon or chaplain	28 (2)	1 (0.2)	4 (1)
Private or seaman	541 (40)	352 (75)	238 (76)
Support role (adjutant, cook, etc.)	124 (9)	31 (7)	6 (2)
Unknown	16	70	3

Source: See notes 2 and 3, this chapter.
Note: All percentages are expressed as a percentage of members whose ranks or terms of service are known. Commissioned officers are those at the rank of captain or above. Noncommissioned officers are corporals, sergeants, and lieutenants, and, in the navy, engineers, ensigns, and mates.

had a relatively high number of veterans who had been wounded, though the fierce fighting done by the Army of the Potomac, in which most of them had served, undoubtedly had more to do with it. Twenty-six percent of the Philadelphia membership reported being wounded in action or discharged for disability, a rate more than double that of the Brockton and Chippewa Falls posts and almost double that of the Union Army.[42] Battle wounds were in some ways the ultimate ranks, clearly showing the sacrifices veterans had made to save the Union. As such, they played an important part in the hagiology of the GAR, with seriously wounded veterans frequently selected for state and national office. The one-armed Lucius Fairchild and the legless James

Tanner, for instance, forged national political careers from their support among Union veterans.[43]

Like all GAR posts, the Philadelphia, Brockton, and Chippewa Falls organizations were made up primarily of former privates. But only 40 percent of the members of elite Post 2 were men of that rank. Instead, Post 2 included an exceptionally high number of former commissioned officers (14 percent of the membership, compared with 2 percent in Brockton and 4 percent in Chippewa Falls) and noncommissioned officers (34 percent in Post 2, 16 percent in Brockton, 17 percent in Chippewa Falls). The preponderance of officers in Post 2 may have been another reason for its large wounded population, since Civil War officers suffered a higher casualty rate than did enlisted men. In any event, the ex-officers in Post 2 were often rewarded with post offices and trusteeships: twenty-five of the thirty post commanders had held ranks higher than private; thirteen had held ranks higher than captain.[44]

By contrast, Webster and Comerford posts had few ex-officers available to fill post offices. In Brockton, only nine of the 540 post members between 1873 and 1900 had held ranks as high as captain, and of these, Alfred Sears was the only one to serve in an office or on a committee. In Chippewa Falls, only twelve members of Comerford Post had been commissioned officers, and while one—colonel and newspaper publisher George Ginty—was a trustee and an active member, none of the others held office at all. The highest rank achieved by any of the eleven Comerford Post commanders was first lieutenant, by William Hoyt; three of the others had been sergeants; one, a corporal; five, privates; and one, a hospital steward. On the other hand, the members of Webster and Comerford posts, three-quarters of whom were ex-privates, still outranked veterans in their respective communities who were not GAR members.[45] And former officers were unlikely to suffer rejection; together, the three posts blackballed only one applicant above the rank of lieutenant. GAR members, in short, showed some slight bias in favor of ex-officers and against short-service men, a preference magnified in elite posts such as Post 2.

Ethnically, the Philadelphia, Brockton, and Chippewa Falls posts were more homogeneous than the population at large, though Comerford Post included more immigrants than the others and probably more Catholics (table 3). American-born veterans made up 84 percent of Post 2; most of the other members were immigrants from Germany or Ireland. While slightly higher than the percentage of

Table 3. Birthplaces of GAR Members, Philadelphia, Brockton, and Chippewa Falls, 1867–1900

Occupation	Post 2, Philadelphia (N = 1,367)	Webster Post, Brockton (N = 540)	Comerford Post, Chippewa Falls (N = 318)
Local	585 (43%)	36 (9%)	1 (0.4%)
Elsewhere in state	293 (22)	228 (57)	18 (8)
Out of state, U.S.	265 (19)	86 (22)	134 (59)
Outside U.S.	219 (16)	48 (12)	76 (33)
Unknown	5	142	89

Source: See notes 2 and 3, this chapter.

Note: All percentages are expressed as a percentage of members whose birthplaces are known. "Local" is defined as a birthplace in the city of Philadelphia (Post 2), Greater Brockton (Webster Post), or Chippewa County (Comerford Post).

foreign-born veterans in Brockton, Post 2's 16 percent was well below the figure for Chippewa Falls and probably somewhat low for the order as a whole. Grant Post 5, for instance, was founded at the same time as Post 2 and drew from the same recruiting base but counted 28 percent of its membership as foreign-born.[46]

The Chippewa Falls post was more diverse, with one-third of its members having been born outside the United States. Most of the immigrant members were either German farmers or French Canadians from the sawmills and lumber camps. But the post membership also included many Irish veterans, as well as natives of Switzerland, France, Norway, England, and Scotland. The post's composition probably gave it a larger number of Catholics than either of the Eastern posts. Data on religious background are not given on membership applications, but the post maintained a plot in the local Catholic cemetery and sixteen of the thirty-nine veterans buried there were members. Comerford Post also sometimes attended the local Catholic church on holidays, something neither Post 2 nor Webster Post ever did, and the post elected the priest, Father Oliver Goldsmith, an honorary member. Still, it is likely that the GAR as a whole, like most Gilded Age fraternal orders, was predominantly Protestant, despite the ineffectual opposition to fraternities on the

part of Protestant evangelical groups such as the National Christian
Association.[47]

If immigrants and Catholics were underrepresented in the GAR, blacks were virtually absent. The Philadelphia, Brockton, and Chippewa Falls posts had only one black member among them—Lemuel Ashport, who acted as the drum major for Webster Post's marching unit. Neither Post 2 nor Comerford Post had any black members, but that was not unusual—few posts elsewhere did either. Sometimes the towns the posts served were mostly white—in Brockton, for instance, the federal census of 1890 found only three black veterans. But where the black veteran population was large, as in Philadelphia, black and white veterans maintained separate posts, an arrangement that caused little comment until a bitter dispute in one Southern department brought the issue to national attention in 1887. As in the Grand Review, as in the Union Army itself, black veterans were accorded separate and unequal status.[48]

Compared with the population as a whole, all three of these posts were native-born and white. Except for the segregation of black members, however, the relatively homogeneous membership of the posts does not indicate active discrimination on the part of the GAR. Rather, it reflects the ethnic makeup of the nation at the outbreak of the war. By the 1890s the U.S. was drawing large numbers of immigrants from countries only slightly represented in the population of 1860. In this way the GAR, like the hereditary Daughters and Sons of the American Revolution, functioned as a kind of passive nativist organization. It did not openly bar nonwhite, nonnative nonmales; it simply drew the line of qualification for membership around participation in a historical event that had occurred too early for the latecomers and too selectively for women and most blacks. An army mostly native-born and white, in other words, produced a social organization mostly native-born and white, in a nation that was becoming more diverse every year.[49]

Of Rules, Lords, and Liquor

The picture that emerges from the GAR membership data reveals an organization with a great deal of local variation. In Philadelphia's Post 2 the typical member was a clerk or an aspiring merchant who paid his dues regularly, wore an expensive badge, and attended a meeting every month or two to transact a little business. In Brockton he was more likely to be a former farm boy turned struggling shoe operative, to whom membership in Webster Post meant bean suppers, an impressive funeral, and, if he was an officer, a chance to exercise authority, which was denied him in everyday life. In Chippewa Falls most members were lumbermen or farmers, many of them immigrants and Catholics, to whom Comerford Post meant a trip to town to share war stories with other men only recently settled in Chippewa County from all points of the compass. Elsewhere in the North, one could find GAR posts dominated by common laborers, farmers, or skilled blue-collar workers.[50]

The class, ethnic and regional differences among members of these posts were evident in their positions on issues ranging from rules and charity to Memorial Day and temperance. In the first place, they interpreted the preoccupation of the national GAR with Union, order, and discipline in significantly different ways. Post 2, for one, made a virtual fetish of rules, as in 1879 when it was faced with the problem of members who simply announced their "resignations" from the GAR. Under the rules it was not possible to "resign"; a member had to apply for and be granted an "honorable discharge." After two unsuccessful attempts to advise would-be "resignees" of that technicality, the post adopted a policy of issuing "honorable discharges" after the fact to those who had announced "resignations."[51] On other occasions the post fined members who failed to wear their badges to meetings, applied for permission from the various state adjutants-general for permission to carry the Post 2 Guard guns to a reunion at Hartford, and insisted on "leaves of absence" for members who planned to be absent from town for short periods. One entire meeting was spent debating the nice point of whether the post could legally remove itself to Springfield, Massachusetts, for the national encampment, a matter settled only by a special "dispensation" from the department commander. In fact, Post 2 often felt the need of such dispensations, as did at least one other middle-class urban post whose records have survived, James Garfield Post 8 of St. Paul, Minnesota.[52]

To less fastidious posts, however, many GAR rules (such as the one requiring a one-week layover between the presentation of a recruit and a ballot on his application) were pointless annoyances that called out to be circumvented. In Comerford Post, the method was simple: the rules were simply "suspended" and the necessary business done. The members' indifference to national procedure is apparent from a meeting in 1890, when those present attempted to make out an application, report on, vote for, and muster one Harry Held on the same night under a suspension of the rules. William H. Howieson, one of the town worthies who lent the post what little continuity it had, objected "that there was no such thing as suspending the rules and regulations of the GAR as they originated in a higher body than this Post. But on the motion being put to a vote it was carried. Said Harry Held was then reobligated without his being balloted upon on the payment of the required fees." In the matter of "resignations," the Chippewa Falls post had too high a turnover to worry about whether they should be called "discharges." The Brockton post was less flagrant, but it too mustered a number of recruits on the night of application, and it frequently dispensed with the formal GAR opening and closing ceremonies as well.[53] The largely working-class veterans of Comerford and Webster posts would have the found elite Post 2's fussiness about rules utterly foreign.

Veterans of different classes also tended to disagree about the Grand Army's quasi-military hierarchy, as evidenced by their attitudes toward the so-called House of Lords affair. This controversy, which first broke out at the national encampment of 1886, stemmed from a prerogative of rank granted just after the demise of the grade system. In 1872 rule changes gave automatic seats in the national encampment not only to elected delegates but also to all present and past national officers and to all past department commanders.[54] Although little-noticed at the time, the inclusion of past officers soon became a major irritant to humble posts like those at Brockton and Chippewa Falls, which rarely saw any of their members elected to departmental office. By the 1880s the GAR had so many past officers that if they all showed up at an encampment they almost outnumbered the elected delegates. The threat of rule by unelected life members—the House of Lords, as one opponent tagged them— loomed.

The campaign against the Lords drew much of its force from its close connection to a drive among some GAR members to lobby Congress for a blanket pension for all Union veterans. The life members, they asserted, were lukewarm toward service pensions and were using their disproportionate influence in the national encampment to block the idea. The "poor soldiers" who made up the majority of the GAR membership could not have their way because of the scheming, well-to-do House of Lords.[55] The politics behind the various pension schemes of the 1880s and 1890s will be examined in detail later; here it is necessary only to stress that well-off members tended to be less enthusiastic about the potential cash boon of a service pension than did the poor soldiers.

In consequence, the haughty Post 2 found itself defending the Lords. After some of its members slipped a resolution supporting a service pension through at a sparsely attended summer meeting in 1884, two of the post worthies—state official James Latta and lawyer Moses Veale—persuaded the post to reverse itself and declare full support for the national encampment's more moderate position, saying it had "acted wisely and well in this matter." Conversely, both the shoemakers of Brockton's Webster Post and the farmers of Chippewa Falls's Comerford Post came out early for the service pension—the former in 1880, the latter in 1883.[56] The service pension was a poor man's cause.

Beyond pension politics, however, the Lords stood for rank and privilege in an order that was, at best, ambivalent about such values. At the 1886 national encampment, held in faraway San Francisco and thus attended mostly by wealthy members, delegates were nonetheless greeted with a host of proposals to bar the life members from their seats, the most radical of which, from the Colorado delegation, also would have barred the Lords from voting on the question of their own exclusion. "How many, outside of the Delegates sent by Posts to San Francisco, are 'poor soldiers'?" cried House of Lords opponent D. T. Brock during the heated debate. When a similar proposal was offered the next year at St. Louis, one of the opponents of the Lords called the existing system of representation "un-American" and "undemocratic" and complained about delegates "whose title to place and power on this floor is only limited by life, and who are in no way responsible to the Departments to which they belong"—a reference to several officers from Massachusetts who had voted to kill the 1886 proposal despite explicit instructions to the contrary from their constituency. But a California delegate objected: "I do not know what class of comrades and men they are in the habit of electing to the office of Department Commander in New York. We in California elect men to the highest office in the gift of that Department, in whom we trust and whom we honor." Both the San Francisco and the St. Louis proposals went down to defeat, but the issue of lifetime tenure continued to be raised at subsequent national encampments and at some state encampments as well.[57]

Life members such as Post 2's Louis Wagner took the insurgency as a personal insult. Wagner, a crusty Philadelphia banker and a charter member of the post, complained that the delegates had "had this hashed until we are tired; and we have had it crammed down our throats by these comrades who come here once in a while, and because they haven't been here before, and never will be again." The anti-Lords forces, which were strongest in New England, replied that the institution was undemocratic and that life members like Wagner were potential aristocrats. As one Massachusetts delegate put it in 1889, life membership was "the European theory; you have to cross the Atlantic to find that monster."[58] The Lords, in short, invoked their stations, their honor, or their long service, while the insurgents replied using the language of republicanism.

No post was more deeply opposed to the Lords than Brockton's Webster Post. With its large working-class membership, low dues, and egalitarian officeholding pattern, the shoemakers' post had long resisted the claims of privilege in the GAR; in its post room, for example, the risers on which officers' chairs normally rested had been deliberately removed. When John A. Andrew Post 15 of Boston formed an association to lobby for service pensions, Webster Post joined willingly and contributed financially.[59] And in 1896 the post took the battle to the Massachusetts department encampment. In a series of resolutions, the Brockton members called for an immediate service pension; a full accounting of expenses incurred by the state officers, which the post suspected had been used for "improper purposes"; and an end to the practice of paying travel expenses of delegates to the national encampment, which one member of the post later asserted were "spent largely in enjoying wine suppers and voting each other expensive presents." The post members also labeled the House of Lords "a privileged class" and "an illegal barnacle," called for its immediate abolition, and pledged the post's department encampment delegation to that end.[60]

When the resolutions reached the floor of the encampment, however, Massachusetts commander Joseph Thayer suppressed them as "inexpedient." Furthermore, the members charged, their proposals were "openly ridiculed from the floor by a delegate who moved that they be referred to his 'barnyard,'" and Department Commander Thayer, as the presiding officer, "not only failed to rebuke this insulting remark, but he also joined in the laugh which it raised." Taking that response as an affront, the post refused to send delegates to the 1897 encampment and declared its intention of boycotting future encampments as well. When department officers visited Brockton in May 1897, they were told that "sending delegates on the part of the

Posts was merely idle work" as long as past department commanders ruled the encampments. For this "insubordination" the new department commander, John M. Deane, revoked the Webster Post charter, an action that the *Grand Army Record*, no friend of the Massachusetts Lords, called "despotic."[61]

For the next two years the Brockton members and their allies in other sympathetic posts denounced the officers' "trivial" and "groundless" accusations and their "abuse of authority"; the officers in return charged the post with refusal to obey orders and use of intemperate language. When three department officers publicly charged Webster Post with insubordination, members of the post, echoing Oliver Wilson's complaint, exploded: "Since when have the rules of our order been so binding in their general application that in all cases they hold every member to as strict an interpretation as army rule and military discipline in time of war?" The affair ended equivocally in 1898 when new Massachusetts commander William H. Bartlett (in real life a Worcester school principal) restored the Brockton charter after an appeal to the national encampment and the passage of some vague resolutions on the part of Webster Post. Neither side apologized, and the *Record* went so far as to claim victory for the levelers. "The free and equal rights of American Citizenship Fully Vindicated," crowed its headline.[62] In the redemption of the Brockton post other humble veterans could take some solace. But the national encampment's continued refusal to unseat the Lords or to endorse the service pension gave elite posts such as Post 2 the real victory.

If the differing class positions of GAR members influenced attitudes toward rules and hierarchy they were also evident in a third area, that of charity for needy veterans. Through all the panics and depressions of the late nineteenth century, Philadelphia's affluent Post 2 continued to dispense its own charity. There is no indication that it appointed even the public committee on veterans' funerals provided for by Pennsylvania law.[63] Most of its members were well-off individuals, longtime (if not lifetime) residents of the city, and veterans of Pennsylvania regiments. Post 2 had many members with money and few who were in desperate need of it; certainly the post did not include many of the chronically poor and unemployed veterans who called on other GAR posts for repeated support. Consequently, its relief fund was larger and faced less severe demands. When members of such an upper-middle-class institution did require money for charity, they did not need to go begging to the city. Instead,

they used private influence to find jobs for each other, dug into their
own pockets, or sought donations from the wealthy men with whom
they socialized.

In part, then, Post 2's minimal recourse to public funds could be
attributed to the social prominence of its membership. But it also
reflected the post's cosmopolitan focus. Unlike the Brockton and
Chippewa Falls posts, Post 2 did not claim to serve all the veterans of
the community; indeed, the occasional referral to Post 2 of charity
cases from other city posts sometimes caused complaints. Rather,
Post 2 was seen within Philadelphia as a leader of translocal charity
efforts: money for comrades burned out in Chicago or flooded out in
Johnstown, jobs for orphans from the state orphans' home, aid for
victims of the Charleston earthquake, even relief for famine victims
in Russia. The post's community of reference was not the geographical one of Philadelphia; it was the same nascent, translocal community of professionals and businessmen served by the Post 2 Business
Directory. For the most part, such veterans as these were not in need
of relief, as their cool attitude toward the service pension would
demonstrate in the 1890s. When they spoke of "manly independence," they did so from a comfortable social position that made
dependence on public charity only a remote possibility.

In Chippewa Falls, by contrast, Comerford Post was at once more
in need of relief money than Post 2 and less able to provide it. When a
new state law in 1888 allowed towns to levy a tax to support poor
veterans and their families, the post leaders seized the opportunity.
Not only did they convince the towns of Chippewa County to impose
the tax, they persuaded the county judge to name post members to
two of the three seats on the commission dispensing the relief.[64]
After the commission began operations in 1888, Comerford Post
abolished its own relief committee and dealt with such needs as
illness and unemployment on a case-by-case basis.

The county-tax approach was a natural choice for a post whose
small elite had a fundamentally local orientation. With the exception
of Colonel George Ginty, whose influence extended at most to the
state level, and Representative John J. Jenkins, these "men of affairs"
were primarily local fixtures, filling such offices as those of county
judge, alderman, district attorney, sheriff, county supervisor and
school board member. Although they had influence, they were by no
means wealthy burghers who could easily fund substantial charity
from their own resources.

Moreover, they superintended a post whose members were mostly farmers or loggers living at some distance from town, few of them pre-war residents of Wisconsin, much less Chippewa County. Whereas Post 2 had clubbish, patron-client relationships between business-men and clerks, Comerford Post had more tenuous connections be-tween Chippewa Falls worthies and Chippewa County farmers and loggers. The Comerford Post officers also were tied to a specific geographical community in a way that the Philadelphians were not: in their eyes, they were responsible for Chippewa County. With influ-ence in local government, limited individual resources and an indi-gent population in constant flux, the Comerford Post officers naturally turned to county-funded charity, especially when the members of the county relief commission were certain to be Comerford Post mem-bers.

In the Brockton post, which had no such relationship to its city, appeals to local government were considerably less successful. In 1889 members brought to the city's attention two state laws that, like the Pennsylvania statute, required towns to fund funerals of indigent ex-soldiers and to name panels of veterans to take charge of them. But Brockton's mayor informed the post members that the laws were "practically of no effect," and the post minutes give no evidence that the city ever appointed any type of veteran funeral commission. As for public aid to living ex-soldiers, Webster Post actually endorsed a petition seeking to *repeal* the state law requiring localities to care for poor veterans outside almshouses—perhaps a grudging admission on the part of the post's veterans that the only charity the City of Brockton intended to give indigent ex-soldiers was what it provided the rest of the population, namely, a place in the poorhouse.[65] Web-ster Post did raise substantial outside aid, but it came from the voluntary donations of honorary "associate members" and guests at post fairs.

The Brockton shoemakers had neither the cosmopolitanism of the Philadelphians nor the powerful local political position that charac-terized the Chippewa Falls members. Just as Comerford Post worried first about Chippewa Falls, Webster Post concerned itself mainly with relief in Brockton; it almost never made donations to state or national relief campaigns. In part, that attitude may have resulted from the same lurking suspicion of the upper ranks of the GAR that led the post to label the House of Lords "an illegal barnacle." Probably, though, it had more to do with the slender resources available to a post of semiskilled shoe-manufacturing workers. In any event, the post's relief was predominantly local in scope.

It was also a reflection of the marginal political position of the

Brockton veterans. Unlike the officers of Chippewa Falls's Comerford
Post, the leaders of Webster Post were men peripheral to the local
power structure. Relatively few merchants and manufacturers belonged to the post, and the few who did were not active in it. In a city
dominated by the shoe industry, Webster Post counted twelve shoe
manufacturers on its roster but elected only three to any office before
1900 and none to the post commandery. With rare exceptions, its
members did not hold local political offices. In return, the citizenry of
Brockton treated the GAR as it did any other fraternal body—as the
recipient of occasional, purely voluntary donations. It is no wonder
that service pension agitators in the late 1880s and early 1890s found
the members of Webster Post among their warmest supporters.

The ethnic differences among GAR posts were evident in other
areas, notably in posts' attitudes toward Catholicism and temperance. The GAR at the national level had a strongly Protestant flavor,
from the tone of its *Services* book, compiled by a Congregational
minister, to the choice of all of its chaplains-in-chief before 1888 (and
probably thereafter) from among the ranks of Protestant pastors.
Moreover, Memorial Day, the most important ritual event on the
Grand Army calendar, was invariably celebrated in a Protestant
church—even in Chippewa Falls, where the local GAR post and the
local Catholic priest were on better terms than in many localities.[66]

For its part, the Catholic church was suspicious of all secret fraternal orders—particularly those with Masonic antecedents—and
viewed the GAR's quasi-Masonic initiation ritual and generic Christian funeral rites as improper substitutes for religious services. Thus,
when Post 51 of Philadelphia tried to use the GAR service for the
burial of a Catholic comrade in 1879, it found the action prohibited by
orders of the archbishop. Three years later, members of a Reading
post refused to remove their GAR badges for a funeral at a Catholic
church; the priests performing the ceremony retaliated by barring
the veterans from the church and refusing to accompany the funeral
procession to the cemetery. A similar incident at Pottsville in 1885,
the *National Tribune* reported, "had the effect of creating a deep
feeling of bitterness between the Catholics and Protestants at the
place." And on Memorial Day in 1882, a Catholic priest in Milford,
Massachusetts, removed the flags placed on veterans' graves by local
Grand Army men, after trying to keep the veterans off the property
entirely. "You get one hundred dollars a year from the town," he
complained, referring to a municipal appropriation for Memorial

Day. "Why not then have solemn mass and service according to Catholic ideas and immemorial usage for the Catholic soldier 'who has fought his last fight,' and has passed from your jurisdiction to that of the church that prays for his soul?"[67]

Despite the generalized Protestantism of the GAR and the hostility of the Catholic hierarchy to fraternal orders, the three posts studied most closely here were not troubled by religious strife. Comerford Post, which probably had the largest Catholic membership of the three, boasted Father Oliver Goldsmith as an honorary member. And when the other, more heavily Protestant posts had Catholic members to bury, as Webster Post did with Michael Casey in 1885 and Post 2 did with John Kennedy in 1887, they were careful to defer to "the rules governing the Church."[68] The Protestant-Catholic strife so visible in other places was largely absent in Chippewa Falls, Brockton, and Post 2 of Philadelphia.

On the temperance question, the largely Yankee Webster Post, located in a dry town, was more austere than were most GAR posts. The Brocktonians made several court-martial inquiries into reports of drunkenness, though they ultimately did not convict any members of the offense. The Webster Post roster listed no one who had anything to do with the liquor trade, while a special post bylaw penalized intoxication in the post room.[69] Post 2, though also dominated by native-born Protestants, was somewhat less agitated. It admitted eleven members who were connected with the liquor trade, some of whom were quite active in post affairs, and the post apparently served liquor at some functions. Still, excessive drinking was frowned upon, and in one incident an applicant whose occupation had been mistakenly listed in a post circular as "bartender" was rejected for membership (he was elected on a second ballot after the mistake was discovered).[70]

On the other side of the question, Comerford Post, with its sizable immigrant membership, had little interest in temperance. The post roster included four saloon keepers, and at meetings the post never reprimanded any member for drunken behavior. Indeed, at one point the members joked about the favorite drink of the teetotalers. When the post adjutant was to deliver resolutions of thanks to someone who had done the post a favor in 1883, it was proposed that if he failed to do so he "be tried by a Drum Head Court Martial and sentenced to be shot with Lemonade, and that Comrade Ginty will see that the Lemonade is properly loaded."[71] Temperance in the

Unity amid Diversity

The differences among the memberships of these
three posts tell something about the diversity of the GAR membership; it will not do simply to say that members were mostly ex-
privates, or mostly businessmen, or mostly Protestants. Yet at least
four general conclusions seem warranted. First, while duration of
service and previous military rank technically meant nothing as far as
joining the Grand Army was concerned, they were important criteria
by which members judged each other. Short-service men were
frowned upon, while former commissioned officers were likely to be
called to serve as post officers. Though not formally barred from
joining, short-term soldiers tended to be excluded by the informal
blackballing of post members; the resulting posts were made up
mostly of men who had served more than one year. And while not
every post had many ex-officers, those that did (such as Post 2)
treated former rank as a strong recommendation for post office.
This practice was even more prevalent at the department and national levels, where former captains, colonels, majors, and generals
abounded.

Second, the limitation of GAR membership to Union Civil War
veterans meant that native-born white men tended to predominate.
While ethnicity was irrelevant in dividing the successful applicants
from the rejects, the GAR's refusal to admit nonveterans or veterans
of later wars would gradually set the members off as racially and
ethnically distinct when the immigrant population of the United
States began to swell in the 1890s. Grounded in the particular historical experiences of its members, the GAR nonetheless shared the
characteristics of passive exclusion with such hereditary organizations as the Society of the Cincinnati and the Daughters of the American Revolution. The ethnic and racial makeup of the order was
beyond the power of time to change.

Third, no matter what the social composition of a post's membership, it tended to serve as a forum for professionals and businessmen
of the middle and upper middle classes. To be sure, there were
exceptions. Industrial workers predominated in posts like the one at

Brockton, while the members of country posts in places such as Lime
Ridge and Dallas, Wisconsin, were virtually all farmers. But even in
Brockton the local burghers held more than their share of the post
offices, and in other industrial cities such as Neenah, Wisconsin, and
Reading, Pennsylvania, GAR posts were founded primarily by high-
status individuals who only later recruited large numbers of blue-
collar workers.[72] In Philadelphia and Chippewa Falls, elite leadership was even more apparent. Both of those posts were usually
commanded by merchants, lawyers, or manufacturers; Post 2 offered
additional benefits for businessmen through its contacts in other
major cities and its in-house business directory. The concentration of
GAR leadership in the hands of the prominent shows most clearly in
the description of national officers' occupations by Robert Beath in
his *History* of 1889, a list that incidentally testifies to the predominance of former colonels and generals in the national GAR leadership. Except for the 17 for whom no occupation is listed, every one of
the 117 national officers between 1866 and 1888 was a businessman,
a manufacturer, or a professional man.[73] The national leadership
was in some sense the local leadership writ large: local notables
selected state notables, who in turn selected national notables.

Finally, despite the penchant for elite leadership, the striking thing
about GAR membership as a whole was its tendency to cut across
class boundaries. The composition of an individual post followed the
occupational and racial contours of the town in which it was located.
When a city's population included mostly industrial workers or
clerks, so did the post; when a county was rural, the post was made
up of farmers; when an area contained different classes of veterans,
they might divide into separate posts on the basis of race or previous
military service. Often the division was based on nothing more than
geography. Like the other nineteenth-century fraternal orders recently analyzed by Mary Ann Clawson, the GAR was not pegged to a
particular social class. Rather, like the early Republican party to
which so many of its members belonged, the order offered its members an alternative to class organization, an alternative based on the
vision of an essentially classless nation.[74]

That vision points to a fourth continuity of GAR membership, one
that does not appear so plainly in the membership data. Above the
many differences among local posts stood the national organization,
with its inclusive membership policy and its putative identification
with the nation. An individual post might bar one class or race of
veterans; the national GAR barred no one who had served honorably

in the Union Army. A post might identify itself with the interest of a
town or city; the GAR claimed to stand for all the veterans of the
nation. To be a member of the order was to wear two hats at once—
that of the local citizen, engaging in social activity with others of a
shared background, and that of the national veteran, an identity
transcending local circumstances and subloyalties and harking back
to the parades of 1865. John Logan was speaking to the local veteran
in his 1869 glorification of the ex-soldier's return to home and hearth.
E. M. Faehtz was addressing the national veteran at the same encampment when, as part of a proposal to create "Grand Army mutual
life insurance," he suggested that leftover money in the insurance
fund be used to pay off the national debt or, failing that, to build "a
monument in the city of Washington to the memory of the defenders
of the nation in the late rebellion."[75]

The tension between local particularism and the cosmology of
Union would continue within and without the GAR until well into the
1890s. Within the GAR of the immediate postwar years, the duality
of the veteran's relationship to the nation had already found expression in the arguments over rank, as the founders' ideal of a unified
and orderly national organization ran up against the reality of a
squabbling and diverse collection of local posts. By the 1880s and
1890s, it would emerge into public life in the form of disputes over
federal pensions, Civil War memories, and insufficiently patriotic
school textbooks. Before any of that could happen, however, the GAR
had to recover from the membership drought brought on by the
collapse of the grade system in 1871. Ironically, it would do so by
transforming itself into just the sort of national fraternal order that
the proponents of grades had envisioned.

CHAPTER 4 POST ROOM

The Philadelphia Centennial Exhibition of 1876, dazzling its thousands of visitors at a site across town from the GAR national encampment of that year, was suffused with images of size, system, and Union. In May, President Grant had thrown the switch to start the giant Corliss engine, a mammoth device that powered every other exhibit in Machinery Hall through a series of belts, while a 7,000-pound master electrical clock governed the hall's timepieces. On the Fairmount Park grounds, twenty-four states (though only Mississippi from the Deep South) had erected pavilions made of native materials, most of which looked like hotels or oversize models of the family home. Strung out around the curvilinear State Avenue

with the huge U.S. Government Exhibition Building as their key-
stone, the pavilions formed a sort of national middle-class neighbor-
hood. At the park gates, veterans of the Union Army stood guard—
the same men who had defended the nation fifteen years earlier had
been specially recruited for Centennial police duty.[1]

The Grand Army encampment delegates meeting that autumn at
Post 2's Spring Garden Street hall were pleased. As they watched the
Philadelphians demonstrate the GAR's elaborate initiation ritual and
prepared to tour the Centennial grounds, they congratulated themselves on the nation's progress. "I feel assured," Commander-in-
Chief John Hartranft told the delegates, "you will experience no
greater pleasure than in the thought that, through your efforts in part,
our great nation was preserved in its integrity for a future of usefulness, honor and glory." Fourth of July orators across the North that
summer had said much the same thing.[2]

But as the national encampment's ability to meet in the modest
quarters of Post 2 suggests, the Grand Army of the Centennial year
had reached rock bottom. Membership had continued to decline ever
since the collapse of the grade system in 1871, and the lingering
business depression following the Panic of 1873 had left many of the
remaining members unable to pay their dues. Some of the GAR
Centennial guards undoubtedly volunteered for the duty not simply
from patriotic motives but because they were out of work. At the
Philadelphia encampment, delegates were informed that Grand
Army membership had sunk to a new low of 26,899. While the nation
was celebrating reunion, the GAR seemed to be undergoing disin-
tegration.

The torpor of the Grand Army was in marked contrast to the
general boom in civilian fraternalism after the Civil War. In 1901 one
observer found 568 fraternal organizations, with a total enrollment of
more than 5 million. Three of the orders—the Masons, the Odd
Fellows, and the Knights of Pythias—reported more than 500,000
members each. Although much of the growth came in the 1880s and
1890s (of the 568 orders in the 1901 study, 490 had been founded
since 1880), some of the larger orders were already flourishing in the
1870s as the GAR went into decline. The Masons, for example, increased their membership by more than 20 percent during the decade, while the Red Men added an average of 10,000 members per
year. With graded ranks and rituals much like those of the dis-
credited GAR system of 1869–71, other orders were prospering.[3]

Some reasons for the GAR's initial failure to join the fraternal parade already have been suggested: political partisanship, the economic depression, the youth of its members. The same factors, however, exerted equal influence on many of the other, highly successful fraternal organizations of the 1870s. The Ku Klux Klan and the Patrons of Husbandry (Grange), for example, were nothing if not political, while most orders—particularly those, such as the Masons and the Odd Fellows, that charged much higher fees than the GAR—undoubtedly suffered from the depression of the 1870s and the rootlessness of young men.

What set the Grand Army apart was its link to the war, a peculiarity that perhaps left its members less in need of the blandishments of fraternalism than were the youthful members of other orders. Mark Carnes has argued that fraternal rituals in Victorian America served to usher initiates into the world of men, allowing them to move beyond childhoods marked by absent or distant fathers and domestic, protective mothers. The orders' ritual tests of courage, overt threats, and patriarchal imagery represented a "pilgrimage for manhood."[4] Insofar as that was true, the allure of fraternalism was probably lost on most Union veterans. They already had been initiated into manhood by passing through the furnace of battle. Perhaps that was why, when faced with the "play soldier" ranks of the grade system, so many of them had simply pointed to their honorable discharges and vowed to "see Grant about it."

In the 1880s, however, the Grand Army underwent a conversion to fraternalism. This is not to say that during the decade the GAR suddenly stopped being a military or a political body and became exclusively a fraternal order; membership continued to carry multiple meanings. But beginning in about 1878, a subtle change of emphasis took place in Grand Army life. Over the next dozen years, the same veterans who had disdained the grade system gradually began finding their way back into an order that by 1890 looked very much like one of the wildly popular "civilian" lodges of the time. The change did not come without a great deal of ambivalence. But as the war receded in memory, the veterans began to find fraternalism less foreign as a model for organizing experience, its nonmilitary features less irrelevant. In part, this softening resulted from the same desire to forget wartime that caused the issues of rank and discipline to fade. At the same time, one cannot explain the GAR's fraternal revival in the 1880s—and the membership gains that accompanied it—without considering that in those years, veteran and nonveteran alike were flocking to lodges and fraternities.

Until fairly recently, historians have had little to say about the prevalence of fraternal orders in the late-nineteenth-century United States, perhaps because the activities of such orders have always seemed somewhat frivolous. Measured alongside the serious social and economic dislocations of the time, the spectacle of hundreds of well-fed white Protestant businessmen exchanging secret grips and lumbering up the street in the guise of Indians, Egyptians, or medieval knights has seemed to most historians at best irrelevant, at worst supremely ludicrous. Even contemporary observers sometimes found it difficult to take the fraternal trappings seriously. An English reporter who viewed the 1891 GAR encampment parade at Detroit, for example, found it a gaudy, nonmilitary procession marred by a "lack of seriousness," in which the uniforms "often looked like the cast-off wardrobe of a third-rate circus company; every army in Europe was, we will not say imitated, but parodied." Scholars have treated the GAR somewhat more temperately, but almost always as a political lobby rather than as a fraternity.[5]

More recent studies have shown that underneath the horseplay of the orders lay meanings of real significance. Lynn Dumenil has found that among Masons, the fraternal tie offered members a spiritual oasis from the world of commerce and a malleable belief system that helped men raised as Protestants adapt to an increasingly secular society. Mark Carnes's close study of the rituals of a number of Gilded Age orders suggests that they helped men overcome anxieties about gender roles and served as a male alternative to an increasingly feminized Protestantism. Mary Ann Clawson notes that fraternal bonding was important not just for the connections it asserted among members but also for the potential connections—such as those of class and those transgressing boundaries of race and gender—that it failed to make. Informal fun certainly was part of the attraction of the fraternal orders, but it is becoming increasingly clear that initiation into an order was, in the words of the 1883 GAR ritual, "no unmeaning ceremony."[6]

By far the oldest and most influential of the fraternal orders was Freemasonry. The Masons attracted prestigious civic and business leaders, erected impressive temples in the middle of major cities, and had places of honor in civic processions and ceremonies—particularly in cornerstone layings, such as that of the Brockton city hall in 1892.[7] The price tag of Freemasonry was the best indication of its prominence: even in small towns the Masonic initiation fee averaged about $30, before annual dues; in large cities the fee might be as much as $100. By contrast, a GAR post was expensive if it charged as much as $5 as a "muster fee."[8] In part because it was usually the oldest fraternity in a community, the Masonic lodge also tended to be at the top of the local fraternal pecking order. Masons in Grand Junction, Colorado, for example, were at the center of a dense network of local fraternities; in Jacksonville, Illinois, the Masonic lodge sent three men to the governor's chair. When Bradford Kingman came to write his *History of Brockton* in 1895, the GAR and others were lumped as "miscellaneous orders and societies"; the Masons got their own chapter. By the turn of the century, the Masons claimed more than 850,000 members, a figure approached only by the Odd Fellows.[9]

Many of the newer orders copied Masonic degree forms, a choice that had less to do with the prominence of Masonry than with the propensity of Masons and ex-Masons to found orders. Major organizations such as the GAR and the Grange were founded by Masons; so were dozens of smaller ones such as the Knights of Reciprocity, a Kansas group opposed to the Farmers' Alliance in the 1890s.[10] By 1900, a remarkable range of voluntary organizations, some purely fraternal or charitable, some predominantly political, employed degree hierarchies similar to that of the Masons. Whereas the Masons gathered in "lodges" to confer the basic degrees of Entered Apprentice, Fellow Craft, and Master Mason, the Improved Order of Red Men had Hunters, Warriors, and Chiefs, gathered in Wigwams; Foresters conferred degrees through three levels of Courts and met in Forest Homes. The Grange was made up of Laborers, Cultivators, Harvesters, and Husbandmen (and, in its female division, Maids, Shepherdesses, Gleaners, and Matrons); the Knights of Labor had several degrees of Workmen and employed quasi-Masonic symbols in their ceremonies. Grand Army members pledged "Fraternity, Charity, and Loyalty," Knights of Pythias vowed "Friendship, Caution, and Bravery," and Odd Fellows demanded "Friendship, Faith, and Charity." Secret orders could be found on both sides of the liquor question, in temperance societies and in such bodies as the Order of the Mystic Brotherhood (founded to fight state prohibition in Kansas in 1882) and the Ancient and Honorable Order of the Blue Goose (formed as a drinking club for Wisconsin insurance men in 1906). On the question of race, the secret Ku Klux Klan would be opposed by the 1920s by the equally secret Knights of the Blazing Ring.[11] Ben-

A GAR post room, with chairs arranged for a meeting, looking from the senior vice commander's chair toward the post commander's chair. In the foreground is the altar; to the left and right (outside the photograph) are the junior vice commander's and chaplain's chairs; along the left and right walls is bench seating for the comrades. This room, formerly that of Post 94, Philadelphia, is still used for meetings by a Sons of Veterans camp. (Courtesy Philadelphia Camp, Sons of Union Veterans of the Civil War)

jamin Stephenson and his cofounders were no different from the rest of the fraternalists, copying whatever worked from the rituals of other orders. As a result, even after the demise of the grade system, the GAR shared with other organizations an allegorical initiation ritual, secret grips and passwords, and an exclusionary admissions procedure.[12]

The GAR post room also shared with the fraternal lodge a highly formal arrangement of space. Posts met in a wide variety of structures, ranging from rented quarters shared with other fraternal orders to impressive "memorial halls," which were to serve as meeting rooms during the lives of the members and as shrines after their deaths.[13] The walls of the room typically were hung with portraits of famous generals, maps of major battles, photographs, flags, and other memorabilia. Souvenirs of the war might be displayed; in some posts leftover cannon were wheeled into the hall; in wealthy posts (such as Post 2) a library of war books and memoirs might be added for the pleasure of the members. The place of meeting and its time— usually one evening each week—were listed in local gazetteers and in "rosters" issued by the department for the information of traveling comrades who might wish to attend a meeting while in the city.[14]

No matter what sort of building a visitor found himself in, he would recognize the standard design of the GAR post room. In the middle of every post room sat the "altar." On this pedestal during muster-in ceremonies rested two crossed swords, their hilts toward the post commander and their points toward the membership; atop the swords was placed an open Bible. A wide, clear space surrounding the altar made it the focal point of the room. The members, seated around the edges of the room on chairs or benches, could not avoid looking at it. The central position of the altar also meant that when a member rose to address the post he spoke "across" or "through" the altar. The altar was the north star around which the post was arranged, its fixed center. When votes on membership applications were held, the ballot box usually was placed on the altar; when collections were taken up, the "hat" was sometimes placed on the altar rather than being passed; in one incident in Post 2, member John Vanderslice's application was placed on the altar for examination after another member questioned Vanderslice's service record. When a nearby post was burned out of its hall in 1886, the first thing Brockton's Webster Post helped it replace was its altar.[15]

At the head of the room, directly behind the altar, sat the post commander, flanked on one side by his adjutant and sergeant major and on the other by his quartermaster and quartermaster sergeant. The commander's chair sat atop a riser or platform; in some posts the chairs of his "staff" also were elevated. This arrangement gave the post quarters something of the air of a throne room, with the commander looking down over the cleared space before him to the altar and to the members seated behind and to either side of it.[16] At the far end of the room, looking directly across the altar at the commander, sat the senior vice commander on his own platform; on the "right and left flanks" of the room sat the junior vice commander and the chaplain on theirs. The lesser officers sat at ground level just in front of the commander's and senior vice commander's platforms. The four ma-

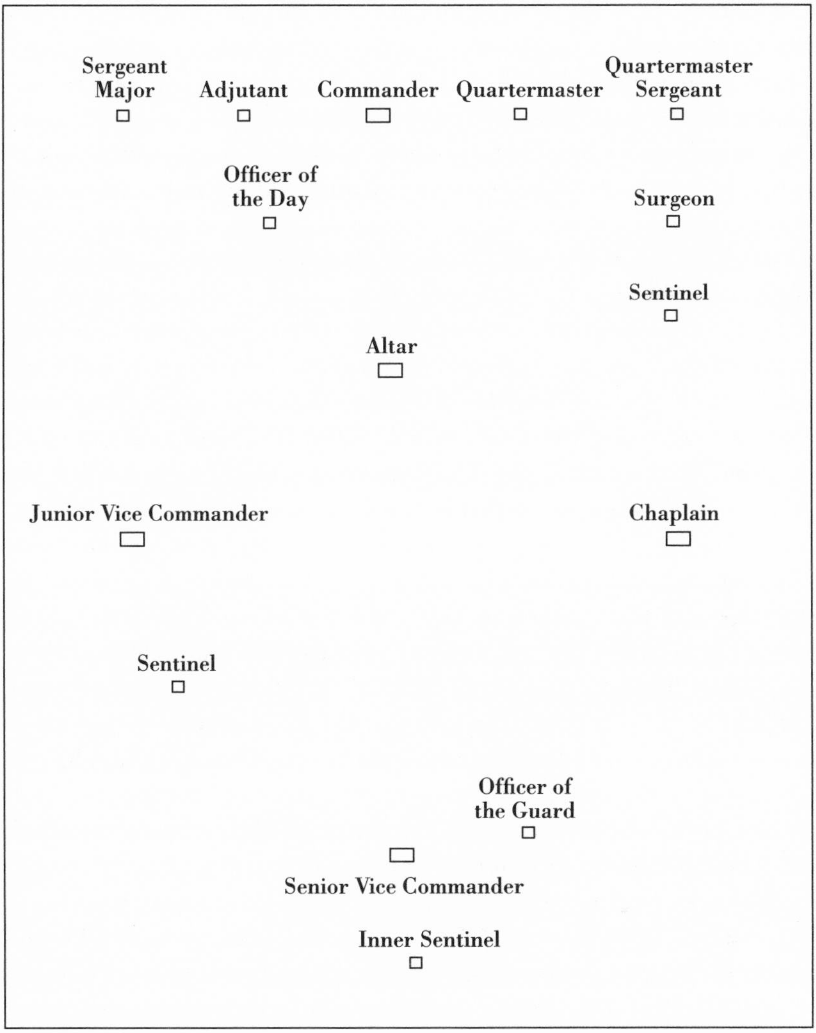

Sergeant Major	Adjutant	Commander	Quartermaster	Quartermaster Sergeant
□	□	▭	□	□

Officer of
the Day
□

Surgeon
□

Sentinel
□

Altar
▭

Junior Vice Commander
▭

Chaplain
▭

Sentinel
□

Officer of
the Guard
□

▭
Senior Vice Commander

Inner Sentinel
□

The design for a standard post room, with officers' stations indicated. Ordinary comrades occupied seats along the walls behind the chaplain and junior and senior vice commanders. (GAR Ritual, 1869) jor officers—the three commanders and the chaplain—were thus positioned so as to form a cross centered on the altar. Aside from the obvious Christian symbolism of the configuration, it emphasized the high stations of the officers, who "surrounded" the post room—one on each flank—and, in posts where platforms were used, looked down on it as well. They faced not the membership but the altar and each other.

Members, as well as officers, sat around the perimeter of the room, not in the middle of it, a placement that turned the central space into a kind of arena, a stage for the various GAR rituals. Within that area, movement was strictly controlled. A member wishing to move from one side of the room to the other, for example, could do so only by passing behind the altar—not between the altar and the commander—and saluting the commander in passing. Officers did not simply wander into the room at the beginning of the meeting; they were announced by the sergeant major and marched to the altar in ranks by the post commander, whence they moved to their chairs. In armed posts, the commander then received a formal "present arms" salute. Only when the commander returned the salute and was assured that "the approaches to this Post [were] properly guarded" and the officers all in their proper stations, did the post open for business. Early rituals also called for visitors to be announced from near the altar and for latecomers to salute the commander from the altar before being seated. In Brockton's Webster Post, a bylaw required salutes of all members entering or leaving the room.[17]

At the post room door, and sometimes inside it as well, guards, or "sentinels," were stationed. The sentinel challenged would-be entrants to give the password and then reported their presence to his superiors. When an official inspector paid a call, for example, the sentinel passed him to the officer of the guard, who reported him to the officer of the day, who reported him to the post commander.[18] Although this cumbersome procedure probably was used only for official visitors, it was an integral part of the ceremony for mustering new members. As in other fraternal initiation rituals, the recruit was escorted through the ceremonial space, on the way being challenged and passed several times.

The visual effect of the GAR post room was that of a highly formal sanctuary. In the center was the altar; around the altar, a cleared area, which focused attention on the altar and provided space for formal ceremonies; around the ceremonial space, officers deployed in the form of a cross; behind the officers, the rows of "comrades."

The concentration of members and officers on the perimeter of the
room represented a boundary: Outside was the profane world, inside was the ceremonial arena, centered on the altar. Outside the circle of members an individual was an unfettered "civilian"; inside it, he was a veteran, expected to exhibit controlled behavior—subordination to officers, marches and salutes, general "conduct becoming a soldier and a gentleman." The symbolic division was made concrete by the posting of the sentinel at the post room door. His challenges were meant to evoke the image of an efficiently run army camp: the "stranger" wandering beyond friendly lines was assumed to be a foe until he gave the proper password at the "outpost"; he was then escorted up the chain of command to "headquarters."

Yet this "camp" bore an uncanny resemblance to a church, and even more to the meeting room of a Masonic lodge, on which its arrangement of space was based (the Masonic officers and altar, for example, were deployed in the same configuration). The confounding of military and quasi-religious imagery suggested an army life that was somehow sacrosanct, orderly, and hierarchical, above the petty scrambling of society. The GAR post room promised not an actual army camp but an idealized model of it—the camp as sanctuary.

A Not-So-Timeless Rite

The design of the post room is of interest in its own right, but it is noted at this point because it provided the stage for several rituals that were central to GAR membership. By far the most significant was the ceremony mustering new members. The muster-in did not involve the question of acceptance or rejection by the post—that already had been decided by a vote at a previous meeting. Rather, it presented the recruit with a series of allegories designed to illustrate the meaning of what might be called "veteranhood": the character that a veteran was to take on and the obligations he was to assume in civilian life as a result of his Union Army service. By taking the GAR membership oath, a recruit acknowledged his bond with other veterans and his subscription to the Grand Army explanation of what that bond meant.

The ritual of 1866 indicates the nature of the order as originally envisioned.[19] Like all later GAR rituals, and like the initiation rituals of other Gilded Age orders, it began at the post room door, where the "stranger" was accosted by the sentinel and held until the officer of the day (in early rituals, the officer of the guard) made his rounds. The sentinel then told his superior he was holding the stranger because "I found him wandering near our lines, desiring to enter the encampment." After a brief examination, which established the detainee's service record and his desire to join the GAR, the officer of the day administered to him an oath of secrecy regarding the proceedings he was about to witness. The officer then reported to the commander that he had in his charge "a former soldier of the Republic—a brave defender of the American Union—who desires to enlist in the Grand Army of this glorious Republic." Upon being so informed, the commander ordered both camp and recruit "prepared for the solemn scenes of enlistment."

The recruit, still in the anteroom, was prepared by being "hoodwinked or blindfolded, divested of his coat and hat, [and] over his shoulders is thrown a torn and otherwise disfigured government blanket, to represent the condition of a prisoner of war." Inside the post room the ceremonial space itself was readied:

> The camp is prepared by placing a box six feet in length, three in width, and two in depth in the centre of the room, labelled upon the lid, in a conspicuous manner, with the name and regiment of some soldier who died in Andersonville Rebel Prison. On the centre of the box will be placed an open Bible and crossed swords, with the American flag draped in mourning. A guard is detailed, armed and equipped, and placed in front of the box. A small stool is placed opposite the guard and near the box, upon which the candidate will kneel. The members of the Post Battalion are drawn up in line (to represent two companies in line of battle) lengthwise with the room.[20]

Into this funereal scene the blindfolded recruit was marched under guard. In the course of a full circuit of the room, the party was stopped once again and challenged by a sentinel demanding, "Who comes there?" The escorting officer of the day replied, "Friends, with the countersign," gave the password to the sentry, marched his charge twice more around the room to the sound of "slow, solemn music," and finally arrived at the altar.

Kneeling before the coffin display with one hand on the Bible, the recruit swore that he would never reveal "any of the hidden mysteries, work or ritual of this band of comrades." He also promised to befriend the ex-soldier, to "employ him or assist him to obtain employment," to give him charity, and to "sustain for offices of trust and profit—other things being equal—at all times the citizen Soldier of the Republic." This done, the officer of the escorting guard commanded: "Attention, Guard! Shoulder arms. Ready! aim!"—and at that point the officer of the guard was to remove the blindfold, interposing with the words: "Hold! This is a soldier and a brother!"

The whole extraordinary initiation sequence of the 1866 ritual bristled with images of secrecy, conspiracy, and mystery very much of a piece with the clandestine political atmosphere surrounding the birth of the order. The blindfold, the repeated challenges, the twice-repeated injunction to secrecy, the thinly veiled threat of the firing squad—all gave the recruit the impression that he was joining a great Unionist cabal at a time when nervous Republicans professed to see secret machinations in the South and treason in the White House.[21] The world moved in secret, and the only way to protect oneself was through hidden organization. "You see, my brother and fellow-soldier," the officer of the day told the recruit after staying the firing squad, "what might have been your fate but for my timely interference on your behalf."[22] The outfitting of the recruit as a prisoner of war emphasized his helpless condition in the absence of aid from his comrades.

At the same time, the ritual offered the camp of veteran "brothers" as a refuge from the hostile world. Although it was impossible to take too much care with a "stranger" at the outpost, once he was shown to have been "a brave defender of the American Union" he could be trusted, for presumably he had shared the experience of war that made veterans unique. The props of the muster service were allegorical explanations of that bond. The coffin was to point out the veteran's kinship with dead comrades: "But oh! many brave men, whose fearless hearts once beat like yours to-night, in holy unison with our glorious Union, are now lying, cold and motionless, beneath the clods of the valley, in a strange, unknown land." The blindfold was to call up "the dark, gloomy days, months and years of the rebellion." The march was to "forcibly remind you of many a lonely midnight hour, in which you have groped your way toward the enemy's camp; or, perhaps, bring to your remembrance some horrid scene of some well-contested field after the battle, where you administered to the wants of your dying comrades."[23]

The service was in some sense a pact with the dead against the living, for the bulk of the post commander's speech to the new recruit that closed the ceremony concerned the need to elect ex-soldiers to office and give them jobs denied them by ungrateful civilians. The

Members of Post 201, Carlisle, Pennsylvania, lined up outside their post hall on Memorial Day for a trip to the cemetery. GAR rituals, including the earliest initiation ceremony, emphasized the ties between living and dead veterans. (U.S. Military History Institute)

war, he told the new member, had begun after "secret political orders sprung up, having for their open and avowed object the destruction of this glorious and God-given Union. . . . This, my fellow soldier, was in part the result of a neglected ballot box." As for the postwar world, "whilst large, healthy and stout men, who never heard a gun fire, are usurping all the offices of profit, a soldier can scarcely get employment—there seems to be a conspiracy against him."[24]

The death imagery, long procession, repeated threats, and theatrical denouement of the 1866 ritual were all common fraternal motifs. Under the terms of the bond the ritual offered, however, the fraternal grade system of 1869–71 was predestined to fail. The true "comrades" of the ex-soldier were those who had been through the dark night of the war with him, and even more so its victims. Living veterans were to band together to protect themselves and the memories of the dead. To this view of veteranhood, the pompous ranks and

ceremonial games of the grade system were irrelevant intrusions
with roots outside the army experience. The petty distinctions of civil
society were not something to copy but something to resist.

The original GAR ritual, then, was a relatively mild expression of what has been called *Frontideologie*: empathy among veterans for their fellows and longing for the world of the military camp, combined with a loathing verging on hatred for civilians and their institutions. Some students of World War I, which produced more than the usual amount of alienation among returning soldiers, have characterized it as a sort of primitive socialism, "the unity of the trenches." Men who had fought together forged bonds of comradeship that transcended social class and gave glimpses of the possibilities of social unity, a unity undermined by weak and selfish civilians in the postwar years. Other writers have emphasized the antipathy of returning veterans toward a civilian society by which they felt victimized.[25]

As expressed by the 1866 ritual, the alienation of Union veterans was less virulent than that of World War I soldiers but not less real. Politically it took the form not of militant socialism or angry alienation but of soldier candidacies and mutual self-help. As Frank Bramhall of New York's Soldiers' and Sailors' League put it in an 1867 speech: "We should place ourselves above the narrow line of Republicanism and Democracy. We should have a Soldiers' Party, standing upon the soldiers' broad platform of loyalty and patriotism, with our own gallant leaders and with a soldiers' press owned, edited and controlled by soldiers, in and for the interests of our great brotherhood."[26] Even in later years such disaffection often led ex-soldiers to exhibit more sympathy toward former enemies—Confederates, Spaniards, Indians, Germans—than toward friendly noncombatants.[27] But especially in the early GAR there remained a tone of victimization, a feeling that soldiers had made a sacrifice without sufficient return from the "large, healthy and stout men, who never heard a gun fire." This unpaid balance—"the only debt we can never repay," as the prophetic banner at the Grand Review of 1865 had put it—would be the sticking point of pension and veteran preference agitation through the 1880s and beyond.

Just as the system of GAR rank was slowly modified, however, the Grand Army ritual was hardly static. In the 1870s and 1880s, the ritual evolved along with the order, marking the GAR's change from a veteran legion with a few Masonic trappings to a fraternal lodge with a few military titles. The original ritual specified the correct alignment of officers, altar, and members only vaguely. Inside the 1866 post room the initiation ceremony was relatively simple: the recruit merely took the oath and listened as two post officers gave addresses that at base were political harangues. By contrast, revisions of the ritual beginning in 1869 provided diagrams specifying the proper arrangement of the post room, gave more detailed instructions to officers, and added speeches more reminiscent of a religious service than a political organization.

The 1869 national encampment made the first major revision in the ritual when it introduced graded ranks. A member now was to pass through three ceremonies in all—one for each "grade" to which he advanced. The full initiation ceremony was applied only to entering members, and in basic form it remained the same. The obligation still was taken on a Bible with crossed swords at the altar; it still closed with the tableau of the firing squad, though the dramatic halting of the execution sentence was replaced by an equally dramatic vocal response by the post members: "BEHOLD THE PROPER DOOM OF THE PERJURED TRAITOR!" But gone were the prisoner of war's blanket, the casket, and the political exhortations by post officers. In their places were a homily on fraternity by the post commander and a prayer by the chaplain, who for the first time had a significant role in the service. Additionally, a post member was assigned to hold the hand of each recruit during the ceremony at the altar.[28]

In the new initiation ritual the emphasis was on fraternity, which the officer of the day informed the recruit was "the great object of the grade upon which you are about to enter." The commander ordered would-be recruits to be admitted to the camp "upon the common bond of fraternity"; when challenged by the senior vice commander, the escorting officer replied that he accompanied "good men and true" who sought to commemorate the war "by uniting with us . . . upon that common bond of fraternity which binds us together as comrades and brothers." To this the superior officer replied that the GAR stood for "that full fraternity of feeling and interest which none can better feel than those who have together fought upon many a bloody field." The chaplain's prayer at the altar, given just before the taking of the oath, thanked God for preserving the recruits from death in battle and expressed the hope that they would "walk in the spirit of true fraternal love to all comrades here." Finally, the commander closed the ceremony by explaining the allegories of the muster-in ceremony as symbols of fraternity. The single rap on the door that had admitted them to the post room signified that "you are received here upon the single principle of fraternity, upon which the

Grand Army of the Republic is erected." The challenges of the sentinels and officers were to "remind you of the scenes through which
you passed during your service in the war, and that as you were then
protected on all hands by faithful sentinels, so we protect ourselves
by these faithful guardians upon our flanks and outposts." The hand-
holding at the altar "was symbolic of that fraternity which is the first
principle of the Grand Army of the Republic, and to which you in
common with all your comrades are solemnly pledged."[29] Dispensing
with politics and funereal imagery, the new ritual recalled the war
chiefly as an event that had brought soldiers together.

The initiation of Recruits, the first rank, was only one-third of the
1869 muster-in ceremony. Similar rituals were required for advance-
ment to Soldier (during which the member participated in allegories
of "charity," the GAR's second principle) and Veteran (during which
he viewed symbols of "loyalty"). But the emphasis throughout was on
camaraderie. In advancing to the rank of Soldier, for example, the
member promised "in all matters of employment [to] prefer comrades of the Grand Army of the Republic to any other person, other
things being equal."[30] This vow, however, was no longer an expression of resentment against civilian society. Rather, it was part of a
general promise of charity toward fellow veterans and their widows
and orphans. "Let the memory of past dangers make you ready to
stand by those who stood by you, to help those who have no earthly
helper," the post commander told the new Soldier. Similarly, the
Veteran vowed not to vote for any candidate "who is not thoroughly
loyal" but otherwise made no political commitments. The political
history of the war was touched on only once in the entire ritual, and
then briefly.[31]

In short, the three-grade ritual began the GAR's transition from
Frontideologie to peaceful civilian fraternalism. It was no wonder
that Radical Republican members such as Oliver Wilson detested the
1869 changes; the modifications altered the stated nature of the bond
between ex-soldiers. Instead of being admitted simply on the basis of
an honorable discharge, veterans now were tested on their adherence to a set of abstract principles that seemed to have been lifted
wholesale from some garden-variety fraternal order. Then they were
treated to a series of ceremonies nearly twice as long as the original
one and, ultimately, promoted through ranks that had nothing to do
with military service.[32] To members like Wilson, who saw something
unique, something not generically "fraternal," in the GAR, the new
forms were disheartening. "Many good and worthy comrades ob-

"Memorial Day," one of a series of allegorical stereopticon slides shown to new members of Post 2 as part of the initiation ritual from the 1870s onward. The sentimental tone of this slide reflects the softening of the ritual, while its funereal imagery suggests the extent to which Memorial Day was considered primarily "the day of our dead." (Courtesy Philadelphia Camp, Sons of Union Veterans of the Civil War)

jected to this process of leveling up as a Veteran, even by name, the man who never got decently far enough to the front to be baptized in an engagement," he complained, adding that during the war the term *veteran* had been applied only to a soldier "tried in action." Wilson regarded the entire fraternal edifice as "a semi-moral-sanctimonious garb of charitable righteousness."[33]

For the Eastern leaders who pushed the changes through, however, fraternalism was a welcome change from the militarism and political partisanship of the early GAR. The most influential of the fraternalists was probably Robert Beath, one of the order's founders in Pennsylvania and its official historian. A partial amputee as a result of wounds suffered at New Market Heights, Beath left the army as a lieutenant colonel, worked for a time as a clerk, and eventually became the secretary of a Philadelphia insurance company. At the time he compiled his *History of the GAR* (1889), he was the most prominent member of a post at Pottsville.[34]

Beath had supported the grade system to the end, giving it up only grudgingly. In his *History* he argued that politics, not civilian intrusions, had been the bane of the GAR, repeating the tale of kindly Dr. Stephenson's grand fraternity of war comrades. The original objects of the GAR, Beath insisted, had been "the formation by ex-soldiers and sailors of a grand union for fraternal and charitable purposes, as fully stated in the organic laws of the organization." Although certain deviant members had steered the organization awry, "the [1869] National Encampment, without a dissenting voice, has forbidden all political or partisan action in any form, and the fruits of this wise and proper policy are now shown in the mingling together of men of all shades of political opinions, working together harmoniously and earnestly for the accomplishment of the noble objects of the Grand Army of the Republic."[35] Beath would spend the rest of his life as a codifier of Grand Army fraternalism, writing the order's court-martial manual, serving as its commander-in-chief, and editing the annual *Grand Army Blue Book* of rules.

Beath's version of the GAR's purpose seems to have been the sense of the order's other leaders in the 1870s as well, for they never tried to undo the fraternalism of the 1869 ritual or seriously question its premises. Even when the grade system failed in 1871, successive national encampments simply compressed the rituals of the three grades into one ceremony that included shortened versions of all the vague homilies—"Fraternity, Charity, and Loyalty—as well as music, prayers, and an optional form for the presentation of the GAR badge.[36] One recommended musical number, "Charity," was particularly cloying:

> Meek and lowly, pure and holy,
> Chief among the "blessed three,"
> Turning sadness into gladness,
> Heaven-born art thou, Charity!
> Pity dwelleth in thy bosom,
> Kindness reigneth o'er thy heart,
> Gentle thoughts alone can sway thee,
> Judgment hath in thee no part.[37]

Other recommended numbers were "America" and "Auld Lang Syne." In the spoken part of the service, biblical quotations and references to Christ that had been added in 1869 were left in place, sparking at least one (unsuccessful) protest.[38] The ritual was becoming an amalgam of lodge initiation, church service, and sentimental concert.

By the same token, the remaining clandestine and semimilitary forms were gradually eliminated. The series of challenges for the password was dropped and the procession around the post room made optional in 1874. The blindfolding of the recruit and the firing squad tableau were scrapped in 1881, and the requirement that the initiate kneel at the altar while taking the obligation was dropped the following year. The obligation itself was purged of any references to voting or employment preferment. The 1883 oath required only that a member "aid all poor and distressed soldiers and sailors, and the widows and orphans of my late comrades, by all the means in my power, so far as I can, without injury to myself or family" and that he "encourage honor and purity in public affairs."[39] At the same time that the veterans were adding quasi-religious features to the ritual, they were softening or discarding political and quasi-military ones.

Because changes in the secret ritual were not debated publicly, it is difficult to know with any certainty why the veterans voted to alter it. For his part, Beath said only that "certain expressions used in the ritual" (meaning, presumably, the references to politics) had been "misunderstood and misapplied."[40] To Wilson, the new ritual represented betrayal by a cabal of Eastern officers. To the great majority of GAR members who joined after 1880, the changes were simply a fait accompli, most of them having been passed by the tiny national encampments of the previous decade. In any case, the changes themselves clearly show the intentions of their authors: militarism and partisanship were out, sentimentality and Christianity were in.

In some ways, the Grand Army ritual after 1880 remained unusual among fraternal initiations. By simplifying the ceremonies rather than complicating them, the GAR ritualists took a path opposite that chosen by other Gilded Age fraternal orders, which spent these years adding new degrees and ritual convolutions. By retaining Christ and Christianity in the rituals, the GAR also broke with standard fraternal practice, which was to dispense with both. The veteranhood promised by the new GAR ritual was simple and egalitarian, with a large dose of evangelical religion. In other ways, however, the revised ritual represented a decay of *Frontideologie* and a compromise with civilian life. No longer were brave and hardy soldiers contrasted with

weak and cowardly civilians; no longer were death and political conspiracy lurking around every corner. To the potential initiate, the lodge room and the post room began to look increasingly similar.[41]

In other areas as well, the GAR of the 1870s moved toward fraternalism. Mutual insurance for members, a common feature of fraternal lodges, was proposed (though not adopted) by the national encampment of 1869; many posts subsequently offered death benefits on their own.[42] The boosting of ex-soldiers for public office was withdrawn as a specific objective of the order in 1869, and the use of the GAR for partisan purposes prohibited. As a substitute, a new objective—perpetuation of "the memory and history of the dead"—was added in 1874 and the change publicized during campaigns to recruit new members. Although the outlawing of partisanship did not have an immediate effect on all posts, outbreaks of local politicking were always reprimanded by the national encampment. The subject had ceased to be a controversial one by the mid-1880s.[43]

To these changes could be added the previously noted easing of membership rules and the increased reluctance of members to follow military usage in day-to-day post activity. And, at least between 1875 and 1878, interest in the ritual *as* ritual, as a performance, seems to have heightened. In each of those years, the ceremony was "exemplified" (performed) for the national encampment delegates as part of the entertainment program—thrice by Post 2, with its stereopticon and musical accompaniment.[44] While in themselves only hints, these and hundreds of other incidents at the local level—joint parades with Masons and Odd Fellows; loans of post guns, flags, and halls to other orders; joint charity arrangements for mutual members; more time spent on musters and social entertainments—leave the impression of an order increasingly fraternal, increasingly civilianized.[45]

The Imaginary Camp

The striking thing about the imagery of most Gilded Age orders, especially the oldest and largest, is the way they seized on some real or imaginary community of the past and re-created an idealized version of it with members filling its roles. The Improved Order of Red Men, for example, imitated pre-Columbian America. Members met in "wigwams"; opened meetings by "kindling the council fire"; kept accounts in "fathoms," "feet," and "inches" rather than dollars and cents; recorded time in "suns" and "moons"; and adopted quasi-Indian names. The Independent Order of Foresters was oriented toward British legends, especially the Robin Hood tales. Masonry wove symbolic narratives around the tools of a medieval guild; the Grange harked back to an ideal agrarian republic of "husbandmen" and "harvesters," "maids" and "shepherdesses."[46] In each case the fraternal ritual depicted a preindustrial, communitarian past—one finds no Brotherhood of the Railroad Train or Order of the Telegraph.

This is not to say that the orders actually re-created communities or anything remotely resembling them; members still spent their real lives laboring in the overheated capitalist engine that was the late-nineteenth-century United States. Rather, the organizations offered communities of the imagination; communities that made up history as the members wished it had happened; communities, perhaps, as they wished the turbulent world they inhabited could be. Inside the lodge room, ranks were straightforward, lines of authority and influence clear, the rules laid out on paper, and—at least in the case of the GAR—the population more homogeneous than in society at large. Outside was a disorganized world filled with strangers. The community of the lodge room was not Sherwood Forest or Arcadia, but it was not Chicago either. By forming lodges, members could shut out confusion; at the same time, they could share the pleasant thought that at some time in the distant past order and true fraternity had been possible.

The Grand Army's version of the ideal community was an army camp that bore only slightly more relation to an actual Union army encampment than the Order of Red Men's wigwam bore to its native American counterpart. Wartime army camps, when not simply scenes of endless tedium, had witnessed death and suffering on a daily basis, as well as a variety of vices that would leave some civilians after the war worried about "lawless" veterans. Marches and orders had been ordeals to be endured because there was no prospect of escaping them, not rituals to enjoy in the expectation of one day being able to preside over them. Enormous numbers had deserted the ranks.[47]

That, however, was not the camp the GAR sought to re-create. Instead, the ideal GAR "camp" offered the picture of self-controlled comrades, voluntarily submitting to a congenial discipline and enjoying fraternity without regard to present or former rank. Orders from

headquarters always arrived on time and were followed, sentinels
stopped every intruder, soldiers said their prayers and abstained
from drink, privates had constitutional rights and took their turns
being officers, space was orderly and movement controlled, marching was strictly for show, and of course no one was ever killed. When
one of the troops died, everyone noticed it; Post 2, for example,
inserted a blank page in the post minutes and left a chair vacant every
time a member passed away. "Within its post halls," rhapsodized
George Ginty, newspaper publisher and prominent member of Chippewa Falls's Comerford Post, "the man who gave the order to com-
mence the battle and the skirmishers of the front line, sit side by side,
bound together by the magic tie of 'comrade'—a title of affection—a
title of respect—a title eminently proper for those who were part of
the Grand Army that stood between chaos and constitutional government."[48]

The fraternal camp also proclaimed the middle-class virtue of self-
control: within the ordered space of the post room, some things were
out of bounds. The broad post-1883 GAR "obligation" did not man-
date specific behaviors, but the decisions of courts-martial make it
apparent that improper conduct involved loss of self-control—disobedience to orders, grasping for undue prerogatives of rank, slander,
embezzlement of funds. On occasion, posts also chastised unfraternal
behavior outside the post room. In 1888, for example, Post 2 cen-
sured member John Barr for testifying before the Philadelphia liquor
license court that one of his comrades "was discharged from his
position as Janitor because of drunkenness, he having frequently
visited the saloon referred to, when in fact such cause of discharge
was not true." Similarly, Comerford Post appointed a committee in
1890 "to investigate the case of comrade John A. Peterson in securing
and accepting the position of janitor of the 1st Ward School when the
position was held by Comrade Villemine," eventually securing Villemine's reinstatement.[49] Most discipline, however, was aimed at
regulating behavior within the post room.

By far the most common offense against discipline was intemperance. Excessive drinking might be viewed as a modal vice in the
GAR, and probably in other orders as well: it represented the failure
of self-denial at the most personal level. Intemperance was the only
recorded cause in the handful of courts-martial in Philadelphia,
Brockton, and Chippewa Falls; it was used by the levelers in the
House of Lords dispute of the 1890s to discredit officers; and it was a
major worry at many national encampments, particularly the 1885

gathering at Portland in the dry state of Maine. John Logan assured the Portland townspeople that they had nothing to fear, since the Grand Army veterans were "trained, drilled and disciplined gentlemen (tremendous applause) and show it wherever they go; and the citizens need not be alarmed."[50] The Portland encampment passed without serious trouble, but as the high incidence of intemperance cases among the court-martial decisions shows, officers often were forced to resort to discipline. A typical case was that of Ed Culberton, who in 1880 entered the post room of Philadelphia's Post 18 "in an intoxicated condition, and did also abuse the Post Commander in the street, using improper language and threats to whip him." Culberton's court-martial was more than justified, in the opinion of Department Commander Chill Hazzard, because "the whole Order suffers in so far as any one of its Posts is made subject to unfavorable criticism by the disgraceful conduct of an individual member."[51] The punishment of intemperance was important not just for the sake of the offender but because it reflected on his fellows' capacity for self-control. By condoning his overindulgence they might be seen as lacking discipline themselves.

If intemperance was the most loudly lamented post room sin, self-mastery was the ultimate virtue. The most respected members were those who renounced self-interest and displayed what was variously described as "character," "honor," or—the most frequent term— "manliness." In arguments that prefigured Oliver Wendell Holmes's famous "A Soldier's Faith," GAR veterans attributed this sterling character to service in a particularly noble war. Comrade John McElroy, editor of the *Toledo Blade*, contended that the war had "found us a people with petty ambitions and low, sordid aims . . . filling our days with little greeds of gaining a dollar here and an acre there." The cure, he concluded, had been the smoke of battle, which had encouraged the development of unselfish character. "How unmanly it is to bewail that we cannot always have balmy skies, and mating birds, and springing flowers," McElroy wrote in 1883. " . . . Wars come to husk off the invidious surroundings of place and circumstance, and show us the real grain of manhood in everyone's nature." George Lemon, the editor of the leading Union veteran newspaper, the *National Tribune*, expressed the same opinion in 1889. The young volunteer of 1861, he proclaimed, "was stronger mentally; was readier to make sacrifices for what he thought was right; was more positive in thought, more unselfish, and higher in motive" than the stay-at-home. The Grand Army of the Republic, said longtime chaplain-in-

chief Joseph Lovering, had "a manliness inherited from those who
have recruited the Grand Army of the Immortals."[52]

The ideal of selfless manliness was held up not only as an inheri-
tance from the war but as a standard of Grand Army behavior as well.
The GAR, Logan told the 1869 national encampment, should "give
the world a practical example of unselfish, manly co-operation"; two
years later he expressed the view that veterans "meet in the strength
and consciousness of our manhood, with a full knowledge of our
freedom and liberty, but with hearts true and loyal to our country and
its laws." When an 1893 candidate for commander-in-chief refused
to engage in the usual horse trading of votes on the encampment
floor, the *Ohio Soldier* lauded his "manliness." Finally the term was
used on both sides of the heated pension debates of the 1880s and
early 1890s. When the *Grand Army Record* editorialized in 1890 on
the relative claims of veterans and bondholders to the federal surplus, its argument was headlined "Manhood Versus Money." As used
by veterans, *manliness* meant self-denial, devotion to high principle,
renunciation of grubby materialism. To be manly was to have control
of one's self.[53]

Advocacy of manliness, or character, was, of course, not limited to
the GAR or, for that matter, to the fraternal orders. Self-control was
the common denominator of a wide variety of postbellum reform
movements, ranging from temperance to abolitionism. Warren Susman has accurately described the general culture of the nineteenth
century as "a culture of character." In this society, one achieved
selfhood by internalized obedience to law and ideals. Manuals and
guides for character development from the period, Susman writes,
invariably described character as relating to key words: "*citizenship,
duty, democracy, work, building, golden deeds, outdoor life, conquest, honor, reputation, morals, manners, integrity*, and above all,
manhood."[54] A commonplace of such advice literature was that character demanded sacrifice in the name of some higher moral law. The
difference in the use of these terms by the fraternal orders was that
they were applied only to members. The saving remnant, committed
to higher ideals, was safe within its sanctuary from a world hope-
lessly gone to greed and self-seeking. In GAR ideology, "character" or
"manliness" was an attribute of veterans in which noncombatant
"civilians" were sadly deficient.

In speaking of the post room, Grand Army members explicitly contrasted its orderliness and camaraderie with the corruption and cold
materialism of civilian life. Commander-in-Chief Samuel S. Burdett,

trying to account for an increase in suspensions in 1886, told the San Francisco national encampment that the GAR included many veterans who "join our ranks looking for immediate and purely material and selfish benefits, and who, finding their expectation slow of realization, properly and naturally fall out." Similarly, General William T. Sherman lauded the GAR post room for promoting character. "No man can, to-day, go to a camp-fire of any Grand Army Post, and successfully boast of deeds not genuine without certain exposure," he remarked after returning from the 1888 national encampment at Columbus. "Brothers reared under the same roof know and love each other well, but a day, or a week, or a year of war comradeship in the same company begets a knowledge of character not possible elsewhere."[55]

This attitude did not mean that veterans were to abstain from seeking pensions from the federal government. In fact, liberal pension legislation typically was defended on the grounds that ex-soldiers deserved the thanks of the nation as a right. What was frowned upon was *individual* avarice and self-indulgence. There were, said the *Grand Army Record* in 1894, "two forces in the Grand Army": one that "uses every effort at camp fires and public gatherings to revive the feeling of public gratitude to the Union Soldiers that so saturated the public atmosphere" during the war, another that "cultivat[es] the small vices" and has veterans "clad in showy uniforms, their breasts shingled all over with brass badges." *National Tribune* editor Lemon put the matter plainly after the highly successful 1882 national encampment at Baltimore. "In the ordinary pursuits of life," he wrote, "greed and avarice, ambition and jealousy, obtrude themselves at every step. Self-interest makes comrades for us to-day, and to-morrow self-interest may change them to foes. It is only when men have suffered in common, faced danger together, braved death side by side, that the true spirit of comradeship is kindled in their hearts." Self-seeking was a civilian vice; veterans, because they shared the memory of an ideal army, met in a spirit of selflessness. Soldiers, said Oliver Wilson, were "the exponents of a faith that leads up to a higher type of manhood."[56]

In some cases, the idealization of soldiering led Union veterans to express empathy for their former enemies, again to the disparagement of civilian society. Commander-in-Chief John Hartranft told the 1877 national encampment: "The Soldiers of the South, who know the cost of disloyalty and the futility of their principles, have also

been the better citizens of that section. . . . On the other hand the
most pestilent classes of the South have been the non-combatants."
Hartranft argued that the war had led to "the cultivation of individual
qualities of the mind and body" but worried that its fruits "may be
gradually lost by the negligence, self-interest and the indifference
of succeeding generations." Similarly, editor Lemon wrote that the
worst enemy of the veteran was not the ex-Confederate but "the
selfish, cold-blooded, low-minded fellow, who cared too little for
anything outside of his own mean little interests to be even an active
rebel or Copperhead." Although other Union veterans continued
to denounce the Confederacy, sentiments such as Hartranft's and
Lemon's planted the seeds of the reunionism that would blossom in
the 1890s, complete with Blue-Gray encampments, a romanticized
Lost Cause, and a studied indifference toward issues of race.[57]

The antagonism toward "selfish" civilians, like the *Frontideologie*
of the early ritual, bears a superficial resemblance to the disillusionment widely expressed by veterans of World War I. The Union veterans' cosmology, however, contained none of the later veterans'
cynicism, their feeling of having been used as cannon fodder in a
meaningless war by a heartless industrial society. Veterans of other
wars and other countries have chosen forms of organization with
widely differing connections to peacetime society—everything from
paramilitary units to the Bonus Army—and other relationships between Northern veterans and the civil society in which they found
themselves were certainly possible. The antagonistic tone of the
pre-1869 ritual hints at one form that the relationship could have
taken, while the open partisanship of veterans like Logan suggests
another. But in the grasping, unsettled world of Victorian America,
the veterans of the GAR chose instead the refuge of an idealized army
camp, just as many of their civilian counterparts were fleeing to
similar bourgeois utopias. "Soldiers' party" politics and pointed antagonism toward civilians were short-lived; in the ritual, they did not
survive 1869. What remained was an ideology of antimaterialism and
self-control that in the late nineteenth century was hardly something
unique to veterans. As a tenet of a veterans' order, it was viable only
so long as veterans could perform the increasingly difficult task of
persuading themselves that civilians were greedy while veterans
were not.

By the 1880s the imaginary camp, with its salutes, sentinels,
guarded approaches, and marches, had been fully joined by the

model of the lodge, with its prayers, music, and broad allegories. The conflation of the two sets of images was complete in the ritual of 1883 and remained so for the rest of the century (the only major change was an 1889 streamlining of what had become a very long service).[58] The combination of fraternal and military imagery seemed to argue that the Union Army camp itself had been a sort of proto–lodge room, a fraternal space that happened to carry with it some military trappings. By that reading, the war had been the catalyst for a bond among soldiers that was stronger, perhaps, than that of the ordinary fraternal lodge, but not fundamentally different from it. Veteranhood might mean affinity for men who had shared the real experience of war as opposed to a fictitious one cooked up in a fraternal initiation, but in the end it imposed the same "manly" responsibilities in civilian society: the middle-class virtues of Christianity, orderliness, temperance, voluntary charity, and unstinting patriotism.

To a great many veterans such a version of veteranhood did not ring true. The new ritual of 1869 was followed immediately by the membership plunge of the 1870s, and the changes left some, like the obstinate Oliver Wilson, steaming for years afterward. "There is *but one comradeship, and that is the comradeship of army life,*" he insisted at the close of his 1905 indictment of the order, "*and such as that formed in the Civil War finds no ties as strong as those that knit the souls of men, on the march, in the bivouac, or on the field of battle.*" As with his attack on the "goody-goody" grade system, Wilson saw the imaginary camp as a "civilian" intrusion. The GAR, he wrote, "was *organized for the soldier.* . . . It was no Young Men's Christian Association. It was no prayer-meeting entertainment. It was a fellowship of Veterans."[59]

To veterans like Robert Beath, however, the fraternalism of the 1870s was a return to first principles. A benevolent and charitable Grand Army, his *History* argued, had happily rediscovered its original purpose and saved itself from the gutter of partisanship. In the long run, there proved to be more Beaths among the ex-soldiers than Wilsons. As the real war faded from memory, large numbers of veterans began to subscribe to the new GAR ideal of the army camp as sentimental refuge. By 1883 the order could boast more than 200,000 members; by 1887, energetic recruiting campaigns under Beath and his successors in the office of commander-in-chief had raised the total to more than 350,000. The GAR, already the largest Union veterans' organization, was on its way to becoming one of the half-dozen largest male fraternal orders in the United States.[60]

The post room space emphasized the GAR's role as a sanctuary. The ritual, after 1883, stressed manliness and fraternity. But several other fraternal features of the order in the 1880s had the ironic effect of making the GAR much less of a refuge from the self-seeking world of commerce than its ritual made it appear. Among these were in-house politicking, commercialization, reciprocal trade patronage, and an exclusive admissions procedure that limited the ritual's implied inclusiveness by allowing those who were already members to veto new applicants.

As has been noted, blackballing of applicants was infrequent, while the types of men rejected did not differ greatly in social status from those elected. But the rarity of rejection did not mean that it was always done in the spirit of worthy comradeship that was enunciated by officers like Beath. Indeed, the evidence from some posts suggests that their charter members used blackballs to establish the types of men with whom they did not want to associate; in later years, those likely to be rejected presumably did not apply. Thus a post might reject a large number of members in the years just after its formation, but very few in later years. The post at Williamsport, Pennsylvania, for example, blackballed fifteen men between 1875 and 1880, but only twelve in the next fifteen years. Philadelphia's Post 94 rejected twelve applicants between 1875 and 1880, but only five thereafter.[61]

Rejections also could stem from personal grudges, racial prejudice, or local political animosities. One veteran in 1875 complained to the judge advocate-general that a vote on his readmission had been "willfully, designedly conducted so as to oust him from the Post" by a member who held against him "an old political bias." In 1885, a Democratic paper in Lebanon, Pennsylvania, charged that the local GAR post had blackballed an exceptionally worthy veteran because he was a Democrat. In the same year two black veterans, one in Ohio and the other in Michigan, complained to Robert Beath that they had been rejected because of their race. In answering those charges, GAR officers invariably argued that better reasons than those alleged probably had prompted a rejection, but if not, it was no one's business but the blackballer's. "No comrade ought to be influenced by personal dislike or malice, but should decide in every case upon his honest convictions," ruled Judge Advocate-General W. W. Douglas in 1872. "Yet, if he does not, he can not be restrained of his privilege. He must answer to his own conscience."[62]

Since the blackball was used only against "strangers" (as the ritual called uninitiated recruits), it was in one sense a tool with which the members defended the purity of their sacred space, their model camp. Read another way, however, the practice of rejection subtly undercut the ideal of fraternity. In the 1875 case, the secret veto allowed a member to vent private animosities and have them recorded as the will of the post. In the Ohio and Michigan cases, it allowed the post as a body to reject black applicants without blame falling on any particular individual. Both instances illustrate the way the blackball system worked against any ideal of selflessness—it allowed the individual an "unmanly" indulgence of passions and the post an evasion of responsibility for its actions. The veto seemed to come not from an identifiable individual but from the post as a thing. As Beath put it to one 1886 rejectee, "The comrade will have to find out for himself where the objection comes from and endeavor to remove it."[63] The blackball reimposed with disturbing clarity the impersonality and coldness against which the GAR was supposed to guard.

The use of rejection to settle scores worried those devoted to the ideal of the post as an inclusive lodge. As early as 1868, Logan, though strongly defending the blackball as "a special and personal privilege which none of his fellows nor the organization have a right to question," warned that applicants "should not be rejected for light and frivolous reasons, and never to gratify personal ill feeling." Similarly, editor Lemon, though noting that the blackball was "an essential institution of every secret organization," argued that something should be done when perfectly worthy veterans were rejected for personal reasons. Such incidents, he said, were giving people the idea that the GAR was exclusive. "The fact that Mr. So-and-so, who served with distinction in the army and has conducted himself since then as an industrious and law-abiding citizen, is known to have been rejected as a candidate for admission to the Grand Army, naturally deters others from applying for membership," Lemon wrote, "and those who have no actual acquaintance with the rules and regulations governing the Order are apt to attribute his rejection to unworthy influences and come to look upon the Order with suspicion, if not positive hostility."[64]

In addition to the blackball, a second divisive force within many posts was the intensity of electioneering for GAR office. In Philadelphia in 1870, for example, it took Post 2 four ballots to elect a chaplain after procedural complications that included one victor who

declined, one incumbent whose reelection was ruled valid by the
commander but invalid by the post, and one slate of three candidates
that produced no majority. Two years later, the same post saw four
offices contested, even though only eighteen members were present
to divide the votes. In Brockton in 1886, George Grant edged Seth
French for the commander's position by two votes on the third ballot
after supporters of a third candidate threw their support to him. In
Chippewa Falls in 1892 it took six ballots to elect Charles O. Law
as post commander even though only twenty men were voting. In the
same year, the Department of the Potomac (District of Columbia) encampment was convulsed by a ballot-stuffing controversy. Throughout the period, national encampments saw spirited contests between
rival claimants to office; indeed, such battles were the main reason
many members attended. When one such member at the 1885 gathering in Portland, Maine, moved to have the election of officers
moved up to the morning of the second day, Comrade Alfred C.
Monroe protested: "Everyone knows who has been at the National
Encampments," he said, "that as soon as the election of the Commander-in-Chief is over, half the delegates leave."[65]

The vigor of GAR politicking is astounding from a twentieth-
century perspective, especially when one considers that GAR office
was almost entirely ceremonial. In general terms, Grand Army electioneering is best understood as a reflection of the highly participa-
tory political culture of its time. Given the national GAR's Republican
coloration, office in a local post also may have served as a marker of
ascendancy in the local Republican party, though the posts studied
here provide little direct evidence of such a connection. The battles
for post commanderships, in other words, may have been surrogates
for larger contests.[66]

Finally, the clientage relationship undoubtedly contributed to the
intensity of the balloting. When most members of a post were sponsored by a few leading businessmen, as in Post 2 of Philadelphia, the
post was really a collection of factions or cliques, each backing its
own headman. In 1878, for example, the two leading proposers in
Post 2, hardware merchant Matthew Hall and salesman Frank Lynch,
squared off for the post junior vice commandery in a test of influence.
It took until 2:40 A.M. to settle the issue, and even then the loser,
Lynch, demanded a recount. Thwarted again when the recount was
completed at the following meeting, his supporters forced a strict
new set of election rules for the following year, when Lynch finally
squeaked to victory, 206 votes to 191. In another Pennsylvania post in

1885, an illiterate working-class veteran, James Kane, refused to support his former sponsor for post office. The sponsor then revealed that Kane's army discharge had been dishonorable, and Kane was court-martialed and expelled from the GAR. It was election scuffles like these that led GAR papers such as the *Grand Army Record* to decry the "scheming and log-rolling" of post politics.[67]

If exclusion and electioneering worked against the ideal of the model camp, so did other aspects of GAR membership that were distinctly advantageous from a business point of view. Most obviously, the GAR offered members who were businessmen the chance to make a profit by selling things to ex-soldiers. *National Tribune* editor George Lemon and his fellow pension agents probably were the most blatant examples of such opportunism. A GAR member and a wounded veteran himself, Lemon set up shop near the Treasury Department in 1877 and used his newspaper to boost both the Grand Army and what ultimately became the most prominent claims agency in Washington. He worked zealously for the broadening of federal pension laws, from which he and other pension agents stood to benefit hugely despite doing little actual work. The sizable pension business generated by his GAR connection allowed Lemon to move into more spacious quarters (the Lemon Building on New York Avenue) in 1892 and to bank a considerable sum of money, though perhaps not the $900,000 profit that one rival paper claimed he had made.[68]

Other businessmen also profited directly from their Grand Army careers. Publisher George Merrill of Lawrence, Massachusetts, threw himself into the business of publishing GAR documents during his year as commander-in-chief, while other commanders awarded that job to associates. Post 2's Joseph Davison turned a profit by manufacturing GAR badges, clothiers sold GAR uniforms, and in cities that landed the national encampment, businessmen of all sorts stood to gain. By the 1880s the encampment had become such a lucrative event that local merchants put up large sums to attract it; in 1885, for example, San Francisco boosters persuaded the California legislature to appropriate $25,000 to lure the veterans to their city, a sum that the city merchants then supplemented.[69]

Reciprocal patronage was equally important. Veteran businessmen like Lemon argued that it should "be made of as much governing force as religion." Members of Post 2, for example, could either find each other through the post's published Business Directory or leave their business cards on a rack in the post reading room. In New York, the editor of *Soldier's Friend* urged veterans to throw their coal business to a GAR member who was an advertiser. In Colorado, the department commander tried to sell stock for a company in which "none but Grand Army men are interested." In Massachusetts, Webster Post gave its orders for flowers for Memorial Day to a florist in the post, saying it preferred to "patronize home industry." If the proprietor of a business was not himself a veteran, he might capture the market through an employee who was. In the Post 2 Business Directory, for example, the drain and sewer pipe firm of Harvey, Moland, and Company advertised its connection with salesman Frank Lynch, while Cook and Brother noted that its custom shirt department was "in charge of Mr. John W. Bonner." "Whenever trade, business, employment, or other advantage can be thrown in the way of a comrade," Lemon advised, "it should be done."[70]

Reciprocal trade patronage was of little use to clerks, skilled workers, and day laborers. Most posts, however, also encouraged veterans to give preference to comrades in hiring. Comerford Post, with its local political influence, was able to dole out the job of watchman at the Chippewa Falls city hall; on at least one occasion, members promised to seek other work for a newcomer to the county. Webster Post of Brockton named a delegate to the Veterans' Rights Union, an organization that lobbied for veteran preference in government hiring, and in one instance advertised for someone to fill in at a shoe factory for a member who was ill. Neither Comerford nor Webster post made any sustained effort to find work for its members, probably because few of them were in positions to give jobs to others.[71]

In Post 2, which had a great many employers among its membership, the posting of vacancies and job seekers was more systematic. The questions "Is any member of the Post out of employment?" and "Does any member of the Post know any positions vacant and that can possibly be obtained?" were added to the regular order of business in 1870, and the Minutes note several cases of unemployed veterans securing jobs with the help of comrades. In 1876 the post began keeping an "Employment Bureau Book" of job seekers, and in 1897 a job register was read aloud at meetings. None of the measures appears to have produced many jobs, and the lone attempt to form a citywide "job bureau" in concert with other posts failed after only one year, in 1879.[72]

In other large cities, however, job bureaus seem to have been more successful. Agencies in New York, Brooklyn, Boston, Buffalo, and Denver sought work for and provided relief to unemployed veterans.

In 1886 the New York bureau reported that it had served 1,500 meals to the indigent, cared for 231 members en route to the state soldiers' home at Bath, buried 137, and found jobs for hundreds of others. Veterans were particularly in demand for jobs involving force—guards, night watchmen, policemen—and during times of labor unrest. In New York, for example, the GAR Employment and Relief Committee advised that it recommended "none but those entirely trustworthy" to employers. In Philadelphia, in addition to patrolling the Centennial Exhibition, GAR members sought railroad jobs in the wake of the 1877 strikes.[73]

In both trade and employment, then, Grand Army members tried to offer preferential treatment to their fellows. Although their record of success was not impressive, their efforts provided some protection for economic performers who otherwise worked without a net. In that sense, employment preference represented the sort of mutual reciprocity pictured in the ritual, "fraternity . . . carried into daily life," in Lemon's words.[74] But it also tended to undermine the conceit that the GAR "camp" was a refuge, somehow above the polluted world of commerce. Fraternity had its uses in the business world as well.

A final feature of the GAR that aided members in commercial pursuits was, oddly enough, the "secret work." The GAR ritual, like those of other oath-bound fraternities, promised practical protection from an evil of Gilded Age social relations that was particularly rife in business—lack of trust. The prevailing scholarship on American communities describes the average nineteenth-century town as an isolated, self-contained "island," dominated by a local elite.[75] But even before the Civil War, no town was really an island; at a minimum each had economic ties to the rest of the nation. While social and cultural links were more tenuous, they did exist, often mediated by businessmen and professionals who doubled as community leaders—the sorts of men who, as we have seen, tended to control GAR posts. After the war, the integration of previously isolated places with a national economy and culture accelerated. In that milieu, the question was not whether to interact with other communities, for interaction was unavoidable. Instead, the problem was one of confidence: in a world of strangers, how could one tell who was honest and who was a mere sharper? In a community where most members knew one another's habits and histories personally—the pure gemeinschaft relationship of much "community history"—it would not have been particularly difficult to figure out who was trustworthy and who was

not. But in the highly mobile, rapidly centralizing society of the late
nineteenth century, the scramble among strangers for local approval (and, more important, for local office or the local dollar) could be bewildering. A politician might turn out to be a champion or a grafter; a railroad promoter might be a savior or a shark; a doctor might be a healer or a quack; even a seemingly worthy alms seeker might be a clever fraud.[76]

There was no guaranteed system for weeding out the deceitful from the trustworthy. But common membership in one of the fraternal orders at least assured that a potential borrower, for example, had subscribed to the same self-denying "principles" or "objects" as the lender, after an examination by men of roughly the same social and economic background, albeit men who might live hundreds or even thousands of miles away. When Comrade Henry Wright, newly arrived from Chicago, applied for aid to Post 8 of St. Paul, for example, the members wrote to his old post to ask about his "character or reputation" and "also as to his family relations, whether needy or not." Similarly, when former St. Paul comrade Winfield Scott Thomas turned up as a recruit at a post in La Crosse, Wisconsin, members there wrote Post 8 to ask whether it had ever rejected Thomas "for keeping a house of ill fame . . . [for] if he is a disreputable character we do not want him." In addition, the secret hailing signs of fraternal bodies supposedly ensured that only the initiated could recognize each other (the GAR "countersign" was provided to recruits as part of the muster ceremony). Such precautions did not exactly provide ironclad security, as attested by the frequent warnings in orders from GAR headquarters against shysters who had gained access to the "secret work" and were using it to solicit money. But like the haphazard attempts to find jobs for members, whatever verification was possible was better than nothing—and in Western towns like Chippewa Falls and La Crosse, nothing was the likely alternative. In the newer communities, one GAR member wrote in 1890, "fraternity has the deeper meaning, and it becomes on occasions another mystic tie, showing its power alike in public and commercial circles, and in social life."[77]

The blackballs, in-house profiteering, reciprocal patronage, and use of the "mystic tie" in commercial circles point up a significant irony in the Grand Army as it existed by the late 1880s: despite all their protestations of self-sacrifice and antimaterialism, GAR members found the order a highly useful tool of business relations. The ritual promised some sort of alternative to the world of commerce, an ideal camp in a fraternal army. But within that form the GAR post gave a businessman the chance to build alliances, reward subordinates, cultivate customers. To workers the post offered occasional job openings, plus credentials of respectability and trustworthiness for employers who required such attributes in candidates for the jobs they offered—such as that of bank guard or strikebreaker. If the post room provided a "refuge" from commercial society, it also supplied weapons for competing in it.

"Weed from Your Ranks the Hangers-On"

In turning toward a businessman's fraternalism in the 1880s, the Grand Army was only following the example of other Gilded Age orders. Yet in thus civilizing itself, the order risked losing its association with the war and becoming just another Elks club or Masonic lodge, for which business clientage and deal cutting were the sine qua non. To those for whom the ideal of the fraternal camp stood as a rebuke to crass materialism, this shift raised the disturbing possibility that the Grand Army had become more a tool of commerce than an alternative to it. Their uneasiness crystallized around two issues: the commercialization of the order and its infiltration by men who were only nominally veterans.

At first, the use of the GAR name or badge in advertising was considered a normal business device. W. W. Douglas, the same judge advocate-general who in 1872 had ruled that blackballing was no one's business but the blackballer's, ruled the following year that a member could use the letters *GAR* on his business sign because reciprocal patronage was one of the duties of membership. To advertise was merely to invite it. "It is difficult to see," he wrote, "why [a member] may not invite the patronage of his Comrades to a lawful business, when he does not ask charity, but gives an equivalent for the aid desired by publishing the fact of his connection with the Grand Army of the Republic, by painting the letters on his sign as well as by wearing the badge or presenting a traveling card or letters of introduction." Douglas compared the case in question to that of a manufacturer who named a brand of cigars "GAR" or a composer who dedicated a piece of music to the order. In such cases, he said, "the connection of the person with the Grand Army of the Republic is used by him to promote his business interests; and if his business is honor-

able, he profits by his membership without injuring the Order, his
Comrades, or the public."[78]

But as the order revived in fraternal guise during the 1880s, members began to have second thoughts about the practice. In 1883 Commander-in-Chief Paul Vandervoort urged veterans not to patronize merchants who used woodcuts of the GAR badge in their advertisements, and in the same year a resolution opposing the use of the order for private business purposes was rejected by the national encampment only on the grounds that such use already was officially frowned upon. Beath, who followed Vandervoort as commander-in-chief, deplored the use of GAR woodcuts on personal and business correspondence. In 1885 the use of the GAR badge to advertise a saloon caused the national encampment to pass resolutions condemning the use of the order for business purposes. That action seemed to change the opinion of the judge advocate-general on the subject, for in 1887 he ruled against a Missouri comrade who had advertised his saloon as "Head Quarters GAR." "The use of the badge and letters G.A.R. is in many cases objectionable though not in my opinion illegal," he wrote, "but when a comrade adds thereto the false and misleading statement that his place is Headquarters of the GAR, I think he is going too far, and is appropriating to his private uses and ends that to which he has no right." In 1887 the national encampment barred the use of the badge or the letters *GAR* for any private business, and by 1889 the principle was well enough established that it was asserted against *non*members. Although no federal statute prohibited outsiders from using the GAR for advertising purposes, the judge advocate-general wrote in that year, such "impropriety . . . could be restrained upon proper application to the courts."[79]

At the same time, some veterans were becoming concerned that the uniqueness of GAR membership was being diluted, both by association with civilian worthies and by the admission of men who had seen only brief or insignificant service in the war. Unlike membership in the other orders, GAR membership was not something obtainable merely through personal connections or the payment of a large fee. As the order gained strength in the 1880s and 1890s, many men who had been only marginally involved in the war—revenue marine officers, cooks, unattached "scouts"—clamored to gain admission, as did those whose military terms had been brief or nonexistent. When these men were also wealthy and prominent local residents, members were sorely tempted to admit them because of the money and prestige they could bring to a post.

In the late 1880s and early 1890s a number of posts began creating what they called "honorary" or "associate" memberships, under which local worthies were admitted to meetings and post social events; in some cases they also received GAR badges.[80] In return they paid hefty fees, most of which usually went to the post relief fund. "Although they never heard the 'rebel yell' . . . they are our good friends and will stand by us," said the *Grand Army Record* in speaking of associate members in 1891, "and will help us privates to obtain something more substantial than 'glory' and 'honor', especially when the 'glory' and 'honor' cost nothing and are good for nothing. Don't you 'catch on', boys?" In Brockton's Webster Post, a "contributing membership" cost $2 per year or $25 for life and privileged the donor to attend post functions and to wear a specially designed badge (not, however, the GAR badge). The substantial Brocktonians who joined included Mayor Z. G. Keith, shoe manufacturer Caleb Packard, Dr. H. H. Filoon, City Marshall Judah Chase, the Reverend Albert Hammatt, and militia captain Charles Williamson. In Worcester, William H. Bartlett reported that the associate members of his post were "the cream of our citizenship." He encouraged the veteran to "reflect that there were many men whose duty to remain at home was as plain as was his to go to the front and that failure to enlist was not necessarily evidence of lack of patriotism."[81]

But veterans elsewhere opposed the idea of allowing civilians to put on the airs of veterans, especially when their aims were less than pure. One member wrote bitterly to the *Record* in 1894:

> A Past Post Commander told me the intention was to elect a few rich men. A very prominent Comrade gave me the names of some six men who would be chosen Associates, and every one of those men was a heavy capitalist, and every one of them a "protected" capitalist. The first on the list was a well known office seeker and chronic office holder, who (as I told the Comrade) has pulled every string, the church string, the militia string, the Irish string, and the GAR string. I am coming to believe that the Plutocracy have debauched the people of this country worse than the Slave Power ever debauched them.[82]

At the national level, complaints about associate membership were heard as early as 1879, and the idea was expressly rebuked by Judge Advocate-General W. W. Baldwin in 1880. "No such membership is known to the Order," he ruled. "The National Encampment has never provided for honorary membership. None but soldiers and sailors who served during the Rebellion are eligible to membership."

Baldwin's position was reiterated in decisions of 1888, 1892, and 1899. Despite official disapproval, however, posts like the one in Brockton continued to admit associate members. Even Beath admitted at one point that his post had a "contributing roll" of citizens who gave money to its relief fund.[83]

Some veterans opposed not only associate membership for civilians but also full membership for veterans who had not served substantial army terms. As has been discussed, some posts blackballed short-term veterans even though GAR rules said nothing about duration of army service. Other veterans got away from the short-service men by joining the more exclusive organizations that began to appear in the late 1880s. The Union Veteran Legion (UVL), organized at Pittsburgh in 1884, was restricted to those who had served at least two years or who had been wounded. The Union Veterans' Union (UVU), formed at Washington in 1886, was limited to veterans with six months' service who had spent at least some time at the front. The Comrades of the Battlefield, announced at the Detroit national encampment of 1891, was limited to those who had served ninety days under fire, suffered wounds, or been held as prisoners of war. Other groups included an ex-prisoners-of-war association and a body limited to those who had responded to Lincoln's first call for troops.[84]

The common aim of all the groups was to limit veteranhood to those who had volunteered (thus excluding draftees and substitutes) or to those who had been under fire (thus excluding many of the "ninety days men"). In recruiting members in 1886, the Union Veterans' Union urged veterans not to "share the glories of [the] field with the men who never served an hour in the army, or at most as general service or emergency men" and to "weed from your ranks the hangers-on." A UVU member told the *Record* in 1891 that while the new order "does not claim to take a higher rank than the GAR, it does claim that the men who were at the front have an experience peculiarly their own, and a feeling for each other which none but themselves can enter into or fully appreciate; hence the Order." UVL national commander J. S. Reed went even further, charging that the Grand Army was full of pardoned deserters and bounty jumpers and characterizing its leaders as men who "seek for the most honors and talk louder than those who quietly and unassumingly went out and fought for years and gave their blood for their country." On Memorial Day, 1888, officers of the UVL and the GAR almost came to blows in Fairmount Park, Philadelphia, over who would be allowed to perform the first services at the statue of General Meade. "We are sick of these militiamen parading as veterans," said the UVL's Francis O'Donnell afterward. "A few veterans have been connected with the Grand Army, and the latter has reaped the benefit of our services on the battlefield. The people at the head of the Grand Army are nothing but militiamen."[85]

Grand Army leaders were not insensitive to such charges, but they never made any serious attempt to limit their order's membership. As a result, neither the UVL nor the UVU ever achieved anything like the size of the GAR, which by the late 1880s was widely regarded as the chief mouthpiece of Union veterans on such public questions as pensions, war, and militarism in schools. Nonetheless, the smaller orders continued to provide a standing challenge to the Grand Army's view of itself as an organization of war-hardened veterans. In the view of these ex-soldiers, the GAR had degenerated into little more than a social organization, much as the antebellum militias had done.

The disputes over commercialization and over short-term and "associate" members showed the continuing tension in the GAR over the veteran's relation to peacetime society. If the order represented a refuge from civil society, as the ritual seemed to promise, it was hardly appropriate for members to use the GAR badge as a tool of trade. But if the GAR existed primarily to facilitate mutual aid among comrades, there was no reason to prohibit members from using the association for what it was worth. If the order's goal was to keep alive specific memories of camp and combat among those who had experienced them, it was counterproductive to allow civilians, who had experienced neither, and short-service men, who had experienced them only fleetingly, to become members. But if the GAR existed only to keep alive a sentimental camp—and war—that had never existed, why should it bar willing civilians any more than the Masons or the Odd Fellows barred eager recruits from their utopias?

Different members answered these conundrums in different ways; some resisted any moves toward commercialism or civilian fraternalism, some embraced them. But in the order as a whole the drift in the 1880s was toward the model of a lodge, complete with sanctuary, secret grip, and business directory. If some members resisted by joining the UVL or the UVU, many more did not. By 1890 the GAR dwarfed all other Union veteran organizations in size, and it continued to do so until it closed up shop in 1956.

In organizational terms, the question posed by the fraternalism of the 1880s was the extent to which the Grand Army would be converted into a civilian fraternal order. But in more personal terms it

was a question of what veteranhood actually meant. If the GAR was simply a mutual patronage society or a social club of people willing to express sympathy for the Union after the fact, then being a veteran was not so different from being an Elk. One went to meetings, participated in a syrupy ritual, traded stories, perhaps cut a few deals; the war did not really enter into it. The memory of the war was something preserved beneath several layers of ceremonial glass. It was remembered as an ideal time of self-sacrifice and antimaterialism, a time not at all like the selfish world of postwar society. That was a pleasant memory, but not one that implied more than reverence on Memorial Day. Certainly it did not extend to refraining from using the GAR badge in one's advertising or denying one's business associates the opportunity to join the club simply because they had missed serving in the war.

But to those for whom the Grand Army represented "a higher type of manhood" than that prevailing in the marketplace, the boundary between veteran and nonveteran was something to be patrolled vigorously. Veteran and civilian alike might share the memory of the war as a time of selflessness, but their memories were irreconcilably different. Noncombatants might grasp the idea of self-sacrifice in the abstract, but the real sacrifices of war were known only to veterans, particularly those at the front. If civilians soon forgot what those sacrifices had been for, the role of the veteran was to remind them by providing "a practical example of unselfish, manly co-operation." To such veterans, the ideal camp was a sentimental creation but also a model of what chaotic peacetime society should look like—orderly, disciplined, selfless, tinged with idealism.

Such a view implied vigilance in admitting new members. To sit in a post with short-service men weakened the boundary that set off veterans as a unique class, since those men had not come near enough to the fighting to risk sacrificing anything. To admit "associate members" was to obliterate entirely the distinction between veterans who had sacrificed themselves and noncombatants who had indulged themselves. Among those who saw themselves as having given up more than others—front soldiers, wounded men, prisoners of war—even fraternization with average veterans was little more than consorting with "militiamen."

As much as these two visions differed over the meaning and implications of veteranhood, they did share a picture of the Civil War as a time of selfless sacrifice. This consonance was, as we shall see, part of a millennial republican view of the war's place in national history that would have disturbing ramifications as the United States inched toward another conflict in 1898. Before that time, however, the cosmology of Union veteranhood would make a more immediate impact on the uproar over military pensions that engulfed the order and the nation from 1879 until almost the end of the century.

CHAPTER **5** RELIEF FUND

The evolution of the Grand Army from political cadre in the late 1860s to fraternal camp in the early 1880s took place largely out of the view of civilians. For GAR members, this internal development was not insignificant. Structurally, the highly decentralized GAR of the 1880s had belied the hopes of its early organizers and the promise of national unity implicit in the Grand Review. Socially, the republican side of the order had come to dominate its military side, as grades, ranks, titles, and quasi-military discipline failed in the face of stubborn egalitarianism. Ideologically, the order had started to drift toward civilian fraternalism and away from the *Frontideologie* of 1867; as Oliver Wilson complained, "certain sentimental notions of fellowship" were replacing the shared bond of war experience among the ex-soldiers. But to the nonveteran, such internal changes were invisible. When civilians of the 1880s noticed the GAR at all, they regarded it as just another miscellaneous order or society; at worst, perhaps, a Republican political club.

All of that would change in the late 1880s and especially in the 1890s as a revitalized Grand Army gained members and political influence. In those years the order began to reach out into public life in an effort to define the proper relationship between Union veteran and civilian. When it did so, prominent nonveterans began to notice and write about the GAR for the first time. And while the Grand Army of the 1890s fought its campaigns on a number of fronts, ultimately its discourse with civilians came to center on three issues, with which it became increasingly concerned: the relief of wounded and indigent veterans, the portrayal of the Civil War in popular culture, and finally, the meaning of American nationalism.

In the broad sense, of course, pensions, remembrance, and patriotism have been staples of veteran-civilian relations after almost all wars. Societies inevitably make some provision for the wounded; wars and warriors sooner or later find their niches in the public memory; veterans' organizations routinely take on some kind of patriotic coloration. But though societies ultimately deal with these questions, they may not always deal with them in the same way. The Civil War, for example, is the most-written-about event in American history, while the Indian conflicts of the nineteenth century, which took longer and probably cost more lives, are usually not even classified as "wars." Similarly, while both Continental Army and Union Army veterans received pensions, the grants differed widely in scale and in the assumptions on which they were based. The veteran-civilian discourse of the Gilded Age was unique, and for that reason it reveals as much about the age as it does about issues particular to veterans. To study pensions is also to study pension granters; to discuss Memorial Day is also to discuss memorialists.

Each of these public issues had engaged some Union veterans from the outset—"charity" and "loyalty," after all, had been among the founding principles of the GAR. But it was not until 1881 that the pension question became prominent on the national agenda, absorbing the attention of lobbyists, editorialists, and politicians as well as veterans. War memorialization and patriotic agitation took even longer to surface, catching the public fancy only in the 1890s. At the risk of some artificial periodization, then, analysis of the GAR's public career begins in this chapter with the question of charitable relief and proceeds subsequently to the issues of war memories and patriotism.

The Limits of Local Relief

Among historians (as, in fact, among editorialists at the time) the GAR is remembered chiefly as a powerful national pension lobby, and rightly so. The organized political muscle of the Union veterans was impressive in an era when wafer-thin margins of victory in presidential races were the rule; the large pension expenditures demanded by the former soldiers had wide-ranging economic ramifications as well. But because the order's agitation for federal pensions is usually the focus, the considerable amount of relief traded among GAR members at the post level—especially in the years before the generous federal pension act of 1890—is often overlooked. The cardinal principle of "charity" was expressed in a variety of quite personal ways—provision of food, coal, a loan, a job, free medical care, or a funeral service; payment of rent or a modest stipend to a widow, schooling or work for an orphan. Such forms of charity offered emergency relief to poor or ailing veterans who otherwise would have been left to fend for themselves. Limited and local in scope, these aids also implied a relationship between veteran and society significantly different from that propounded by later advocates of federal pension legislation.

The vehicle of a post's charity was its relief fund. Until 1888, when the maintenance of such a fund was made optional, every Grand Army post was required to set aside money "for the assistance of needy soldiers and widows and orphans of deceased soldiers."[1] The method of raising a charity fund varied somewhat from post to post. In Chippewa Falls's Comerford Post, for example, money raised through dues and muster fees was simply earmarked for relief as necessary, with members of a standing relief committee responsible to the post for its expenditure. In Brockton, money for relief came primarily from fairs and other public solicitations; the Webster Post bylaws explicitly required "all money received by this Post, in response to a direct appeal to the public" to be set aside for relief. Philadelphia's Post 2 had enough well-to-do members that it could have funded relief entirely with voluntary contributions. But after considering that idea in 1872, the post chose instead to designate a given fraction of all dues—formally set at one-third in 1877—to build a charity fund. Nationally, the GAR reported giving more than $1.5 million in charity between 1871 and 1888. In 1887, a typical year, the combined charity expenditures of all posts were $253,934.43.[2]

To discuss post aid using dollar figures, however, is something of a deception, since most of it came in forms other than cash. Medical services, to cite the most conspicuous example, usually were rendered at no charge or were funded by the post. The post surgeon was expected "to professionally care for the needy sick comrades of his Post, and widows and orphans who may need his services and yet be unable to pay for them; and to see that the money value, at current rates, of the services he may so tender and donate to his Post be entered upon the returns as a part of the amount disbursed for charity." Pharmacists (the post surgeon often was a pharmacist rather than a physician) might give drugs or other medications to a suffering comrade gratis, or he might be reimbursed later for doing so. In 1873, for example, Post 2 thanked a drugstore on the ground floor of the building that housed the post hall for furnishing free medicines to members "for a long time." During a typical year, 1888, posts nationwide reported treating 3,900 veterans and expending $14,500 on food and medicine.[3]

Another common form of relief to the sick was the appointment of "watchers" to minister to the needs of bedridden members. Brockton's Webster Post paid its watchers small fees for their trouble; in Chippewa Falls, Comerford Post regarded the duty as an obligation of membership and assigned members to it without pay. Most posts assigned members to visit sick comrades, a practice made systematic in Webster Post by the appointment of one charity committee member from each ward of the city.[4]

Post-funded medical care of this sort was almost always aimed at meeting a one-time emergency, such as a winter illness or an injury on the job. Where permanent disabilities or chronic injuries were involved, other solutions had to be found. In 1875, for instance, Post 2 had to decide what to do about Jerome Gates, a veteran living solely on a pension of $5 per week from another fraternal order—barely enough to pay his board. "This case may last a long time," the charity committee reported. "We propose in conjunction with other Posts to pay $3 per week as our turn comes." In Brockton, a similar case in 1889 produced a similar solution: Webster Post, the local Masonic lodge, and other orders to which an ailing member belonged agreed jointly to pay him a $15-per-week stipend. In Chippewa Falls, Comerford Post was so strapped for funds that it sometimes had to turn down pleas for long-term assistance. In 1884, the watchers assigned

to the seriously ill John H. Brown were informed that "owing to the financial condition of the Post further aid from now will cease." The post relented so far as to vote a one-time $20 stipend to Brown's widow after he died, but when she applied for more relief seven months later she was told the post did not have the resources to pay her any more.[5]

In the worst cases, a post could arrange to send permanently disabled or dependent veterans to one of the newly erected federal and state soldiers' homes. As early as 1868, Commander-in-Chief John Logan called for the Grand Army to be represented on the boards of soldiers' homes and orphan asylums. By the mid-1880s members of the order sat on such panels in many states (the Vermont and Pennsylvania boards were made up entirely of GAR men) and for several years in New York actually administered the home itself. GAR posts could be instrumental in arranging admissions to the state homes. "In order to obtain admission into the Penna Soldiers and Sailors Home at Erie," Post 2 adjutant Charles Kennedy informed applicant Charles Weissert, "you will be required to have some member of the Grand Army of the Republic to recommend you as to habits, character, etc." Another would-be resident was advised that he "must be of good moral character and not addicted to the *Canteen*." The Brockton and Chippewa Falls posts arranged similar admissions to the Massachusetts and Wisconsin soldiers' homes.[6]

Some posts resorted to insurance schemes to meet long-term needs, paying members disability or death benefits in return for a dues surcharge. In 1876, Post 2 instituted a death benefit of a sort by assessing each member 25 cents upon the death of another; this plan apparently continued on a voluntary basis after the GAR judge advocate-general ruled against forced contributions in 1879. But the 1869 national encampment rejected the idea of national GAR insurance, and for most posts the risk involved in providing insurance benefits was too high to make the idea worthwhile. As a sociologist examining contemporary fraternal beneficiary societies in 1901 pointed out, most such schemes were unstable because they were statistically unsound, either assessing too little in dues or promising too much in benefits. The GAR carried an additional handicap in that, unlike other fraternal orders, it could not constantly recruit new members to pay the premiums needed for the relief of older veterans.[7]

Moreover, any plan that did maintain an adequate cash reserve was always under the suspicion (often justified) that its real reason for existence was to provide capital for speculators. GAR posts were jealous of their relief moneys, and many members probably balked at the idea of giving trustees control of a large insurance fund. The 1869 proposal for national GAR insurance, wrote Oliver Wilson, was perceived by many members as "an additional device for somebody to make money off the Order."[8] Its failure left the field to death-benefit assessments such as that of Post 2, which was really a one-time collection of alms. Grand Army aid to survivors of dead members, like its medical care of living ones, remained largely a system of emergency donations rather than a program of ongoing relief.

A veteran might require aid from his fellows even if he was not sick; he might be poor, out of a job, stranded in a strange city, or all three at once. Posts were not always very successful in trying to place unemployed veterans in jobs. Still, most at least made the effort, particularly in the neediest cases. In addition to its intermittent "employment bureau" and the occasional hiring of members by members, Post 2 aided job seekers such as John Shillas, a Maine veteran who was given $2 and promised $5 more by the relief committee "provided they do not succeed in obtaining work for him tomorrow"; and William F. Harding, a wool carder whose train fare home to Cohoes, New York, was paid after he failed to find work in Philadelphia. In Brockton, Webster Post tried to place constantly indigent member John Linehan in a job at a city park; in Chippewa Falls, members of Comerford Post passed the hat for a comrade recently arrived from Pennsylvania and promised to seek work for him and for his son.[9]

Philadelphia's Post 2 was equally solicitous of unemployed widows and orphans of soldiers. In 1880 it passed a resolution calling for the restoration of a widow to her job at the Treasury Department, while post leaders Samuel Bachtell and Moses Veale were zealous members of the statewide GAR committee on soldiers' orphans, which regularly investigated conditions at the state orphans' home and sought jobs for its inmates when they reached employable age. In one extraordinary case, Post 2 even helped apprehend and convict the employer of a soldier's orphan who had subjected his charge to such harsh treatment that the boy was "brought home in a dying condition, and after a few days of intense agony, died." The post put up a reward for the employer's arrest, one member testified at his trial, and another provided free legal services to the prosecution.[10]

Posts gave aid in many other forms to Union veterans, widows, and orphans who were temporarily unemployed or impoverished. A poor veteran in Weymouth, Massachusetts, received a stove to warm himself during the winter; George Raymond of Plymouth, Massachusetts, had his back rent and bills paid; Mary Edson, a widow in Brockton, obtained help in collecting some bills due her; a veteran from Natick, Massachusetts, had his train fare paid. John Sayles's post in Chippewa Falls reimbursed a post at Rice Lake for his fare home from that place, purchased firewood for member P. W. Kibbey, and gave a widow $15 even though its charity committee "had come to the conclusion that she had ought to be sent back to Minnesota." In Philadelphia, veteran John C. Stewart received money to help him get his clothes out of a pawnshop; Mansfield Wood had one week's board paid and member Joseph McCullough one month's rent; and the family of deceased member Samuel Beers obtained money to pay his outstanding bills. In 1884, even delegates to the national encampment pitched in to relieve a Dakota Territory veteran crippled in a train accident on his way to the gathering.[11] Such minor disbursements occupied the agenda of almost every post meeting.

Probably the most common form of local charity in the GAR was providing for the funerals of members. The Brockton, Chippewa Falls, and Philadelphia posts all paid funeral expenses frequently and maintained cemetery lots for veterans; Post 2 also required at least two officers "to visit the home of the deceased comrade, make such arrangements as may be necessary for his proper burial, and determine the amount, if any, to be spent therefor." When post members felt the family of the deceased could afford a funeral, however, or when the request was for burial of a lapsed member, they sometimes refused to provide the money. In 1887, Post 2 informed the widow of James Dougherty that it would not fund his funeral because members were "of the opinion that the funeral expenses should have been paid from the estate of the late Comrade Dougherty." Similarly, Comerford Post declined to pay for the burials of Thomas Kiley in 1893 and William Wilcox in 1899. Kiley, a longtime Comerford Post adjutant, had forfeited his claim on the post by moving to Hayward. As for Wilcox, the Chippewa Falls members decided that since he "during his life and good health (being financially able) to attend the meetings of the Post and pay his regular dues thereto Failed to do either, that the Post were under no obligations to turn out for his funeral."[12]

If asked, a post also would perform the GAR funeral service, a simple rite marked by allusions to "the great review" and "the merciful Captain of our salvation." Otherwise, post members would turn out in GAR uniforms for a conventional religious ceremony. Some churches frowned on the wearing of uniforms and arms or, as with the Catholic church, on the quasi-religious form of the GAR funeral service. Such a response could prevent a post from performing the GAR rites. When Post 2 member Joseph Cusack died in 1885, for instance, post officers were allowed to attend the funeral, but not in uniform. When John Kennedy died in 1887, "Mrs. Kennedy, while appreciating the kindness of the Post, had concluded because of the rules governing the church in which the family worship that it will be better to have no military display and the funeral will therefore be private."[13]

Even if a deceased veteran's church permitted the GAR rites, however, there was no guarantee that the post members would participate. In Philadelphia, Post 2 generally managed to have some representative at the funerals of members. But with dozens of members dying every year by the 1880s, some of them virtually unknown to each other, it was difficult to muster an impressive showing every time. In 1881 and again in 1889 commanders of the post complained that turnouts at funerals were disappointingly light. But when Commander James Whitecar suggested in 1889 that notices be sent out whenever a member died, his adjutant gently informed him that this "had been the former custom, with but little good result."[14] Members were not about to shoulder a duty that in the winter months of some years would have involved almost weekly attendance at funerals.

Instead, the adjutant suggested that Whitecar send out funeral notices whenever he thought they were "appropriate"—a polite way of saying that they should be sent only on the deaths of prominent members. That, in fact, was standard practice not only in Post 2 but also in Brockton and Chippewa Falls, posts that did continue to fund and attend the burials of lower-status veterans but that turned out in force and attached great ceremony only to the funerals of notable members. The Philadelphia post left a blank page in its minutes and an empty chair in its post room on the death of any member. It performed the GAR funeral rites for such humble members as paperhanger William Hazlitt and government assessor Peter Sides. But upon the death of Robert Orr—prosperous merchant, prominent post member, former colonel wounded in action—Post 2 held a full-blown GAR funeral at the post hall, presided over by the department chaplain and including a funeral procession with a drum corps, delegations from the federal customhouse and the Sons of Veterans, the uniformed Post 2 Guard, and a detachment of state militia. When Brockton's Alfred C. Monroe—department adjutant, twice state representative, war amputee—died in 1891, Webster Post staged a large

funeral, started a statewide fund to build a monument to him, and acquired a portrait of him that not only was insured but also was attached to a block and tackle so that it could be rescued quickly in case of a fire at the post hall. In Chippewa Falls, the funeral of Colonel George Ginty (a newspaper publisher and Republican state senator) was attended by former Wisconsin governor and GAR commander-in-chief Lucius Fairchild, with round-the-clock honor guards assigned to the casket beforehand.[15]

This is not to say that posts neglected the funerals of ordinary members, only that funerals of poor and prosperous veterans were treated as events of different sorts. For a family of low or middling status, a funeral was a major expense, while the promise of burial with semimilitary honors was a strong reason to maintain membership in a post. When such a veteran died, post members usually were aware of the circumstances of the survivors; if not, the charity committee soon ascertained them. The post then provided its services at the funeral, money for the burial, sometimes a small stipend for the widow. Like the provision of free medical care to indigent veterans during life, funeral services were charity for comrades who otherwise could not have afforded them.[16]

The families of prosperous veterans such as Orr, Monroe, and Ginty, on the other hand, obviously could afford to pay funeral expenses; they did not choose the GAR rite simply because they had no other option. Unlike their less privileged comrades, these upper-middle-class veterans had never needed to ask for post charity. Indeed, they had been instrumental in deciding how to hand it out. Consequently, their funerals were treated not as charity events but as pageants. Bristling with military trappings, their rites were celebrations of successful businessmen who located the meaning of their lives in their brief army careers and wanted everyone to know it (Ginty, for one, is said to have asked for "a strictly Grand Army burial" with his last breath).[17] Post members participated in such events not out of a sense of duty to the unfortunate; those funerals drew small crowds. Rather, through the funeral members reaffirmed their essential comradeship with veterans wealthier and better known than themselves. In short, while most GAR funerals represented relief to needy comrades, the most heavily attended services were not "charity" at all.

Medical services, aid to the destitute and the unemployed, and funeral assistance were the three most common forms of GAR charity. Less-regular donations included cash gifts to individuals or to other posts (those burned out of their halls, for example) and relief campaigns organized after such disasters as the Chicago fire of 1871 and the Johnstown flood of 1889.[18] GAR charity seemed impressive when considered in the aggregate, which is generally the way it was listed. In the 1870s, for instance, the posts of New York reported spending between $18,000 and $30,000 annually on charity; in 1872, Adjutant-General Roswell Miller reported almost $75,000 expended on charity by all posts of the order. In 1888 Robert Beath added all GAR relief disbursements since 1871 and came up with the staggering total of $1,643,598.22.[19]

Congratulating themselves on such a fine showing, members were fond of pointing out that the GAR, unlike other fraternal orders, provided relief for Union veterans whether they belonged to the order or not. The Grand Army, George Lemon argued, "spends more for real charity—very much more—than any other Order or Society in the country." Societies such as the Odd Fellows and the Knights of Pythias, he wrote, "are mainly life and health assurance associations, and the money they pay out is not in the nature of charity, but payment on policies. The G.A.R. benefactions are charities pure and simple."[20] In 1881, for example, more than one-third of the Brockton post's charity expenditures went to nonmembers; between 1881 and 1883 the post aided 22 members and 53 nonmembers. In Philadelphia's Post 2, 80 of 108 persons assisted in 1876 were nonmembers or their relatives; in 1884 the Pennsylvania department surgeon reported giving free medical examinations to 47 candidates for entrance to the state soldiers' home, only 13 of whom were GAR members.[21]

Despite the large totals, however, the typical relief expenditure was not very large. In Beath's tabulations, for example, the posts of the order reported spending $215,975.19 in the year ending March 31, 1888. But that sum was divided among 23,810 different persons— thus averaging about $9 per case. Similarly, Brockton's Webster Post reported spending $362.91 to relieve 33 persons in 1881—an average of about $11 each, with almost one-third of the total spent on a single member. Only 3 of the 7 members relieved by Webster Post got more than $20 in the course of the year; the 26 nonmembers averaged $5 each.[22] While the GAR as a whole provided a great deal of relief, it did so in very small doses.

The proximate cause of the slimness of post-level charity often was a spending limit imposed in cases that promised to be costly or prolonged. In 1881, Webster Post took up a collection to pay George

Raymond's back dues and reimbursed a post in Plymouth for his medical care, but when the bills began to mount (the post ultimately spent $112.97 on him), the Plymouth post was instructed to limit expenditures for him to $10 per month. In Chippewa Falls, Comerford Post voted $5 in aid to John McAfee, turned out for his funeral, and paid his widow's rent for two months after his death. But when she continued to petition the post monthly for rent money, the members—after considering building her a house—referred her to the relief committee, a body that was not allowed to make a disbursement larger than $5.[23] The low average expenditure also resulted from strict limits on single payments. Webster and Comerford posts both required explicit post approval for relief expenditures greater than $5; Philadelphia's Post 2 required approval for payments of more than $20 to members and $5 to "deserving soldiers."[24]

Behind the restrictions, however, was a general conception of charity that was distinctly limited. Though not insignificant to the beneficiaries, post donations of money and services clearly were never intended as substitutes for the ongoing support of a pension. Temporary and local, they were one- or two-time gifts to tide a member over a difficult period. The small cash donations were usually earmarked for specific purposes—rent, coal, train fare—and administered by a committee or, in a practice common in Victorian fraternal orders, by a committee of women from the auxiliary Woman's Relief Corps.[25] By the same token, money granted without a specified purpose rarely amounted to more than $5. Small sums might help a veteran or his widow out of a tight spot, but they were not likely to be of much help in cases of long-term illness, disability, or financial insolvency.

Problems of such magnitude were not solvable through limited, voluntary charity, and when faced with them, posts tended to fall back on some form of mutual self-funding, like insurance or death dues. The veterans, in other words, saw post-level relief in conventional nineteenth-century philanthropic terms: as a local, personal, specific way for individual soldiers to help each other weather individual crises.[26] The system was based on voluntary contributions, which could be just as freely withdrawn. It assumed no continued dependence on the part of the recipients; it implied no continued obligation on the part of the donors. Like the injunctions to follow GAR "orders," appeals to charity carried only as much force as the members cared to give them.

This limited notion of charity was based on a genuine fear of dependence or, to put it in more positive terms, a desire for independence. Freedom from obligation to others was at the root of the idea of manliness espoused by leading veterans. Manliness, as we have seen, was put forward as a counterweight to the ethic of self-interest that ruled the capitalist marketplace. It generally was taken to mean selfless behavior—even self-sacrifice—in the interest of some higher ideal. But the manly relinquishment of self presumed the existence of an independent self; one cannot sacrifice what is not one's own to begin with. As an editorialist in 1879 put it, "[Men] must have a sense of manliness and proper responsibility which would prevent them, under any circumstances, from depending on anybody but themselves for the maintenance of their family."[27] Autonomy thus was a prerequisite for manly behavior. Long-term charity threatened to sap the manliness of members by placing too much power over their lives in the hands of others. In a culture that placed a premium on self-reliance, to accept large handouts indefinitely—even from comrades—was to admit failure.

GAR speakers usually pictured the Union veteran as an independent man who, when driven to seek relief, preferred the aid of his fellows to any sort of public alms. "Thousands of our poor, helpless, crippled comrades have been placed in positions where they could not earn their own bread," Benjamin Stephenson reported to the 1868 national encampment, "who, but for our instrumentality, would be left to seek their support from the cold hand of charity, *and the Union soldier disdains to beg.*" At Denver in 1883, J. G. B. Adams put forward the idea that autonomy had been the first thought of returning veterans in 1865 and that only the overwhelming need for relief had led them to organize. "We swore when we got through [with the war] that we would call no man commander, but would run our own machine; but when we found crippled men who came to the strong and hearty and wanted help, and widows and orphans, the boys came together . . . and organized the Grand Army, which, as a charitable organization, is the greatest the world ever saw."[28]

Because posts worried about dependence, they tried in various ways to spare relief recipients its stigma. In particular, they tried to keep indigent veterans from being herded into almshouses or buried in paupers' graves. Many states had laws by 1890 preventing ex-soldiers from meeting either fate, while Congress in 1872 extended the privilege of burial in national cemeteries to all destitute veterans with honorable discharges. A typical case was that of a veteran in Mansfield, Connecticut, who would have been buried in a pauper's grave had the undertaker not notified the local GAR post. The post

arranged for a GAR graveside service and authorized the man's burial in its lot. "There was not a relative at the grave," the *Grand Army Record* reported, "but nearly forty members of the Post attended the funeral, although the veteran was not a member of the order and a stranger to nearly all."[29]

Some posts also tried to protect the anonymity of their relief recipients. Post 2, for instance, usually recorded charity disbursements in its minutes only as "given to a member of this post." Many posts protested a move in 1883 to publish pension lists. In 1892, Webster Post asked the Brockton newspapers to refrain from printing lists of pension applicants drawn up at public meetings. And in 1893 the order stopped requiring reinstated members to take the ceremonial "obligation" a second time after Pennsylvania department commander Thomas Sample protested: "If he has been dropped for nonpayment of dues you compel that man to stand up before the Post and admit his poverty, and there are a number of people who are out of the Grand Army who will not consent to do anything of that kind."[30]

The GAR's constricted system of mutual self-help may have allowed some veterans to maintain a sense of autonomy, but it unfortunately provided nowhere near enough relief to cope with the vicissitudes of American economic life in the late nineteenth century. Following the Panic of 1873, GAR Surgeon-General Hans Powell noted with some pride that "the services of Department and Post Medical officers, have been in great demand." But by early 1877 the charity committee of Post 2 was urging members to "exercise great care" before referring aid applicants; too many members were out of work, and the post was being forced to tap its general revenues to provide for them. Two years later, the post quartermaster complained that "Post 2 is not a *mint*" and asked other Philadelphia posts to stop sending him so many charity cases.[31]

During the next serious slump, in 1887, Post 2's adjutant had to discourage at least two applicants for post aid. "I regret that it is not in our power to provide a situation for you," he wrote veteran James Lawry. "You are no doubt aware that our city is large and there are many persons, especially 'Old Soldiers,' seeking employment, and in our own post there are at this time several, out of employment." Ten days later he told H. E. Brown that a request for substantial charity (probably a post-funded pension) to a veteran's widow was "a task too delicate to undertake with the comrades of the post" and might establish a precedent that would lead to "unfortunate complications." "I think," he concluded hopefully, "that some good angel will bring to the family of our late Comrade, comfort and happiness."[32]

The most severe depression was that of the 1890s, which threw many veterans out of work at a time when they were well advanced in age. Post 2's response to the crisis was to create an "employment bureau," which during its brief existence received such plaintive missives as this one from George Cook in 1897:

> Dr Sir and Bro:
> For the first time in my life I am out of employment. And very anxious to be employed. Was for years Salesman for Wholesale Dry Goods House. Then in business for my self. And later Manager of Merchant Tailing Establishment to Jan 1st, 1897. Am very active. Can sell, manage, or buy goods, or take charge of office or counting room. Understand credits, also the handling of men. Am only 49, as yet, but feel as young as my boys.

From scant surviving records, however, it appears that only two of the seventeen men who listed themselves with the Post 2 bureau found employment during its tenure, George Cook not among them.[33]

On the West Coast, a California officer warned in 1895 that "the procession of veterans that is coming this way broke, expecting to enter one of the Soldiers' Homes in this state immediately upon arrival" would be disappointed. "During the financial depression our Posts have all they can do to take care of their own members," the California adjutant wrote Oregon commander S. B. Ormsby in 1895, "and sojourners get left, and at this time San Francisco is about the worst place in the world for a man out of a job and without money."[34] In short, the posts did what they could to help veterans through hard times, given the resource constraints imposed by an ideology of self-reliance. But when that relief was not enough, as it often was not, the unfortunate comrade was thrown back on his own resources or those of "some good angel."

Dependent Pension and Service Pension

By 1890 at the very latest, the GAR system of voluntary relief was an anachronism. Post-level charity did not disappear even after the maintenance of a post relief committee was made optional in 1888; posts continued to dispense aid well into the

next century. But in a world increasingly dominated by large corporations, railroads, centralized government, national communications
networks, and mass political parties, the idea of the autonomous,
"manly" individual, dependent on no one, no longer made sense. As
previously insulated communities came to rely more heavily on each
other, individuals began to realize that they were at the mercy of
forces and events outside their control or even their understanding.
The phenomenon that Thomas Haskell has called "recession of causation" was at work.[35]

The new situation of dependence on others made most people
uncomfortable for the same reason veterans worried about being
sent to almshouses: it represented a loss of the autonomy necessary
to live a moral life as it was commonly understood. For the dependent, there could be no manly self-sacrifice; more likely, he would
experience only degradation and manipulation. To some social reformers, that seemed to be exactly what was happening. Yet in the
complex, industrializing economy of 1880 it was impossible not to be
affected to some degree by translocal forces, and continued reliance
on purely local philanthropy was an invitation to hardship. Although
Union veterans in the 1880s and 1890s still pictured the GAR as a
brotherhood of independent, selfless volunteers, they were not about
to sacrifice themselves on the altar of personal autonomy at a time
when no one else showed much inclination to do so.

Comrade George Lemon, who perceived the change earlier than
most, was already calling for the melding of local networks into a
national lobby in 1877. "Each man of you is the center of a circle of
influence," he told his veteran readers in agitating for federal legislation to equalize bounties paid as inducements during the war. "Each
man is a component part, a scattered drop, of a current which, if
united, will sweep to success with a majesty of strength."[36] In an 1885
editorial, Lemon argued that organizations based on locality alone
were becoming obsolete:

> Our population has become so large, and our social system so
> complex, that subdivisions into societies, associations, orders,
> etc. has become imperative. In earlier and simpler days neigh-
> borhoods furnished all the subdivisions necessary. Every little
> community was a large family in which everybody knew every-
> body else, and was quite ready to do proper acts of kindness,
> friendship, or charity. . . . With increasing density of population
> the duties and obligations of "neighborliness" are rapidly declin-

ing. We feel less brotherly toward our next-door neighbor now than our fathers did to the man who lived miles away.[37]

As a Washington-based claim agent, Lemon had an obvious interest in advocating public aid to veterans. But following the Arrears Act of 1879 (the passage of which owed much to Lemon's influence), a great many other former soldiers came around to his view that local post philanthropy was not enough.

Some posts eased the strain by tapping outside sources of local relief. The Chippewa Falls post made use of county tax revenues, while the Philadelphians dunned their wealthy friends; in 1871, for example, Comrade Thomas Ellis, a storekeeper, told the other members of Post 2 that if he brought the matter of a dwindling relief fund before the public, he "felt assured of contributions from the wealthier classes." In some posts the "associate membership" about which so many veterans complained continued to flourish because it was a useful fund-raising tool. In Brockton, two fund-raising events modeled on wartime sanitary fairs raised $3,500 for the Webster Post charity fund. In other places, the local congressman was lobbied to push through private pension bills. "It should be fully recognized," said Commander-in-Chief Charles Devens during the depression following the Panic of 1873, "that in many instances generous assistance has been afforded to the posts by the communities in which they are situated, from a feeling that whatever is entrusted to them is carefully expended, with the fullest and tenderest regard to the just pride of brave men who have been compelled, sometimes, most reluctantly, to accept assistance."[38]

Local relief efforts, like the in-house charity provided by posts, were hardly equivalent to pensions. But that had never been intended. Posts doled out aid in one- and two-time doses; localities provided whatever relief was usual for indigent and unemployed persons. In no case was there any promise of sustained relief. The standard view held that pensions were reserved for soldiers crippled in federal service; other veterans, even poor or unemployed ones, had to take care of themselves. "We believe that the utmost which the country owes [veterans] is the payment of pensions to those who were disabled in the service, and to their families after their death," stated one body of conservative veterans, trying to preserve the status quo in 1890. " . . . We believe that every American owes to his country in time of peace the duty of earning his own living; and that this obligation is not cancelled or weakened by army service."[39] For

veterans hampered by illness or thrown out of work by a business
depression, this view provided cold comfort.

With local public aid available only sporadically, Union veterans in the 1880s began pushing in almost every Northern state legislature for statutes ensuring special treatment for ex-soldiers. Some of the new laws required localities to provide extra relief or to bury indigent veterans; some required veteran preference in government hiring; still others provided large appropriations for soldiers' homes and soldiers' orphans schools. In every case, state veteran legislation represented a significant expansion of the sphere of public responsibility. And in almost every case, the GAR had much to do with the passage of the new laws.

The provision of state-level aid to veterans came at a time when states were taking the first steps toward regulation in other areas of social life as well—public health, labor, railroads, and especially centralized charity. Although there were significant precedents for federal relief of the suffering—notably the wartime United States Sanitary Commission and the Freedmen's Bureau—those agencies had been allowed to atrophy in the postwar period.[40] Instead, charity cases increasingly were dealt with either by private voluntary organizations or by one of the new state boards of charity.

The state boards, often neglected in examinations of nineteenth-century reform, could be strong forces if they were adept lobbyists. As William R. Brock points out, they "mark the beginning of a new era in which government would accept responsibility for the treatment of ills that had formerly been regarded as inevitable, incurable, and decreed by an inscrutable Deity." Most of the agencies, however, were underfunded and purely advisory. They were only as strong as the public pressure they could bring to bear on legislators.[41] What made state legislatures responsive to calls for relief of Union veterans was the ex-soldiers' political power—unlike the poor, veterans voted in a recognizable bloc—and their overt identification with the nation rather than with any given locality, class, or industry. If any group could make a plausible claim for state charity, the veterans could.

In Pennsylvania, for example, the Grand Army was influential in securing many forms of aid, beginning with appropriations for soldiers' orphans schools. Post 2 maintained a standing committee after 1873 to lobby legislators in Harrisburg on the subject, while the state GAR department worked to ease restrictions on entrance to the schools, inspected them regularly, and drafted legislation. "By their numerical strength, and by their social and political standing," a historian of the Pennsylvania orphans schools wrote of the GAR members in 1877, "they have been enabled so to shape legislative action as to obtain favorable results."[42]

While the orphans were still being taken care of, some members of the Pennsylvania GAR thought it would be "inexpedient . . . in view of the State finances" to demand money for a state soldiers' home. But in 1884, GAR investigators found 150 old soldiers in public alms-houses; the department adjutant reported 199; another investigation in 1885 found between 300 and 400. Robert Beath, who headed the 1885 inquiry, expressed shock that "men who at Gettysburg stayed the advance of an invading enemy, whose success would have cost the people of our State many millions in money, and would have pro-longed the war, appear to be forgotten in their old age, or when decrepitude has overtaken them, and they live miserably as paupers, instead of being the honored wards of a grateful Commonwealth." Beath recommended asking the state for $50,000 to fund a soldiers' home, with the other $20,000 needed for the project to be raised the old way, through voluntary subscription. In lobbying for the measure, however, the committee concluded that "the finances of the state would not be pressed too severely if we asked for a larger sum," and upped its request to $101,500.[43]

The bill breezed through the Pennsylvania legislature without a dissenting vote, and the new soldiers' home opened in 1886. On its eleven-member board were nine GAR members, including Beath, Louis Wagner, Post 2's John Vanderslice, and Comrade Isaac B. Brown, the bill's legislative sponsor. In the same year, Comrade Thomas Stewart, a state legislator from Montgomery County, pushed through a companion bill to provide for state burial of indigent vet-erans. Here, too, Beath reported in 1889, Grand Army men had been appointed "in nearly all the counties of the State to report all such cases and attend to the necessary details."[44]

What happened in Pennsylvania also happened elsewhere. With GAR prodding, state after state in the 1880s moved to aid the Union veterans. Maine appropriated $35,000 annually to fund pensions for its veterans, with the rate in specific cases to be determined by local aldermen. In New York, an act of 1887 required towns and cities to provide "such sum or sums of money as may be necessary" to be drawn on for relief purposes by the local GAR post commander and quartermaster; in Massachusetts, each town was allowed to dispense such aid itself, though it could authorize the local GAR post as a disbursing agent by a special vote. Ohio, Wisconsin, and Iowa pro-

vided for special county taxes to relieve indigent veterans and their
families; Minnesota instituted a state tax for the same purpose. New Hampshire, Massachusetts, New York, and Wisconsin required communities to maintain indigent veterans in some location other than the poorhouse. New York, Massachusetts, Ohio, and Kansas gave preference to veterans in public hiring. Twelve states in addition to Pennsylvania provided money to bury veterans whose families were too poor to afford it. And between 1879 and 1888, a steady procession of new state soldiers' homes opened: in New York (1879), Massachusetts (1881), Vermont (1884), Illinois (1885), Rhode Island (1886), Pennsylvania (1886), Michigan (1887), Wisconsin (1887), Iowa (1887), Minnesota (1888), Ohio (1888), and Nebraska (1888).[45]

Even state aid, however, continued to be based on the narrow grounds of service-related disability, and when it was not—as with statutes ordering towns to care for poor veterans outside almshouses—it was difficult to enforce. Although evidence on enforcement is sketchy, one suspects that there were many localities in which the state laws were "practically of no effect," as Brockton's mayor had put it. Aid continued to be limited to those suffering from service-related wounds and illnesses and to survivors of those killed in the war. As with the post charity efforts, there was no promise of ongoing relief.

The federal pension statute adopted during the war accurately reflected the same narrow point of view.[46] Under the general law of 1862, Union Army soldiers who had suffered permanent bodily injury or disability as a direct consequence of military service were eligible for federal relief at monthly rates ranging from $8 to $30 (depending on rank) for total disability, with lesser amounts paid for partial disability. In the event of an ex-soldier's death from service-related causes, a pension at the full-disability rate was payable to his widow, his dependent mother or sister, or his orphaned children under the age of sixteen. One section of the 1862 act, which later proved to be important, stipulated payment from the date of a veteran's discharge only if he filed his claim within the ensuing year (or, in the case of a widow, within one year from the date of the veteran's death). Otherwise, the pension was to start on the date the claim was allowed by the Pension Bureau. The law allowed no pension simply for indigence and none for injuries not proved to be of service origin.

The 1862 statute was liberalized on occasion over the next seventeen years. Higher rates were added for severe disabilities such as loss of sight, the commissioner of pensions was empowered to set intermediate rates for injuries not specified in the original law, and in 1873 the limitation for claims was extended from one to five years (a change primarily benefiting widows, since almost all Civil War soldiers had been mustered out of service by 1866). With those minor modifications, the law of 1862 remained the basis of all federal pension payments until 1879. Under it, pension expenditures averaged $26.5 million annually between 1866 and 1878. The pension roll in 1878 numbered 223,998 names.

By the standards of previous American wars, the general pension act of 1862 was an eminently generous and just piece of legislation. Although still based on service-related disability, it included more classes of dependents and paid higher rates than any previous law. Nevertheless, it excluded some who felt they should have been eligible. Writing in 1918, William Glasson outlined the perfect hypothetical case:

> A soldier was discharged from the army in 1864. He married in 1865 and was able to support himself and his wife by his usual occupation. After a few years he was in poor health, and in 1871 he died of tuberculosis, never having applied for a pension. Not connecting his death with army service, his widow filed no application within the five year period. However, in 1878, she was informed that she could probably establish a valid pension claim. She filed an application and secured evidence that her husband suffered from a severe attack of bronchitis while in the army, and that he was unusually susceptible to colds after his discharge. A combination of military, medical, and lay testimony connected the tuberculosis from which her husband died with the attack of bronchitis as a cause. The Pension Bureau allowed the claim and placed the widow on the roll at eight dollars a month to commence with the date of filing the last evidence in the case.

Had this widow filed her claim two years earlier, however, she would have been able to collect the full arrears from the time of her husband's death—a lump sum of about $500. "The contrast in the settlement obtained by a widow who filed her application within the prescribed time limit and that obtained by the widow who applied after the expiration of the five year period," Glasson commented, "was undoubtedly calculated to produce a feeling of dissatisfaction in the mind of the latter."[47] Other vexed claimants included veterans who could not amass evidence to prove that their injuries had originated in army service, those whose claims had been disallowed, those whose applications had been delayed in the Pension Bureau, and those who experienced dire poverty as a result of injuries or illness suffered *since* the war.

Talented pension agents played expertly to these disaffections. George Lemon, the leader of the pack, complained in 1877 that as a result of delays in pension payments, "many widows and orphans of soldiers who died in defense of the country are in great want and destitution, and cases have been reported where families have been turned into the streets." When Pension Commissioner John A. Bentley began taking a hard line with some applications, Lemon launched a series of savage attacks on him, ending with a large engraving of the commissioner on the front page of the *National Tribune*, captioned "The Arch Enemy of the Soldier" and "The Man who Cannot bring himself to Believe the testimony of the Soldiers."[48] In all likelihood, the person who informed Glasson's hypothetical widow that she could establish a valid pension claim would have been a pension attorney.

The result of the combination of ambitious pension attorneys and dissatisfied veterans was a constant flurry of pension bills in Washington commencing almost as soon as the war ended. One scheme called for the government to issue warrants to all honorably discharged veterans good for free land in the West. Another called for veterans to be given the difference in value between their wages (which had been paid in greenbacks) and the price of gold at the time. A third proposal, backed strongly by Lemon, called for federal payments to equalize the varying bounties given to volunteers at different stages of the war. The bounty equalization measure actually passed Congress in 1875, only to be vetoed by President Grant on the grounds that it was too lavish for a government in the midst of a depression and that it would mostly benefit "claim agents and middlemen." The *New York Times*, a foe of large pension outlays, reported the introduction in 1878 of bills to pension Revolutionary War survivors or their descendants, "volunteers" who had helped out in local actions of the War of 1812, and anyone who had served as long as fourteen days in the Mexican War. "One more step," the *Times* complained, "will bring us to pensioning all the North-western pioneers who have ever in Government service held themselves ready to defend their own ranches."[49] The only measures to become law in the 1870s, however, were minor rate adjustments that did not alter the basic disability requirement for federal aid or significantly affect the number of claims filed.

The first of two major changes in the Civil War pension system was the Arrears Act of 1879, which, strictly speaking, was also a modification of the general law rather than a wholesale overhaul. It did not change the service-related disability basis for claims. It did not tamper with the rates. All the act did was provide that veterans and widows who had already established claims to pensions *or who established new claims prior to July 1, 1880,* were henceforth to receive payment effective from the date of the soldier's original discharge. Thus a veteran discharged in 1865 who had not been granted a pension until 1871 could collect all the money that would have been paid him had the claim been approved in 1865.

The new act neatly solved the problem of inequity posed by Glasson's hypothetical "widow"—now all pensions would have a common starting point. But it produced a stampede on the Pension Bureau. In 1880, new claims, to say nothing of new petitions from existing claimants, numbered 138,195, a total higher than those of the previous five years combined. In June, the last month before the deadline, the bureau received 44,532 new applications.[50]

The cause of the rush is not hard to determine. For a man already on the pension roll, the Arrears Act might mean several years' worth of back pensions, a single payment of hundreds of dollars at a time when towns and posts were doling out charity in $5 lumps. A veteran who successfully prosecuted a *new* claim—or found enough new evidence to resurrect an old one—might receive more than $1,000. Not only that: claims now could be based on ex parte affidavits rather than on military records alone, a system that Pension Commissioner Bentley called "an open door to the Treasury for the perpetration of fraud."[51] Assessing the damage in 1889, pension reformer Leonard Woolsey Bacon scoffed:

> What wonder, considering the infirmities of human nature, that the invitation to step up and take a thousand dollars apiece, with an annuity, out of the Treasury "on a mere *ex parte* affidavit," should be accepted in the same large spirit in which it was offered; that men in comfortable circumstances who had been ashamed to ask for twelve dollars a month, should find the offer of a thousand dollars in a lump sum to be quite a different matter; and that men in comfortable health should become conscious all at once of hitherto unsuspected disorders, traceable through subtle lines of causation to a longer or shorter military service?[52]

The strong cash incentive to file, combined with the easing of evidence requirements, made the Arrears Act an expensive piece of legislation. In 1880, the first full year of the act's operation, federal pension expenditures were more than double what they had been in 1878. By 1885, the commissioner of pensions estimated that the measure had cost $179.4 million in arrears alone.[53]

Despite this sudden largess, the Grand Army showed only a passing interest in the Arrears Act. True, Commander-in-Chief John Robinson and at least two state departments endorsed the idea, while many individual members undoubtedly responded to Lemon's constant agitation for arrears. But the national encampment took no formal action on the bill, and GAR officers engaged in none of the lobbying that would soon make the order notorious. At the local level, neither Post 2 nor Webster Post took any notice of the measure (Comerford Post was not yet in existence).[54]

In large part the Grand Army's neglect of the act reflected the organization's preoccupation with other matters. Mired in the recruiting drought of the 1870s, GAR leaders did not conceive of their small, widely dispersed organization as the voice of all Union soldiers. The encampments of the decade concerned themselves with rules, ritual, and the shoring up of a fragile national structure rather than with pensions. The real movers behind the Arrears Act were not Grand Army officers but pension agents (who stood to make a $10 fee from each successful new claim) and politicians solicitous of the "soldier vote" in the upcoming 1880 elections. Insofar as such agitators considered the GAR, they viewed it as one soldiers' organization among many. Within four years, however, the order would be on the rebound and at the forefront of pension agitation.

The revival of the Grand Army owed much to George Lemon, who sensed the possibilities early. From the inception of his *National Tribune* in 1877 he had urged veterans to concentrate their fire, to "present before the Congress of the United States the same unbroken front which won many a glorious battle field." The success of the Arrears Act—and the business it generated—reinforced his feeling that great things could be achieved if the "soldier vote" could be marshaled in a single bloc. "The truth is that no political party can any longer afford to ignore the soldier," he editorialized buoyantly in 1882. "As compared with two years ago, when there was a lack of all organization among our comrades to secure the recognition of their claims, the situation is decidedly cheering. Our veterans are beginning to awake to a consciousness of their power."[55] Lemon planned to awaken this consciousness, and there were politicians aplenty from both parties, though chiefly among the Republicans, ready to help him. But if Union veterans were to be organized as a national political pressure group, they had to think of themselves as distinctive, as veterans first and as members of other groups only secondarily. The Grand Army, with its national scope, quasi-military ranks, and ritual emphasizing the "sacred tie" of veteranhood was ideally suited to the task.

Lemon sought the patronage of GAR posts in the first issue of the *National Tribune,* and from 1880 onward he worked ceaselessly to build the order up to fighting strength. Urging members to "amalgamate, organize and move on the enemy in solid columns," he gave much space in his paper to GAR affairs and helped organize some posts by mail. Commander-in-Chief Paul Vandervoort, a true booster who named Lemon an aide-de-camp (and was later employed by him in return), also used the military metaphor in drumming up an unprecedented number of new members in 1883. "Comrades, I call upon you to go to work; the harvest is ready," he wrote in one National General Order. "Recruit all along the line."[56]

Whether it was the influence of Lemon or simply reawakened self-interest, the GAR became much more active on the pension issue in the wake of the Arrears Act. In 1881 the national encampment appointed a committee on pension legislation to serve as its official lobby in Washington. The committee's first report, made in 1882 as the Arrears Act was still pumping huge infusions of cash into the economy, was exceptionally mild: it called only for higher pensions for maimed veterans, and for increased appropriations to the Pension Bureau and the surgeon-general's office to hire the extra clerical and medical help needed to process pending claims. But by 1884, with GAR membership more than tripled in size since 1880, the order was pressing aggressively for new legislation. The national pension committee report of that year called for an extension until 1885 of the limit on filing arrears; special pensions for former prisoners of war; equalization of bounties; a $100-per-month pension for severely disabled veterans, with similarly large increases for lesser injuries; higher rates for widows and orphans and the continuance of widows' stipends even when their husbands had died of non-service-related causes; a relaxation of the standards of proof required to establish claims; and—most important—a bill to pension all veterans, disabled or not, who had become dependent on others for support.[57]

Even that ambitious program was less than what some delegates

were advocating. The encampment declined to endorse several other, more radical ideas—land warrants, compensation for greenback wages, and a "service" pension that would have rewarded every man who had served a minimum term in the Union Army. The more extreme proposals, which continued to be put forward at subsequent encampments, usually were rejected on the grounds that they were not likely to pass Congress. But as the GAR continued to swell in size and influence, the tone of the pension radicals became shrill enough to give politicians pause. "Who are in the lead on this question, Congressmen or the comrades of the Grand Army?" cried Indiana delegate Thomas Bennet during debate over service pensions at the 1886 encampment. "I do not want a Congressman to tell me what he wants. I want to tell him what I want on this question."[58]

The politics of pensions became particularly acrimonious in the 1880s because electoral support for the two major parties was almost equally divided. The presidential elections of 1880 and 1884 were decided by tiny margins (9,464 and 23,005 votes, respectively), while in the contest of 1888 the loser, Grover Cleveland, actually outpolled the winner, Benjamin Harrison, by almost 100,000 votes. Like the Irish vote in New York City or the German Lutheran vote in Ohio, the veteran vote could provide the margin of victory in important swing states. Thus the capture of the soldier vote was never far from the minds of representatives who were drafting pension legislation. But as Bennet's comment suggests, in the late 1880s the pension clamor began to take on a life of its own.

At this point it is worth emphasizing that the Arrears Act did not alter the *basis* of pension payments. Although it stimulated a flood of new applications, it did not add any new classes of pensioners to the rolls. To qualify for pension relief, a veteran still had to prove that he was sick or disabled, that his sickness or disability was the direct result of his military service, and, where a full, or "total disability" pension was to be granted, that his disability left him unable to perform manual labor. The simple fact of disability was not enough to establish a claim; neither was poverty. Pensions continued to be based, as they always had been before the Civil War, on *war-related disability* (or, in the case of widows' pensions, war-related death).

Beginning with the 1884 committee report, GAR pension agitation was aimed at eliminating that fundamental eligibility requirement. The change is reflected in GAR legislative proposals between 1884 and 1890, which were of two basic types: "dependent" pension bills and "service" pension bills. Bills of the former variety called for the pensioning of all ex-soldiers who were unable to support themselves because of infirmities, whether those infirmities had anything to do with war service or not; they were, in a sense, extensions of the local and state-level efforts to keep ex-soldiers out of almshouses. Bills of the latter type were proposals to pension every honorably discharged soldier who had served a given term (usually sixty or ninety days), regardless of his physical or financial condition. Service pensions obviously were more inclusive and costly than dependent pensions, but both required the jettisoning of the old idea that pensions were compensation for injuries suffered *in war*. Under the new plans, veterans would be guaranteed benefits simply because they were veterans.

With the aid of heavy GAR lobbying, the first of a series of dependent pension bills moved through Congress in 1884. A measure passed by the Democratic House in that year tried to redress the grievances of needy ex-soldiers who could not prove that their injuries were war-related by relaxing the rules of evidence in cases in which disabilities were "probably" of service origin. The Republican Senate simultaneously passed a more liberal measure: eligibility was to be extended to any Union veteran of ninety days' service who depended on his own labor for support and suffered from a disability, war-related or not. Both measures died at the end of the session when the two houses could not reach agreement on them.[59]

The next scheme, put forward in 1887, came even closer to becoming law. In 1886, President Cleveland had included in his annual message to Congress a statement of sympathy for veterans who had been "reduced to destitution and dependence, not as an incidence of their service, but with advancing age or through sickness or misfortune." Encouraged, Congress in January 1887 passed a bill described by its House sponsor as a measure to get the ex-soldiers out of the almshouses. It provided a pension of $12 per month to any veteran unable to earn a living as a result of mental or physical disability. Like the 1884 Senate bill, the 1887 dependent pension measure required only that the claimant's disability not be the result of his "vicious habits or gross carelessness," a restriction that in practice ruled out almost no one save drunkards and syphilitics. It also required the claimant to prove that he could not support himself—a "pauper" provision inserted over the objections of GAR lobbyists.

Despite those safeguards, President Cleveland vetoed the dependent pension bill in February 1887. Not only would the new claims

cost too much, he argued, but it would be impossible to decide who
was "dependent." "What is a support? Who is to determine whether
a man earns it, or has it, or has it not?" he wrote in his veto message.
"Is the government to enter the homes of claimants for pension, and
after an examination of their surroundings and circumstances settle
those questions? Shall the Government say to one man that his
manner of subsistence by his earnings is a support, and to another
that the things his earnings furnish are not a support?"[60] It was the
sort of question that might have worried a local post charity committee trying to avoid promiscuous giving.

The GAR, by now boasting more than 350,000 members, responded to the veto with righteous outrage. Commander-in-Chief
Lucius Fairchild asked posts to send their opinions of the veto to their
congressmen, and hundreds did so. Lemon called Cleveland's argument regarding dependence "mere word twisting" and said of his
argument that the bill would impose too heavy a burden on the
nation: "Who is bearing that burden now? The G.A.R. posts and the
State, Township and municipal treasuries of the country." George
Merrill, chairman of the GAR national pension committee, reminded
members that all around them were veterans and widows "whom
you know to be amply deserving of pensions, but who are unable to
obtain them under existing laws, because of some technicality in the
record, or from loss of evidence" and urged them to "make the air
ring with their vigorous and emphatic protest."[61] The bill's supporters, however, were unable to round up the votes to override the veto.
A similar bill passed the Senate the following year but died in the
House.

In his 1887 veto message Cleveland insisted on referring to the
dependent pension bill as a "service pension" measure, and in comparison with existing laws it must have seemed so. Certainly it would
have pensioned a great many persons whose main claim to government preference was service in the Union Army. But a "pure" service
pension was one that required no proof whatsoever of disability or
dependence, and by 1887 just such a law was being loudly called for
in many quarters of the Grand Army. In Brockton, for example,
members of Webster Post knew about the dependent pension bill
and the president's veto—member Seth French had read them a
paper on the subject in March 1887. But in July they voted 43–0 to
repudiate the bill their national officers had worked so hard to pass.
Instead, the post became active in the Service Pension Association, a
Boston-based confederation of Grand Army men working to promote

unlimited service pensions. Other nonelite posts, such as the one at Chippewa Falls, simply favored pensions—the more the better—and endorsed both service and dependent pension bills.[62]

It was elite GAR locals such as Philadelphia's Post 2 that held out against the service pension idea. Resolutions favoring the service pension were sneaked through one of Post 2's sparsely attended summer meetings in 1884, but they were soon repudiated and replaced by resolutions stating that the national encampment had "acted wisely and well." In general, the service pension found support not among the leading posts but among the same humble posts that during these years attacked the privileges of the GAR's "House of Lords." A disapproving *New York Times*, noting as "an ominous sign" the charge made by service pension advocates that comrades who disagreed with them were snobbish "shoulder straps," concluded that the agitation was the work of "the thoroughly democratic tendency of those who are joined by a common covetousness."[63]

The clamor for service pensions was particularly disturbing to the national GAR officers because it flared up just as they were trying to lobby for the more modest dependent pension bill. In 1884, Commander-in-Chief Robert Beath was driven to condemn John A. Andrew Post of Boston, ringleader of the Service Pension Association, for undermining the work of the national committee. The 1,496 posts that had signed Andrew Post's pro–service pension circular, Beath said, were "unwisely giving ear to opinions and counsels proceeding from no recognized authority."[64] Nonetheless, advocates of the service pension brought it to the floor of every encampment after 1883, and in 1888 and 1890 they managed to push through favorable resolutions. In 1889 the national pension committee acquiesced to the agitation so far as to prepare bills of *both* types, which competed for attention in Congress. In early 1890 the Senate passed a dependent bill similar to the one vetoed in 1887; at the same time the House approved a measure to pension every veteran over the age of 62.[65]

The compromise bill that eventually emerged from this welter of competing proposals, the Dependent Pension Act of 1890, was the second major piece of Civil War pension legislation. As approved by President Benjamin Harrison, who had campaigned in 1888 on the pledge that it was "no time to be weighing the claims of old soldiers with apothecary's scales," the act contained no service pension provision. But service pension proponents were able to force the removal of the "pauper" clause—the section requiring applicants to prove dependence. The result was a law that granted a pension to every

honorably discharged soldier of ninety days' service who suffered
from any disability that incapacitated him for manual labor, no matter what his financial situation and no matter how the disability had
been incurred. "While not just what we asked," the GAR national
pension committee reported triumphantly in 1890, "it is the most
liberal pension measure ever passed by any legislative body in the
world, and will place upon the rolls all of the survivors of the war
whose conditions of health are not practically perfect."[66]

In time, the measure would do more than that. Liberal construction
by administrators—including the practice of interpreting age as a
pensionable "disability"—created what was for all practical purposes a service pension system. The number of pensioners grew from
537,944 in 1890 to 676,160 in 1891, 876,068 in 1892, and 966,012 in
1893. Between 1890 and 1907, payments under the act totaled more
than $1 billion.[67]

"Manhood Versus Money"

The debates of veterans with each other before
the act of 1890 and with vocal civilian pension reformers afterward
reveal an important change of attitude. The assumption behind the
original pension law of 1862 had been that the federal government,
having contracted for the services of soldiers, was liable only for
injuries they sustained while in its employ. Mere service as a Union
veteran did not entitle a man to any special consideration, even if he
happened to be sick, jobless, or destitute. Upon being mustered out,
he had become a civilian, and, like other civilians, he had to take his
chances in the marketplace or accept the minimal public relief provided in the almshouse. The national pension laws, like the charity
practices of most localities, assumed a body of ex-soldiers who had
returned to lead independent lives as private citizens. With the exception of a limited group of seriously wounded or ill veterans, those
ex-soldiers had no more claim to the public treasury than did any
other group.

Even the moderate proponents of dependent pensions had rejected that idea by 1884. As posts found voluntary charity at the local
level steadily less effective, they turned to state statutes to compel
localities to keep veterans out of almshouses and potters' fields. At
the same time, the success of the Arrears Act and the clamor of
claims agents like George Lemon awakened veterans to their poten-

tial political power at the national level. They began to think of broadening the pension act to include all needy veterans, not just those who could link their ailments to military service. The dependent pension proposals of the 1880s, far from assuming an easy metamorphosis of veteran into civilian, treated ex-soldiers as a special class, to whom ordinary charity arrangements did not apply. They assumed that the nation owed the ex-soldier a support.

Yet in defending their proposals in disputes with the advocates of more radical plans, the dependent pension champions invariably fell back on the conventional language of independence and manliness. Commander-in-Chief Robert Beath, attacking the service pension idea in 1884, said agitation for them "does not become those who are suffering from no disability and are able to earn a living."[68] Comrade A. B. Campbell, a Kansas delegate to the national encampment of 1886, protested an $8-per-month service pension bill on similar grounds:

> I believe every man in this country who fought for the flag, and who retains his physical manhood, who came out of it hale and hearty and well, and who has not yet been disabled in the great battle of life, resents the proposition, and that he does not want that $8 a month. I don't want it until disease has racked my body, until, in the struggle of life, I am staggering through. I do not want it; but I do want this: Whenever I get into trouble, whenever I get disease, whenever in the struggle of life I become unable to take care of myself, I then have a right to go to the Government, for which I risked my life in her hour of trial, and say to her, "You shall protect me in my hour of trial."[69]

Comrade Samuel S. Burdett attacked the same bill on the grounds that it was unmanly. The $8 service pension, he said, "sends patriotism to the auction block, and measures it by a price as does the huckster his wares. I protest that if we must go upon the market that the measure of compensation has been put at too low a figure. Eight dollars a month is not my price."[70]

A majority of the national pension committee members in 1890 recommended that the encampment simply thank Congress for the Dependent Pension Act rather than pressing on to demand service pensions because "every pension granted ought to be a badge of honor . . . and not procured by the eager efforts of any combination or organization, banded together to urge or demand recompense for services rendered." And in the same year a new conservative ex-soldiers' group, the Veterans' Patriotic League, argued that "every

veteran (not disabled in the service) who accepts a pension while able to support his family is lowering the tone of American independence and patriotism," adding that any expansion of the pension system beyond the Dependent Pension Act, "especially in the direction of a 'service pension,' [is] unnecessary, demoralizing and pernicious."[71]

There were practical political reasons as well for moderation in pension demands. "Twenty years after the war," former commander-in-chief George Merrill cautioned the service pension radicals in 1886, "can any reasonable man expect that Congress is going to pass a pension bill that will take more money than the surplus in the Treasury, and that they will lay a new war-tax in order to pay pensions? If we ask too much we will get nothing, in my judgment." Similarly the *National Tribune* conceded in 1885 that while service pensions might be a good idea, they were a political impossibility. Often such "practical" advice was couched as a reminder that most civilians still held to the sorts of notions about public charity embodied in the act of 1862. "Public opinion everywhere is almost unanimously opposed to granting a pension to an able-bodied man as a service pension," Lucius Fairchild told the 1890 encampment. "But public opinion everywhere says that any man who falls into disability shall be aided, and ought to be aided, by the United States government."[72] In short, even those who favored making every dependent ex-soldier eligible for federal charity felt obligated to do so by stressing the Union veteran's rugged self-reliance.

The advocates of more radical pension schemes were at some pains to respond to these arguments. Some took the Keynesian approach of Comrade George Patch, who argued that the economy needed "not a contraction of the currency, not a hoarding of it up in vast sums, but a broad and universal distribution of it among the people; and this money would go into the homes of every comrade of the Order." Some may have believed Comrade Edward Loring, a service pension zealot from Massachusetts, when he claimed in 1886 that his bill would cut out the pension agent middleman by "making every man's honorable discharge his pension certificate." Some even argued that service pensions would end the problem of pension fraud because universal eligibility would eliminate the incentive for it.[73]

By far the most common rebuttal, however, involved the declaration of a new principle: that the Union veteran had a prior claim on the nation's treasury, not as compensation for illness, not as a gratuity, but as an absolute *right*. The Service Pension Association's Frank Farnham, calling the GAR "the representatives of the men who saved the country, by the greatest of sacrifices," argued that "any reasonable demand" of the veterans should receive the public's "unqualified support." Opposition to the Grand Army, he said, came mostly from ex-Confederates, ex-Copperheads, and Mugwumps. "The whole Order," Farnham wrote in 1894, "yea, every survivor of the Union Armies is daily insulted and the value of his services questioned and belittled, not only by those whose very lives are a forfeit to the country which they betrayed, but by thousands who forget that all they have, and all they are is due to the sacrifices of the Union Soldiers."[74]

The implication was obvious: if the government had money (and in the 1880s and 1890s the Treasury bulged with surpluses), it should spend it on the men who had saved the nation. *"The sacred faith of the country, the promises of all the great men who were entitled to speak for it was pledged that thereafter no Union Soldier should ever know want,"* Farnham concluded, *"but that every one of them should pass the remainder of his days in comfort as a ward of the nation!"* The image of veterans as national saviors was reinforced in a constant drumbeat of encampment addresses, ceremonial toasts, and political speeches. As the minority report of the 1886 GAR pension committee put it, service pensions were warranted on the grounds "that the financial condition of the country permits it; that ample precedents support it; that a majority of G.A.R. posts have petitioned for it; that the failing health and energies of the veterans require it, and that the justice and honor of the country demand it." New York supporters of the $8 service pension bill were even more blunt. "The GAR," they proclaimed in 1886, "own this country by the rights of a conqueror."[75]

The idea that Union veterans had some sort of preemptory claim to the national domain was manifested not only in pension agitation but in a wide array of schemes. Between 1883 and 1890, the GAR national encampment considered resolutions asking the federal government for everything from veteran ownership of Yellowstone Park (asked "What would we do with it?," the proposal's backer replied that a new soldiers' home could be built there and the veterans employed as tourist guides); to free land in the West ("If we had been a monarchy," said the boosterish Paul Vandervoort, "we would have confiscated the soil we conquered and given it to the victors"); to a national "Dome of Freedom" to house meetings and war relics in Washington; to the privilege of naming one of the new Western states; to the substitution of blue for gray uniforms in the federal

postal service.[76] None of these proposals was seriously entertained,
but that they were made at all gives some indication of the veterans'
conception of their relationship to the nation. A more pragmatic
demand was for veteran preference in government hiring, and the
GAR-endorsed Veterans' Rights Union, founded in New York in 1882
to advocate the hiring policy, met with considerable success. By 1888
the VRU could point to veteran preference laws in New York and
Kansas and strong support among GAR posts elsewhere.[77]

At base, the service pension advocates argued that the Union veteran's service in saving the nation was in the nature of a contract: in
return for it he was owed public support, regardless of his physical or
financial condition. Gone were the expressions of worry about self-
reliance that had marked charity efforts at the post level and, to a
lesser extent, agitation for dependent pensions. Service pension advocates did not conceive of pensions simply as handouts from a
generous nation; instead, they talked about pensions as a right. "In no
sense are the pensions 'a generous gratuity,'" wrote Lemon, expressing that view in 1885. "The assumption that such is the case is a
humiliating insult. . . . Pensions to disabled soldiers were as much a
part of the contract as interest to the bondholders, and it is downright
dishonesty to deny them."[78]

Moreover, the contract was an open-ended one: the saving of the
Union had been such a great service that anything given in return was
of necessity incomplete. Ideologically, that approach solved the problem of dependence rather nicely. When moderate veterans and reformers called the service pension "demoralizing" or "pernicious"
because it gave money to men who were not in need, its proponents
replied that present need was not the point; past service to the nation
was. Pensions could not produce "demoralizing" dependence because they were payments for services already rendered.

Politically, the result was what reformer Charles Francis Adams,
Jr., called the "entering wedge" effect: when arrears were paid,
agitation for dependent pensions was begun; when those were paid,
service pensions were demanded; when almost every veteran was on
the rolls, calls for rate increases were heard; when the increases
were forthcoming, demands for public land and other bonuses mate-
rialized. Even under "the most liberal pension measure ever passed
by any legislative body in the world," the payments were never
enough. Lemon, who had not endorsed the service pension at the
time he wrote his 1885 pensions-as-a-right editorial, soon did so; by

the time the Dependent Pension Act was passed, he was calling it "merely the first installment of the debt the nation owes the men who saved its life at enormous cost to themselves."[79]

It is impossible to make almost one million people "wards of the nation," however, without paying a colossal bill. As pension expenditures began to mount following the Dependent Pension Act in 1890 (they would not peak until 1913), the interest of civilians was at last drawn to the issue. Although Southerners seem to have opposed the pension mania from the outset,[80] they were joined after 1890 by genteel Northerners such as Adams, a former Union Army general, and Edwin L. Godkin, editor of *The Nation*.

These Mugwump reformers had several reasons to be concerned about the swelling pension roll. For one thing, they wanted to reduce the extremely high tariffs then in place, a feat more easily accomplished when the Treasury was full to overflowing than when it was being drained by pension payments. They were also appalled by the large number of apparently fraudulent pension claims, which seemed to offer further proof of the corruption they deplored in Gilded Age political life. Some of them were interested in reconciliation with the South. But most pertinent to the argument advanced here is the reformers' conception of pension eligibility, which by 1890 was coming to seem rather old-fashioned: they continued to hold that the only legitimate basis for pension payments was service-related disability. In the Mugwump view, military service was a duty, not a claim for later payment.

Godkin, who first took notice of the issue during the debates leading up to the Dependent Pension Act, found service pensions appalling in principle. As Congress was considering a proposal to pension all veterans over the age of sixty, he wrote:

A large proportion of the half-million of people who are to be added to the pension roll are persons who have no possible claim to consideration. Some of them were worthless as soldiers during the war; others are now "hard up" simply because they have grown shiftless and dissipated since the war; others are well-to-do, and in no possible need of any increase to their income. The simple fact about the matter is that any old "bummer" who can establish the fact that he was connected with the Union Army in any way for ninety days, even if he got no further than the recruiting camp, may now have his name placed on the pension roll and draw $8 a month for the rest of his life; and so, too, may any prosperous comrade who has amassed a competence since the war.[81]

The service pension would give money to men who had suffered no injury as a result of the war and who in some cases had become positively rich in its aftermath. To Godkin, that was not only a waste of public money but immoral as well: it was turning perfectly healthy and prosperous veterans into mendicants. "'Veteran' is becoming in their eyes a synonym for 'bummer' or 'dead beat,'" he wrote, "and [nonveterans] begin to listen to the clamor for pensions very much as they listen to the arguments by which the street casual enforces his demand for a quarter on a cold night."[82]

Godkin dismissed the contention of service pension advocates that pensions were payments for services already rendered. If that was the case, he said, all the Grand Army talk about manly self-sacrifice was so much hokum. "To the patriot of the future," he scoffed in 1891, "all the brave talk about repelling the invader and preserving the Union, of defending home and liberty, will be meaningless. To all this he will reply: That is all very fine, but how much money is there in it for me?" The Grand Army itself he branded as a selfish political lobby. "For fifteen years," he wrote in 1895, "these men, who professed to have fought for pure love of the Union, have devoted all the energies of a great organization to the extracting of money from the public treasury, without the smallest regard to truth, honor or decency."[83]

Like-minded reformers echoed Godkin's charges for the next two decades. Edward F. Waite, writing for *Harper's*, argued that most pensions were "in their legal aspect, pure gratuities," not entitlements. Veteran Allen R. Foote attacked the service pension proponents as "mercenaries" and announced a "Society of Loyal Volunteers," dedicated to the idea that military service was a duty, not a cash transaction. William Bayard Hale suggested that it was "questionable ... whether men whose service to their country consisted in spending three months on a junket for which they were paid and for which their expenses were provided, should, years afterward, demand that the Government give them an income." And in 1909, the Reverend E. H. Hall went so far as to blame a rash of Spanish-American War pension claims on the decline of "self-respecting traditions" since 1861.[84] All of the pension opponents insisted that anything more than a disability pension was a pure gratuity, an assumption in harmony with the law of 1862 but not with that of 1890.

For their part, veterans pictured genteel critics as ungrateful evaders of a sacred debt. Copying the rhetoric of contemporary greenback agitators, they branded their opponents as "bondholders," begrudging pensions to the poor veteran while calling loudly for the redemption of war bonds in gold. "The value of the bonds of the United States Government depended wholly upon the success of our arms in the late war," insisted GAR surgeon-general Azel Ames. Soldier papers routinely compared pensions paid to soldiers and interest paid to bondholders, in one instance under the headline "Manhood Versus Money." Lemon's *National Tribune* carried a facetious conversation between "Swellhed" and "Koupon" at the "Gilt-Edge Club," complaining that pension expenditures were driving up the price of liquor and kid gloves. "It is not the middle-class people or the poor men who complain of the amounts paid out for pensions," the editor told his veteran readers. "It is the rich whose luxuries are taxed." When Bishop H. C. Potter told a Harvard audience in 1891 that the existing pension system was "pauperizing," the *Grand Army Record* dismissed him as "voic[ing] Harvard College and all that those words imply."[85]

The debate came to a head in an 1892 exchange between reformer William M. Sloane and GAR member C. W. Miller, the commander of a post at Latrobe, Pennsylvania. In an article in *Century*,[86] Sloane argued that military service was a duty owed the nation and that pensions were therefore gratuities. An individual's "personality, his manhood, his right to life, liberty and the pursuit of happiness" were his main concern, Sloane wrote, but "all these come to him only in organized society; and in the necessary sacrifices, even to the risk of life, which he has to make for it under the safeguards of constitutional government he is merely performing an act of enlightened selfishness." Because he was acting primarily for himself, "the citizen soldier has neither a moral or legal right to a pension." That most nations pensioned disabled soldiers was therefore a credit to human nature, prompted by "gratitude, wisdom, and a sense of merciful compassion." Veterans disabled outside their military service, Sloane argued, belonged in the hands of local authorities, while those who were not disabled were simply "increas[ing] their income and their comfort by drawing from other taxpayers what they do not really need." The extravagant pensioning of hundreds of thousands of veterans was "simply the distribution to one class in the community of what belongs to another," and for that Sloane had a word. "We are no longer on the verge of socialism, we are in it," he concluded. " . . .

Nothing can explain our tolerance of the present and prospective
pension expenditure but socialism of an extreme and dangerous
type." The alternative to the 1862 disability law, it seemed, was
socialism.

Replying in the *National Tribune*,[87] Miller first disputed the idea
that an individual existed only in organized society: "Organized society has no function and no rights except such as have been dele-
gated by the individuals composing it; nay, it has no existence except
by the will of the individual." True, the citizen owed a duty to the
state, but that vested him with a legal and moral right *against* the
state, just as if it had been a contract. "The Union soldier," Miller
argued, "surrendering his personal liberty for a term of years, enduring hardship and hard fare, exposing himself to disease and wounds,
suffering maiming and death, lays the State under the highest conceivable obligation to him."

The denial of that obligation was "the blind selfishness of despotism." It turned the offer of a pension into a gratuity, an implication
that the soldier deserved only what a benevolent state chose to give
him. Such a pension, Miller asserted, was an insult to the Union
soldier. "We will have none of your charity; we want no benefactions,
because they are not consistent with our manhood," he told Sloane.
" . . . The poorhouses of our counties are open to us, and there we
have undoubted right, equal, at least, to that of the recently arrived
immigrant." If the nation wanted "to maintain a standing army,
awarding maimed veterans the paltry pensions of European Governments," he concluded, "the way is open." Instead of disability pensions and socialism, the alternatives posed were service pensions
and monarchy.

The striking thing about the whole pension debate from the mid-
1880s into the twentieth century is the way all parties asserted that
they stood for independence and manliness, no matter what policy
they were advocating. Proponents of the dependent pension bill of
1887 were proud that their measure, unlike the service pension,
would give money only to those in need; it would not sap the self-
reliance of veterans. But Grover Cleveland, in vetoing the same bill,
said it confused wounded veterans with those who were "willing to
be objects of simple charity and to gain a place upon the pension-roll
through alleged dependence."[88] Advocates of the Dependent Pension
Act of 1890 billed it the "first installment" on a contract freely drawn
by the government with independent individuals. But reformers held
that the act created "knaves and loafers" and "mendicants" and

argued that the original disability statutes were less likely to be "demoralizing." Service pension backers in the 1890s said that any kind of charity based only on disability or dependence made veterans "paupers before the country whose very existence we have preserved"[89] and argued for pensions as compensation for services rendered. Mugwump reformers like Sloane replied that only unmanly individuals went to war for money or depended on pensions when they were perfectly capable of working. Every party to the debate attempted to paint the others as advocating some kind of plan to turn veterans into helpless dependents, while picturing its own scheme as a bulwark against the decline of self-reliance.

The sticking point between reformers and Union veterans by the 1890s was this: while the reformers saw veterans in the present tense, as civilians who were former soldiers, the veterans had come to see themselves in the past tense, as ex-soldiers first. To the reformers, the past heroics of an ex-soldier were irrelevant to his pension; he either needed public assistance, much as any other citizen might, or he did not. To the veterans, it was the ex-soldier's present condition that was irrelevant; he had served honorably and expected to be rewarded for it. To the reformers, manliness or self-reliance was something established in postwar civilian life, defined by relationships to other persons in a community. To the veterans, it was a characteristic rooted in wartime, when some had offered themselves and some had offered only cash ("Manhood Versus Money").

That supreme offering had created a reciprocal obligation on the part of the nation, an open-ended contract, "the only national debt we can never repay." In some ways, the most remarkable thing about the GAR, as compared with veterans' organizations of other American wars, was its fixation on its members' past services, even as it put forth a present-day political agenda of pension demands. Thus while veterans and civilian reformers both applauded the virtues of independence, they were talking about different things, even, in a sense, about different times.

The Sacred Debt

The conception of an open-ended contract between the nation and its veterans was an idea not seen in the aftermath of previous wars; some public protest was certainly understandable. Yet despite the pleas of genteel opponents like Sloane and

Godkin, the cry against pensions never became general. Pension laws continued to be liberalized, and pension expenditures, already high by historic standards, continued to rise until the eve of World War I. The veterans' numbers were declining, but public provision for them was increasing.

In part, the growth of the national pension apparatus was a response to inadequate local and state-level relief efforts: if needy veterans were to be aided, some large-scale agency would have to do it. But need alone cannot explain the willingness of civilians to grant unprecedented sums for the relief of the Union veterans. Other and needier groups—immigrants, sharecroppers, exploited factory operatives—went begging in the Gilded Age, indeed until the New Deal years. What made the veterans' arguments for entitlement persuasive even in such a hostile climate was the linkage of important Victorian values like independence and manliness—the same values that historically had justified only local and intermittent charity—with participation in the war. In arguing for pensions as an absolute right, the Union veterans were exploring new ground, but they were justifying the change by appealing to traditional values. Moreover, they were playing to a public inclined to regard the war as a success and the Union as increasingly important.

The linkage between manliness and Civil War duty was one the reformers never seriously tried to break, no matter how much they disparaged the veterans' service as "three months on a junket" or "a summer's escapade."[90] They never questioned the war or its objects and almost always started from the premise that most veterans were honorable heroes. Instead, they attacked the GAR or its leaders, although a certain amount of circumspection was evident even in those complaints. Typically, the GAR was pictured as an order noble in its origins but led astray by some scheming group—pension agents, selfish leaders, politicians.

Godkin, for example, argued that the early GAR had been a patriotic society, animated by ideals and held together by bonds of comradeship forged in wartime. Noting the charitable objects listed in the organization's first constitution, he commented: "Not a word here about pensions, not a word about offices. Mutual assistance and good citizenship were the end and aim." But since then, he argued, it had gone through a "rake's progress" and arrived at its low state as an outright pension lobby, an army of grasping shirkers. Similarly Charles McKnight Leoser, a former GAR commander from New York, wrote in 1893 of the GAR's "perversion from its original praiseworthy ideals," while the *New York Times* complained that the order had become diluted through the indiscriminate recruiting of men who "experientially know not the difference between gunpowder and cheese."[91]

If would-be reformers found it a delicate matter to oppose pensions, ordinary Northern civilians found it even more difficult to express reservations, for fear of being labeled as stingy. Noncombatants, said the Society of Loyal Volunteers in 1892, "feel a delicacy in taking a position on the subject of pension legislation which will give an excuse to any man who has suffered to point to them and say: 'You are not with us, because you are not of us.'" Pension investigators sometimes had difficulty obtaining information on accused frauds from civilians. William Sloane said that juries were reluctant to convict in pension fraud cases, while William Bayard Hale reported that in some communities during the second Cleveland administration, "public sympathy was violently against the special examiners sent out to unearth frauds, and attempts were made to mob them." When civilians did complain about pension expenditure, they tended to do so indirectly, most commonly by blaming pension agents for leading the virtuous soldiers astray. "Why does not some soldier of national standing call a halt?" pleaded an exasperated *New Haven Palladium* in 1890. "Protest cannot well come from civilians, for at once the cry of 'ingratitude' is raised."[92]

In the face of a hesitant public opinion, the politicians who made the pension laws were hardly prepared to resist what by 1890 had become probably the most powerful single-issue lobby in Washington. Local and national officeholders graced the platform at every Grand Army encampment, candidates ran for office as "the soldier's friend," and Mary Dearing has even argued that the organized veteran vote swung the exceptionally close presidential election of 1888.[93] In their public statements, Northern politicians adopted an almost apologetic tone (though perhaps few were as deferential as the mayor of Wilkes-Barre, Pennsylvania, Thomas Broderick, who introduced himself meekly to the Pennsylvania GAR encampment of 1883 as "a man who never was a soldier, yet who possesses the chief and noblest characteristics of a soldier"[94]). General Charles Francis Adams, Jr., who dismissed the whole species of veteran political flattery as "cant and fustian—nauseating twaddle, perhaps, would not be too extreme a term," nonetheless admitted that "any member of Congress representing a district north of the Potomac, who dares to criticize, much less to challenge a measure involving an increase in the appropriation for pension payments, practically takes his politi-

cal life in his hand."[95] The pension reformers, in short, were in the
minority, and the politicians were wise enough to know it.

At one level, then, the pension legislation after 1879 was simply an
exercise in power politics, the reward of a well-organized, one-issue
lobbying campaign. But such complete success, continuing even as
veteran numbers dwindled in the early twentieth century, could not
have occurred without the acquiescence, and even the support, of a
great many civilians. Behind the unprecedented entitlement grants
to veterans was a persuasive presentation of the war and the veterans' role in it. Veteran mythology pictured the war as the central
event of national life—a time in which the Union had been saved,
manhood established or lost, debts incurred that lasted indefinitely.
In this curious use of history, veterans became virtually living statues:
saviors, examples of true manhood, creditors to the nation until the
day they died.

Some civilians, notably Southerners and Mugwump reformers, obviously did not accept such a use of the past against the present. But
to a great many Northern members of the war generation, the war
experience—their own, if not the heroic version of the veterans—
undoubtedly held some meaning that was worth asserting against the
troubling realities of peacetime life. Endorsing the "manly," "independent" veterans against the grasping, disorderly present of the
1890s was one way of expressing that sympathy. Among members of
the younger generation, however, there was no guarantee that the
history of the war would be employed in the correct way. As the
veterans aged and saw their children grow up in a nation that took its
saved status for granted, they faced the question of a remembered
war in a postwar world.

CHAPTER **6** **CAMPFIRE**

> *Great God, was ever such measure of patriotism reached by any man on this earth before. That is what your monument means. By the subtle chemistry that no man knows, all the blood that was shed by our brethren, all the lives that were devoted, all the grief that was felt, at last crystallized itself into granite, rendered immortal the great truth for which they died and it stands there to-day, and that is what your monument means.*
> —General James Garfield on the stump at the soldiers' monument, Painesville, Ohio, July 3, 1880[1]

If civilians after 1880 were willing to fund an unprecedented level of public spending for military pensions, it may have been because they were constantly deluged with reminders of the glorious sacrifices of Union soldiers. The image of veteran as savior, close to the hearts of service pension advocates, was not their invention alone. It was a commonplace of a postwar popular culture with a weakness for nostalgia and sentiment. Between 1880 and 1900, fond tributes to the warriors abounded in every conceivable form. Some, like Garfield's, were campaign speeches. Others took the form of syrupy odes ("Cover Them Over with Beautiful Flowers"), war dramas ("The Drummer Boy of Shiloh"), war lectures, war memoirs, Memorial Day orations, and monuments erected by adoring towns.

A GAR post often was at the heart of such cultural productions, and even when it was not, the order was urging civilians to remember not just the war but a particular version of it. The Grand Army, through personal narratives, civic commemorations, and its own unique re-creation of the wartime camp—"the campfire"—tried to institution-alize the memory of the war as a radically unique event, a one-time-only drama of national salvation. It was a view with implications not only for pension legislation but for postwar society in general.

The boom in reminiscence after 1880, like the simultaneous up-surge in pension agitation, was in marked contrast to the lull of the 1870s. During that time of Reconstruction headaches, modest pensions, and struggling veterans' organizations, the nation had hardly given the war a second thought. Fewer war novels were published in the 1870s than in any other decade; magazines rarely ran articles about it; the regular army was allowed to languish. The GAR oc-cupied itself chiefly with fraternalism and post-level charity. It was, as Gerald Linderman puts it, a decade of "hibernation."[2]

Yet even when interest revived in the 1880s, it was characterized by a superficiality that has left almost all recent students of Civil War literature echoing Walt Whitman's famous remark that the real war did not get into the books. Rather than coming to terms with the sectional divisions that the war laid bare, the suffering it caused, or the black slaves it freed, postwar authors drowned in "reams of special pleading and irrelevant minutiae," Daniel Aaron has written. The war, he concludes, "was not so much unfelt as unfaced. Northern writers found it easier and more reassuring to portray it as an exalted example of national redemption than as a grisly historical moment when the political system broke down and the nation took a 'moral holiday.'" Following the virtual amnesia of the 1870s, Northerners of the 1880s embarked on (in James Moorhead's characterization) "a sea of self-congratulatory chauvinism."[3]

Contradicting the nostalgic view of the war, of course, were the gruesomely detailed battle narratives of such writers as John W. De Forest and Ambrose Bierce (who were Civil War veterans) and Stephen Crane (who was not). In their works, the war was bloody, confused, and certainly an ambiguous triumph if not exactly a hollow one. But this grim realism, often considered the major literary side effect of the Civil War, took some time to manifest itself. Bierce's Civil War collection, *In the Midst of Life*, did not appear until 1891; Crane's *The Red Badge of Courage* came out in 1895; the novels of De Forest, though published earlier, were not widely appreciated in his time. Like those of the later realists, De Forest's novels flew in the face of almost everything written or said about the Civil War in the late nineteenth century.[4]

Instead, public taste ran to stately memoirs or sentimental treacle. The most widely read accounts of the war were the battle reminiscences of generals, especially Grant's *Personal Memoirs* (1885–86), which quickly assumed a place on parlor tables across the North. Four months before the first volume of *Memoirs* was to be delivered, 300,000 sets had been ordered from the wounded veterans who sold it door to door. It went on to become one of the most widely read books of the Gilded Age and, in the opinion of at least one critic, a work whose taut prose style influenced later writers.[5] The recollections of other generals also were commercial successes. The multi-authored "Battles and Leaders of the Civil War" doubled the circulation of the *Century* soon after it began appearing in serial form in 1884; it ran for two years and in 1888 was issued in book form. Among veterans, formal military chronicles and dissections of individual campaigns were popular. By 1886 the Post 2 library in Philadelphia contained dozens of regimental histories as well as the complete set of official government war records. Elsewhere, periodicals such as George Lemon's *National Tribune* reached thousands of veterans with regular features recounting the campaigns of the war.[6]

The Union officers who authored these works tended to play down the disturbing aspects of battle in favor of grand strategy. Ulysses Grant's one-sentence description of the burning of Atlanta—"Atlanta was destroyed so far as to render it worthless for military purposes before starting, Sherman himself remaining over a day to superintend the work and see that it was well done"—usually is cited as the ultimate example, and in fact Grant in his *Personal Memoirs* seems to

be standing on something of a plateau overlooking the battlefield.
This most famous of Civil War memoirs has, as William McFeeley
puts it, "conciseness, totality, and strength," the result of the general's "extraordinary capacity to see certain of his life's experiences
with a forbidding wholeness." But that very stress on the totality
of campaigns, Edmund Wilson once observed, mutes their terrors.
"The very objectivity of Grant's method of describing the war always
works to eliminate its tragedy," Wilson commented. "His mind seems
so firm and clear that no agony or horror can cloud it."[7]

Contributors to the *Century*'s highly successful "Battles and Leaders of the Civil War" series showed a similar inclination to dwell on
the big picture at the expense of personal introspection. In one piece
General William T. Sherman cited "the great Napoleon" as his precedent for operations in Georgia and described the March to the Sea as
"in strategy only a shift of base for ulterior and highly important
purposes." In another, partisans of George G. Meade and Daniel
Sickles spilled much ink debating the tactics of each general at Gettysburg. The great majority of contributors concentrated on strategic
expositions of major battles and campaigns. When they faced the
problems of the postwar period at all, the generals tended to be
sanguine. Though not all of them agreed with Grant's pronouncement that it was "probably well that we had the war when we did,"
most would not have quarreled with his characterization of wars in
general as "not always evils unmixed with some good." Certainly few
cared to dwell on the personal suffering and manifold dislocations
that the war produced.[8]

It was in this climate of self-satisfaction that the obscure, low-
ranking veterans who made up the average GAR post tried to assess
the meaning of the war as they passed through middle age in the
1880s and 1890s. One might, perhaps, expect the foot soldier memorialists to have favored the realistic view—after all, they had borne
the brunt of hard fighting from a vantage point considerably less
Olympian than that of Grant. For the most part, however, Grant's
troops followed one of two paths in putting the war behind them:
either they copied their officers in trying to connect the small parts of
the overall struggle that they could perceive to the broad tactics and
campaigns or they dwelt on sentimental "scenes of camp and battle."
The confusion and bloodshed of combat, so apparent in the wartime
letters and diaries of the men, tended to disappear from their postwar accounts.[9] So did the ambiguity of the war's outcome for ex-
slaves and defeated Confederates. Instead, the tellers adhered to a

prewar, millennialist tradition of national history that reaffirmed such Grand Army credos as the goodness of militia organization, the sanctity of the fraternal camp, and the national saviorhood of Union veterans.

Tactical Memoirs and Campfire Tales

The broad-gauge reminiscences of the generals were echoed in the GAR post meeting, where members related personal stories of their army careers, sometimes in the form of prepared papers. In 1886, the *National Tribune* suggested to posts that they set aside certain meetings for the discussion of particular battles, complete with prepared maps and papers. In Philadelphia, Post 2 tried assigning a different member to give a paper each week in 1871. In Chippewa Falls, Comerford Post commander Charles Law announced a policy of having comrades "give some of their experiences while serving in the Army" in 1893. In Cincinnati, Fred C. Jones Post published its members' reminiscences.[10]

Although few of these ephemera have survived, many GAR posts also compiled books of "personal war sketches," in which individual veterans told of their army careers. Their narratives, though obviously intended as formal permanent memoirs, probably give a fairly good indication of the types of stories related as "entertainment" at GAR meetings.[11] They are remarkable not only for their precise, often petty, detail but also for the effort the writers made to grasp their places in the larger scheme of battle. Consider this summary, from Private John C. Miller of Simon Cameron Post 78, Middletown, Pennsylvania:[12]

> The most important events during his enlistment took place at Petersburg, morning of the 2d. At the recapture of Fort Greg, two battalions took the open field in front of said fort, while the infantry came in on the left and captured the fort. They were exposed to the fire of three forts that day and held the position all day and laid there all night, [and] on the 3d followed Lee to his capture at Appomattox.

Or this, from Corporal Phillip Snyder, of the same post:

> In his second term of enlistment, the events of his military life were many and varied in front of Petersburg. June 18–19 the Co.

had hard fighting and lost many of their best men and officers.

Colonel Prescot of the 32nd Mass. commanded the brigade[;] he
was killed the 18th of June. [Snyder] helped to carry him to the
rear, and one of the four that carried him back was killed and one
wounded so there was two returned to their command, one out
of each regiment.

Or this, from Private Rudolph Pfanmiller:

To him the most important event while in the service was that
they kept the confederates near Petersburg for the time and
prevented their interference with Sherman's March to the Sea.
His entire, though short military service was full of interesting
events. He rejoices that he has been able to do an humble part in
re-establishing the union of the states, emancipating the colored
man, and making his adopted country, in fact, the land of the free
and the home of the brave. All honor to the boys in blue.

Some foot soldiers even used their memorial records to rebuke their
superiors. Private Samuel Arbuckle of Acker Post 21, St. Paul, Minnesota, noted:

The one thing in my military career that I have to criticize was
the loss of lives and suffering caused by the blunder of Genl.
Sibley in sending Co. A 6th Regt. Minnesota Vol. with forty other
volunteers into an enemys country where a few days before
Capt. Marsh's Co. B 5th Minn. Infantry had been annihilated,
when he could just as well have sent a Whole Regiment.

Similar criticisms were made by Sergeant George Blotcher of Middletown:

When the battle was fought at Winchester, June 13–14–15,
[18]63, under General Millroy, if Gen. Millroy had left Winchester on Friday night June 13, 1863, with his 12,000 men, and
returned to Martinsburg, and then to Frederic City, Md. he
would not have lost a man and in such event would have given
Gen. G. G. Meade a helping hand at the battle of Gettysburg. By
not so doing they lost all their artillery wagons, and over 2,000
soldiers were taken prisoners.

In these narratives and hundreds of others like them, foot soldiers
tried to locate themselves in the panorama of the campaigns, related
encounters with the great and the near-great (such as Colonel Pres-

cot), and occasionally, as with Private Pfanmiller, drew moral lessons from the conflict. Although they also included tales of personal hardship and wounds, the personal sketches were always firmly anchored in the context of specific battles, campaigns, and objectives. Asked what the most important incident of their service had been, the great majority limited themselves to summary listings of ranks held and battles witnessed, or gave replies like that of Colonel David J. Higgins of Bryant Post 119, Minneapolis: "No very important events except what was common to all soldiers who did their duty." The stress, in short, is less on personal reactions to combat than on the broad actions of armies. Rather than trying to explain the war's effect on himself, the individual veteran sought to explain his own contribution to the Union Army's success.[13]

Given the late date at which the authors wrote their sketches—the Minnesota narratives, for example, date from the 1890s, while the Middletown sketches were compiled in 1896—their obsession with detail undoubtedly reflects the influence of previously published generals' memoirs and campaign histories. A more direct influence was the structure of the interview on which the sketch was based. Each veteran was asked first to give basic service data (muster dates, regiments served in, ranks attained, battles witnessed, wounds suffered); only in closing did he speak about "intimate acquaintances" and "striking incidents." In Middletown he signed his account at the bottom to "certify that the Sketch of my War Service as above written is true as I verily believe"; in Philadelphia and Minneapolis, the personal war sketch form warned that "great care and mathematical accuracy must be observed in the matter of Names, Dates, Localities and Events." The main concern was with getting minor details right.

But while the personal war narratives make tedious reading today for anyone save a genealogist, the intent of their authors is plain: as far as they were concerned, they were writing history. James Shaw of Rodman Post 12, Rhode Island, laid out the objective clearly in 1869. In his post, Shaw explained, a member was detailed at each meeting to read a "personal reminiscence of the war," but only one containing "such facts as came under the *personal observation of the writer.*" If other posts followed this scheme, he said,

> it will bring out and add to the history of the war an immense mass of material and evidence that would otherwise never be written or placed in any enduring form, and for which future generations would have to depend on tradition, always unreli-

able. . . . Written by men who saw and knew of what they write,

read in the presence of others who were with them at the time
and can correct errors, if they should be made, these sketches
cannot fail to be correct. Let writers remember the importance
of being as nearly correct as possible in regard to dates, for when
these papers are gathered together we shall have a full and
complete history of the war.[14]

For Shaw and veterans like him, the war was graspable only by the
men who had seen it firsthand—anything else was "tradition, always
unreliable." That was why the veteran narratives were so important:
once these men died, the only reliable record of the conflict would die
with them. If, on the other hand, the fragments of battle could be
collected, the country would have a record of what each individual
soldier was doing within each army during each significant battle of
the war, a sort of national diorama.[15]

While the individual soldier might not be able to make sense of the
individual engagements in which he had been involved, he retained
confidence that such incidents would mean something when added
up. His sketch was his contribution. The history of the war, to this way
of thinking, was an accretion of personal narratives, a collection of
small stories whose larger truth eventually would become evident, if
it was not evident already. Somewhere beneath the confusion of
battle there was a moral involving the army as a whole. "If we cannot,
some of us, be proud of anything we did," Thomas B. Reed told the
national encampment of 1885, "we belong to the organization, and
can be proud of the things other men did." Bryant Post's Higgins made
the same point in his war sketch: "Every event was a link in the chain
that was welded into the blood of the Soldier which was to bind our
Country into a Strong Republic."[16] In looking back at the war, the ex-
soldier pictured himself as part of a huge fighting machine, the "moving mass of glistening steel" that had swept up Pennsylvania Avenue
in 1865.

On a few occasions, posts tried to export the panoramic view of the
war to civilians by sponsoring public war lectures or exhibitions of
battle paintings. In 1870, for example, Post 2 put on two war lectures,
one by a Mr. Nasby and another by a Dr. Allen; in 1878 it sponsored a
talk by Colonel J. R. Bachelor on the battle of Gettysburg; in 1884,
post member Louis Fortescue lectured on his escape from Libby
Prison; in 1893, the post and its guests listened to a speech on the
career of Admiral David Farragut. In Brockton, Webster Post spon-

sored "illustrated lectures" on the war in 1887 and an "illustrated exposition" of the Gettysburg fight in 1888.[17]

If the posts studied most closely here are an indication, however, war lectures for civilians were decidedly mixed successes. The Allen and Nasby lectures, for instance, lost $100 for Post 2, while Webster Post, after an initially optimistic forecast that it could sell 1,500 tickets to a series of winter war lectures in 1886, abandoned the project when it appeared unlikely that the costs would be covered. When the Brockton members were approached about sponsoring another lecture by "Major Thomas" in 1888, they informed him "that as the Post has not been very successful with lectures in the past they must decline the offer."[18] Although the evidence is hardly conclusive, it does suggest a limit to the amount of battle exegesis the public would tolerate. For the most part, battle narratives remained in-house entertainments.

An alternative path of remembrance that ultimately proved much more appealing to civilians was to pass over the fighting entirely in favor of sentimental vignettes of camp life, both printed and re-enacted. "Scenes of camp and battle," as the written reminiscences often were called, were the lifeblood of such soldier paper features as the *National Tribune*'s "Fighting Them Over" and *Field and Post Room*'s "Recollections." Alongside the tactical rehashing of battles, these accounts served as lighter fare: the story of a friendly encounter with a Confederate picket, the details of life in a tent, the joys of foraging, the clever rejoinder of the private to the sergeant.

In the *National Tribune* of May 14, 1891, for instance, "Fighting Them Over" consisted of first-person accounts of General Kilpatrick's raid and fighting at Waynesboro and Knoxville, but also an account of life at headquarters written by an orderly, a story of "humorous traits" in the character of General S. S. Carroll, and the tale "A Balky Mule." Other issues included stories about dogs in camp, the tale of a letter mistakenly opened in camp that led to a marriage proposal, and amusing incidents in the life of a provost marshal. Although *Field and Post Room*, a veteran magazine published at Harrisburg, Pennsylvania, billed the reminiscences filling its columns as "exciting narratives rehearsed around the camp-fire or in the post-room," most were closer in spirit to the "irrelevant minutiae" of the officers' memoirs. These tales represented what Thomas Leonard aptly terms "a sort of petty realism—the recollection of such trivial, everyday details of life at the front that the battlefield seemed like a normal environment and suffering was lost sight of."[19]

Camp as spectacle: members of the 120th New York Infantry on stage and in uniform at an 1875 reunion in Kingston, New York. GAR campfires featured similar scenes, including mockups of wartime camps, drilling exhibitions, group singing, and theatrical presentations of the GAR initiation ritual. (U.S. Military History Institute)

A more elaborate form of camp nostalgia was the GAR campfire, an all-veteran social gathering at which certain practices of the war-time camp were resurrected for an evening. Usually held in the winter months, the campfire typically began with an invitation from one post to another to visit its hall, sometimes with a marching escort provided from the train station. Once at the hall, the visitors partici-pated in a program that might include such activities as "an old-time army meal" (coffee, hardtack, beans), clay-pipe smoking, drinking, war stories, the blowing of army calls on a bugle, and the singing of war songs.

At a campfire hosted by Cameron Post of New York City in 1880, for example, visitors from other city posts discovered a room decorated with tattered battle flags, stands of arms, and knapsacks with rolled blankets. Smoking clay pipes, they were entertained by the beating of

Cooks work to prepare the Great Barbecue at the 1895 national encampment at Louisville. At national encampments, many of the delegates relived the experience of camp, eating group meals, living in tents, and sharing stories around bonfires in the evenings. (Library of Congress)

"Reveille," a war poem ("The Return of the Standard"). and a speech by Corporal James Tanner. The evening closed with the singing of war songs. In January 1885, Brockton's Webster Post treated visiting posts from Lynn and Harwich to a meal of "beans, hardtack and coffee, etc.," followed by addresses and music; a campfire the following month included harmonica duets, a silent military drill exhibition, songs, speeches, and dinner. An 1882 gathering at Lynn, Massachusetts, included an actual campfire blazing away on the opera house stage. Chippewa Falls's Comerford Post hosted a hardtack supper and campout for out-of-town posts visiting the county fair.

In the 1880s and 1890s, similar scenes were repeated throughout the order.[20]

Campfires also figured prominently in the entertainment programs of department and national encampments. A campfire at the 1877 national encampment at Providence, for example, included not only the fire but "miniature tents pitched among the Juniper trees [which] made the scene appear very realistic to the 'boys.'" Most other encampment campfires were even more "realistic," since their singing, smoking, and speech making took place outdoors amid the pitched tents of the delegates. In 1881, a typical state gathering at Lafayette, Indiana, gave notice that it would feature "drills, dress parades, camp-fire chats, songs, etc. . . . rations and tents furnished free to soldiers and sailors who will go into camp and comply with the discipline of the same." Until the 1890s, when most veterans had become too old to sleep in tents, national encampments included the same sorts of facilities for those who wished to live in camp again. At the Columbus encampment of 1888, the *National Tribune* reported, carefully platted rows of tents were available to house tens of thousands of veterans, while dining halls were ready to serve 12,500 men at a sitting. At Denver in 1883, a camp housed between 10,000 and 15,000 men, as did "Camp Beath" at Minneapolis in 1884. The temporary tent camps, with their straw bedding, army meals, bugle calls, and nightly campfire chats were as close as the Union veterans could come to re-creating their wartime lives under canvas.[21]

No matter what the form of war reminiscence in the Grand Army—personal sketch, war lecture, written camp scene, campfire performance—three themes recurred. In the first place, the wartime camp was remembered as a place of camaraderie and sentiment, where brothers in arms "drank from the same canteen." The ideal fraternal camp promised by the post-1869 initiation ceremony and bounded by the orderly space of the post room was played out in the ritual indulgences of fraternal pleasures—singing, storytelling, smoking, drinking—at campfires. Whereas the new initiation ritual portrayed the wartime camp as an orderly proto–lodge room, the campfire pictured it as a place of singing, backslapping, and general gemütlichkeit.

By focusing only on the stage props of military life, both campfires and written scenes of camp and battle abetted the initiation ritual's picture of a sentimental bivouac rather than a messy war. Such performances left out the same thing lost in most contemporary popular accounts of the Civil War—a sense of tragedy, or even of

The national diorama: Grand Army encampment of 1892 on the Ellipse in Washington, D.C., where tents and stands were arranged to reproduce the position of the Union armies at the close of the war. A notable anomaly in the scheme was the display of the USS Kearsarge, *visible near the center of the photograph. (Library of Congress)*

history. The shock of modern combat, the discouragement of Reconstruction, the hardening of social attitudes that George Fredrickson once dubbed "the twilight of humanitarianism," were nowhere to be found. Instead, the message of the war was one of brotherly camaraderie, a message with few ramifications for the postwar world. By venerating artifacts of the war—pipes, bugles, tents, uniforms, hardtack—as symbols of a long-lost camp rather than as harbingers of postwar society, the Grand Army encouraged a memory of the war that was essentially static.

In the pining for camp it is easy to see simply an exaggerated version of the nostalgia that infiltrates all veteran reunions, and undoubtedly some veterans did have fond memories of the war. One suspects, however, that the sentimental conventions of postwar Victorian culture simply did not allow the ex-soldiers to express the doubts and confusions they had about the war or its aftermath. Certainly the progressive disillusionment expressed in the volunteers' wartime writings argues for such a view. And even in the memoirs of the 1880s and 1890s, there were hints of ambivalence

around the margins of remembrance. Passing references to the carnage of battle ("a day I shall never forget") seeped from the cracks of
the impassive personal war narratives. A fascination with the suffer-
ings of prisoners of war permeated the columns of the soldier papers,
as indeed it permeated much nonveteran discourse about the war. In
fiction, veterans like those of Sherwood Anderson retold war stories
until "a something snapped in their brains and they fell to chattering
and shouting their vain boastings to all as they looked hungrily about
for believing eyes."[22] It may even be that the stories related at closed
campfires, for all the levity chronicled in the post minutes, actually
included tales of suffering and confusion that veterans could only tell
each other. Since those narratives, unlike the personal war sketches,
passed unrecorded, there is no way of knowing; they are lost to us, as
they were to nonveteran contemporaries. In any case, the veterans'
recourse to camp camaraderie as a way of commemorating the war
virtually smothered the less pleasant aspects of the fighting. It was, as
John Ruskin wrote to Charles Eliot Norton, like "washing your hands
in blood and whistling."[23]

Ossified as such war commemorations were, when they were
broadened to include civilians (as Post 2's open campfires and most
national encampment gatherings were), they risked turning into pure
lodge entertainments. At best the open campfires offered nonveterans the same sort of nostalgia with which the veterans toasted themselves. At worst, they degenerated into the sorts of carousing parties
lampooned in an 1879 poem dedicated to Philadelphia's Post 8:

> You are blushing like a rose,
> Husband mine, husband mine.
> There's a blossom on your nose,
> Husband mine, husband mine.
> Your track's a crooked lane
> And you've drawn a map of Spain
> With your latch-key round the key-hole,
> Husband mine, husband mine.[24]

Although Commander-in-Chief Paul Vandervoort, a booster of fraternalism in the order, called open campfires "sources of great and
lasting good to the Order," other GAR officers worried about them—
particularly "the very injurious effects of Sunday Camp Fires," as one
Pennsylvania commander put it. Commander-in-Chief Louis Wagner
in 1881 decried campfires at which "the song, the story, or the personal conduct of some present overstepped the bounds of propriety,

and where the desire to appear 'funny' resulted in bringing our Order into disrepute." Still, open campfires were popular among nonveterans, particularly politicians. After one such campfire, city council member William Ward told the *Chester* (Pennsylvania) *Evening News* that he "had attended so many camp fires that he already felt as if he was a 'half-cut' military man already, and he liked to attend them because he always met so many good fellows."[25]

Some campfires were even more inclusive, admitting women and children to the proceedings. Here the picture of the wartime camp was, if possible, even less warlike. Some of the "mixed" campfires included "living tableaux," those stock features of Victorian civic pageantry in which participants assumed stationary poses as parts of "scenes" meant to illustrate historical events.[26] Like the campfires generally, these tended to portray camp rather than battle. An 1886 "ladies' night" entertainment in Post 35 of Chelsea, Massachusetts, for example, featured ten tableaux, none of which had much to do with fighting: "Off to the War," "The Soldier's Return," "Foraging," "The Committee Meeting," "Gypsy Camp," "Day's Work Begun," "Day's Work Done," "The Soldier Boy's Promotion," "Presentation of the Flag," and "The Grand Army of the Republic." A Memorial Day entertainment put on in 1889 by the wives of GAR members in Leominster, Massachusetts, featured a broken column representing "Our Unknown Dead" and a tableau of "The Goddess of Liberty." Post 10 of Worcester every year performed "The Drummer Boy of Shiloh" for the town, interspersed with tableaux of "The Battle Charge," "Decoration of the Soldiers' Graves," "Guardian Angels," "Surrender," and "Justice and Angels of Peace."[27]

Other campfires attended by women were simply standard Victorian parlor entertainments under another name—musical quartettes, lavish dinners, formal toasts, group singing. In 1883, for example, Webster Post held a campfire with the Twelfth Regiment Association that included the presentation of a war relic but also a large dinner with wives, children, and invited guests, and "entertainment consisting of readings by Miss Mowing, selections on piano by Mr. Howard, speeches, stories, etc." In 1891, Philadelphia's Post 2, which maintained its own orchestra for such affairs, held a reception for ladies and gentlemen who had accompanied the post to the national encampment at Detroit; in 1896 it staged a lavish "thirtieth anniversary campfire."[28]

The only link some of these campfires had to the war was the singing of "Marching through Georgia." But if the commemoration of

camp steadily tended toward fraternal hoopla, it was only because
the order as whole was becoming civilianized; ranks and military
discipline were giving way to "associate membership" and voluntarism, and *Frontideologie* was being superseded by fraternal clientage
and deal cutting. Camp nostalgia was yet another way in which the
realities of the war were tamed to suit Victorian preferences for
order and sentiment. As Commander-in-Chief John Logan told the
national encampment as early as 1871, "To keep the scenes of war
with all its horrors vivid before the mind, without some still more
important motive, would hardly meet with the approval of this intelligent age."[29] Two decades of civilianization later, the Grand Army's
model camp would be scarcely distinguishable from the meeting
place of any other up-to-date lodge.

A second theme that emerged from GAR memorializations of the
1880s was that the war had a broad meaning, not to say a moral, that
transcended individual combat experiences. With occasional exceptions such as Private Pfanmiller, the authors of the personal war
sketches left the moral unstated. But in campfire speeches and war
lectures, the repeated lesson was one of national salvation: the war
had maintained the Union. Prewar social and economic differences
between the sections, issues of free labor and political power in the
West, and especially the questions of blacks and slavery received
scant mention in celebrations of the war's outcome. Instead, the
grand achievement of the Northern armies had been to rescue the
indivisible nation as it had existed before "the late unpleasantness"
and, if anything, to cement it more tightly. The war was a mission
accomplished; the nation, something maintained intact rather than
something greatly changed. It was a rhetoric of preservation.

At the Denver national encampment of 1883, for example, Colorado governor J. B. Grant, an ex-Confederate, told a campfire audience that the principles of the Union Army "were not only triumphantly vindicated by the sword in 1865, but are today enshrined in
the hearts of the people from Maine to Georgia, and under their
guiding influences friend and foe are gleaning alike the blessings of a
free, a prosperous and a united country." As for the Confederates,
their principles could "never again rise to the surface of American
politics. They are dead forever." At the Indianapolis national encampment campfire of 1881, Indiana governor A. G. Porter told the
audience that those who had fallen in battle "are here in the remembrance of great deeds imperishable. They are here in their good work
still going on. The workman may fall, but his work goes on immortal."

Later on the same evening, Benjamin Harrison and James Tanner made similar pleas, Tanner saying that the Union veterans were all that had stood "between a united country and Mexicanization."[30]

Among the side effects of Grand Army preservationism was one whose impact on the pension debate has already been noted: it encouraged the Union veterans to think of themselves as national saviors. Offering a toast at an 1879 encampment at Albany, Governor Charles Van Zandt of Rhode Island argued that "but for the Union soldiers, there would have been an end to the country"; the nation, he said, must be handed down to the last generation "as unmutilated, as pure, as brilliant . . . as you meant that it should be." At the Denver encampment of 1883, a Colorado legislator argued that without the soldiers of the GAR there would have been no state of Colorado. Both Logan and General Thomas Wood compared the GAR man to the soldier of republican Rome, a patriot who, Wood said, represented "self-dedication, even to martyrdom, for the preservation of the State." A national encampment committee of 1885 chose a biblical metaphor, comparing the Union veteran's loyalty to "the purity and piety of the Christian martyrs." All of the rhetoric went to make up the bombast that so repulsed the pension reformers of the 1890s.[31]

Despite the rhetoric of preservation, however, the third theme of GAR reminiscence was that the nation, having been saved once, did not require further saving. The incidents of the war deserved to be memorialized in song and stone, but the issues over which it had been fought had been settled so finally that no further agitation on the part of the veterans was required. In campfire speeches the war became more a monument than a living presence. "All we ask," Congressman William McKinley told the Boston national encampment campfire of 1890, "all we have ever asked, is that the settlements of [the] war— grand settlements, made between Grant and Lee at Appomattox, and which were afterwards embodied in the Constitution of the United States—shall stand as the irretrievable judgment of history and the imperishable decree of a Nation of freemen." Similarly, merchant James Hodges told a national encampment campfire at Baltimore in 1882, "The nation now knows no North, no South, no East, no West." Even Frederick Douglass, called upon to make a speech to the same audience, sidestepped postwar sectional and racial conflicts to talk about the wartime accomplishments of black soldiers and the "loftiest feelings of patriotism" of the city of Baltimore. Perhaps the most complacent view was that of Grant. At the close of his *Personal Memoirs*, the general suggested that the war had produced "such a commingling of the people that particular idioms and pronunciation

are no longer localized to any great extent." The great work of restoration being complete, he concluded, there was "but little to do to preserve peace, happiness, and prosperity at home, and the respect of other nations abroad." Most of the Union veterans who twice helped elect Grant to the presidency would have agreed.[32]

Defining themselves as national saviors might easily have led the veterans to pronounce on issues of public policy. With the understandable exception of the pension question, however, it is remarkable how little the Grand Army used its exalted platform to lecture the nation. At encampments and post meetings, occasional speeches denouncing Mormonism or "anarchy" were heard, but they do not seem to have captured the order's attention.[33] In particular, the GAR showed little interest in the military issues that have so concerned twentieth-century veterans' groups—funding for the armed services, more and bigger weapons, overseas expansionism. The one major change that the Grand Army sought in postwar political life—a broadening of the pension system—seems an exceedingly modest demand, in any case one that was not met until twenty-five years after Appomattox. Even the GAR's "patriotic" campaign of the 1890s was, as we shall see in the next chapter, mild compared with the efforts of later veterans' groups.

In short, although the Grand Army wore military trappings and acted as custodian of a war of national salvation, it never developed into a full-fledged militarist organization. As the House of Lords agitation of the 1890s amply demonstrates, one reason that it did not was that the ranks and discipline of military life did not translate well to the setting of a voluntary fraternity. Ideologically, however, the lack of a militarist ethos in the GAR had more to do with the members' memory of the conflict as a one-time, monumental event. In Garfield's perfect metaphor, the war represented tears and grief crystallized into granite, rendered immortal, and still standing in the middle of town.

The sole obeisance that the GAR insisted the public make to the war was the observance of Memorial Day, and even here the tone of commemoration is revealing. Memorial Day (originally Decoration Day) had come into being as the result of a pronouncement by Logan in 1868.[34] GAR posts treated the day with great reverence, appointing large standing committees to make arrangements for it and decrying civilian indifference. In Chippewa Falls, Comerford Post denounced as unpatriotic "any citizen or society taking part in or placing before the public any games of Base Ball or any other games that will entice the public and thereby detract from the proper observance of the day." Other GAR orators condemned the "giving of balls, the holding of camp-fires, picnics, excursions, or other form of public entertainment," and attacked President Grover Cleveland for supposedly fishing on Memorial Day. When Otis Thatcher of Dartmouth, Massachusetts, questioned a public appropriation for Memorial Day at a town meeting in 1892, he was rebuked by Comrade William H. Potter, who "spoke of those who remained at home 'during the Dark Days of the Rebellion', and made a scathing allusion to the 'Home Guard' patriotism of the previous speaker, retiring amid wild applause. . . . During the balloting the old town hall was rocked with National War Songs amid the wildest enthusiasm."[35] Memorial Day was virtually the only occasion for which the Brockton and Chippewa Falls posts practiced drilling.

But while Memorial Day called to life memories of the war, it was even more "the festival of our dead," as the GAR cemetery service put it. The official service included prayers that "the memory of our dead shall encourage and strengthen in us all a more loyal patriotism"; in "this silent camping-ground of our dead, with soldierly tenderness and love, we garnish these passionless mounds." Every soldier's grave was "the altar of patriotism"; the flowers strewn on the graves were to "endure until the touch of death shall chill the warm pulsebeat of our hearts"; Memorial Day was "to our dead their day of coronation." In 1884, Post 2's Charles Kennedy even thought it necessary to ask permission to solicit individual contributions to cover Memorial Day expenses "notwithstanding the implied prohibition contained in Sec. 1, Art. 14 of the By Laws" (the section barring subscriptions for funerals). Like their ex-Confederate foes, whose own memorial observances focused primarily on bereavement, the Union veterans saw Memorial Day as a time to contemplate loss.[36]

The order of service itself varied little from year to year and place to place. First came a special sermon on the Sunday before Memorial Day, and GAR members often attended church in uniform. On the day itself, the post assembled and marched to the local cemetery to decorate the graves of the fallen, an enterprise meticulously organized months in advance to assure that none were missed. Finally came a simple and subdued graveyard service involving prayers, short patriotic speeches, and music, which itself was typically funereal, and at the end perhaps a rifle salute. An 1887 Chippewa Falls service, which could stand for any of the thousands of such ceremonies performed across the North before 1900, consisted of prayers,

patriotic oratory, and four typically doleful musical numbers: "Strew
Blossoms on Their Graves," "Cover Them Over with Beautiful Flowers," "Cheers and Tears," and "God Save Our Union."[37]

Certainly the most extraordinary use of the funeral motif was at a
citywide memorial service held at Philadelphia's Academy of Music
in 1879. In the ceremony, a mock funeral was staged on Memorial
Day as a dramatic entertainment to raise money for GAR relief in the
city, with Grand Army members (including several from Post 2) playing the parts. As the *Philadelphia Press* described it:

> A soldier's funeral, with the eulogy pronounced upon him at
> the subsequent meeting of his comrades in arms, was the simple
> plot of the piece, the dramatic action of which was elaborated
> merely by the process of setting the stage with scenery; and the
> play told just so much of a soldier's history as his "Post" had to
> concern itself with after his decease. In the first act the slain
> warrior is supposed to be brought in his coffin into the Post room.
> In the second, the military funeral forms and marches to the
> grave; and in the last the comrades are seen assembled in their
> Post room to listen to their chosen orator as he rehearses the
> noble qualities of their departed friend.

The *Press* found the memorial service "a sacred operatic drama,
solemn, impressive, pathetic, every way beautiful" and said it "was
greatly heightened by the solemn ritual of the Grand Army, which is
scarcely inferior to the services of the Church."[38] Even in an era
fascinated by death, the idea of staging a funeral as a fund-raiser
seems fairly extraordinary. But it does illustrate the extent to which
Memorial Day was considered a time to commune with the fallen
rather than to proclaim the lessons of the war.

Monumentality

At the center of Grand Army war memories was a
paradox. On the one hand, the attention to detail in battle narratives
and the rhetoric of preservation in campfire speeches suggested that
the war had a great lesson still to teach. "Let each and every one that
belongs to the organization . . . read a history from his memory to
every child he meets, that he may learn that patriotism which lives in
the hearts of good and true and brave men," Logan told the national

encampment of 1885. "My comrades, it is from you that the truthful history of the war will be written." On the other hand, the nostalgia of campfire performances, the disengagement from military issues, and the funereal imagery of Memorial Day argued for a war that was irrevocably past, unconnected to the concerns of contemporary life. The memory of the war loomed over the present; at the same time, it was strangely distant. As Marcus Cunliffe aptly put it, involvement in the war was "intense yet oddly superficial."[39]

To understand such a pattern of remembrance we must keep in mind the ways in which native-born, white, Protestant men of the type predominant in the late-nineteenth-century GAR conceived of historical change in general. At base, such conceptions owed a great deal to the bundle of attitudes labeled by historians as republicanism. Rooted in English Whig or Commonwealth ideology, republicanism emphasized the virtue of the independent yeoman, the corruption inherent in centralized power (and consequently the need to remain on guard against it), the superiority of citizen militias to standing armies, and the timeless, millennial nature of the Republic.[40] As Dorothy Ross points out, in the early nineteenth century, Americans typically saw their Revolution as a millennial event and the nation's subsequent history as a story of virtue maintained. Such change as took place was merely epiphenomenal—the revelation of "God's plan," the varied expression of ingrained national traits, the playing out of timeless "principles." No matter what happened on the surface, Ross writes, "the essence of American republican institutions, of American history, had always been and must always remain the same."[41]

So pervasive was that ideology among native-born whites that historians have found it almost everywhere they have looked, from the platforms of the Democratic party to the broadsides of nascent labor organizations. Both Civil War armies invoked republican traditions; both pointed to the same Revolutionary symbols.[42] Indeed, the shadow of republicanism was evident in the day-to-day life of the GAR: in the anticorruption rhetoric of the House of Lords opponents; in the insistence, despite the unprecedented entitlement payments of the 1880s and 1890s, on the manly independence of Union pensioners; and in the militialike organization of the order itself.

The other great influence on popular historical thinking during the antebellum years was evangelicalism, which modified both the secular nature of republicanism and its emphasis on timeless preservationism. In the North, evangelical crusades against sin, culminating in the antislavery movement, drew on images of battle and the Apoc-

alypse. When the war finally came, Yankee reformers pictured it as
the crossroads of human history, Armageddon, a climactic struggle
from which the nation would emerge redeemed.[43] Hymns urged
patriots to march; ministers spoke of millennial change. No longer
was the Republic seen as an entity perfectly formed at the beginning;
it needed to be actively saved, not passively preserved. History was to
be shaped, not studied for examples of virtue.

For many Northerners, the millennial promise of 1860 soon faded.
In fact, the postwar years marked something of an intellectual water-
shed, in which republicanism itself was called into question as a way
of understanding history. Among historians, the war shook faith in
the perfectly formed Republic and sent scholars burrowing in a direction that would ultimately emerge as Progressive historicism.
Some prewar reformers found in the conflict a reason to give up
humanitarianism in favor of force and social conservatism (the position expressed in Logan's famous 1871 riposte to the Universal Peace
Convention: "The Grand Army is determined to have peace, even if it
has to fight for it"). Others pointed to the army as a model of order
and to the strenuous military life as a corrective for the flabby civilian
world.[44]

While instances of disillusionment can also be found in the early
GAR (in the *Frontideologie* of the 1866 ritual, for example), by the
1880s the veterans' memorializations told a different story, one that
the millennial republicans of 1860 would have found utterly familiar.
In that telling, the war was an apocalyptic event in which an ineluc-
ably pristine Union had been preserved. The timeless meaning of the
event was not deducible from evidence—it was the starting, not the
end point of discussion. The personal war sketches, minor battle
details, and nostalgic camp performances merely *illustrated* a grand
theme that had never been in doubt. When collected in Shaw's "full
and complete history of the war" the moral would be self-evident.
Taken individually, however, the details had a radically unique, one-
time-only quality. None of them would ever happen quite the same
way again; that was why it was so important to record as many of
them as possible.

Such a characteristic Victorian attitude, which historians of museum and cemetery practice have dubbed "the pastness of the
past,"[45] perhaps makes more understandable the funereal emphasis
of the GAR Memorial Day. Individual deaths, like "striking incidents
witnessed" and the nonrecurring behaviors of camp, were irrevoca-

bly (and not a little wistfully) past, but in GAR cosmology they were surface phenomena. Beneath them, the unchangeable principles of the Republic went on without end.

Indeed, in retrospect the process of saving the Union acquired the same aura of inevitability that its founding had always had for true republicans. In their personal war sketches, veterans like Corporal Charles Parker of St. Paul attributed their escape from certain death to divine Providence ("Though a *thousand* shall fall at thy side," read the psalm that reached him from his mother the day after three near misses at Chickamauga, "and *ten thousand* at thy right hand, it *shall not come nigh thee*"). Even during the most desperate moments of the war, recalled Minneapolis GAR member (and former chaplain) Moses Jones Kelley, he "was sure of success and could not help saying so." Although obviously not all GAR members were as sure of Providence as Parker and Kelley were, the oft-repeated rhetoric of such members had much in common with that of antebellum Yankee preachers.[46]

At the same time, the overwhelming importance of the Republic's preservation required permanent and public commemoration. Veterans proclaimed the message of national preservation in Congress, where on pension questions they drew pointed inferences regarding the duty of the nation to its saviors. And in city after city, new monuments refuted in stone any notion of the Civil War's "pastness." Mostly neoclassical in style, didactic in intent, columns and statues were raised not only in cemeteries but in the most public places imaginable. In Indianapolis, an enormous Soldiers' and Sailors' Monument, built at a cost of $250,000, towers over the square in the center of the city, while in Lancaster, Pennsylvania, a more modest monument does the same. In Hartford, a memorial arch occupies part of the Connecticut state capitol grounds. In Brooklyn, a replica of the Arc de Triomphe dominates centrally located Grand Army Plaza. In Washington, the national Grand Army memorial is situated on Pennsylvania Avenue halfway between the Capitol and the White House. These were not markers of a vanished past; they were intended to teach a lesson. "Fellow citizens," Garfield told his audience at the Painesville, Ohio, monument, "that silent sentinel, that crowned granite column, will look down upon the boys that walk these streets for generations to come, and will not let them sleep when their country calls them." In the words of the GAR dedication services, monuments were "an incentive for the display of public valor and virtue in all coming time."[47]

A monument decorated for Memorial Day in Santa Fe, New Mexico, 1880. Like many Civil War markers, the Santa Fe monument was located in the center of town—in this case, on the main plaza, facing the Palace of the Governors. (U.S. Military History Institute)

The monumental version of republicanism was equally apparent in the attitude of Union veterans toward their defeated enemies. As long as ex-Confederates did not question the moral lesson of the war, they were treated cordially—in fact, they were sometimes contrasted favorably with "loyal" noncombatants. Especially after 1880,

posts and encampments occasionally socialized with veterans from
the other side. In 1885, for example, Webster Post welcomed former
Confederates to its citywide memorial services for Grant. In 1887,
Post 2 invited former Confederates to meet General Philip Sheridan,
who was visiting, and in 1890 a former aide to Stonewall Jackson
gave a lecture to the post. Almost two dozen Blue-Gray reunions
between 1881 and 1887 included GAR posts, and in 1889 the national
encampment formally endorsed one such reunion at Vicksburg.
"There was no personal feeling between the men of the south and the
men of the north," Comrade John Jenkins told Comerford Post in an
1894 lecture. "They were always pleasant to each other when they
met, but it was the great question that existed between the two
factions. The responsibilities of the late war cannot be placed on the
backs of the southerners, because they fought for what they thought
was right."[48]

By the time Jenkins spoke, white Northerners and white Southerners were engaged in a veritable love feast of reconciliation,
complete with Blue-Gray reunions, Lost Cause nostalgia, and Confederate war monuments (including the first to be permitted at Gettysburg). A few communities began holding joint Blue-Gray Memorial
Day services. In 1884, the *Century* launched its "Battles and Leaders"
series, which avoided politics and carefully balanced Northern and
Southern military viewpoints. By 1902, Confederate general James
Longstreet, who had become a Republican after the war, could even
join Union officers to review the Grand Army parade at Washington,
while the GAR's own commander-in-chief solicited donations for
Confederate veterans' homes.[49]

When it came to drumming the lessons of the war into the next
generation, however, the ex-Confederates were doomed forever to
play the heavy, always on the side of error, always vanquished by the
hosts of the righteous. In the words of GAR commander-in-chief
William Warner, "we were eternally right and . . . they were eternally
wrong."[50] The line dividing cordiality from hostility ran between
those actions (such as lecture invitations) that implied only sociability
between former foes and those (such as the erection of Confederate
monuments and the waving of the Confederate flag) that seemed to
be aimed at subverting the message of national salvation.

Union veterans commonly expressed the division by saying that
while the former rebels might be fine fellows, their *principles* were,
and always would be, wrong. In 1874, for example, Comrade A. B.
Underwood of Massachusetts objected to the decoration of Confed-

"Bygones," a nostalgic watercolor of 1911 that hung on a Philadelphia post hall wall, is typical of the reunionist sentiment that prevailed after 1890. Over drinks and a cigar, a relaxed GAR man and an intense ex-Confederate, both in uniform and seated in what appears to be a plantation setting, argue the details of some past battle. (Courtesy Philadelphia Camp, Sons of Union Veterans of the Civil War)

erate graves on Memorial Day by saying he "had none but the kindest feelings toward those who fought against us, respected their gallantry, bore them no malice, and would bury past differences and unite under one flag; but Memorial Day is the day on which we commemorate the memory of our fallen comrades, and let it be forever understood that we distinguish between loyalty and disloyalty; the latter is the treason against which we fought, and the former we pay respect and tribute to." In 1881, the *National Tribune* commended a display of Confederate battle flags to its readers by writing: "As ensigns of an unholy cause the Confederate flags are, and of right ought to be, odious to the eyes of loyalty; but as the exponents of manly daring, fortitude, and devotion to an idea (although a wrong one) they are entitled to the respect of all men and well worthy the reverence of those who upheld them so bravely on the field of martial strife." In

1891, Commander-in-Chief John Palmer allowed that the Confederates had been gallant and said the GAR was willing to accept them as fellows "on the broad grounds of American citizenship and unconditional loyalty." But he went on to denounce several GAR men who had marched in an Atlanta parade that included the Confederate flag. "Do you propose to surrender what you fought for, and what your comrades, who sleep in heroic graves, fought for?" Palmer asked. "As the stars are fixed in the sky, so I believe your patriotism is fixed and immovable, to preserve the memories and fruits of that great struggle."[51]

At the local level, opportunities for righteousness were less frequent but by no means absent. In Brockton, for example, members of Webster Post refused to make a donation to a Confederate veterans' home in Texas. In New York, a GAR member was dishonorably discharged for toasting Jefferson Davis at a Southern banquet. In Washington, D.C., Lincoln Post objected to a proposed "Blue and Gray" reunion and exhibit at the Chicago World's Columbian Exposition on the grounds that "we were right in '61 to '65, and our opponents were wrong." In Philadelphia, Post 2 denounced a Chicago Confederate monument, a New York Blue-Gray reunion, and a Philadelphia Blue-Gray parade.[52]

In general, Grand Army posts objected most strenuously to those behaviors or symbols that implied honor to the Confederate *cause*—a flag, a monument, a toast to a president, flowers on a grave. The worry was not so much about the lauding of individual Confederates (unless they were symbolic individuals such as Davis), for they would die eventually. Nor was it with the proper exegesis of battles, for those conflicts were by definition one-time-only events. Instead, GAR posts worried about transmitting the moral of the war to the next generation intact. If monuments were to call forth "public valor and virtue in all coming time," the lessons of the war could not be subject to historical change. And if the virtue of the Union was to be timeless, so must be the infamy of the Confederacy.

In short, the Grand Army memory of the war represented the persistence into peacetime of the millennial, republican vision widely prevalent in the North before 1860. Although gentleman-historians and disillusioned intellectuals were wrestling with new conceptions of history and the nation as early as 1880, the older ideology of republicanism lived blissfully on in the campfires of the GAR until at least 1900. In that view, the virtuous nation, saved until Sumter from the ordinary travails of history, had come through the war purified of the blot of slavery and ready to lead the rest of the world into the sunshine of universal democracy. Despite the painfully obvious failure of Gilded Age America to live up to that vision, the Grand Army of the Republic (the name of the order itself is highly significant) strained to see the nation in those terms.

The past was the past. With the Republic secure, its saviors could return to lives as simple citizens. "There is not in human history, a case cited except ours, in which a million of soldiers were, in a day, removed from belligerent to peaceful life," Logan had told the 1869 national encampment. "Probably, there is no government on earth, except our own, that would have dared try the experiment. I am confident there is no other in which such trial would be safe." As for the future Republic, it was as secure as destiny could make it. The Union veterans, General W. H. Gibson told the 1880 national encampment, had only "to carry forward in the future what has been made in grand prophecy during the past."[53] These were not the words of realists trying to come to grips with a bloody and divisive war, nor those of militarists with a present-day political agenda. The members of the Grand Army had no such words in their vocabulary. Instead, they spoke the language of monuments.

John A. Logan: The Volunteer Soldier of America

The Union veterans' devotion to the republican model of history was visible in their victory columns and in their treatment of former Confederates. But it was at its most pronounced in their hagiolatry of General John Alexander Logan, a soldier whose name has recurred frequently here. In the life and writings of the GAR's chief founder lie important clues to the meaning of Grand Army veteranhood.

Considered solely in the light of Logan's opportunistic political career, the adulation accorded him is hard to comprehend.[54] A Douglas Democrat before the war, Logan followed the course of political expediency in Congress during the secession crisis, supporting conciliatory measures toward the South while at the same time backing military appropriations. Until the last minute, he held out hope for a peaceful settlement. After the first battle of Bull Run, however, Logan became a staunch supporter of the war; when he returned home after adjournment, it was to raise a regiment of volunteers. Over the next four years he served with distinction, sustaining two wounds and ending as a corps commander under Sherman. He also became the soldier-politician par excellence, returning home in 1864 to stump for the Republican ticket while using his military record to keep his own political star ascendant.

After the war Logan discarded his Democratic allegiance, throwing in his lot with the Radicals, first in the House, where he was one of the managers of Andrew Johnson's impeachment trial, and then in the Senate. In the 1870s and 1880s he became known for his Stalwart views, bloody-shirt oratory, and attention to the wants of Union veterans. After helping to found the Grand Army, he served three times as its commander-in-chief (1869–71) and became a fixture at GAR national encampments.

Throughout his military and political life, Logan seems to have been motivated primarily by a desire to please the electorate. In the army, Sherman regarded both Logan and General Frank Blair "as 'volunteers' that looked to their personal fame and glory as auxiliary and secondary to their political ambition, and not as professional soldiers." In peacetime Logan was, as his biographer delicately puts it, "a pragmatic politician constantly motivated in his choice of tactics by self-preservation."[55] In 1884 his career peaked in an unsuccessful run for the vice presidency on a ticket headed by James G. Blaine; two years later, he was dead.

This is hardly the stuff of which monuments are made. Yet Logan was without a doubt (again in the words of biographer James Pickett Jones) "one of the most popular and well-known figures of his time."[56] His distinctive handlebar mustache and booming, spread-eagle oratory were fixtures on the Republican national campaign circuit; when he entered the hall at GAR encampments, there were cheers and calls for a speech. He was popular enough to be mentioned seriously for the presidency in 1884 before settling for second place on the ticket. When he died unexpectedly in 1886, the list of subscribers to the fund for his widow read like a who's who of the Gilded Age: Henry Hilton, George Pullman, Hamilton Fish, Cornelius and William K. Vanderbilt, C. P. Huntington, Leland Stanford, James Eads, Russell Alger, George Washington Childs, A. J. Drexel, John D. Rockefeller, John Wanamaker, Whitelaw Reid, John Sherman, J. L. Routt, Marshall Field. Thousands of mourners passed his bier in the Capitol Rotunda; after funeral services in the Senate chamber, thousands more lined the route to Rock Creek cemetery as General Sheridan led the funeral procession. Webster Post of Brockton can-

The body of John A. Logan lying in state in the Capitol Rotunda, 1886. Logan's funeral was held in the Senate chamber; his body was buried in Rock Creek Cemetery but was moved to a newly built tomb three years later. In 1901 an equestrian statue of Logan (the $65,000 cost of which was covered primarily by a $50,000 congressional appropriation) was unveiled at Logan Circle. (Library of Congress)

vassed its membership ward by ward to collect money for a Logan monument; Post 2 passed resolutions of sorrow, something it did for only five other generals (Grant, Sherman, Garfield, Burnside, and Philadelphia's own George Gordon Meade). He is one of a handful of Union generals honored with a major statue in Washington.[57] Why was so much adulation focused on Logan?

For GAR members, of course, the obvious answer was that Logan was a founder of their order and a staunch advocate of their pension demands in Congress.[58] But for members and nonmembers alike, there was a deeper reason: Logan was the republican volunteer personified. Unlike Grant, Sherman, Sheridan and other prominent Union generals, Logan had not attended West Point. Instead, he had worked his way to an army command through the time-honored techniques of militia service, political wire-pulling, and personal popularity with the troops he led.

Logan had raised his original regiment, the Thirty-first Illinois, with the same sort of forceful stump speaking that brought him political laurels; he was a successful recruiter because he was a successful politician. When he spoke to encourage reenlistment in a regiment commanded by Ulysses Grant (then a colonel) Grant later recalled that Logan "inspired my men to such a point that they would have volunteered to remain in the Army as long as any enemy of the country continued to bear arms against it."[59] Moreover, unlike many of the soldier-politicians who raised similar regiments, Logan proved to be a highly capable battlefield commander; in engagements from Fort Henry to the Carolinas, he showed himself brave under fire and at least as able as the professional generals alongside whom he fought. He was a self-made success.

Logan's achievements offered reassuring evidence that the old American system of volunteer militias and soldier-politicians—the arrangement so wickedly lampooned in prewar militia musters—still constituted a sufficient bulwark for the defense of the nation. He was living proof that the volunteer republic was not dead; in time of war, yeoman farmers and mechanics could be relied upon to rush to its defense. As Logan put it in an 1883 campfire speech (which, incidentally, gives a fair introduction to his florid oratorical style):

> These [GAR delegates] are the representatives of the men who, when they first heard the rumblings of discontent, quietly listened for the thunderings from the first war cloud, and when it broke forth in sullen tones, left the plow in the furrow, the plane on the bench, the hammer on the anvil, the scythe in the swathe, the garden and the dairy, the flock on the hill, and the herd in the valley, their stores closed, their clerks' desks unsupplied, their cases in court unargued, their sick in the hands of nurses, their Bibles closed on their stands, the pulpit vacant—with one embrace for the wife, a kiss for the little darling, a loving glance at the sweetheart, and a farewell for all, they came forth with the patriotic declaration, "My life belongs to my country."[60]

The war, Commander-in-Chief John Hartranft told the GAR national encampment of 1877, had "proved that our nation could rely upon the patriotism and gallantry of its people. It solved the problem of a strong free government, abolished standing armies except as a police, and returned to the old days of a nation in arms without falling

into anarchy on the one hand, or despotism on the other." Because
citizens like Logan could still emerge as military leaders, then sub-
merge themselves again in the body politic, the country had no need
for that traditional bane of republics, the standing military force.[61]

Logan's own belief in the efficacy of the volunteer system, combined with his lingering resentment over the one disappointment of
his military career, the refusal of West Pointer William T. Sherman to
give him permanent command of the Army of the Tennessee, led him
to become "the scourge of the regular Army" in Congress after the
war. From a position on the Military Affairs Committee, he argued for
reductions in the armed forces, lower salaries for generals, and all
manner of changes in the administration of West Point, which he
considered an "aristocratic" institution. The reforms that he advocated ran directly counter to the struggles of the reduced military
services to professionalize and depoliticize themselves in the postwar period.[62] But they demonstrate the continuing attraction of the
volunteer ideal to soldiers like Logan—and, one suspects, to his GAR
admirers as well—who had grown up in an era when local militia
units were also social clubs and stepping-stones to political office.

Logan's love for the volunteers and his animus toward West Point
also drove him to spend the last years of his life writing *The Volunteer
Soldier of America*.[63] Published the year after his death, the remarkable, sprawling, 615-page volume was a clear distillation of the same
millennial republican interpretation of the war that infused practically every GAR campfire speech, personal narrative, and monument dedication. In it, Logan attempted not just to show the importance of volunteer soldiery but to place the Civil War in a world
historical context dating back to the beginning of time.

Whereas professional soldiers such as Grant and Sherman had
focused narrowly on battles in their memoirs, Logan began by announcing that "the late war between the American States was the
legitimate climax of several cooperating forces." The North American continent, he wrote, had been providentially reserved for European civilization through "a marvelous ordering of events." The Revolution, though it "arrested the attention of the world," was actually
the product of trends dating back "forty centuries." The Civil War, by
removing the blot of slavery, had rendered the Declaration of Independence "the Magna Carta of all mankind, destined to last while the
human race endures."[64]

The hero of this history was not the professional officer, the hired

mercenary, or the draftee. Rather, Logan maintained, the savior of
the nation was the citizen-soldier, who was uniquely qualified to
perform the task for three reasons. First, unlike the subject of a
monarchy, he had "a personal and direct interest in the government."
Second, the blessings of universal free education had made him "a
man of intelligence . . . an umpire whose judgment seldom errs."
Third, his upbringing gave him "a character of independence, of self-
reliance, of quick action, and ready command of expedients"—particularly on the frontier, "where he becomes a *quasi* soldier through
force of surroundings and mode of life."[65] Here were all the elements
of standard republican history collected in one place: the pure nation
on the virgin continent, rescued from the ordinary course of history
by "a marvelous ordering of events"; the Declaration of Independence as a millennial document; the common man as a reservoir of
virtue; the free schoolhouse and the frontier as vital molders of
character.

The main threat to this yeoman's paradise was "class distinction,"
both in the slaveholding South and at "aristocratic" West Point.
Tracing the history of government from the Greek commonwealths
through the aristocracies of his own century, Logan argued that the
Southern slave system had been "the legitimate child of monarchy."
Although the inevitable clash between the Southern system and that
of the North had been bloody, the outcome had never been in doubt.
"As man was never born to die," Logan wrote, "so his last and best
hope on earth was never created to perish so prematurely. The
disease which had attacked the nation was terrible in its deadly
strength, but the remedy was close at hand and indigenous to the soil.
It lay in the patriotism of the people, and in the strong arm and
courageous heart of that marvelous power, the American volunteer
soldier."[66]

Once cured, the country presumably could return to its pristine
state, provided that "class distinction" did not come back to ravage it.
To avoid that fate, Logan wrote, the "restrictive, inadequate, and
wholly un-American" military academies needed to be overhauled in
the interests of democracy. Much of the rest of *The Volunteer Soldier
of America* was devoted to proving that many service academy gradu-
ates had deserted to Confederate service at the outbreak of the war
and that West Point class leaders had gone on to have undistin-
guished military careers. Genius, Logan argued, "is not made by art,
nor created by education." Faced with the uncomfortable truth that
Grant, Sherman, and Sheridan were all West Pointers, Logan simply

noted "foreshadowings" of natural military genius in Grant's early

life and pointed out that none of those generals had finished at the top of his class. "Lucky, indeed, was it for the perpetuity of the Republic," he wrote, "that such men as Grant, and Sherman, and Sheridan, and many others—accidents of the system—were . . . born soldiers."[67]

If the naturally valorous American volunteer was to be preserved, Logan concluded, the national system of military instruction needed four improvements. First, the rudiments of military instruction should be taught at every state university, not just at the academies. Second, West Point and Annapolis should be "finishing schools," with admission by competitive examination administered by an impartial national board. Third, the public schools should "include, as part of the education given by them, the daily practice of gymnastics and the regular drill of the infantry soldier, under competent teachers." Fourth, each state should strengthen its militia system and encourage young men to attach themselves to it. This plan, he said, would be "wholly adapted to our peculiar form of government."[68]

Certain aspects of Logan's program—for example, regular drill for schoolboys, military instruction in state colleges—strike the modern eye as militaristic. Yet he presented the scheme as *anti*militaristic, as an alternative to a system that concentrated military power in the hands of a dangerous minority. "To constitute a small body of men the sole military experts of the nation," Logan warned, "is to invest them with a tremendous power for evil, should they, in the course of human weakness, ever see fit to use it."[69]

The near miss of the war, in which the nation had been saved by the valor of the volunteers and the "accidental" loyalty and competence of a few West Pointers, proved the point to Logan's satisfaction: what the nation needed to do was rejuvenate the old militia system that had had such good results in the past. The volunteer regiments had produced good officers (including, not so incidentally, John Alexander Logan). They had included, if the posts studied here are any indication, somewhere between 80 and 97 percent of all GAR members.[70] If the militia system that produced the volunteer regiments was improved and extended to the schools, it might continue to be the bulwark of the Republic. In the process it would restrain the "aristocratic" military academies. Most important of all, it would assure the continuation of an important republican institution, the militia, as a model for the next generation.

Here, as in so many other areas, GAR leaders espoused an ideology of conservation or preservation rather than significant change. The

GAR's veneration of the volunteer hero Logan—like its quasi-militia structure, "national saviors" pension campaign, and monumental war remembrances—portrayed the Civil War not as a social and political earthquake but as the preserver of a timeless Republic. As the "Armageddon of the republic," the "legitimate climax of several cooperating forces" of world history, the war had a cosmic significance that stood outside mundane history. It was a one-time-only event that conferred upon its veterans a special character as saviors. The preservation of the Union had been uniquely their accomplishment.

Under that reading, personal memories of camp and battle, of death and dying, of ambiguity and fear, could be safely consigned to the past. At best they could be shared among the men who had experienced them; they had no relevance for civilian society. What needed planting in the minds of the next generation was the timeless moral of the war. If that moral did not literally stand in the middle of town, as at Painesville, it might be communicated by other means— bloody-shirt oratory or militia training, for example. That a generation raised on apocalyptic interpretations of the struggle should go to war thinking in such terms is understandable. That it should continue to think in the same terms thirty years later, even as veteran memoirists like Bierce were beginning to recover some of the war's ambiguity, is, perhaps, somewhat more unsettling. At the very least, it shows the extreme rigidity of Protestant Victorian culture in the face of challenges to its worldview that were rapidly accumulating by 1890.

Toward the 1890s: Fathers and Sons

In a more melancholy way, public reaction (or rather, lack of reaction) to Grand Army war commemorations in the late 1880s and 1890s showed the tension between the inherited apocalyptic view and the realities of life in a society long since saved. The mixed success of public war lectures and the tendency of open campfires to decay into lodge parties already have been mentioned. At the same time, the ritual denunciation of the Confederate cause and the booming of the Union volunteers in spread-eagle speeches were beginning to sound worn. More of the former foes were dying, and few of those who remained looked likely to lead a second insurrection. In 1895, the Grand Army held its national encampment in a former slave state for the second time, at Louisville (Baltimore in

1882 was the first).[71] Blue-Gray reunions were becoming the rule of

the day. And the spread-eagle style itself was falling out of fashion: Charles Francis Adams was not the only one who was tired of it. When Logan, one of the last great practitioners of the art, gave a typical Memorial Day address at Grant's Tomb in New York shortly before his death in 1886, for example, one Illinois Republican told Shelby Cullom it was "the d——dest performance I ever saw . . . such remarks would disgrace a freshman in a Western college."[72]

The early monuments in cities such as Indianapolis and Brooklyn were impressive, but in other places the idea of commemorative structures fell victim to meager funding, disinterest, or more-pressing civic priorities. In Chippewa Falls, for example, Comerford Post twice set out to erect a monument to the war dead of Chippewa County in the courthouse square. The first time, in 1891, the post was able to raise some money through a public dance and appropriated $500 to the project, but when the need for a new post hall became urgent the following year, the money was reappropriated to that use. In 1898, the post managed to raise $1,500 for a monument—mostly from public subscriptions—but three months later decided that the project was "not expedient" and gave up on the idea. Comerford Post also lost $17.45 by investing in a GAR memorial at Decatur, Illinois, that was not built.[73]

In Brockton, a typically difficult situation between Webster Post and the townspeople resulted from the post's desire to have the city fund a "memorial hall" and some city residents' wishes to build a badly needed library or city hall instead. The result was that from 1882, when the post first began holding fairs and bazaars to raise money for the project, until 1894, the city built neither. When one opponent of the hall complained in 1890 that "the present GAR quarters are comfortable and well adopted for their purpose and will house the post for years to come," Webster Post's George B. Lawton replied with some exasperation: "It is to be a *memorial hall*, not a GAR hall. It is to be sacred to the memories not only of the local post but of the things that were precious and patriotic in the days of '61– '65."[74] The war was becoming so distant that the very idea of a memorial had to be explained.

Despite Lawton's plea, several Brockton citizens sued to stop the city from expending public money on any such edifice, and in 1891 the state supreme court agreed with them, finding that the erection of a hall for the use of a GAR post was "not a public purpose." Instead, Brockton proceeded to build a city hall, which included a "memorial frieze" of the war in its rotunda as a compromise. The outcome of the dispute so piqued the veterans that they first considered suing to recover their share of the money raised for the project, then petulantly voted not to attend the cornerstone-laying ceremony of the new building. Although they eventually relented, the actual laying of the stone was done by the Masons.[75]

As for the resurrection of the militia drill, it never came about in quite the way Logan envisioned in *The Volunteer Soldier of America*. School drill did become popular in the 1890s, but enthusiasm for it proved to be short-lived and generated no major changes in the way American military forces were raised and trained. Certainly nothing like Logan's projected overhaul of military education ever took place.

Probably the most telling example of the GAR's difficulty in transmitting the apocalyptic view of the war to the next generation was the order's problematic relationship to a new auxiliary organization, the Sons of Veterans. Founded in 1878 (though not completely consolidated until 1886), the S of V was open to the sons of honorably discharged Union veterans. It was intended as a hereditary organization and is, in fact, still in existence. The new order was also a response to the desire among younger men for military display, a desire that led some civilian orders in these years to establish "militant" wings.[76]

Many GAR members who supported the new organization also held out hope that it would perpetuate the GAR's quasi-military tradition, drilling itself as a volunteer militia. In their minds, the S of V was to stand as the country's new safeguard against resurgent rebellion, its "chief bulwark against sedition, anarchy and intestine disorder on the one hand, and the subversive and corrupting influence of enormous wealth and great corporations on the other." It would give a "firm assertion of patriotic principles, which must be continually asserted in order to impress them upon the rapidly developing Nation, which every year receives millions of foreigners, who have no conception of our National ideas and what it cost to maintain them."[77] As early as 1878 some Grand Army members called for the admission of sons of members to the GAR itself, or at least to its meetings and campfires.[78]

But while the GAR national encampment officially endorsed the Sons of Veterans as an auxiliary in 1888, the S of V and the GAR never amalgamated.[79] Indeed, in some places the new order was indifferently received. In Philadelphia, Post 2 resisted the formation of a Sons camp for years before finally agreeing to support one in 1892 (though it appears to have been fairly successful thereafter). In Chippewa Falls, Comerford Post declined to form a Sons of Veterans camp in 1888; the only recorded participation of its sons in post activities was in 1886, when they were permitted to join the Memorial Day parade. In Brockton, a camp of Sons organized in 1883 joined in such activities as campfires and Memorial Day services. But in 1886 its members talked of surrendering their charter, and by 1889 the members of Webster Post expressed the opinion that it would be better to disband the camp. Although a Sons camp in Brockton was resuscitated the following year, it was soon engaged in wrangling with the post over the proceeds of a joint fair, and by 1893 was no longer being invited to the annual installation dinners—if, in fact, it was still in existence.[80]

In part, the distance maintained between the GAR and the Sons resulted from a feeling among Grand Army members that the Sons did not understand the meaning of the mantle being conferred on them. Just as the veterans worried about the dilution of their own order by civilian commercialism, they perceived a regrettable tendency among the Sons to equate membership with gaudy, fraternal display. As early as 1881, for example, the national encampment warned members of the fledgling organization not to use GAR titles and instructed them to adopt some uniform "to distinguish them from the Grand Army of the Republic." In 1883, Commander-in-Chief Paul Vandervoort scolded one branch of the Sons for "scatter[ing] commissions throughout the country. . . . Generals and Lieutenant-Generals by brevet have been created by the score." The following year Commander-in-Chief Robert Beath told the encampment he had nothing to say about the Sons "further than that we should insist on the abrogation of the many high-sounding titles they have distributed with lavish profusion, and that they be required to wear a uniform that will not be confounded with that of the GAR." In 1886 the *National Tribune* deplored the "stupid and insipid" overuse of the secret Sons of Veterans "grip" among its members.[81] Although the GAR had its elements of militia and lodge practice, it also had a direct link to war service that was missing from the Sons of Veterans. No matter how reverently the sons treated the memory of the war, it could not be the same thing to them that it was to their fathers.

The differing experiences of GAR and S of V members, however, offer only a partial explanation of the failure of the two orders to amalgamate. A deeper reason can be found in the persistence of the apocalyptic cosmology that led Grand Army members to view their war experience as unique, nonrecurring, and monumental. Revolutionary War veterans, to take the most pertinent counterexample, ensured the continuity of their organization through heredity: the Society of the Cincinnati is still in existence because membership is passed down from fathers to sons. Twentieth-century veterans' organizations such as the Veterans of Foreign Wars and the American Legion have perpetuated themselves through different means: the admission of veterans of later wars. But because Grand Army members viewed "their" war as a radically unique event and themselves as the nation's saviors, they resisted such hereditary principles to the end. The GAR was an organization strictly bound by time, fated to pass away with the death of its last member. "The GAR, unlike other societies, is limited by the constitutional law of nature," Comrade George Ginty told Chippewa Falls's Post 68 in 1885. "When the last survivor of the war disappears, its mission will have been accomplished; its cause will have been won."[82]

Ginty was voicing a view that soon became a commonplace. After 1890, when it had become clear that the life of the order would not be extended, national encampments of the GAR took on a poignant quality. Proposals for a "retired list" of homebound members surfaced occasionally; in 1896 the rules were changed to provide for mergers of declining posts and retention of inactive "nonresident" members.[83] Encampments of the decade are suffused with references to "the line of graying heads" and the GAR's "march into the sunset." In the twentieth century, the photograph of the last surviving Union soldier of a town, regiment, or state would become a staple of local photojournalism.

As for the Sons, although these "worthy sons of patriot sires" deserved plaudits, they could never comprehend the essence of the Civil War experience. "I do not favor any kind of merging of any other association with ours," Commander-in-Chief John Kountz told the national encampment of 1885. "I am opposed to the perpetuation of the Grand Army, believing the mission of our great comradeship will have been fulfilled when the last comrade has joined the final muster-out." Three years earlier, Commander-in-Chief George Merrill had put the matter even more bluntly: "No one, not even our sons, can appreciate the memories of camp and march, of bivouac and battle, as those who were participants therein; the scenes of the great struggle can never be to them what they are to us." When the last GAR veteran passed on, Merrill suggested, "let there close with him, except in its glorious record and bright memory, the last scene of the life of the

Grand Army of the Republic."[84] The memory of the GAR would stand
as a monument, but the door to membership was closed forever.

Of course, the sons would have their own opportunity for glory in 1898, as the Spanish-American War claimed the nation's attention. But while the example of the Union veterans would hang over the heads of the volunteers embarking for Cuba or Manila, it was a model they could never really emulate. The nation of 1898 was not the nation of 1861, nor were its wars thought of in the same way as they had been in the apocalyptic days before Sumter. The Union could be saved only once. After that, it became a granite monument, standing silently and unapproachably in the center of the courthouse square.

CHAPTER **7** FLAG

In 1890, the year of the generous Dependent Pension Act, GAR membership peaked at just over 400,000. The next year it began to decline, until by the turn of the century the order could count only 276,662 members, the great majority of them in their fifties and sixties. With younger men barred from joining the order, its future decline was a certainty.[1] In a sense, the Grand Army had aged along with its membership: Republican partisanship in the late 1860s, when young veterans were eager to snare political patronage jobs from victorious soldier-candidates; fraternalism and local charity in the late 1870s and early 1880s as up-and-coming businessmen and ambitious clerks strove to make their marks; pension lobbying and war reminiscences in the 1880s and early 1890s as the ex-soldiers became infirm and longed for their younger days.

Yet in the Union veteran's natural history before 1890 was a social history as well. Even in its internal development, the Grand Army had wrestled with many of the public problems of its time: the tenuous nature of republican equality in a corporate age; the threat that money posed to manhood; the destruction of island communities; the question of entitlement to charity. In each case, the veterans had made the adjustment to industrial capitalism, while continuing to speak the language of republicanism.[2]

With the pension campaigns and war memorials of the 1880s, the Union veterans had begun to make direct forays into the realm of what has been called "public culture."[3] Their declarations of their own national saviorhood, while aimed at securing private benefits, were also propositions about the public duty of civilians. By the same token, although the veterans' millennial republican memories of war were clearly based in their own historical experiences, such memories were also rebukes to more modern, civilian forms of recall—professional historicism, Confederate intransigence, popular apathy. The ex-soldiers intended their cosmology to apply not only to themselves but to nonveterans as well.

After 1890, such forays would become even more explicit and prescriptive as the Grand Army embarked on a series of public, patriotic crusades aimed directly at civilians. In their loyalty campaigns, Union veterans would try to shape a public culture in which they, like the prewar generation generally, were a declining minority. Many Americans no longer fit the contours of the millennial historical mold. Many others, like the Sons of Veterans in their gaudy uniforms, were too young to understand it. And in 1898 the Union veterans faced a new war that fit their conception of national history only with difficulty. Nonetheless, members of the GAR held fast to a vision of the nation that thirty years of massive social upheaval outside their order had done little to shake.

The GAR Nation

The 1890s have long been recognized as a decade of patriotic offensives among native-born, white members of the American middle class. Nativism and jingoism flourished as never before in groups such as the American Protective Association; worries about anarchism and other "foreign" agitation led to campaigns for immigration restriction. In intellectual circles, Social Darwinism and scientific racism became fashionable. In social life, exclusive hereditary societies such as the Sons and Daughters of the American Revolution sprouted like weeds. In the press, William Randolph Hearst's jingoistic *New York Journal* whipped up sentiment for war with Spain. In public education, calls were heard for the placing of flags on schoolhouses and the military drilling of students, while "patriotic" bodies vied with each other to censor textbooks. The flag itself became the object of a sudden and intense cult that would ultimately produce Flag Day and the Pledge of Allegiance. While such older, ritually oriented fraternal orders as the Masons seem to have held out against the tide of secular patriotic activity until its second crest in the 1920s, many others were thoroughly engulfed by 1898.[4]

Given the GAR's rhetoric of monumentality and national savior-hood in the 1880s, it should come as no surprise that its members joined the patriotic onslaught of the 1890s early and enthusiastically. Because Union veterans had, in the stock phrase of many an encampment speaker, "stood on the right side of the line that divided loyalty from treason" in 1861–65, they felt uniquely qualified to say where that line was in 1890, in 1898, or in any other year. George Lemon's *National Tribune*, for one, became an outspoken advocate of immigration restriction; in 1898, the national encampment would enthusiastically endorse the war with Spain. And local GAR posts worried incessantly in the 1890s about patriotism in the public schools.

All of this may seem perfectly predictable in light of the activities of later veterans' organizations such as the American Legion and Veterans of Foreign Wars. Yet because Americans have become so accustomed to assumptions of patriotic prerogative on the part of veterans' groups in this century, we tend to forget how novel they were in the context of the 1890s. In the first place, powerful veterans' lobbies like the GAR had no more precedent in American life than had the massive Grand Review in 1865. The political power that the Union veterans commanded enabled them to make unprecedented pension demands; on the other hand, it generated opposition among civilians who were not prepared to rethink old ideas about voluntarism and charity to suit the "national saviors."

Moreover, the GAR's relatively homogeneous membership was becoming increasingly unrepresentative of the American population at large. The GAR never managed to enroll even half of the eligible Union veterans, while those it did enroll made the order overwhelmingly white, predominantly native-born, and (though class composition varied from place to place) largely middle class or lower middle class. In a political environment like that of the 1890s, marked by racial, class, and ethnic strife, claims to national saviorhood by such a group were bound to be problematic.

Finally, the Grand Army's interpretation of the Civil War as a one-time-only event of national salvation made access to the true "nation" somewhat remote, even for the ex-soldiers' white, native-born, middle-class children. If no one but Union veterans could claim guardianship of the Republic and if (to overstate the case somewhat) no one but native-born, middle-class, white men over the age of fifty could be Union veterans, then the inclusiveness of the flag was perhaps not so inclusive after all. It was a "nation" based on a conception of history that passively excluded a great many people.

To illustrate, it is worth considering in some detail the GAR's strained relationship to four large groups of Americans who did not fit its cosmology particularly well: immigrants, industrial workers, blacks, and women. These four groups, which have been the focus of much of the best recent historical writing on the nineteenth century, were either largely absent from the Grand Army worldview or appeared as disturbing, disruptive elements. They were not, it should be repeated, actively excluded from membership, though blacks were relegated to second-class status and women to an auxiliary order. Rather, they were passively barred by a cosmology that looked backward to a nation more homogeneous than the one in existence by 1900.

The immigrants in GAR posts, for example, were almost all from the British Isles, Canada, or Germany; the few who came from elsewhere were novelties and sometimes sources of amusement. One post in Pennsylvania, for example, bragged that it could "claim as a member what no post heretofore heard from can, to wit, a full-fledged Chinaman," while Post 2 enjoyed hearing Comrade Charles Schuellerman tell humorous stories involving Germans. The early years of the order saw little rancor over nationality, though the national encampment did decline to print a German version of the ritual—a move warmly supported by a German-born commander from Washington, D.C. The veterans' tone, in short, was assimilationist. The *National Tribune*, in welcoming immigrants in 1880 and 1881, recommended "a smart country school teacher" to "make a good American out of a green Norwegian in six months."[5]

As the massive Southern and Eastern European influx began in the

1890s, however, some members of the GAR began to worry. When
New York's Lafayette Post presented flags to the Rhinelander School
in 1897, it was careful to note that the banner had been accepted by
Master Hess of the school drill company; when it gave a flag to Baron
de Hirsch English Day School the following year, "a Russian girl pupil
five years old" accepted it. Others within the order made more
threatening noises. "Shall American Labor Be Trampled Under the
Heel of Italian Lazzaroni Immigration?" the *National Tribune* asked
editorially in 1888. From that point onward, the paper became a
steady opponent of foreign immigration, supporting the immigration
restriction bill of 1890, attacking antipension newspapers as being
under the control of "Jew and Gentile aliens," and attributing labor
troubles in Pennsylvania coal mines to the hiring of Hungarians—
"half-savage aliens," who, the paper said, brought only "brigandage
and trouble." Similarly, the national encampment's "patriotic instruction" committee of 1892 raised the question of "whether some
restriction must not be placed upon that portion of the tide of immigration sweeping upon our shores which represents only the poverty
and crime of other lands." Such fulminations may not have had much
effect; there is little sign of overt nativism in the activities of the posts
studied here. But the protestations undoubtedly contributed to the
self-satisfied jingoism of the period preceding the war with Spain.
And if GAR members were largely native-born, the Sons of Veterans
were almost entirely so.[6]

The underrepresentation of industrial workers in the GAR was
even greater than that of immigrants (and, given the large number of
industrial workers who were immigrants, probably not unrelated to
it). Though by no means absent from GAR posts, laborers and semiskilled workers were relatively scarce there, and certainly, once
members, they held few of the high ceremonial offices so central to
membership. In some posts, it has been suggested, the high muster
fees and a prevailing business-club atmosphere made it difficult for
people from those groups to participate. But it also reflected the
Grand Army's attitude toward labor, which was rooted in the same
independent producerism that led Grand Army speakers to mytholo-
gize the farm boy volunteer and to defend pension expenditures in
the name of manliness. Even if labor and capital could no longer be
consolidated on individual farms, they were nonetheless the same
interest and could only harm one another by quarreling. Such a
view echoed the "harmony of interests" theory first propounded by

economist Henry C. Carey in the 1840s: labor strife only produced
disorder.[7]

Thus Commander-in-Chief John Robinson could call the railroad strikes of 1877 "a *seeming* conflict between capital and labor" and offer the GAR's services as a police force to the president. "While this organization, true to its principles, will advocate justice and equal rights," he told the national encampment, "it will discountenance every attempt at anarchy or insurrection." In Post 2, members formed themselves into rifle companies "in defense of law and order." Some were sent to Pittsburgh to suppress the riots there, while others volunteered themselves to work railroad jobs. In the late 1880s, a fresh outburst of labor strife brought thanks from a post in Racine to the governor of Wisconsin for suppressing "anarchy" and a speech by Commander-in-Chief William Warner in which he declared the GAR "the great conservative element of the nation." It also produced such rejoinders as *The Volcano Under the City*, a history of the 1863 draft riots penned by a Union veteran, which ended by calling on working-men to be "the community's real bulwark against disorder."[8] These were not sentiments calculated to endear the GAR to unionists, particularly when Grand Army members were rushing to join militia units that were battling strikers.

In the 1890s the great and violent strikes at Pullman and Homestead provoked even more hostile reactions from Grand Army speechmakers. In 1894, for example, Pennsylvania department commander William Emsley declared, "When the lines are drawn between right and wrong, deeds of violence and destruction of property find neither advocacy nor supporters among our comrades. . . . The boys who wore the blue will be found on the side of America and its institutions." Oregon department commander S. B. Ormsby issued a similar order, saying it was "not the province of the Grand Army of the Republic to discuss theories at this time, nor to endeavor to lay the blame, or place responsibility for the trouble now upon us. It is sufficient for it to know that the law has been defied, property destroyed, and human life sacrificed or put in jeopardy." The *National Tribune*, while placing part of the blame for the Homestead strike on the Carnegie Steel Company, nonetheless denounced the course of the workers and dismissed as "mischievous nonsense" the idea that the militia was a tool of employers. "The National Guard cannot become the oppressor of any class of our people," Lemon wrote. "It is the agent of the whole people, organized to carry out the will of the people by insuring obedience to the law. We must have obedience to the law under all circumstances. If the laws are not obeyed and respected there is no protection for anybody." Similar indictments of "anarchy" marked Commander-in-Chief John Palmer's address to the 1892 national encampment at Washington.[9]

In the harmony-of-interests tradition, Grand Army members avoided class rhetoric and usually tried to appear evenhanded in their public positions on these conflicts. The *National Tribune*, for example, came out for the right of telegraphers to strike in 1883. The paper assigned blame to the companies in a railroad dispute of 1885 and again at Homestead in 1892. The *Grand Army Record* similarly urged members not to "disgrace the badge" by signing up as Pinkerton detectives, while commanders such as Robinson and Warner prefaced their denunciations of labor unrest with disclaimers that the order supported "justice and equal rights" or "the dignity of labor."[10]

But when push came to shove, the GAR was always to be found in the camp of order and property rights. Whereas once phrases such as "equal rights" and "the dignity of labor" had been invoked to attack slavery and promote free-soil settlement of the West, now they served mainly to obscure the reality of industrial capitalism. Indeed, the GAR's continued devotion to harmony-of-interests rhetoric can perhaps best be understood as a variant of the ideology of the Republican party, to which so many GAR members belonged. Even in the late nineteenth century, as their party was becoming the party of big capital, Republican candidates from Grant ("the Galena Tanner" of 1872) to Logan ("the volunteer soldier of America" of 1884) continued to invoke independent producerism on the stump. Although Republican rhetoric continued to diverge from Republican economic policy for the rest of the century, Union veterans as a group rarely grappled with the contradiction. The House of Lords affair of 1886–98 was perhaps one of the few instances in which it surfaced, and then only in symbolic form.[11]

Harmony-of-interests rhetoric was understandably congenial to businessmen's posts, such as Philadelphia's Post 2. More surprising, perhaps, was the deafening silence on labor issues in Chippewa Falls, where Comerford Post included many loggers, and especially in Brockton, where Webster Post was filled with shoe factory workers and where local politics were influenced by a strong socialist organization and a thriving Boot and Shoe Workers Union. In seventeen years of Comerford Post minutes (1883–1900), there is no mention

whatsoever of unions, strikes, or labor unrest in Chippewa Falls or
elsewhere. In the sixteen surviving years of Webster Post minutes
(1877–93), there are only two passing references to labor: in 1885,
when the post declined to supplement its charity committee's efforts
to relieve the families of local strikers, and again in 1886 when the
post declared that demands on members for charity in the wake of
another strike had left them too poor to get up a subscription for a
widow.[12] While neither Comerford nor Webster Post supplied militiamen or strikebreakers (unlike Post 2), both seem to have been
largely unconcerned with the problems of workers.

Black Americans posed a much starker challenge to the GAR
worldview than did new immigrants or industrial workers. Immigrants and workers fell outside the Grand Army's preservationist
cosmology because they had, by and large, appeared on the scene
since 1865. Blacks, by contrast, had been present before the war;
most had undergone a marked change of legal status as a result of it,
though after the waning of Reconstruction in the late 1870s it became
glaringly apparent that the war had effected no revolution in race
relations. The question for Grand Army posts was whether blacks—
specifically black veterans—should continue to be segregated and
ignored or whether the war had mandated a new attitude.

In considering that question, the Union veterans were pulled in
several different directions. Radical members like Logan and former
officers of black regiments like Philadelphian Louis Wagner continued to stand up for the rights of black ex-soldiers, while occasional
encampment speakers like Frederick Douglass reminded the members of the central place of emancipation in the war's legacy. On the
other hand, the same wave of reconciliation sentiment that was
inspiring Blue-Gray reunions and Confederate veterans' homes in
the 1890s was also heightening GAR ambivalence about race relations. And even those members who insisted on a reconstructed
South were not always in favor of "social equality" in the North.[13]

For the most part, Grand Army members took the stock position of
the Victorian Northern middle class, arguing that blacks were entitled to equality before the law, though not necessarily to anything
more. Although a few Northern posts had a black member or two,
separate black and white posts were the rule where the black population was large, just as they were in civilian fraternal orders such as
the Masons. In the South, where the GAR had always been perceived
as a Radical front group (prospective members of the Ku Klux Klan,
for example, were required to swear that they had never been GAR

A unit of black musicians heads a predominantly white military parade on Memorial Day in Santa Fe, New Mexico, 1880. A few black troopers are visible toward the rear of the company. This was a regular army parade; Grand Army processions were more segregated, with white and black troops marching separately. (U.S. Military History Institute)

members or supported its aims), integrated posts were out of the question, particularly in the early years, when the order's survival was in doubt. Some Southern GAR departments did not survive 1868; the rest were defunct by the early 1870s. Although the order revived in the South in the 1880s, it did so under decidedly non-Radical white auspices.[14]

Here again, the Grand Army conception of the war was pivotal: because the members viewed the conflict primarily as a battle to preserve an existing Union rather than as a crusade to free slaves or establish social equality, they felt no compulsion to change their views of blacks once the war ended. The one instance in which a GAR commander-in-chief took notice of the ongoing decay of Reconstruction—John Hartranft's call on Southerners in 1877 to "give up the pistol and the lash, concede free speech, a free press and free votes, and submit to the decision of the ballot"—was prefaced by praise for Confederate veterans and assurances that the GAR "would impose no restrictions which freemen ought not to endure, or ask any submission which freemen ought not to give."[15] Because Northern campfire speakers tended to remember the war in preservationist rather than liberationist terms, they became exercised easily by counter-Unionist symbols such as the Confederate flag but hardly ever by reports of Southern mistreatment of blacks. By the 1880s, the question of race was rarely broached in the order.

Incidents in two of the belatedly reconstituted, all-white Southern GAR departments illustrate best the ambivalence with which Grand Army members viewed black veterans. In 1887, a Wisconsin national encampment delegate challenged the Tennessee and Georgia department commander's refusal to grant a charter to a black post and offered an amendment to the order's rules and regulations that would permit the commander-in-chief to overrule him. One Southern member protested that blacks did not know how to organize themselves properly, while another, Comrade Graham, argued that the GAR was "a social organization. Those who are in have rights and those who are out have no rights except what are given by those within. Otherwise what would be the use of the ballot?" But Northerners, including the forceful and belligerent Wagner, disagreed sharply. One delegate, Comrade Salomon, went so far as to suggest that the offending Southern department commander be removed from his position and added that black members were always to be preferred to ex-rebels. "I for one say that I would rather shake hands with the blackest nigger in the land if he was a true and honest man, than with a traitor," Salomon told the encampment. The amendment passed, but the matter was allowed to die quietly; the new posts were not formed.[16]

In 1890 the issue came up again, and this time it gained widespread attention outside the order. The immediate cause of the renewed furor was a factional fight in the Department of Louisiana and Mississippi, where Commander Jacob Gray had tried to offset his opposition's advantage in the department (opposition engendered, ironically, by Gray's attendance at Jefferson Davis's funeral) by hurriedly creating five new—and predominantly black—posts just before the department encampment. The existing white posts, however, refused to seat the black delegates, who then proceeded to meet on their own. Asked to decide the question, the GAR judge advocate-general ruled for the exclusion of the black posts on the technical grounds that they had not been mustered in time. Nowhere did his lengthy opinion mention the race of any party to the dispute. When Comrade William Murrell of New Jersey protested, "Why is it that you shut out black comrades?" Comrade Joseph O'Neall of Ohio defended the decision by arguing that it was simply a matter of rules, pointing out that "no man can tell by the record whether it was a white post or a colored that was excluded."[17]

There the national officers certainly must have hoped the issue would die, as it had in 1887. When it did not, some Southern members proposed to solve the problem by creating separate departments for black and white posts. Commander-in-Chief Wheelock Veazey gave that idea official endorsement in 1891, saying he believed that majorities of both black and white veterans preferred such an arrangement. The *National Tribune* also found the proposal "well worthy [sic] the most serious attention" and touched on a fear that probably lay at the root of the uproar, even for some Northern posts: the specter of black officers commanding white members. To bring blacks into the existing Southern departments, the paper said, "would be to at once convert those departments into thoroughly negro organizations, which would destroy their value as teachers of loyalty, and drive out many white comrades who dread the censure of their Southern neighbors for their affiliation with negroes, and marching in Posts and Departments under negro officers."[18] In supporting the separate-departments proposal at the 1891 encampment, Graham of Louisiana made the same point even more bluntly, appealing to the Northern veterans' distaste for "negro domination":

In your Posts at the North it is a very different thing. You may have three or four colored men, nice men, respectable men, whom you all know and speak to every day on the street. They come into your Post and you treat them well. They are respectful to you. They take no part in the arrangements; they do not elect the officers. You do all the business and everything of that kind. With us it is very different. Should we open the doors, there would be eight or ten or fifteen white men, perhaps, in a Post, perhaps twenty-five and there would be two or three hundred colored men, and it would be a case of the tail wagging the dog.[19]

To this way of thinking, a department in which blacks commanded whites could not properly teach "loyalty."

Despite such pleas, delegates at the 1891 encampment were aware that civilians were watching their deliberations with keen interest. If Union veterans were formally to endorse the idea of a "color line," it would be interpreted in some quarters as a significant retreat from the ideals for which the war had been fought and in others as an acceptance of the Southern social system. Furthermore, many members still were not willing to abandon the black veterans. "During that fierce struggle for the life of the nation, we stood shoulder to shoulder as comrades tried," read the report of one committee that included three past commanders-in-chief. "It is too late to divide now on the color line." When advocates of separation pointed to segregation in churches, schools, and other fraternal orders, past commander William Warner replied: "They are matters of sociability. Comrades, when these black men or white men, or whatever color or nationality they may have been, shouldered the musket in defense of the Union, it was not a question of etiquette, a question of sociability. It was a question of patriotism and loyalty."[20] In that case, the idea of a separate "veteran" identity was put to work in the service of social change.

Ultimately the proposal for segregated departments was rejected, and ultimately the rejection had exactly the effect predicted by the Southerners: the withdrawal of white members from the affected departments. In attempting to enforce the encampment's decision, newly installed Commander-in-Chief John Palmer was forced to suspend the white commander, the senior vice commander, and the junior vice commander of the Louisiana and Mississippi department; he also had to reorganize the department itself when the white posts tried to surrender its charter.[21]

In its last major public debate on the subject, then, the Grand Army stood its ground against segregation. While the color line was officially repudiated, it remained in force nonetheless. It was there in the informal blackballing of black members who attempted to apply to white posts, word of which occasionally leaked into the newspapers.[22] It was there in the separation of black from white posts, if not black from white departments. And in the South, it was there in the disregard of other Southern departments for the antisegregation order of the national encampment—a directive that, like other GAR orders, proved impossible to enforce without the consent of the membership. By 1898, when Commander-in-Chief John P. S. Gobin returned from a tour of the South to report that "race prejudice remains and the chasm seems to be widening," the national encampment had given up trying to assert its authority in the matter. When a similar dispute split the Woman's Relief Corps in the late 1890s, the GAR's sister organization simply divided the affected departments on the color line.[23] Black veterans, in short, were admitted to the GAR on terms of formal equality accompanied by informal discrimination.

Like blacks, women were not so much excluded from the GAR worldview as they were relegated to secondary positions within it. Early in the order's history the national encampment rejected the idea of "side degrees" for wives and daughters of veterans, and even after it recognized the Woman's Relief Corps as an auxiliary in 1881, women, like sons of veterans, were never admitted to membership.[24] Instead, they were expected to strike standard Victorian poses as "angels of the home": making curtains for the post room in Brockton; arranging flowers for Memorial Day in Chippewa Falls; waiting in the hallway outside the post room for invitations to a dance in Philadelphia; giving motherly injunctions to "be true to God" and "acquit yourselves like men" to a Sons of Veterans camp in Muskegon, Michigan; sewing flags for post halls; preparing food for post social functions; serving lunch to the national encampment; raising charity funds—and then turning them over to the veterans for disbursement.[25] "Loyal women" could participate in the patriotic project, but only within a clearly delimited sphere. They were to inculcate patriotism in children; otherwise, they were to wait on the wishes of the ex-soldiers.

From their positions as guardians of the home, women could, of course, launch telling criticisms of veteran vices, particularly intemperance. In 1883, for example, one woman from Kansas complained to the *National Tribune* that GAR encampments were nothing but drinking sprees, which caused "a strong prejudice against the Grand

Army among outsiders and among the women folk generally." Recall-
ing drunkenness at a recent commercial exposition, Olive Wright of
Denver in the same year urged members to bring their wives along to
the national encampment there so that "our beautiful city will be
spared the shame and humiliation of a scene similar to the 'business
men's barbeque' of last summer." And at the Detroit national encampment of 1891, the scene of a drunken banquet of unprecedented
proportions, the Woman's Christian Temperance Union tried and
failed to put the veterans on record against the serving of spirits to
old soldiers (past commander-in-chief Samuel Burdett, however,
commended their "goodness of heart and purpose").[26]

But at bottom, the world of the veterans remained a male one.
Women had a modicum of influence, but it was essentially limited to
matters affecting home and family. Indeed, the opportunity to escape
into the all-male sphere of the post room seems to have been a prime
attraction not only of the Grand Army but of Victorian fraternities in
general.[27] The Woman's Relief Corps (again, the name speaks volumes) might offer aid and comfort, but its officers always struck a
deferential tone when addressing the veterans. As its president, Kate
B. Sherwood, told the national encampment in a typical speech of
1884, the WRC was "organized for work, and because the Grand
Army called for us. We are equally ready to disband and go home
whenever the Grand Army are through with us." Perhaps the most
apt metaphor for the women's spectator status came from the California WRC in 1893. Declining an invitation to join Grand Army men
on parade, the women declared that they would rather remain as
they had been at the victory parades of 1865, when they had "stood
on the sidewalks and cheered their fathers, brothers, sons and
lovers."[28] In the static world of the GAR, men marched while women
cheered.

In the Union veterans' relationship to immigrants, workers, blacks,
and women lay a vision of the "nation" that was at base an effort to
freeze the social relations of 1865 and hold them against all comers.
While the GAR's positions on specific issues were by no means reac-
tionary (the national encampment's antisegregationist position of
1892, in fact, actually represented a call for major change in the
South), the thrust of its worldview was conservative and suspicious of
change. For immigrants, that translated into training in the meaning
of "American institutions" from a "good country schoolmarm." For
workers, it meant employment only on liberal capitalist grounds—

they could choose to work or not to work on terms offered by an employer. For blacks, it meant the legal rights guaranteed by the postwar amendments, but no more. For women, it meant relegation to sentimental guardianship of the home. That was the nation as deposited by war on the shore of the 1870s, and the GAR meant to preserve it intact into the twentieth century. Even when advocating the vast expansion of the federal pension system, one of the major public policy changes of the nineteenth century, the veterans tried to justify the move by linking it with prewar ideals of manliness and independence.

The "nation" of Grand Army cosmology was still the redeemer of the world, a chosen place not bound by the ordinary constraints of history. It was a place in which farm boy volunteers could be relied upon to drop the plow and race to the front, leaving their wives to tend (in Logan's phrase) "that place of Heaven called home."[29] It was also, in GAR rituals and ceremonies, an orderly place, a peaceable kingdom from which disorder and diversity were shut out. In the fraternalism that took over the order in the 1880s, the wartime camp was idealized as a place of camaraderie and order, a happy (if never-existent) community much like those propounded by other fraternal orders of the time.

In the public culture of the 1890s, however, the Union veterans' version of the "nation" had to fight it out in the ideological arena with a number of other views. Among academic historians, the historicists were beginning their work of demolition, looking for cause and process rather than deep, unchanging truth in the nation's past. In the cities, immigrants with no knowledge of the war or its hagiography were arriving in great numbers. Impersonal industries were coming to overshadow the farms of Logan's imaginary volunteer plowboys. And everywhere, blacks and women were showing increasing disinclination to accept the positions tendered them as part of the white man's Victorian utopia. It was an unsettling time for many, and none more so than the men who had been reared on the millennial version of the nation, had fought a bloody war ostensibly to preserve it, and now, in their old age, found themselves living in a strange country. The reaction of the veterans, by and large, was to wish that it could be 1865 again.

But the GAR nation was not simply an exercise in nostalgia. Especially in the ultrapatriotic context of the 1890s, it had real political consequences. By tying the preservation of the Union to the preservation of the antebellum Northern social order, the GAR put forth a

strong proposition about American nationalism, a proposition to
which future versions of the "nation" would feel obligated to respond. To understand why that was so, it is important briefly to consider the various guises nations have worn in other parts of the world and to keep "nationalism" separate from a term with which it is often confused, namely "patriotism."

Patriotism—literally, the love of one's ancestral soil—describes the affection people feel for a particular place or group, a loyalty based originally on kinship organization.[30] It is not specific to the modern state or the capitalist economy but is a constant feature of social relations. In the words of Carlton J. H. Hayes, who first made the point half a century ago, "Human beings are social animals and do appear equipped with traits which render it possible and necessary for them to live in groups, but the groups do not have to be nationalities."[31] The mission of the nationalist propagandist is to conflate such elemental affections with loyalty to the nation, which is exclusively a phenomenon of the modern world. Arising with industrialization and the modern state, nationalist movements invariably begin by identifying a particular linguistic and/or cultural group as a "nation" and then proceed to demand that that group have either a state of its own or a sphere of autonomy within a state controlled by others.

Not surprisingly, studies of nationalism have tended to focus either on how linguistic-cultural groups come to see themselves as nations, or on the relationship of nations to state formation. At first, intellectual historians such as Hayes and Elie Kedourie concentrated on debunking the romantic nationalist notion of the nation as a "natural" entity with a "soul" or "national will" that required only the conjuring of the nationalist to come to life. More recent scholarship has examined the social roots of nationalist movements, explaining them variously as handmaidens of economic modernization (Ernest Gellner), devices to gain state power (John Breuilly), or "imagined communities" resulting from the rise of print capitalism (Benedict Anderson). While these writers differ on matters of causation, they are all concerned primarily with the origin of the modern nation-state.[32]

Compared with such movements, American nationalism of the 1890s such as that espoused by the Grand Army exhibits three significant differences. In the first place, despite the homogeneity of GAR membership, its version of the nation was not based on any linguistic or cultural principle. Rather, it stressed conformity with liberal capitalism; in theory, "American" was a voluntary identity. In Europe, by contrast, the interplay between capitalism and an explicitly linguistic or cultural nationalism was considerably more complex, particularly as it related to state power.[33] This dissimilarity has often led theorists to categorize national identity in the United States as different in kind from nationality elsewhere, or to remove the U.S. from comparative discussion entirely.[34] One is tempted to conclude, as some have, that liberal capitalist ideology and American nationalism of the sort championed by the GAR were the same thing. However, given the number of passive exclusions from the American nationalism of the GAR worldview—blacks, immigrants, industrial workers, women— it seems more accurate to say that for Union veterans at least, liberal capitalism was the broad context within which a narrower American national identity was argued out, beginning with the struggles of the 1890s. From that point of view it could be argued that American nationalism, despite its eighteenth-century Revolutionary origins, is basically "gradualist," a term that A. D. Smith applies to national movements in Canada, Australia, and Brazil—nations that, so to speak, came to themselves slowly.[35]

Second, the millennial tone of much GAR agitation, already apparent in the rhetoric of monumentalism and "national saviorhood" in the 1880s, was curiously backward-looking. Its "nation" was based not on language, race, class, or gender but on the vision of a specific *time*: the prewar ideal of a virtuous, millennial Republic, extending on through the postwar world, the decisive victory of 1898, and, presumably, infinitely. This was the world of the independent producer, of entrepreneurial capitalism, of the citizen-soldier volunteer. And while it is always risky to generalize about the experience of an entire birth cohort, it is at least possible that the GAR's republican model of history had meaning even for nonwhite, nonnative, non-middle-class Northerners of the prewar generation. Throughout the postwar period, black and working-class veterans continued to join the Grand Army even though they were relegated to subordinate positions. Outside the order, nonveteran voters continued to support unprecedented pension expenditures.

Finally, unlike nationalist movements in the early modern world, the GAR of the 1890s functioned within an *established* state. Theorists of nationalism generally pass over poststatehood nationalist lobbies with little comment, and they offer some sound reasons for doing so. As John Breuilly, who explicitly excludes "nationalist pressure groups" from his analysis, points out, in the established nation-

state, "any route that is taken can be called nationalist. Anyone can,
and does, use some sort of nationalist rhetoric in a world where the nation/state is the basic political unit and where it is difficult to locate cultural groups distinct from the public state. As a consequence nationalism is reduced to mere emotion or pragmatism."[36] To see the cogency of Breuilly's objection, one has only to look at the abundance of present-day political lobbies that find it expedient to mask their demands by invoking the "national interest," "national security," or the "national economy."

Yet even as nationalist appeals have become common coin, certain groups have been more prone to wield them than others. It is one thing to argue, as almost every pressure group does, that the "national interest" demands some specific policy. It is quite another thing to claim guardianship of the nation and privileged access to its "real" meaning. Such claims, even when put to use in struggles over public policy, are what distinguish nationalist lobbies such as the GAR from other pressure groups within established states.

Moreover, the assertion of privileged access to the nation is simultaneously a rebuke to privilege based on other potential classifications—race, class, gender, region, religion. Geoff Eley has found, for example, that in Wilhelmine Germany nationalist lobbies such as the Navy League had specific enemies in mind; what those groups offered, he concludes, was "a polemical refutation of the class analysis of the Socialists." Although the political context of the Gilded Age United States was quite different, the GAR nation was similar in that it served to buffer the membership from a variety of threatening alternatives: industrial unionism, immigration, racial equality, feminism. And like the German leagues, the GAR recruited members disproportionately from the petty bourgeoisie—a class worried about dissension and, other authors have argued, particularly attracted to nationalist movements.[37]

Grand Army nationalism, then, combined allegiance to liberal capitalism of a distinctly antebellum variety; a view of history that was backward-looking, preservationist, and faintly evangelical; and loyalty first to the national state rather than to race, class, gender, region, religion, or any other particularism. Operating within an established state, it functioned not only as an endorsement of that state but also as a negative statement about potential alternative nationalisms that sought to alter it. Shaped by the same forces at work on nationalist movements elsewhere in the nineteenth-century world—industrialization, state centralization, mass politics—GAR nationalism nonetheless represented the unique response of a particular group of men, situated in a particular social space, who had undergone a particular set of historical experiences.

In the 1890s, the Grand Army moved to gain a public hearing for its version of American nationalism. Union veterans could be found in most "loyalty" movements of the decade, but they concentrated on three issues: school textbooks, military drill, and the flying of the national flag over schoolhouses. In each case, the focus was on children in the public schools, that is, on the future of the Republic. And in each case "patriotism" was linked to the millennial republican version of national history that veterans had been teaching through campfires, monuments, and pension agitation for twenty years.

The Patriotic Boom: Texts, Drill, Flags

The GAR's campaign for "correct" Civil War histories began in 1888 with the discovery by some Wisconsin members that commonly used school history texts often presented a version of the war significantly at variance with the Grand Army's evangelical nationalist view. In a report presented to the national encampment, the Wisconsin veterans charged that because of the publishers' need to find a Southern market, many texts glossed over the events of the war "to the extent that a student after finishing the study is unable to comprehend the differences between the two sections that resulted in the war, and is left unable to comprehend which was right and which wrong; indeed to discover that even there was a right or wrong side to that struggle for the preservation of the Union." Worse, some of the books used in the South went even further, "teaching a thoroughly studied, rank, partisan system of sectional education."[38]

Among other things, the Wisconsin members claimed, pro-South histories justified secession and nullification as legitimate responses to an overbearing Congress, upheld the theory that the Union was simply a voluntary association of independent states, attacked Lincoln as a warmonger, portrayed the Confederate leaders as martyrs and self-sacrificing patriots, and charged that the Union armies were made up mostly of European mercenaries and penniless draftees. This view was hardly consistent with Logan's picture of virtuous farm boys rushing to the front to face the Armageddon of the Republic.

The time had come, the Wisconsin members concluded, "to cease

toying with treason for policy, and to cease illustrating the rebels as
heroes, as is the case in some of our own school histories. It is not
reviving sectional issues or animosities to advocate that this matter
be dealt with strictly in accordance with the true facts of history." The
national encampment endorsed the Wisconsin report and deputized
a "Committee on a Systematic Plan of Teaching the Lessons of Loyalty to Our Country and One Flag" in 1891. That committee's report
in 1892 recommended, among other things, the "correction" of insufficiently loyal school history texts. Many of the volumes in use, the
committee said, tended "to omit, gloss over, and even to misinterpret
the history of the war."[39]

With the encouragement of national and department officers, individual posts soon began to prod text publishers and local boards of
education on the issue and used other means to influence students'
views of the Civil War as well. In Wisconsin, for example, several
posts instituted "children's campfires," where veterans related the
Union version of the war to young people; in Chippewa Falls, members were detailed to visit schools on Memorial Day. In Philadelphia,
Post 2 members invited high school classes to visit the post hall, tried
to institute a series of lectures by post members in area schools, and
designated their own committee to deal with "patriotic instruction."
University of Pennsylvania historian John Bach McMaster even went
so far as to submit the manuscript of his school history to a GAR
committee in Chicago, hoping for an endorsement. Other authors
scrambled to revise texts, but it was 1898 before the GAR's school
history committee could find "substantial improvement in the tone
and sentiment" of histories of the war and 1900 before it could
declare that "the general character of these histories is satisfactory."[40] By that time, the Union veterans would be championing flag
displays, school drill, and a host of other patriotic activities.

What GAR members meant by "satisfactory," of course, was a
history in line with their own millennial view of the Civil War. Post 2's
"patriotic instruction committee" of 1894, for example, pronounced
one text, *Ellis' Universal History of the United States,* an "insidious
work" that "vilely belittles and aims to detract from the fidelity,
courage, and patriotic work performed by the soldiers of the Union
armies." Despite the publisher's offer to purge the text of any objectionable passages, the post members were not appeased. In a nationally circulated report, the Pennsylvanians complained that textbook authors never used the words "treason" and "rebellion" to
describe the Confederacy, and seemed "content . . . to give the causes

on each side which led up to the Rebellion, leaving the reader to his own conclusions as to the right or the wrong of it."[41]

It was exactly the text authors' attempt at neutrality and nuance that the Union veterans found most offensive. Their own personal war narratives had been contributions to a national diorama of victory, their monuments "silent sentinels," not tombstones. The patriotic instruction committee report of 1897 put the matter in terms that read like a religious confession of faith:

> We insist that our youth shall be taught that the war was more than a mere bloody contest to gratify selfish ambition or to test the military strength of the two sections of our country. We demand that it shall be plainly and clearly taught that it was a war, between the Government of the United States, and a part of its citizens in revolt against it; that it was prosecuted by the National Government for the maintenance of its constitutional authority, and the enforcement of its laws; and we further insist that it be made clear and beyond doubt, that those who fought for national unity in this struggle were right.[42]

No accurate history could portray the two armies as equally worthy; one had to be right and the other wrong. The war could not be a "mere bloody contest" or a test of strength; it had to be seen as a war of principle, unsullied by mean motives.

As for the publishers' pleas that the truth had to be hedged to serve a national market, the veterans insisted that any history telling a truly national story, as opposed to those tainted with sectionalism, could have only one theme: the theme of Union. The eternal nature of the Republic was not open to question. As the 1894 Pennsylvania committee put it, taking issue with one text's seemingly innocuous claim that "the issue of the conflict decided that the Nation should be henceforth 'one and inseparable'": "If only the issue decided the indivisibility, before that issue was framed it must have been a question whether the Union had a right to maintain itself."[43] To the members of the Grand Army, such a conditional war was not an admissible possibility.

Moreover, a proper appreciation of the Civil War had to place the conflict in the pantheon of truly apocalyptic, transhistorical events. In *The Volunteer Soldier of America*, John Logan had gone all the way back to ancient times to place the war in context, and even then he had found only two really comparable occurrences: the creation of the world and the founding of the Republic. Under that view, Union

Union and Confederate veterans tour the Peach Orchard during a reunion at the Gettysburg National Military Park, 1913. The park, established by Congress in 1895, preserved a memory of the war somewhat different from that of GAR textbook agitators. One seat on its governing board was reserved for a Southerner, and by 1930 it included several impressive Confederate markers. (U.S. Military History Institute)

veterans were connections not just to the war but to History. As such, they expected to be included in all sorts of commemorative events— the Fourth of July, for example, or the marking of the four-hundredth anniversary of Columbus's landing in 1892. As the Pennsylvania chairman of the National Public School Association put it, the participation of GAR members in the 1892 celebration offered "the conspicuous linking of the patriotic achievements of the past with the patriotic hopes of the future." Similarly, posts sometimes presented flags to schools on unrelated national holidays, such as Washington's Birthday.[44] And when the 1892 patriotic instruction committee came to recommend a national holiday to mark the Civil War, it suggested a virtual smorgasbord—Lincoln's Birthday, Appomattox, the Emancipation Proclamation—whose very diversity of meaning is revealing. To the committee, at least, the question of which event the country should celebrate—a martyrdom, a military victory, or the freeing of the slaves—was less important than its acknowledgment of the overriding importance of the war.[45]

It was important to implant the millennial version of the war in the minds of schoolchildren. But it was equally important to expose them to a more immediate symbol of patriotism, namely the American flag. At the same time that they raised the textbook issue, Union veterans began calling for the display of an American flag over every public schoolhouse. In 1888, two socially prominent "leading" posts in New York City, Lafayette Post 140 and Hamilton Post 182, began competing with each other in presenting flags to schools. After the national encampment endorsed the practice in 1892, it spread throughout New York and to other states as well.[46]

Like wartime presentations of regimental colors, postwar school flag presentations invariably were elaborate affairs, girded with marches, patriotic music, and speeches. In these ceremonies, the national banner took on an almost religious significance. When Lafayette Post presented a flag to Columbia University in 1896, for example, the ceremony included an escort by the Seventy-first Regiment of New York National Guard, prayers, the presentation of formal resolutions, and the singing of "The Star Spangled Banner" by all present. In his speech presenting the flag, Admiral Richard Meade offered several biblical passages in support of his assertion that "the flag is to us what the cross was to the Christian apostles, what the cross on the sword was to the knightly crusader," and he concluded that "loyalty to the colors, whether to victory or defeat, whether to life or unto death—these are the marks of the true believer."[47] Similarly, Commander-in-Chief William Warner told the national encampment of 1889 that the reverence of schoolchildren for the flag should be like that of the Israelites for the Ark of the Covenant. The Oregon GAR encampment demanded that weekly singing of "The Star Spangled Banner" be required in schools, while in Utah, GAR member E. W. Tatlock offered his opinion that school flag presentations in his state in 1897 were tempering Mormon hostility to the federal government. "It was encouraging and inspiring to hear Mormon children, many of whom had never before seen a flag, singing with earnestness and patriotic zeal 'The Star-Spangled Banner,' 'America,' and other songs of like nature," Tatlock reported to the national encampment.[48]

Outside the order, North Dakota and New Jersey in 1890 made the flying of flags at schoolhouses mandatory; other states soon followed suit. By 1900 a number of states had recognized Flag Day, the Ameri-

can Flag Association was agitating to make the holiday national (a
campaign that finally succeeded in 1916), and New York had become,
in 1897, the first state to bar the use of the flag in commercial
advertisements. In that year, the GAR patriotic instruction committee could report that the flying of flags over schools and other public
buildings had become "almost a universal custom." The 1898 report
found 35,049 schoolrooms with flags, 26,352 in which the Pledge of
Allegiance was administered, and 1,619 in which the Declaration of
Independence was posted.[49]

The veterans practiced the same flag ritualism that they preached.
The 1891 national encampment at Detroit instituted the practice of
standing for the playing of "The Star Spangled Banner," while Commander-in-Chief John Palmer (who two weeks earlier had denounced
a Southern GAR post for marching in a procession that had included a
Confederate flag) suggested singing along with the music as well, a
practice taken up at the New York department encampment the next
year. Palmer ordered the use of the Stars and Stripes in post meetings
and suggested a form for the presentation of colors adapted from U.S.
Army tactics. Brockton's Webster Post, for one, took up Palmer's
suggestions quickly. In November 1892 it added the presentation of
the flag to its post opening ceremonies; at a joint dinner two months
later, Brockton Woman's Relief Corps members presented the post
with a new flag, entering the hall to the strains of "The Star Spangled
Banner."[50]

Among the veterans in Palmer's Detroit audience, of course, veneration of the flag already had roots in the attachment they felt to
particular stands of colors carried or captured in battle. Certainly the
Union veterans had demonstrated loyalty in the famous battle-flag
incident of 1887, in which President Grover Cleveland had proposed
to return captured Confederate battle flags to the Southern states as
a gesture of reconciliation. The "flag order" had provoked such outrage in GAR quarters that it had been hastily revoked.[51]

These banners, as well as the tattered Stars and Stripes that survived the war, were prized not simply because they were national
flags but because of the specific associations they carried. Post 2 of
Philadelphia, for example, was under constant solicitation from regimental associations, civic societies, and other groups to loan out its
colors for parades, not because those organizations could not obtain
flags otherwise but because the *particular* war associations of the
Post 2 banners gave them a special significance. When veterans at the
Detroit encampment failed to march with authentic battle flags, it

was cause for complaint from at least one British observer: "Flags there were in plenty; but they were as a rule the trumpery pennons of individuals, or the brand-new gaudy banners of the different Posts, and not in the least historical or important."[52]

What was new in the flag ritualism of the 1890s was the emergence of the flag as a symbol of abstract nationalism. As late as 1889, most schoolhouses did not fly flags, such recognitions as Flag Day and the Pledge of Allegiance were not yet in existence, and the practice of taking off hats and singing at the playing of "The Star Spangled Banner" was followed only in a few localities. Even in 1898, when a second Columbia flag ceremony was to be held, university president Seth Low expressed doubt that the student band knew the tune.[53] By the turn of the century, the display of the flag at schools was law in most states, Flag Day was on its way to federal legal status, and patriotic exercises such as the Pledge of Allegiance and the singing of "The Star Spangled Banner" were commonplace.

Thus while the flag was an important symbol before 1890, it was only in the last decade of the century that the national banner acquired semisacred trappings. In that high decade of what some have called the "civil religion" of the United States, the flag was the chief icon. For Union veterans especially, what had been a banner carrying particularistic associations of battle became a universal symbol of American nationality.[54] And after American victories in Cuba and the Philippines, it seemed to some GAR zealots that the flag was destined to sweep not just the country but the planet. "A flag for the national capital; a flag for every temple of justice; a flag for every schoolhouse; a flag for all the world," Chaplain-in-Chief Frank C. Bruner exulted in a prayer opening the 1898 national encampment. "All hail the banner of the free!"[55]

Along with textbooks and flags, the GAR in the 1890s promoted patriotic instruction through military drill in the public schools. John Logan had first advocated drill for schoolboys in his 1888 history of the American volunteer; in the years before the Spanish-American War it became something of a national craze. Some advocates of school drill, of course, were primarily interested in the discipline that they thought drill would impart to unruly youths, especially the urban poor. Military instruction, they said, would teach "executive ability," "self-confidence," "subordination," "obedience and a proper respect for authority."[56]

But the virtues of order and patriotism tended to be closely linked.

The national encampment endorsed the concept of school drill in
1893 and again in 1894, the worst years in a period of depression and labor strife that lasted most of the decade. These encampments appointed "aides for military instruction in the public schools" as well as "patriotic instructors," and in some years combined the two positions. In New York City's Lafayette Post 140, the instigator of the flags-for-schools campaign was also the chief promoter of military drill.[57]

The drill movement gained a prominent spokesman in 1894, when Lafayette Post induced former president (and GAR member) Benjamin Harrison to write a national magazine article in which he called the idea "good in every aspect of it—good for the boys, good for the schools, and good for the country." Not only would drill produce better physical coordination, Harrison argued, but in a country that (here echoing Logan) "will never have a large standing army, our strength and safety are in a general dissemination of military knowledge and training among the people." Although writers for genteel magazines protested that military drill prepared boys for "fame through slaughter," schoolboy soldiering was widely popular, at least until the marching became definitely routed toward Havana. One report in 1896 found 30,000 members of an "American Guard" in sixty schools, with others in church and temperance society drill clubs. Another, in 1894, reported the existence of one hundred companies of a "Baptist Boys Brigade," drilling under army regulations with blue uniforms, guns, and cartridge boxes containing New Testaments.[58]

Harrison's call for a "general dissemination of military knowledge and training among the people" drew on the same fondness for antebellum militias that informed the GAR organizational structure, Logan's attacks on West Point, and many a "corrected" history of the Union volunteers. Like the writers of those histories, the school drill advocates looked backward in order to preserve. And like both the textbook and the flag campaigners, what they tried to preserve for schoolchildren (and through them for posterity) was more than just abstract reverence for the flag. As the *Grand Army Record* put it in 1894, "all this blow and bluster about the 'Flag,' the 'Flag,' etc., many times repeated, is merely senseless bosh, and mystifies rather than enlightens and educates unless the speaker has sufficient sense and patriotism, at the same time, to crystallize and to make clear what that emblem represents and is used for."[59] What the Union veterans sought in the text, drill, and flag agitations was a particular *version* of American nationalism that made sense in light of their own historical experience, a version in which right and wrong were apocalyptically clear, orderly militiamen filled a volunteer army, and social ills like Mormonism and pauperism disappeared in the folds of the national flag.

The Grand Army flag campaigners of the 1890s, in short, took a possessory interest in defining the "nation." But it was a peculiar kind of nationalism: one that embraced an antebellum form of liberal capitalism rather than linguistic-cultural prescription, emphasized republican preservation rather than dynamic change, and treated the Civil War as an unassailable monument rather than as an equivocal triumph. It was peculiar because it described the United States of 1860 better than it described the United States of 1890. To embrace independent producerism in 1890 was to ignore the ways in which trusts and monopoly industries were busy subverting it. To see the Union as simply "preserved" was to overlook the many things war had changed about American society, independent producerism among them. And to treat the war as an unequivocal triumph was to disregard the demise of Reconstruction and the rise of Jim Crow in the South.

Rather than acknowledging these unpleasant truths, the Union veterans drifted toward a version of the nation identified with the existing state almost to the exclusion of other characteristics. Again and again in the turbulent last decade of the nineteenth century, GAR leaders insisted on, in the *National Tribune*'s phrase, "obedience to the law under all circumstances," a position reminiscent of Grant's famous remark that the best way to secure repeal of a bad law was to enforce it. Oregon commander S. B. Ormsby perhaps put the matter most clearly during the strikes of 1894: "Whatever [the federal] government may desire to do in Oregon, it is our duty to see that it is done."[60] "Loyalty" did not mean loyalty to a nation defined by race, culture, language, or class. It did not mean loyalty to abstract principles of racial or social justice. It meant loyalty to the national state, with which the veterans were uniquely associated. It meant loyalty to the power relationships that happened to be in existence: loyalty to order itself, loyalty to the status quo. This version of the nation was well suited to middle-class white men who had more to lose than to gain from the serious social dislocations of the 1890s. But it was equally congenial to men weaned on the idea of the American nation-state as a timeless repository of virtue, with a mission in the world.

The culmination of the Grand Army's patriotic crusade was the war with Spain in 1898, an event greeted in the order with unrestrained enthusiasm, if not actual relief. Upon the declaration of hostilities, GAR members started support funds for the families of servicemen, made speeches to raise local regiments, volunteered their own services, offered their pension moneys to replace the battleship *Maine*, and flooded the commander-in-chief with "proposals of inventions, which the inventors believed were calculated to destroy the entire Spanish Army by entirely new methods."[61]

In Brockton, Webster Post and its Woman's Relief Corps formed a committee to distribute medicine, coal, and rent money to the wives of men in service, the money being raised by a public "Citizens' War League." In Chippewa Falls, Comerford Post members worked to encourage enlistments and denounced a local antiwar editor and his newspaper as "unpatriotic," "un-American," and "traitorous." In Philadelphia, Post 2 offered the services of its armed parade unit, the Post 2 Guard, to the mayor of the city, the governor of Pennsylvania, and Secretary of War Russell Alger. A few members of the post and its associated Sons of Veterans Camp 299 actually did enter active service, bringing back souvenirs of the *Maine* for the post's war relic case (among them the ship's flag, which was greeted with cheers, then sealed in a fireproof case, "to be exposed only on muster nights and special occasions").[62]

Following the quick American victory, Grand Army speakers were equally quick to describe the triumph both as the culmination of ten years of flag and textbook agitation and as the overseas extension of the Union army's millennial crusade. In New York, Lafayette Post donated six hundred American flags for the schoolhouses of newly conquered Puerto Rico. In a prayer opening the 1898 national encampment, Chaplain-in-Chief Bruner thanked God for the national flag, an "emblem that we are to carry forth for civilization and to make the nations who have been blackened by superstition and darkness, brighter and more beautiful." The flag, he said, was "a patriotic schoolhouse, a symbolism of those elements which make good government." In his formal speech, Bruner argued that both the GAR and the common school system "had a paramount significance in moulding the race into a more sublime civilization," which was now on the march. "The Union soldier ha[s] been the harbinger in the declaration of a great truth," Bruner told the delegates. " . . . The hand of God is upon it. It is the mission of the Chaplain-in-Chief to advocate this boon of heaven and give it incentive that it may outgrow sectarianism and flow to all the world."[63]

Similarly, Commander-in-Chief John P. S. Gobin's keynote address to the 1898 encampment noted that the Union veterans "for over a third of a century have taught love of country and adoration of the flag," and boasted that "our organization and our teachings during the last thirty years, has [sic] been effective in preparation for this glorious result." Like the troops of 1861, Gobin said, most of the men of 1898 were volunteer "citizen-soldiers," committed "to enforce the decrees of humanity and civilization among those who disregard their teachings"—though in this case the transgressors were "upon the islands of our adjacent seas." With proper vigilance, the commander concluded, "we believe the Nation will still continue under the providence of Almighty God to the higher position which He has evidently designed for it." John M. Thurston, senior vice commander-in-chief of the Sons of Veterans, spoke in much the same terms, lauding "a flag of growth," praising the valor of the volunteers, and telling the aged Grand Army veterans to "be gloriously content, the Union you preserved remains forever, and liberty, equal rights and justice, is your heritage to your descendents even unto the judgment day."[64]

Unfortunately for the nation of 1898—and, it could be argued, ever afterward—the rhetoric of the crusade ill fit the realities of the sordid four-month clash with Spain. The foe was obviously weak and openly conciliatory; the selfish economic interests of Americans in Cuba were too close to the surface; and in the war's aftermath, the moral dilemma of administering conquered territory became acute. Only four years earlier, Grand Army members in Pennsylvania had complained that pro-Southern school histories ignored the essentially moral nature of U.S. wars. "In but a single instance has this country engaged in war of conquest," they wrote. "Its other wars were fought to maintain a right, and always has the right triumphed. It is [as] essential that that right should begin with the war as that it should be established by the war."[65] Now, with the United States standing precisely in the position of a conqueror, the standard of moral "right" had become a difficult one to apply.

Although Cuban and Philippine independence could be, and were, construed as the overseas extension of a vital American principle of self-determination, it was not an extension hallowed by tradition. Moreover, it seemed not to be fully appreciated by its recipients. The longer the Philippine insurrection against American rule continued, and the more the American volunteers came to dislike their Cuban

allies—who, much to their surprise, turned out to be dark-skinned—
the harder it became to justify the war as a vindication of universal
rights.[66] To see civilization triumphant and the flag serving as schoolhouse to the world under such circumstances required a certain
amount of creative obliviousness.

Some sense that the war of 1898 differed from the struggle of
1861–65 appeared in the ongoing preoccupation of GAR members
with the memory of "their" war and in their refusal to amalgamate
with veterans of the more recent conflict. "They are entitled to all the
honor we can give them," Gobin said of the Spanish-American War
veterans, "and will no doubt receive the thanks of a grateful people;
they will doubtless, if they have not already done so, organize a
society of their own, but there can be no merit in their becoming
members of our organization, founded under different auspices and
based upon entirely different principles."[67] Nevertheless, Gobin and
other Grand Army speakers, like most civilians, continued to charac-
terize the new war as the glorious continuation of a national crusade.

Although the events of the Spanish-American War itself are outside the scope of this study, in at least one way the inherited millennial conception of the new war may have adversely affected the men
organizing and fighting it: by contributing to the notorious wreck of
American war preparations in Florida and Cuba. It is well known that
only 379 of the 5,807 men who died on the American side of the
conflict fell in combat. The rest, as Gerald Linderman has shown,
were victims of simple unwillingness or inability to adopt those un-
glamorous practices of camp—sanitation, clean water, proper food,
medical care—that did not fit the nation's preconception of war as a
morally charged "personal encounter" with the enemy.[68] A great deal
of the responsibility for the losses to disease, of course, rested with
the government. In its rush to award limited combat opportunities to
as many of the clamoring volunteers as possible, Alger's War Department neglected such details as food supplies, camp training, and even
ambulances. The result was a health disaster.

But even the War Department's best efforts at warding off disease
likely would not have overcome the attitudes of soldiers who, Linderman persuasively argues, saw the war as an opportunity for personal
and national glory rather than as a mundane exercise in latrine
digging and water boiling. Embarking from Tampa, the volunteers
expected a battle of clear right and wrong against an identifiable
enemy, a fight to give an enslaved people "liberty, equal rights and

justice" and to hasten the coming dawn of worldwide republican-ism—exactly the sort of war pictured at Grand Army campfires during the preceding thirty years. Arriving in Cuba, they found impersonal death by long-range rifle, debilitating disease, and an ally in many ways stranger (and, before long, more despised) than the supposed enemy.[69] In short, the ideology of war as a battle-filled moral crusade, affirmed by the only federal veterans available to advise the recruits of 1898, not only was difficult to apply to the new situation—it could actually be dangerous.

Despite the postwar revelations of these shortcomings, the patriotic boom was not dampened in the GAR or, for that matter, in the rest of the country. Whatever doubts members may have had privately about the righteousness of the cause or the waste of lives from disease, the public position of their organization was one of satisfied celebration and open chauvinism. At the 1898 encampment Commander-in-Chief Gobin described the spectacle of the United States flag flying over distant islands as "indicative of a higher civilization and a purer evangelization," while Chaplain Bruner's prayer ("We thank Thee that we are on a mighty move to bring peace to all the world") was as much self-congratulation as it was an invocation of divine blessing. As for the deaths from disease, the veterans seemed content with Alger's official explanation that disease was unavoidable and natural in war, Gobin saying only that "the Government . . . was in capable hands," while Sons of Veterans officer Thurston referred to "the necessary incidents and shortcomings" of an army put in the field in haste.[70] Certainly McKinley and Alger—both GAR members, the latter a past commander-in-chief—were in no danger of attack from the old soldiers.

Instead, the Grand Army pushed on with the campaigns it had launched a decade earlier, presenting flags to schools, pressuring publishers for patriotic texts, encouraging military drill, visiting schools on holidays. When the national encampment returned to Washington in 1902, the delegates reenacted their great march of thirty-seven years earlier, parading up Pennsylvania Avenue. Then they met on the convention floor to hear Commander-in-Chief Ell Torrance denounce anarchy; national patriotic instructor Alan C. Bakewell give a state-by-state report on textbook revision, Flag Day, and military drill; and Secretary of War Elihu Root declare that the government's harsh antiinsurgency campaign in the Philippines would "purg[e] all elements and conditions against the authority of the government of the United States."[71] The same men who had begun their march in 1865 as disorderly, localistic citizen-soldiers had ended it as defenders of order and the national state.

The irony of Grand Army cosmology in the twentieth century was that the nation the veterans had saved in 1865 no longer existed by 1900. The volunteer militias of evangelical republican legend had fought their final war in 1898, with mixed results. The ideals of independent producerism and manliness were under increasing strain in an economy of centralization and trusts. The bloody shirt had given way to Blue-Gray reunions and alms for indigent Confederates. Most important of all, the groups left on the sidewalks at the Grand Review of 1865 were demanding places in the national parade line. Inside the post room, women were still a "lovely galaxy of ministering angels"; outside, they were agitating for the vote. Inside, laborers were independent yeomen; outside, they were forming unions. Inside, black veterans continued to be relegated to second-class status; outside, writers like W. E. B. Du Bois were trying to resurrect the radical heritage of Reconstruction.[72]

The power of the GAR in the nineteenth century lay in the effective use by the Union veterans of their own group history as culture. In campfires, personal narratives, pension editorials, and the day-to-day life of their organization, the veterans constructed a history that explained both the Civil War and the nation in the millennial vocabulary of the prewar generation. At the same time, they tried to satisfy newer Victorian preferences for sentimental fraternity, order, and middle-class respectability. What emerged was a cosmology of some durability. The inherited burden of national saviorhood still hung heavy over the volunteers of 1898 (and perhaps even the recruits of 1917), while the linkage of Americanism and middle-class Victorianism would prove even harder to break. In the new century, the GAR "nation" would be a stubborn cultural obstacle in the path of all variety of revisionists: not only Du Bois but William Dunning and Charles Beard as well.

Yet the GAR worldview at bottom was an artifact of its time. Useful as it was in pension debates, it was couched in language that few in the new century understood. Whereas the Union veterans claimed only to have saved the nation, newer patriotic societies claimed to own it; whereas they practiced patriotic instruction, younger voices called for immigration restriction; whereas they stood for independence and manliness, their sons worked in large organizations. When the last Grand Army member died in 1956, the order, in all its "glorious contentment," would expire with him.

The disjunction between the old soldiers' view of the nation as a millennial republic with a civilizing mission and the reality of a burgeoning, culturally diverse population engaged in wars that were not easily construed as moral crusades did not become apparent until after the horror of World War I. It was only then that the disillusioned battle memoirs so conspicuously absent from Civil War literature began to appear. And it was only then that early critics of nationalism began to ask what the "nation" really was and where it had come from. The question seems to have faded from the scholarly agenda somewhat since then. But in an era in which virtually every public policy is justified by its relation to the "national" interest, it is a question still worth asking.

NOTES

PREFACE

1. Foner, *Reconstruction*; Mitchell, *Civil War Soldiers*; Linderman, *Embattled Courage*; Foster, *Ghosts of the Confederacy*; Maris A. Vinovskis, ed., *Toward a Social History of the American Civil War: Exploratory Essays* (New York: Cambridge University Press, 1990).

2. Mary Dearing's *Veterans in Politics* is a political history of the GAR. Aside from Dearing's national work, three studies of Union veteran involvement in politics at the state level have been made: Heck, *The Civil War Veteran in Minnesota Life and Politics*; Lankevich, "The GAR in New York State"; and Noyes, "History of the GAR in Ohio from 1866 to 1900." Primm, "The GAR in Missouri, 1866–1870," covers the early years of the order in that state. Wallace E. Davies's *Patriotism on Parade* treats the fraternal and social aspects of the GAR, but only as one among several veterans' and hereditary societies spanning a period of more than a century.

Lankevich, for one, finds GAR members in New York in support of Democrats and concludes that they supported candidates of both political parties (Lankevich, "The GAR in New York State," pp. 53–54, 168–73, 202–4, 300).

CHAPTER ONE

1. *Philadelphia Bulletin*, May 23, 1865, p. 3; *Philadelphia Inquirer*, May 25, 1865; Wainwright, *Diary of Battle*, p. 528.

2. Wainwright, *Diary of Battle*, pp. 526, 527, 528.

3. Upson, *With Sherman to the Sea*, pp. 176–77 (entry misdated May 20, 1865); Gerrish, *Army Life*, p. 297.

4. For Meade and Sherman parade orders, see n. 1 above. *Philadelphia Inquirer*, May 24, 1865, p. 1; *New York Tribune*, May 24, 1865, p. 1; *New York Times*, May 23–25, 1865, p. 1; *Philadelphia Public Ledger*, May 25, 1865, p. 1.

5. Leech, *Reveille in Washington*, p. 510; *New York Tribune*, May 24, 1865, p. 1.

6. *Philadelphia Inquirer*, May 25, 1865, p. 1.

7. *New York Times*, May 25, 1865, p. 1.

8. *Philadelphia Public Ledger*, May 22, 1865, p. 2; *New York Tribune*, May 25, 1865, p. 4; *Philadelphia Inquirer*, May 26, 1865, p. 2.

9. Weld, *War Diaries and Letters*, p. 399; Emily Apt Geer, *First Lady*, p. 78; Allen Morgan Geer, *Civil War Diary*, p. 224; *Philadelphia North American and U.S. Gazette*, May 23, 1865, p. 2.

10. Sherman, *Personal Memoirs*, 2:377.

11. *Philadelphia Inquirer*, May 24, 1865, p. 1; *Philadelphia Bulletin*, May 23, 1865, p. 3. See Associated Press dispatch in many newspapers of May 24, 1865, e.g., *New York Tribune*, p. 1.

12. *Philadelphia Inquirer*, May 25, 1865, p. 1.

13. Gerrish, *Army Life*, p. 299.

14. On the countervailing parade traditions of Philadelphia's upper-class militias and working-class burlesquers, see Davis, *Parades and Power*, pp. 49–111.

15. *Philadelphia Inquirer*, May 24 and 25, 1865, p. 1.

16. Wainwright, *Diary of Battle*, pp. 529, 530.

17. Upson, *With Sherman to the Sea*, pp. 169–75, 177; Gerrish, *Army Life*, pp. 299, 298.

18. *Boston Post*, May 23, 1865, p. 1; see also the fears of the *New York Sunday News*, March 22, 1868, reprinted in the *Soldier's Friend*, May 1868, p. 4.

19. Wainwright, *Diary of Battle*, p. 530.

20. The snub was much remarked upon in newspaper coverage of the review. Sherman mentions it himself in his *Personal Memoirs*, 2:377. One of Sherman's adjutants, Henry Hitchcock, reports in his diary about Sher-

man's "giving Stanton the cut direct *on the stand* on Pennsylvania Avenue"
(emphasis his); see *Marching with Sherman*, p. 320.

21. *Philadelphia Inquirer*, May 25, 1865, p. 1.

22. *New York Tribune*, May 25, 1865, p. 1; *New York Times*, May 25, 1865, p. 1; *Philadelphia Inquirer*, May 24, 1865, p. 1.

23. Wainwright, *Diary of Battle*, p. 527; Dearing, *Veterans in Politics*, pp. 51–52. Other accounts of the banner appear in contemporary press reports of the parade.

24. On the survival of the state-centered federal structure, see Hyman, *A More Perfect Union*. On soldiers' and civilians' local loyalties, see Mitchell, "The Northern Soldier and His Community," and also Mitchell, *Civil War Soldiers*, pp. 16–17; Doyle, *Social Order of a Frontier Community*, pp. 227–59; and Baker, *Affairs of Party*, p. 321.

25. *Philadelphia Inquirer*, May 24, 1865, p. 1; *Boston Post*, May 26, 1865, p. 1.

26. Upson, *With Sherman to the Sea*, pp. 180–81.

27. *Eau Claire* (Wis.) *Free Press*, August 17 and July 13, 1865.

28. Ibid., July 13 and 6, 1865.

29. *Boston Post*, June 1, 1865, p. 1; *Boston Transcript*, June 2, 1865, p. 1; *Boston Post*, June 14, 1865, p. 4. See reports of local testimonials in towns around Boston in *Boston Post*, June 12–15, 1865.

30. *Philadelphia Inquirer*, June 12, 1865, p. 2.

31. *Philadelphia Public Ledger*, June 10, 1865, p. 2.

32. *Philadelphia Inquirer*, June 12, 1865, pp. 1–2; *Philadelphia Public Ledger*, June 12, 1865, p. 1.

33. *Philadelphia Public Ledger*, June 10, 1865, p. 2; *Philadelphia Bulletin*, June 10, 1865, p. 4.

34. Bull, *Soldiering*, p. 248; Bloodgood, *Personal Reminiscences*, p. 219; Gerrish, *Army Life*, p. 297; Tilney, *My Life in the Army*, p. 241. In the 1890s, hundreds of Grand Army of the Republic veterans recorded "the most important events" in their army careers in "personal war sketches." The Grand Review was frequently listed, especially by former musicians— for instance, by Corporal Charles Parker, Drummer E. F. Kenrick, and Fifer James Harroll, all of St. Paul, Minnesota. These are among the personal war sketches of Acker Post 21 (box 56, v. 182A) and Garfield Post 8 (no box number, v. 230), Department of Minnesota Papers. For more on these sketches, see discussion in chap. 6.

35. "The Reunion of the Grand Army of the Republic," p. 655; *Journal of the National Encampment*, 1892, "unofficial proceedings," p. 298. (The last flourish regarding Sheridan was a bit of fancy. Sheridan was not at the Grand Review, having already departed for Texas and a post as a military governor.) For similar comments, see General Order #2, Oregon Department Commander H. H. Northrup, August 10, 1892, Oregon Collection, GAR Papers; and *New York Times*, September 21, 1892, p. 1.

36. Harte, "A Second Review of the Grand Army," in *Writings of Bret Harte*, pp. 17–19.

37. Long, *The Civil War Day by Day*, p. 705; United States Bureau of the Census, *Historical Statistics of the United States*, ser. A119–134, p. 15; Vinovskis, "Have Social Historians Lost the Civil War?," pp. 3–7.

38. *Historical Statistics of the United States*, ser. A119–134, p. 15; ser. Y-135, pp. 1079–80; and ser. Y-27, p. 1072; United States Bureau of the Census, *Compendium of the Eleventh Census, 1890*, pt. 3, pp. 572–86.

CHAPTER TWO

1. Dearing, *Veterans in Politics*, pp. 113–47, esp. pp. 134–47.

2. On the reduction of the army, see Huntington, *The Soldier and the State*, pp. 226–30.

3. *Proceedings of the National Encampment*, 1869, p. 33.

4. See, for example, the fears of the *New York Sunday News*, March 22, 1868, reprinted in the *Soldier's Friend*, May 1868, p. 4; *Boston Post*, May 23, 1865, p. 1.

5. Long, *The Civil War Day by Day*, p. 705; Wiley, *Life of Billy Yank*, p. 303; Rorabaugh, "Who Fought for the North?", pp. 695–701.

6. Beath, *History of the GAR*, pp. 659–81; "Patriotic Societies of the Civil War"; Heck, *The Civil War Veteran in Minnesota Life and Politics*, pp. 70–83. On the traumas faced by Confederate veterans, see Foster, *Ghosts of the Confederacy*, pp. 11–35; Donald, "Generation of Defeat," pp. 7–18.

7. Thomas Leonard, *Above the Battle*, p. 15.

8. *Proceedings of the National Encampment*, 1879, p. 645; *Journal of the National Encampment*, 1885, p. 234.

9. On the understandable nature of the Civil War, see Thomas Leonard, *Above the Battle*, pp. 9–24, esp. pp. 9–13. Leonard argues, however, that the veterans tended to remember the war as being more orderly and understandable than it actually had been. Such selective memory kept soldiers in later, even more chaotic wars from understanding what was happening to them.

10. From "Picket Shots," a column of letters from readers in the *National Tribune*, February 10, 1887.

11. On the World War I experience, see Leed, *No Man's Land*, pp. 125–28, 150–52, 180–86.

12. Ibid.; Turner, *The Ritual Process*, pp. 94–130.

13. Leed, *No Man's Land*, pp. 12–33, 73–75.

14. Ibid., p. 14.

15. *Boston Post*, June 12, 1865, p. 1; Dearing, *Veterans in Politics*, pp. 56–57.

16. Leed, *No Man's Land*, pp. 200–203; Tuttle, *Race Riot*, pp. 10–31.

17. Stephenson, *Dr. B. F. Stephenson*; Dearing, *Veterans in Politics*, p. 81; Robert B. Beath, preface to *Proceedings of the Pennsylvania Department Encampment, 1867–72*, p. vii.

18. Dearing, *Veterans in Politics*, p. 84. On the political origins of the

GAR and the election of 1868, see ibid., pp. 80–184, and Beath, *History of the GAR*, pp. 33–52.

19. Among other early officers, for example, 1866 Commander-in-Chief Stephen Hurlbut was elected state senator and later named ambassador to Peru by President Grant; 1866 Senior Vice Commander-in-Chief James McKean was elected to Congress and became a judge in Utah; 1866 Chaplain William Pile served in Congress and as Grant's ambassador to Venezuela; and Logan's junior vice commander, Joseph Hawley, became governor of Connecticut. Beath, *History of the GAR*, pp. 68–378, gives capsule biographies of these and other officers through 1884.

20. General Order #6, Commander-in-Chief John Logan, February 18, 1868, National General Orders Book, Sons of Union Veterans Collection.

21. *Proceedings of the National Encampment*, 1869, p. 35; Oliver M. Wilson, *The GAR under Its First Constitution and Ritual*, p. 153.

22. Dearing, *Veterans in Politics*, pp. 1–49; Fredrickson, *Inner Civil War*, pp. 177–80, 225–28; Holmes, cited in ibid., p. 220; and on martial language in antebellum campaigns, see Baker, *Affairs of Party*, pp. 287–91.

23. *Proceedings of the National Encampment*, 1869, p. 36.

24. Ibid., pp. 40, 41; on the debt and inability to fund an inspector, see ibid., 1870, p. 83.

25. From Beath's report as assistant adjutant-general, *Proceedings of the Pennsylvania Department Encampment*, 1867–72, p. 50.

26. The first committees are recorded in the reconstructed minutes of the meeting of January 28, 1867, in Post 2 Minutes, Sons of Union Veterans Collection.

27. On the badge and local productions of it, see Beath, *History of the GAR*, pp. 653–57, and *Journal of the National Encampment*, 1883, p. 120. Adjutant General William Collins complains about the frequent changes of ritual in *Proceedings of the National Encampment*, 1870, p. 85.

28. The best evidence of variation in the rituals is in the department inspectors' reports once the system became established in the late 1870s. There the inspectors rate post performances of the ritual and state whether the officers performing it have memorized their parts completely, partially, or not at all. See also the clip from the *Scout and Mail* in the *Grand Army Record*, July 1889, p. 8.

29. *Proceedings of the National Encampment*, 1869, p. 47.

30. Ibid., pp. 37, 36.

31. On Masonic degrees, see Dumenil, *Freemasonry and American Culture*, pp. 32–41. The GAR grade system proposal is laid out in *Proceedings of the National Encampment*, 1869, pp. 64–67. Oliver Wilson says that he warned Shaw that grades were a bad idea; *The GAR under Its First Constitution and Ritual*, p. 152.

32. *Ritual of the GAR* (hereafter *Ritual*), 1869, p. 14; *Rules and Regulations for the Government of the GAR* (hereafter *Rules and Regulations*), 1869, chap. 1, art. 5.

33. Beath, *History of the GAR*, p. 100; on the Red Men's Adoption Degree, see Carnes, *Secret Ritual*, pp. 98–104.

34. *Proceedings of the National Encampment*, 1869, p. 64.

35. General Orders #11 and #12, Pennsylvania Department Commander Oliver C. Bosbyshell, October 15 and November 19, 1869, Pennsylvania Department General Orders Book, Sons of Union Veterans Collection.

36. See, for example, Post 2 Minutes, January 3 and 10 and February 13, 1870; May 25, 1871; and, on the remission of dues, January 20, 1870, Sons of Union Veterans Collection.

37. *Proceedings of the National Encampment*, 1870, pp. 83, 88.

38. Beath, *History of the GAR*, pp. 379ff; membership figure from ibid., p. 651.

39. *Rules and Regulations*, 1869, chap. 5, art. 11; see also *Proceedings of the National Encampment*, 1869, p. 73.

40. Personal war sketch volume of Acker Post 21, St. Paul, Minnesota, box 56, v. 182A, Department of Minnesota Papers; *Journal of the National Encampment*, 1883, p. 121; *New York Times*, August 28, 1879, p. 5.

41. Oliver M. Wilson, *The GAR under Its First Constitution and Ritual*, p. 173.

42. Other frequent disputes included arguments over what privileges came with which ranks (56 cases) and over the legality of courts-martial (40 cases). Since some decisions touched on more than one issue (a court-martial ruling dealing with privileges of rank, for example), these categories are necessarily approximations. Most decisions, however, were single rulings on single disputes. The tabulation is made from the rulings in Carnahan, *Decisions and Opinions* for cases before 1884, and from the judge advocate-generals' reports in the *Journals of the National Encampment* for subsequent years. The 378 cases are classified according to the judge advocate-general's perception of the main issue involved, as indicated in his synopsis.

43. Carnahan, *Decisions and Opinions*, pp. 50–51; Post 2 Minutes, April 27 and May 4, 1876, Sons of Union Veterans Collection; *Journal of the National Encampment*, 1881, p. 752; ibid., 1889, p. 110; Beath, *Blue Book*, 1884, p. 53.

44. *Baltimore Sun*, October 14, 1880, p. 1; Post 2 Minutes, August 25, 1887, Sons of Union Veterans Collection; *National Tribune*, October 22, 1881, p. 4.

45. Oliver M. Wilson, *The GAR under Its First Constitution and Ritual*, pp. 156–57; 173–78; 68; 195. See also Wilson's comments on the grade system, pp. 151–55, 182, 188.

46. This version is as recited by Commander-in-Chief William Warner at Milwaukee, *Journal of the National Encampment*, 1889, p. 34. The verse was a staple of soldiers' reunions.

47. *Proceedings of the National Encampment*, 1871, p. 114.

48. Beath, *History of the GAR*, p. 100.

49. Oliver M. Wilson, *The GAR under Its First Constitution and Ritual,*

p. 9.

50. Ibid., pp. 146, 171.

51. General Order #7, Pennsylvania Department Commander James F. Morrison, October 27, 1899, Pennsylvania Department General Orders Book, Sons of Union Veterans Collection.

52. *Journal of the National Encampment,* 1884, p. 246.

53. Oliver M. Wilson, *The GAR under Its First Constitution and Ritual,* p. 182.

54. *Rules and Regulations,* 1869, chap. 1, art. 2.

55. On the railroads' innovations in the management of large organizations, see the work of Alfred D. Chandler, Jr., esp. *The Visible Hand,* pp. 81–187, and "Organization of Manufacturing and Transportation," pp. 137–65. On the problems of discipline in Civil War armies, see Shannon, *Organization and Administration of the Union Army,* 1:151–92; Mitchell, *Civil War Soldiers,* pp. 56–59; McPherson, *Ordeal by Fire,* pp. 169–73; Paludan, *A People's Contest,* pp. 56–60; Donald, "Died of Democracy."

56. Faust, "Christian Soldiers," pp. 72–77; Fredrickson, *Inner Civil War,* pp. 98–112, 166–98; Weber, *Northern Railroads in the Civil War,* p. 232; Chandler, *The Visible Hand,* p. 95; Livesay, *Andrew Carnegie,* p. 33; Paludan, *A People's Contest,* pp. 142–43. On the war and industrialization, see Cochran, "Did the Civil War Retard Industrialization?"; the essays by Stephen Salsbury and Stanley L. Engerman in Andreano, *Economic Impact of the American Civil War,* pp. 167–209; and Wright, "The More Enduring Consequences of America's Wars."

57. Post 2 Minutes, July 23, 1877, Sons of Union Veterans Collection; *Journal of the National Encampment, 1889,* p. 34.

58. Carnahan, *Decisions and Opinions,* p. 30.

59. Ibid., pp. 34–35; *Journal of the National Encampment,* 1891, pp. 160–62.

60. Carnahan, *Decisions and Opinions,* p. 162; *Journal of the National Encampment,* 1890, pp. 56–60; ibid., 1891, pp. 139–40; ibid., 1887, pp. 103–7; ibid., 1888, pp. 99–100.

61. Carnahan, *Decisions and Opinions,* p. 154; *Journal of the National Encampment,* 1887, p. 107; ibid., 1892, p. 160.

62. *Rules and Regulations,* chap. 5, art. 6.

63. Figures for Philadelphia posts are culled from convictions published in Pennsylvania Department General Orders, 1875–1900, Sons of Union Veterans Collection. For the elaborate court-martial form, see Beath et al., *Manual,* pp. 31–39.

64. Dumenil, *Freemasonry and American Culture,* pp. 80–88. For two typical GAR cases, see Fletcher Webster Post 13 (Brockton, Mass.) Minutes, August 23 and 30 and September 6, 20, and 27, 1877; and James Comerford Post 68 (Chippewa Falls, Wis.) Minutes, October 21 and November 4, 1885, Local Post Records Collection.

65. Post 2 Minutes, September 14 and 21 and October 26, 1893, Sons of

Union Veterans Collection; Proceedings of Post Court-martial, Garfield Post 8, St. Paul, Minnesota, September 30, 1886, versus Edwin J. Walsh, Minnesota GAR Records (53.I.10.10F).

66. Webster Post Minutes, July 19 and 26 and August 9, 1877.

67. *Journal of the National Encampment*, 1884, pp. 178–80; General Order #5, Department Commander A. Wilson Norris, December 29, 1874, Pennsylvania Department General Orders Book, Sons of Union Veterans Collection; *Journal of the National Encampment*, 1886, pp. 112–14.

68. Carnahan, *Decisions and Opinions*, p. 43.

69. Ibid., pp. 68, 94, 97.

70. Ibid., pp. 96, 153; *Proceedings of the National Encampment*, 1874, p. 297; ibid., 1876, p. 411; ibid., 1878, pp. 559–60.

71. Webster Post Minutes, January 12, 1887; *Grand Army Record*, February 1889, p. 4.

72. Minnesota Department Adjutant's Notebook, February 17, 1890, Minnesota GAR Records (53.I.9.7B).

73. *Grand Army Record*, September 1886, p. 4; *National Tribune*, August 14, 1884, p. 4; Lankevich, "The GAR in New York State," p. 199; *Journal of the National Encampment*, 1886, pp. 153–67.

74. Letter to *Grand Army Record*, June 1895, p. 48.

75. Carnahan, comp., *Decisions and Opinions*, p. 167.

76. *Journal of the National Encampment*, 1891, p. 165.

77. Compare the *Rules and Regulations* of 1869 with subsequent editions through 1899; similarly, compare the *Blue Book* of 1884 with subsequent revisions.

78. *Journal of the National Encampment*, 1887, p. 145; letter, Minnesota Department Adjutant to Junior Vice Department Commander C. H. Parker, January 29, 1890, Department Adjutant's Notebook, Minnesota GAR Records (53.I.9.7B).

79. Letter to *Grand Army Record*, September 1897, p. 68.

80. Beath, *Blue Book*, 1895, p. 4.

81. Cunliffe, *Soldiers and Civilians*, pp. 186–92, esp. p. 188; Davis, *Parades and Power*, pp. 58–67. British volunteer militias in the nineteenth century also served largely as social outlets; see Cunningham, *The Volunteer Force*, pp. 103–26. On life in the earliest American militias, see Fred Anderson, *A People's Army*, and Shy, *A People Numerous and Armed*, esp. pp. 23–33.

82. Cunliffe, *Soldiers and Civilians*, p. 192.

83. Ibid., p. 230.

84. *New York Times*, April 2, 1878, p. 4; Bierce, "The Wooden Guns," in *Fantastic Fables*, pp. 23–24; Linderman, *Mirror of War*, p. 66; Reinders, "Militia and Public Order," pp. 91–94. The *Times* editorial was penned after what the editors regarded as the dismal performance of the Pennsylvania militias in quelling the railroad strikes of 1877. The militias sent to Pittsburgh, the *Times* said, "have drifted, demoralized, piecemeal back to Philadelphia" after "fatally blundering. . . . Three or four well-drilled regi-

ments and battalions have always done the show work for the State, and the rest of the system has been one of shreds and patches" (*New York Times*, July 26, 1877, p. 4).

85. On the New Jersey joint encampments, see *New York Times*, August 30, 1878, p. 2; September 13, 1881, p. 5; September 6, 1883, p. 5. At many national encampments, state militia companies paraded with the veterans. Philadelphia's Post 2 also sponsored competitive shooting matches and at one point entertained a proposal, later withdrawn, to share a new armory with the Pennsylvania National Guard. See, for example, *Springfield Republican*, June 5, 1878, in Post 2 Scrapbooks; Post 2 Minutes, September 9, 1881; October 5, 1882; September 30 and November 4, 1886; Sons of Union Veterans Collection.

86. Post 2 Minutes, July 23 and 26 and August 2, 1877; *Proceedings of the National Encampment*, 1878, p. 522; letters, J. T. Hickman (commander of Post 2 Guard) to Philadelphia Mayor Charles Warwick, Pennsylvania Governor Daniel H. Hastings and Secretary of War Russell Alger, June 2 and 3, 1898, inserted in Post 2 Minutes of July 30, 1898, Sons of Union Veterans Collection. Letter, Henry P. Marvin to Comerford Post, April 23, 1898, ser. 1, box 12, Local Post Records Collection.

87. Cunliffe, *Soldiers and Civilians*, p. 191; Davis, *Parades and Power*, pp. 73–111.

88. Pittsburgh *Telegraph*, July 31, 1882, recorded as part of "unofficial proceedings" of Gettysburg summer encampment in *Proceedings of the Pennsylvania Department Encampment*, 1882, pp. 210–12; *Philadelphia Times* account, recorded as part of "unofficial proceedings" of Bellefonte summer encampment in ibid., 1884, p. 277. Susan Davis has pointed out the continuity of such transvestism with older folk burlesques of authority (*Parades and Power*, p. 106).

89. Comerford Post Minutes, October 16 and November 6, 1889, Local Post Records Collection; Webster Post Minutes, October 25, 1893; Post 2 Minutes, February 6, 1873, Sons of Union Veterans Collection.

90. *Journal of the National Encampment*, 1884, p. 35; ibid., 1873, p. 53; ibid., 1887, pp. 93, 112.

91. Ibid., 1892, p. 48.

92. Ibid., 1884, p. 247.

CHAPTER THREE

1. *Journal of the National Encampment*, 1889, p. 34.

2. Tabulation of post memberships and total veteran populations in the three cities is from the following sources: Comerford Post Quarterly Reports, 1885 and 1895, ser. 1, box 11, Local Post Records Collection; manuscript State of Wisconsin special census of surviving Union soldiers and sailors, 1885 and 1895, reels 27 and 38, State Historical Society of Wisconsin; Webster Post Adjutants' Quarterly Report, 1890, Massachusetts State

House Collection; *Proceedings of the Pennsylvania Department Encampment*, 1890, pp. 213–25; United States Bureau of the Census, *Compendium of the Eleventh Census, 1890*, tables 101 and 102, pp. 583–86. National figures are from *Journal of the National Encampment*, 1890, p. 79, and *Compendium of the Eleventh Census, 1890*, 3:573.

3. Statistics in the remainder of this chapter on the membership of the Philadelphia, Brockton, and Chippewa Falls posts, unless otherwise indicated, are tabulated from the records of the posts themselves. For a more extensive treatment of the posts, see McConnell, "Who Joined the Grand Army?" For a fuller description of the records used, see McConnell, "A Social History of the GAR," pp. 114–16 (n. 19). For Philadelphia Post 2, the primary documents are the post Descriptive Books, 1866–1900; Business Directory, 1886; Roster, 1896; and Minutes, 1866–67 and 1870–1900, all in the Sons of Union Veterans Collection. For Fletcher Webster Post 13 of Brockton, the primary documents are the Adjutants' Quarterly Reports, 1873–1900, Massachusetts State House Collection; 1886 Roster, published in the *Grand Army Record*, April 1886, p. 6; Bureau of the Census, 1890 special census of Union veterans and widows, National Archives (M123, reel 11); Brockton city directories, 1869–70, 1876–77, 1882, 1889, 1894–95 and 1900, Brockton Public Library; and Webster Post Minutes, 1876–93, which were made available from the private collection of Mr. Ken Oakley, Randolph, Mass. For James Comerford Post 68 of Chippewa Falls, the primary sources are the Adjutants' Quarterly Reports, 1883–97; Minutes and Membership Applications, 1883–1900; and Roster, 1889, all in ser. 1, boxes 10–13, Local Post Records Collection. Those sources were supplemented by information from French, *Chippewa Falls, Wisconsin*; Chippewa Falls city directory, 1907, Library of Congress; city directories, 1883, 1885, 1893–94 and 1894–95, Chippewa County Historical Society; city directories, 1887–88 and 1889–90, Area Research Center, University of Wisconsin at Eau Claire; Bureau of the Census, 1890 special census of Union veterans and widows, National Archives (M123, reel 116); Forrester, *History and Biographical Album of the Chippewa Valley*; and *History of Northern Wisconsin*.

4. *Proceedings of the Pennsylvania Department Encampment*, 1867–1872, pp. vi and vii. The connection of fraternal orders to urbanization was, of course, made long ago by Arthur M. Schlesinger in *The Rise of the City* (1933). Wallace Davies, a student of Schlesinger's, makes the same point regarding the GAR and other patriotic societies in *Patriotism on Parade*.

5. Descriptive Book, Cavalry Post 363, MG-60, box 7, Pennsylvania Historical and Museum Commission Archives (hereafter PHMC Archives); Lankevich, "The GAR in New York States," pp. 110–14; on black posts, see *National Tribune*, February 10, 1867, p. 6. On residential segregation, see Baltzell, *Philadelphia Gentlemen*, pp. 173–222; Jackson, *Crabgrass Frontier*, pp. 99–102, 114–15; Sam Bass Warner, *Streetcar Suburbs*.

6. The top posts usually can be found in the "unofficial proceedings" of

the national encampments, hosting dinners or providing escorts to national
officers. See, for example, the "unofficial proceedings" attached to *Proceedings of the National Encampment*, 1876, pp. 420–28, at Philadelphia, when Post 2 was the host; or ibid., 1877, pp. 490–507, when Prescott Post 1 of Providence was host.

7. Childs, *Recollections*, pp. 131–37. Post 2 Minutes, September 15, 1887; November 20, 1889; and October 23, 1886, Sons of Union Veterans Collection. Post 2 adjutant E. G. Lippert later said that he had been asked to allow Grant to join Post 2 in a specially arranged muster ceremony but had rejected the idea because "whilst Post 2 would be very glad and honored to have the General in our Post, yet we could not go out of our way to coax any man to become a member of Post 2" (*Philadelphia Ledger and Transcript*, December 21, 1879, in Post 2 Scrapbooks, Sons of Union Veterans Collection). This explanation was somewhat disingenuous, since the post had done exactly that in 1866, offering to muster General John Geary at any time and place he found convenient (Post 2 Minutes, November 20, 1866, Sons of Union Veterans Collection).

8. *Proceedings of the National Encampment*, 1876, pp. 420–42; Post 2 Minutes, September and October 1899, Sons of Union Veterans Collection; *Proceedings of the National Encampment*, 1877, pp. 483–84; ibid., 1878, p. 569.

9. *Springfield Republican*, June 5, 1878; *Providence Morning Star*, June 28, 1877, both in Post 2 Scrapbooks, Sons of Union Veterans Collection.

10. Rejectees were identified from Post 2 Minutes, 1866–1900, Sons of Union Veterans Collection. In addition to the rejectees, nine other recruits were allowed to withdraw their applications before a vote when it looked as though they would fail, a tactic barred by a post bylaw between 1879 and 1888. In all, fewer than 3 percent of Post 2 applicants were blackballed.

11. Rejectees were identified from Department of Pennsylvania General Orders, 1875–95, in Pennsylvania Department General Orders Book, Sons of Union Veterans Collection; sizes of posts were determined from report of the department inspector in *Proceedings of the Pennsylvania Department Encampment*, 1896, pp. 168–83.

12. *Philadelphia Transcript*, February 16, 1879, in Post 2 Scrapbooks, Sons of Union Veterans Collection; *Veteran*, September 1891, p. 10; Lankevich, "The GAR in New York State," p. 114.

13. For a study of the way social organizations (including a Union veterans' club, the Union Veterans' Union) served to integrate the commercial elite of Wilkes-Barre, Pa., see Edward J. Davies, "Class and Power in the Anthracite Region."

14. The occupational categories employed here are basically those used by Stephen Thernstrom in *The Other Bostonians*, app. B, pp. 240–72, which in turn are only slight modifications of categories devised by a census statistician in the 1930s. The major modification I have made is to create a separate category of "proprietors." That change follows one made

in the same scheme by Dumenil in *Freemasonry and American Culture,* app. B, pp. 226–29, and for the same reasons: First, I was working with records that do not permit the kinds of fine distinctions among levels of property ownership that Thernstrom's census figures allow; second, I was interested in studying clientage within the GAR. Because of differences in our samples, it seemed wise to create three other categories not used by Thernstrom—active duty military men, farmers, and those who were retired or listed no occupation. Finally, gaps in the early data, especially in Brockton, made a category of "unknowns" necessary. For a comparison with seventy-nine other posts in Pennsylvania and Wisconsin, see McConnell, "A Social History of the GAR," app. C. For comparable data on the class composition of some other nineteenth century lodges (Masons, Knights of Pythias, Odd Fellows), see Clawson, *Constructing Brotherhood,* tables 3:1–3:4 (pp. 95, 97–98, 100).

15. The lack of property data makes it impossible to distinguish between petty and large proprietors, a problem that Dumenil acknowledges in using the same category. Some wealthy individuals probably are included among the proprietors, just as some minor contractors probably are among the major ones included in the high-status category and some small business owners probably are among the skilled workers.

16. The actual number of members in this class probably was somewhat lower than that indicated by the membership data because clerk and bookkeeper positions typically were first jobs for young men who later became managers, proprietors, or executives. Especially between 1866 and 1880, when more than half of those listed as low-status, white-collar employees in Post 2 joined the order, the "clerks" could have been men just entering the workplace (most were in their thirties), who later attained more-prestigious white-collar jobs. On the other hand, Post 2 continued to draw large numbers of low-status, white-collar workers even in the 1880s and 1890s—100 in the 1880s and 83 in the 1890s, compared with 245 between 1866 and 1880. By then, most applicants were over forty—too old to be considered clerks just starting out. Although not conclusive, these later data may indicate that many of the applicants of the early years who were listed as "clerks" and "bookkeepers" actually remained clerks and bookkeepers.

17. Descriptive Books of Posts 21, 22, 23, 76, and 94, MG-60, boxes 5 and 6, PHMC Archives.

18. For all posts, offices included in this tabulation are post commander, senior and junior vice commander, quartermaster, surgeon, chaplain, officer of the day, officer of the guard, adjutant, sergeant major, quartermaster sergeant, and the several members chosen as delegates to the annual department encampments. Of the two trustees in question, one "clerk," Oliver C. Bosbyshell, is later listed by the post business directory of 1886 as working in the city controller's office and seems to have been employed even later as an official of the U.S. Mint. The other, Abram G. Rapp, is listed as a bookkeeper at the time of his application in 1874. Although that

may have remained his occupation, the impressionistic evidence makes one suspicious. For one thing, he was once post chaplain, a position usually reserved for a veteran of high status. In addition, he was elected delegate to the department encampment six times between 1884 and 1899, an honor not generally conferred on wage workers since it involved an extended trip out of town.

19. Rejectees in Post 2 were identified from Post 2 Minutes; occupations were compiled from circulars announcing applicants in Post 2 Scrapbooks, both in Sons of Union Veterans Collection.

20. Letter, Post 2 Adjutant Charles F. Kennedy to "Frank" [Taylor], March 10, 1887, Adjutant's Letterpress Book, Sons of Union Veterans Collection; *Ritual*, 1869, pp. 10, 12, 14; for a case in which "friendly discussion" continued even *after* the balloting, see the case of Orrin Bosworth, Webster Post Minutes, May 27, June 17, July 15 and 22, and August 5, 1885.

21. On the GAR initiation ceremony, see chap. 4; on the father-son theme in Gilded Age fraternal rituals, see Carnes, *Secret Ritual*, 94–127.

22. List of proposers compiled from Post 2 Minutes, 1877, and Post 2 Orders Book, 1878–87, both in Sons of Union Veterans Collection.

23. The prominence of building contractors is even more apparent in Post 2's Business Directory of 1886, Sons of Union Veterans Collection; for another post dominated by members in the building trades, see the Descriptive Book of Post 591, Bryn Mawr, MG-60, box 8, PHMC Archives. In addition to the directory, Post 2 kept a rack for members' business cards in its anteroom.

24. Bedford, *Socialism and the Workers in Massachusetts*, pp. 107–36; Brockton Board of Trade, *Manual*, pp. 64–65; "Brockton, A City of Enterprise," pp. 67–80; Webster Post Minutes, July 23, 1890.

25. Because some of the early records of Webster and Comerford posts have been lost, occupational and birthplace data on members of these posts are less complete than those for Post 2. In the text, percentages are given relative to the number of members for whom a given characteristic (occupation, birthplace, rank, duration of membership) is known. In Brockton, it is something of a problem in this period to distinguish between "shoemakers" and "shoe manufacturers." The post, however, seems to have been aware of the distinction in recording occupations. A check through Brockton city directories reveals that all of those listed in the post records as "shoe manufacturers" are also listed in the directories as heads of manufacturing establishments. None of those identified by the post as "shoemaker" is so listed.

26. Brockton Board of Trade, *Manual*, p. 65.

27. Distinguishing semiskilled shoe factory operatives from skilled shoemakers also is a difficulty. Although not a perfect solution, those listed as "shoemakers" in post records were classified as semiskilled unless the city directories listed them as proprietors of small shoe shops or as shoe repairmen.

28. Webster Post Minutes, March 4, 1880, and May 19, 1881; information on Sturtevant and Handy from Webster Post Adjutants' Quarterly Reports, Massachusetts State House Collection; on arrearages, see McConnell, "Who Joined the Grand Army?," table 6.4.

29. Dumenil, *Freemasonry and American Culture*, p. 40, indicates the importance of fraternal funerals to Masons; Clawson, *Constructing Brotherhood*, pp. 34–35 and 42–43, traces the practice back to early modern guilds and religious fraternities.

30. Webster Post Minutes, April 7 and 14, 1886.

31. French, *Chippewa Falls Wisconsin*, pp. 137–41; *Chippewa County, Past and Present*, p. 151.

32. Comerford Post Minutes, March 15, 1883, Local Post Records Collection.

33. 1903 *Roster* of George Thomas Post 5, Chicago, pp. 53–75, Special Collections, Chicago Public Library. Of this post's 981 members, 296 had served in Illinois regiments, 595 in regiments of other states, and 90 in United States service.

34. Compare the memberships of Posts 34 (Whitewater), 129 (Neenah), 130 (Fond du Lac) and 207 (Marinette), as tabulated in McConnell, "A Social History of the GAR," app. C.

35. Comerford Post Adjutants' Quarterly Reports, 1888; muster fee from Comerford Post Minutes, April 4, 1883, Local Post Records Collection.

36. Comerford Post Adjutants' Quarterly Reports, 1884, Local Post Records Collection.

37. Doyle, *Social Order of a Frontier Community*, esp. pp. 92–118; Alcorn, "Leadership and Stability," pp. 685–702. Similar patterns are found in the host of studies of transience: see Curti, *Making of an American Community*; Barron, *Those Who Stayed Behind*; Katz, Doucet, and Stern, "Migration and the Social Order"; Robbins, "Opportunity and Persistence"; and Underwood, *Town Building*.

38. Howieson is listed variously in Chippewa Falls city directories between 1883 and 1907 as a millwright, foreman, carpenter, carpentry contractor, and mechanic—another illustration of the difficulty of assigning a single occupation to a member. Three of the eight directories list Howieson as a millwright, which in this case seems to have meant a builder of sawmills. In 1874, Howieson erected a $2,000 house for himself in the city, a rather lavish dwelling if he was only a carpenter, and in 1879 he was elected a city alderman (*Chippewa Herald*, January 2, 1874, and March 28, 1879).

39. Proposers in Comerford Post were tabulated from Membership Applications and Minutes, 1883–1900, Local Post Records Collection.

40. In Post 2, for example, 20 percent of those in high-status white-collar occupations were former commissioned officers, compared with 14 percent of the low-status white-collar employees and 9 percent of the skilled workers.

41. Post 2 Minutes, June 25, September 3 and 24, 1885, Sons of Union Veterans Collection. Data on Post 2 rejectees were compiled from Pennsyl-

vania Department General Orders Book, 1878–87, and the Post 2 Descriptive Books, Black Book, Minutes, and 1896 Roster, all in Sons of Union Veterans Collection. Rejectees from Comerford Post are identified from Membership Applications, 1883–1900, Local Post Records Collection.

42. The best estimate for the Union Army is 13.9 percent (277,401 wounded out of approximately 2 million who served); see Long, *The Civil War Day by Day*, pp. 710–11. On the higher casualty rates in the Army of the Potomac, see McPherson, *Ordeal by Fire*, p. 479.

43. Tanner was appointed commissioner of pensions by President Benjamin Harrison. Fairchild was elected governor of Wisconsin and later served as U.S. consul in Liverpool and Paris; he also was commander-in-chief of the GAR in 1887. The elevation of wounded members to high office is yet another way in which the GAR differed from civilian orders such as the Masons, which usually rejected disabled applicants; see Carnes, *Secret Ritual*, pp. 142–43.

44. For all posts, commissioned officers include generals, colonels, majors, and captains. Noncommissioned officers include lieutenants, sergeants, and corporals, and—in the navy—engineers, ensigns, and mates. The category of "privates" also includes naval seamen and landsmen. Separate classifications were made for surgeons and chaplains, and for those who served in noncombat roles—cooks, quartermasters, teamsters, adjutants, musicians. On the higher casualty rates among Union officers, see McPherson, *Ordeal by Fire*, p. 173.

45. For a comparison of members' and nonmembers' ranks and service terms in Brockton and Chippewa Falls, see McConnell, "Who Joined the Grand Army?," Tables 6.5 and 6.6.

46. Post 5 Descriptive Book, MG-60, box 5, PHMC Archives.

47. The cemetery plot is still in existence; a list appended to Comerford Post Minutes for 1893 gives the names of some of the members buried there, and a check of the tombstones reveals those buried after 1893. On Goldsmith, see Comerford Post Minutes, November 22, 1887, Local Post Records Collection; on the National Christian Association, see Carnes, *Secret Ritual*, pp. 72–79, 88–89.

48. United States Bureau of the Census, *Compendium of the Eleventh Census, 1890*, tables 101 and 102, pp. 583–86. Annual debates on the issue of black veterans in the GAR begin in the *Journal of the National Encampment* of 1887 and continue well into the 1890s; see discussion in chap. 7, and also Wallace E. Davies, "The Problem of Race Segregation in the GAR." On racism in other Gilded Age fraternal orders, see Clawson, *Constructing Brotherhood*, pp. 132–35.

49. Whether immigrants joined the Union Army in proportion to their share of the antebellum population is another question. Although the most extensive treatment of the subject, Ella Lonn's *Foreigners in the Union Army and Navy* (1952), seems to indicate that they did, more recent studies argue that they did not. See McPherson, *Ordeal by Fire*, pp. 358–59; Vinovskis, "Have Social Historians Lost the Civil War?," pp. 16–17;

Rorabaugh, "Who Fought for the North?," p. 697. Kemp, "Community and War," pp. 67–68, suggests that immigrants were underrepresented among early volunteers but overrepresented among those recruited later through the offer of bounties.

50. Compare the occupational structures of other Pennsylvania and Wisconsin posts in McConnell, "A Social History of the GAR," app. C.

51. Post 2 Minutes, October 30, 1879, Sons of Union Veterans Collection.

52. Post 2 Minutes, May 30, 1878; November 8 and 15, 1877; April 28, 1881; July 22 and August 26, 1886; Sons of Union Veterans Collection. Many dispensations for Post 8 are included among the voluminous, but only partially organized, records of the post in Minnesota GAR Records.

53. Comerford Post Minutes, May 21, 1890, Local Post Records Collection; Webster Post Minutes show many meetings "opened and closed without form" and at least twenty-one same-night musters. Another way around the one-week layover provision was to have the department issue a "blanket" dispensation to muster new members whenever the post found it convenient, a practice deplored by successive commanders-in-chief.

54. *Proceedings of the National Encampment*, 1872, pp. 175, 187; *Rules and Regulations*, 1872, chap. 3, art. 2, and chap. 4, art. 2.

55. See, for example, the letter of D. T. Brock to the *Grand Army Record*, September 1886, p. 3.

56. Post 2 Minutes, May 1, June 5, and December 11, 1884, Sons of Union Veterans Collection; Webster Post Minutes, December 2 and 9, 1880; Comerford Post Minutes, December 5, 1883, Local Post Records Collection.

57. Letter of D. T. Brock to *Grand Army Record*, September 1886, p. 3; *Journal of the National Encampment*, 1886, pp. 193–94; ibid., 1887, pp. 247, 248; ibid., 1888, p. 187; ibid., 1889, pp. 181–85; ibid., 1890, pp. 179–92.

58. *Journal of the National Encampment*, 1890, p. 187; ibid., 1889, p. 182.

59. Webster Post Minutes, December 2 and 9, 1880; August 3, 1887; December 12, 1888.

60. *Grand Army Record*, June 1897, p. 44; *Brockton* (Mass.) *Enterprise*, May 20, 1897, quoted in ibid., May 1897, p. 36.

61. *Grand Army Record*, July 1897, p. 51; *Brockton* (Mass.) *Enterprise*, quoted in Ibid., May 1897, p. 36; ibid., September 1897, pp. 65, 67; and December 1897, p. 94.

62. *Grand Army Record*, October 1897, p. 76; July 1897, p. 51; September 1898, p. 68; *Journal of the National Encampment*, 1898, pp. 271–75.

63. See General Order #15, Pennsylvania Department Commander Austin Curtin, June 20, 1885, Pennsylvania Department General Orders Books, Sons of Union Veterans Collection.

64. Comerford Post Minutes, January 5, November 2, and December 7, 1887, Local Post Records Collection.

65. Webster Post Minutes, July 24 and 31 and February 6, 1889.

66. Lovering, *Services*; Beath, *History of the GAR*, pp. 68–378. In the

eighteen years for which Post 2 Minutes specify the church attended, the post attended the churches of Presbyterians (five times), Baptists (four times), Episcopalians (thrice), and Methodists, Congregationalists, and Jews (once each), as well as meeting once in an unidentified church and once in its own hall. Webster Post worshiped with the Congregationalists seven times and the Methodists twice; in other years more than one church (always Congregational, Methodist, Baptist, or Universalist) was designated. Comerford Post attended Methodist services four times, Episcopal services three times, Presbyterian and Baptist services once each, and a church of undetermined denomination once.

67. *New York Times*, August 26, 1879; *National Tribune*, March 25, 1882, p. 8, and June 4, 1885, p. 4 (a similar incident in Pittsburgh is recorded in ibid., June 7, 1888); *Journal of the National Encampment*, 1882, pp. 896–97. On the Catholic church's hostility to the GAR and other fraternal orders, see Lankevich, "The GAR in New York State," pp. 125–26; Carnes, *Secret Ritual*, p. 4; Preuss, *Dictionary of Secret Societies*, esp. p. 33.

68. Webster Post Minutes, October 31, 1885; letter, Post 2 Adjutant Charles Kennedy to "Commander," November 25, 1887, Adjutant's Letterpress Book, Sons of Union Veterans Collection.

69. Webster Post Minutes, August 23 and 30, September 6, 20, and 27, 1877. A similar situation prevailed in the Masons; Dumenil reports that the national order did not exclude brewers, liquor dealers, or saloon keepers, but local lodges often did (Dumenil, *Freemasonry and American Culture*, pp. 80–88).

70. Post 2 Minutes, February 28 and March 13, 1884, Sons of Union Veterans Collection.

71. Comerford Post Minutes, September 19, 1883, Local Post Records Collection.

72. Compare Descriptive Books, Post 20, Janesville (box 4, folder 1); Post 129, Neenah (box 42, folder 2); Post 174, Lime Ridge (box 29, folder 4); Post 144, Dallas (box 26, folder 1); all ser. 1, Local Post Records Collection; and also Descriptive Books, Post 94, Philadelphia, and Post 78, Reading (MG-60, boxes 5 and 6), PHMC Archives. On the similar predominance of middle-class veterans in the United Confederate Veterans, the GAR's counterpart in the South, see Foster, *Ghosts of the Confederacy*, pp. 106–8.

73. Beath, *History of the GAR*, pp. 68–378.

74. Clawson, "Fraternal Orders and Class Formation," and *Constructing Brotherhood*, pp. 249–59; Foner, *Free Soil, Free Labor, Free Men*, pp. 29–39.

75. *Proceedings of the National Encampment*, 1869, p. 61.

CHAPTER FOUR

1. Trachtenberg, *Incorporation of America*, p. 41; Post, ed., *A Treatise Upon . . . 1876, A Centennial Exhibition*, pp. 188–205; United States Cen-

tennial Commission, *Grounds and Buildings,* map following p. 18; Post 2 Minutes, October 18, 1875, Sons of Union Veterans Collection.

2. *Proceedings of the National Encampment,* 1876, p. 384. On Centennial Fourth of July orations, see Glassberg, *American Historical Pageantry,* pp. 9–14.

3. Meyer, "Fraternal Beneficiary Societies," p. 655; Dumenil, *Freemasonry,* app. A, p. 225; Carnes, *Secret Ritual,* p. 99.

4. Carnes, *Secret Ritual,* pp. 93–127.

5. "The Grand Army of the Republic," p. 133.

6. Dumenil, *Freemasonry and American Culture,* pp. 31–111; Carnes, *Secret Ritual,* esp. pp. 107–27; Clawson, "Fraternal Orders and Class Formation," pp. 689–95, and *Constructing Brotherhood,* pp. 249–59; *Ritual,* 1883, p. 22. Other useful analyses of fraternalism in particular contexts include Doyle, *Social Order of a Frontier Community,* pp. 178–93; Gilkeson, *Middle-Class Providence,* pp. 151–60; Thernstrom, *Poverty and Progress,* pp. 167–71; Walkowitz, *Worker City, Company Town,* pp. 156–66; Barron, *Those Who Stayed Behind,* pp. 124–27; and Scott, "As Easily As They Breathe . . ." and "Women's Voluntary Associations," in *Making the Invisible Woman Visible,* pp. 261–94.

7. Kingman, *History of Brockton,* pp. 767–68.

8. Dumenil, *Freemasonry and American Culture,* p. 13; Post 2's muster fee can be compared with those of other Pennsylvania posts in the reports of the department inspectors, *Proceedings of the Pennsylvania Department Encampment,* 1881–1900. Nationally, muster fees are averaged in the *Proceedings of the National Encampment,* 1873, pp. 221–29; ibid., 1874, pp. 286–91; and sometimes thereafter in the reports of the inspectors-general (e.g., in *Journal of the National Encampment,* 1883, p. 68).

9. Underwood, *Town Building,* figs. 3 and 4, pp. 102 and 104; Doyle, *Social Order of a Frontier Community,* p. 190; Kingman, *History of Brockton,* p. 483. Dumenil, *Freemasonry and American Culture,* app. A, p. 225.

10. Preuss, *Dictionary of Secret Societies,* p. 228; Stevens, *Cyclopaedia of Fraternities,* pp. 303–4, 395–99.

11. Dumenil, *Freemasonry and American Culture,* pp. 32–41; Cook, *Five Standard Rituals;* Preuss, *Dictionary of Secret Societies,* pp. 35, 180–82, 183–87, 301–4, 376–77; Stevens, *Cyclopaedia of Fraternities,* pp. 233–34, 238–47, 388–94, 395–99.

12. Stephenson actually devised a system patterned partly on that of the Soldiers' and Sailors' League of St. Louis (Beath, *History of the GAR,* pp. 33–52), but the ritual was indebted to his Masonic experience as well; see Wallace E. Davies, *Patriotism on Parade,* p. 123, and Stevens, *Cyclopaedia of Fraternities,* pp. 366–67. On the mutual copying of rituals, see Carnes, *Secret Ritual,* p. 6, and Clawson, *Constructing Brotherhood,* pp. 126–29.

13. GAR memorial halls survive in a number of places: inside the original Chicago Public Library, on the courthouse square in Terre Haute, Ind., in the basement of the Massachusetts State House, Boston, and (until 1988) in the dome of the Wisconsin State Capitol. The Sons of Union Vet-

erans Collection is housed in the former hall of Philadelphia's Post 94. In
Brockton, a memorial frieze survives inside the city hall, and the GAR
shares the honor of a War Memorial Building, though a separate GAR memorial hall was torn down in the 1960s to make way for a parking lot.

14. For a view of Post 2's elaborately furnished hall as it appeared in
1887, see the photo in Beath, *History of the GAR,* facing page 168.

15. Post 2 Minutes, March 31, 1881, Sons of Union Veterans Collection;
Webster Post Minutes, December 9, 1886. When Comerford Post was
burned out in 1889, it replaced its altar Bible first (Comerford Post Minutes, February 20, 1889, Local Post Records Collection). The ensuing discussion of post room design, unless otherwise noted, is based on the
standard diagram included in each version of the *Ritual* before 1900. It
first appeared on p. 2 of the 1869 *Ritual.*

16. Webster Post, however, dispensed with the platforms under its officers' chairs after 1877 (Webster Post Minutes, September 27, 1877).

17. *Ritual,* 1869, p. 5; *Rules and Regulations of Fletcher Webster Post 13,*
art. VII, War Memorial Building Collection.

18. The form of inspection is detailed in *Journal of the National Encampment,* 1883, pp. 105–7.

19. Discussion of the original ritual, unless otherwise noted, is based on
Proceedings of Enlistment and Muster.

20. Ibid., p. 4.

21. Dearing, *Veterans in Politics,* pp. 134–47. See also editorial in a soldier newspaper, the *Great Republic,* January 17, 1867, p. 285: "It is as important that the enemies of the Union be routed in this contest with the
ballot as it was that the same enemy should be by the bayonet and the bullet on the late fields of battle. If the loyal people of the nation shall be
beaten now, the sacrifices of the war will have been made in vain, and trai-
tors will triumph at last."

22. *Proceedings of Enlistment and Muster,* p. 6.

23. Ibid., p. 7.

24. Ibid., pp. 9–11.

25. Diehl, *Paramilitary Politics in Weimar Germany,* pp. 212–13; Leed,
No Man's Land, pp. 80–96, 196–204; Mitchell, *Civil War Soldiers,* pp. 67–
68, 82–88.

26. *Great Republic,* February 21, 1867, pp. 358–9. A similar organization
in New York City, the United Service Society, announced in 1865, "existing
parties having failed" to prevent the war, "it is the right and duty of those
who have fought in such a conflict to assert an important influence in the
public politics, in adjusting the revolutionary consequences of so vast a
war" (*Soldier's Friend,* March 1865, p. 1). See also the letter from "A Soldier" to the *Eau Claire* (Wis.) *Free Press,* July 27, 1865, and the editor's response, August 10, 1865.

27. Thomas Leonard, *Above the Battle,* pp. 59–73.

28. The ensuing discussion, unless otherwise noted, is based on *Ritual,*
1869.

29. Ibid., p. 14.

30. Ibid., pp. 18–19.

31. Ibid., p. 27, 29.

32. The 1869 *Ritual*, including opening and closing ceremonies, is twenty-four pages long; the 1866 version is thirteen pages. While it is possible that the 1866 version nonetheless took more time to perform, that seems unlikely, since the 1869 version calls for marches and challenges between officers' "stations" and contains a number of time-consuming prayers and musical numbers.

33. Oliver M. Wilson, *The GAR under Its First Constitution*, pp. 190, 195.

34. Descriptive Books, Post 23, Pottsville, Pa., PHMC Archives, MG-60, box 5; Beath, preface to *Proceedings of the Pennsylvania Department Encampments, 1867–72*, p. vi; Beath, *History of the GAR*, pp. 270–71.

35. Beath, preface to *Proceedings of the Pennsylvania Department Encampments, 1867–72*, p. vii.; Beath, *History of the GAR*, pp. 35, 100.

36. The national encampment of 1871 did away with the three-grade ritual, as well as the grade system (*Proceedings of the National Encampment*, 1871, p. 135, 138). Other changes were made at the encampments of 1874 (ibid., 1874, p. 305) and 1881 (*Journal of the National Encampment*, 1881, p. 797). After 1881, changes were few and minor.

37. *Ritual*, 1883, p. 16.

38. *Journal of the National Encampment*, 1887, p. 179.

39. General Order #4, Commander-in-Chief Charles Devens, June 15, 1874, National General Orders Book, Sons of Union Veterans Collection; *Journal of the National Encampment*, 1881, p. 797; ibid., 1882, p. 889; *Ritual*, 1883, p. 22.

40. *Proceedings of the Pennsylvania Department Encampments, 1867–72*, p. 102.

41. Carnes, *Secret Ritual*, pp. 47–48, 59–60; Semmel, "Sociology of Secrecy," pp. 488–89.

42. *Proceedings of the National Encampment*, 1869, pp. 57–63. On "beneficial posts," See Wallace E. Davies, *Patriotism on Parade*, pp. 142–43; Lankevich, "The GAR in New York State," pp. 117–18; *Proceedings of the National Encampment*, 1873, pp. 221–29, and ibid., 1874, pp. 286–91.

43. On publicizing the change, see *Proceedings of the National Encampment*, 1874, pp. 278–79. A good measure of partisan political activity in the GAR is the extent to which commanders-in-chief felt obligated to deny such activity or explain it away in their annual addresses to the national encampment. Following the 1869 resolution, commanders-in-chief either denied or denounced partisanship in the GAR in 1870, 1871, 1874, 1876, 1877, 1878, 1882, 1883, 1884, 1885, 1887, and 1888. Political agitation also was deplored at the openings of the encampments of 1872 (by the GAR adjutant-general) and 1880 (by the head of the Dayton Soldiers' Home, site of the encampment that year). After 1888, the issue was not raised in opening addresses and only rarely on the encampment floor. Well before that time, comments by the commanders-in-chief had changed from defen-

sive denials of charges made by outsiders (such as that of Commander-in-Chief Charles Devens, *Proceedings of the National Encampment*, 1874, pp. 269–70) to occasional rebukes of particular posts that strayed from an agreed-upon nonpartisan policy (such as that of Commander-in-Chief George Merrill, *Journal of the National Encampment*, 1882, pp. 868–69).

44. *Proceedings of the National Encampment*, 1875, p. 372; Beath, *History of the GAR*, p. 165, 192; *Proceedings of the National Encampment*, 1877, pp. 483–84; ibid., 1878, p. 569; circular, April 9, 1877, in Post 2 Scrapbooks, Sons of Union Veterans Collection. The demonstration of 1878, says Beath, was performed "in numbers so great as to literally pack the hall" (*History of the GAR*, p. 192).

45. See, for example, the participation of groups ranging from the Odd Fellows to the local Catholic glee club in Chippewa Falls's 1884 and 1887 Memorial Day exercises, and the same post's attempt to form a drum corps in conjunction with the Ancient Order of Hibernians (Comerford Post Minutes, May 30, 1884; May 18, 1887; and November 16, 1887; Local Post Records Collection); Webster Post's arrangement with the local Masons and other orders to provide a joint stipend for an ailing comrade, its invitations to other fraternal bodies to join the 1890 Memorial Day parade, and its frequent loaning of its hall (Webster Post Minutes, October 30, 1889, April 23, 1890, January 24, 1878, and October 13, 1881); and Post 2's loaning its flag to parading organizations—a group of postal workers, for example (Post 2 Minutes, October 19, 1882, Sons of Union Veterans Collection). Similar examples could be cited almost ad infinitum.

46. Stevens and Preuss in their encyclopedias give details of the imagery of these and the other fraternal orders of the period. Clawson makes a persuasive general argument similar to the one advanced here, linking fraternalism to changes in the workplace and to new conceptions of masculinity (*Constructing Brotherhood*, pp. 172–77, 211–213). See also Semmel, "Sociology of Secrecy," pp. 491–92, and Carnes, *Secret Ritual*, pp. 143–44 (on the bucolic ritual of the Modern Woodmen).

47. On camp, see Mitchell, *Civil War Soldiers*, pp. 73–74; on desertion, see McPherson, *Ordeal by Fire*, p. 468, and Lonn, *Desertion during the Civil War*. For an ex-officer's complaints about the high incidence of desertion—especially among the "seven dollars a pound fellows" who enlisted for bounty money—see Adams, "Pensions," pp. 330–33. Many more, of course, simply never reported for duty; see Levine, "Draft Evasion in the North during the Civil War."

48. Speech to 1885 Wisconsin department encampment, included in Comerford Post Minutes, February 4, 1885, Local Post Records Collection.

49. Post 2 Minutes, April 12, 1888, Sons of Union Veterans Collection; Comerford Post Minutes, September 3 and 17, 1890, Local Post Records Collection.

50. On the use of the temperance issue against the "House of Lords," see *Grand Army Record*, August 1891, p. 5, and November 1891, p. 8. On the Portland controversy, see *National Tribune*, July 2, 1885, *Journal of the Na-*

tional Encampment, 1885, pp. 327, 333 ("unofficial proceedings"), and *New York Times*, June 23, 1885, p. 5.

51. General Order #4, Pennsylvania Department Commander Chill Hazzard, April 12, 1880, Pennsylvania Department General Orders Book, Sons of Union Veterans Collection.

52. *National Tribune*, December 27, 1883, p. 3; ibid., January 10, 1889, p. 4; *Proceedings of the National Encampment*, 1877, p. 469. See also *National Tribune*, January 10, 1884, p. 4, in which Lemon rebuts the argument that good swearers make the best fighters. Citing Cromwell and Washington (who is said to have prayed regularly at Valley Forge), he concludes: "The fact is . . . that profanity, so far from being a sign of bravery, is simply an indication of a lack of self-control on the part of the person who is addicted to it, and self-control is essential to good discipline."

53. *Proceedings of the National Encampment*, 1869, p. 34; ibid., 1871, p. 105; clip from *Ohio Soldier*, reprinted in *Grand Army Record*, October 1893, p. 80; *Grand Army Record*, April 1890, p. 4. For a discussion of the terms "manliness" and "effeminacy" as applied during the war, see Moorhead, *American Apocalypse*, pp. 146–49.

54. Walters, *American Reformers*, pp. 82–83; Foner, "Causes of the American Civil War," pp. 206–7; Susman, " 'Personality' and the Making of Twentieth-Century Culture," pp. 214, 220. On the different uses to which "manliness" was put in the workplace, see Clawson, *Constructing Brotherhood*, pp. 170–72.

55. *Journal of the National Encampment*, 1886, p. 29; Sherman, "Camp-Fires of the GAR," p. 502.

56. *Grand Army Record*, January 1894, p. 8; *National Tribune*, June 24, 1882, p. 4; Oliver M. Wilson, *The GAR under Its First Constitution*, p. 203.

57. *Proceedings of the National Encampment*, 1877, p. 445; *National Tribune*, January 13, 1887, p. 4. On the reunion sentiment of the 1880s and 1890s, see Foster, *Ghosts of the Confederacy*, esp. pp. 67–70. On the images Union and Confederate troops had of each other during the war, see Mitchell, *Civil War Soldiers*, pp. 24–55.

58. The 1883 *Ritual* apparently was to be brought back as a result of action by the 1890 national encampment, though it is not clear from the debate whether that decision was actually implemented. See *Journal of the National Encampment*, 1889, p. 185, and ibid., 1890, p. 193.

59. Wilson, *The GAR under Its First Constitution*, pp. 198–99, 132.

60. Beath, *History of the GAR*, p. 651. An 1897 tabulation (Harwood, "Secret Societies in America," p. 620), although it does not include "military societies" such as the GAR, is the most complete comparison we have. It lists four orders larger than the GAR, which in 1896 numbered 340,610 members: Masons (974,000 members), Odd Fellows (940,350), Knights of Pythias (475,000), and Ancient Order of United Workmen (361,301). The figures for the Masons and the Odd Fellows include black members, who were segregated in separate lodges in both orders. Because Harwood's tabulation omits labor organizations as well, the Knights of Labor—the only

labor order with more than 300,000 members in 1897—also should be included. Had such a tabulation been done in 1890, of course, the GAR
(which at that point had more than 400,000 members) probably would
have ranked fourth.

61. Rejectees in Williamsport and in Post 94, Philadelphia, were compiled from Pennsylvania general orders, 1875–95, Pennsylvania Department General Orders Book, Sons of Union Veterans Collection.

62. Carnahan, *Decisions and Opinions*, p. 84; *National Tribune*, April 16,
1885, p. 4; ibid., November 12, 1885, p. 4, and December 31, 1885, p. 4;
Carnahan, *Decisions and Opinions*, pp. 28–29.

63. *National Tribune*, June 24, 1886, p. 4. Post 2 went so far as to pur-
chase "a little hood" for the ballot box to preserve the anonymity of blackballers. Interestingly, the motion to buy the hood was made by Maurice
Fagan, one of the members who was adamant about not admitting short-
service men to the post; see Post 2 Minutes, June 3, 1880, and November 9,
1882, Sons of Union Veterans Collection.

64. General Order #10, Commander-in-Chief John Logan, April 13,
1868, National General Orders Book, Sons of Union Veterans Collection;
National Tribune, March 15, 1883, p. 4.

65. Post 2 Minutes, December 29, 1870, and December 26, 1872, Sons of
Union Veterans Collection; Webster Post Minutes, April 14, 1886; Comerford Post Minutes, December 7, 1892, Local Post Records Collection;
Journal of the National Encampment, 1892, pp. 168–90; ibid., 1885, p. 119
(a similar complaint is voiced in the *Grand Army Record*, September 1886,
p. 4).

66. Local post records almost never allude to partisan politics, though
this may be precisely because the national encampment had banned such
expressions in 1869. See the revealing comment of the *Grand Army Record* (April 1898, p. 26) on the actions of Commander-in-Chief John P. S.
Gobin during the House of Lords affair: "Commander-in-Chief Gobin
sought and obtained the office to which he has been elected solely to aid
his chances in being nominated as the Republican candidate for Governor
of Pennsylvania. The 'House of Lords' machine in Pennsylvania is omnipo-
tent. If the Commander-in-Chief should help an anti-'Lords' State Commander out of his dilemma the Commander-in-Chief would lose his 'pull'
in Pennsylvania."

67. On Lynch and Hall, see Post 2 Minutes, February 14, December 12
and 19, 1878; September 25, October 9, and December 4, 1879; and December 1, 1881. On Kane, see *Journal of the National Encampment*, 1885,
pp. 262–93; *Grand Army Record*, November 1887, p. 4.

68. On the work of pension lawyers, see Boynton, "Fraudulent Prac-
tices," p. 230; *Journal of the National Encampment*, 1883, p. 139; *New York
Times*, July 15, 1887, p. 4, and April 15, 1892, p. 4. On Lemon's career, see
Glasson, *Federal Military Pensions*, pp. 150, n. 1, 185, n. 1, 188, n. 1, 214–
18; Dearing, *Veterans in Politics*, pp. 268–77; Lankevich, "The GAR in New
York State," pp. 17–18, 142–45; *New York Times*, October 27, 1883, p. 4,

and July 15, 1887, p. 4; *Journal of the National Encampment*, 1886, p. 217; and of course Lemon's own *National Tribune*. The estimate of Lemon's profits is from the *Grand Army Gazette*, reprinted in *Grand Army Record*, April 1886, p. 1; for Lemon's places of business in Washington between 1875 and 1897, see Washington city directories, Washingtoniana Collection.

69. On the commanders, see the publication credits on the frontispieces of *Journal of the National Encampment*, 1882, 1884, and 1885. On Davison, see ibid., 1876, pp. 387–90, Beath, *History of the GAR*, pp. 653–57, and *National Tribune*, May 29, 1884, p. 6. On the San Francisco encampment, see *Journal of the National Encampment*, 1885, p. 127.

70. Post 2 Minutes, November 8, 1877, and July 25, 1878, Sons of Union Veterans Collection; *Soldier's Friend*, August 21, 1869, p. 2; *National Tribune*, June 7, 1883, p. 4; Webster Post Minutes, March 8, 1877; *Journal of the National Encampment*, 1887, pp. 49, 109; Post 2 Business Directory, pp. 6, 8, Sons of Union Veterans Collection; *National Tribune*, April 7, 1887, p. 4.

71. Comerford Post Minutes, January 21, 1891, Local Post Records Collection; Webster Post Minutes, January 23 and July 24, 1889.

72. In Sons of Union Veterans Collection, see Post 2 Employment Bureau Book, and Post 2 Minutes, September 1 and 15 and November 3, 1870; June 8, 1871; March 30, 1876; December 13, 1877; April 24 and May 22, 1879; October 2, 1884; and January 21, 1897.

73. Lankevich, "The GAR in New York State," p. 116; *New York Times*, April 12, 1885, p. 3; Post 2 Minutes, October 18, 1875, and August 2 and 23, October 4 and 25, 1877, Sons of Union Veterans Collection.

74. *National Tribune*, April 7, 1887, p. 4.

75. This, of course, is the argument of Wiebe, *Search for Order*. See, however, Bender, *Community and Social Change in America*, which questions Wiebe's assumption that the late nineteenth century—or any other period, for that matter—saw a sudden change in American communities from primarily gemeinschaft to primarily gesellschaft values. Instead, Bender urges that these two categories be considered as Ferdinand Tönnies first proposed them—as contending and simultaneous influences in society rather than as "stages" in a model of community decay.

76. Haskell, *Emergence of Professional Social Science*, pp. 27–47, esp. pp. 81–85; Bender, "Cultures of Intellectual Life," pp. 181–92; Doyle, *Social Order of a Frontier Community*, pp. 178–80.

77. Letters, Adjutant A. Lammey of Godfrey Weitzel Post 425, Chicago to Post 8, October 29, 1886, and anonymous commander of La Crosse, Wis., post to Post 8, March 10, 1890, both in Minnesota GAR Records, 53.I.10.10F; Kilmer, "The GAR As Seen from the Inside," p. 154. Hardly a year of national general orders went by without several warnings from headquarters about imposters, as one example among many, see General Order #5, Commander-in-Chief John Hartranft, November 16, 1876, National General Orders Book, Sons of Union Veterans Collection.

78. Carnahan, *Decisions and Opinions*, pp. 53–54.

79. *Journal of the National Encampment*, 1885, pp. 209, 294; ibid., 1887, pp. 109, 256; GAR *Rules and Regulations*, 1887, p. 32; *Journal of the National Encampment*, 1889, p. 105.

80. Proposals to create some sort of "honorary membership" were in the air from the first (*Proceedings of the National Encampment*, 1868, p. 23, and ibid., 1872, p. 192), but were never recognized at the national level. For evidence of associate membership in Pennsylvania, see *Proceedings of the Pennsylvania Department Encampment*, 1880, p. 5. Also see Post 2 Minutes, May 22, 1879; clip from *Hartford Evening Post*, June 6, 1878, in Post 2 Scrapbooks; and letter, Post 2 Adjutant Charles F. Kennedy to James S. Lowell, May 14, 1888, Adjutant's Letterpress Book, all in Sons of Union Veterans Collection.

81. *Grand Army Record*, quoted in *Veteran*, August 1891, p. 6. Webster Post Minutes, December 21, 1887; September 10, 1890; March 25, October 14, November 4, and December 2, 1891; and April 6, May 4, June 22, and August 31, 1892. *Grand Army Record*, April 1893, p. 28.

82. *Grand Army Record*, June 1894, p. 46, letter from "a Comrade in a New England city."

83. Carnahan, *Decisions and Opinions*, p. 136. *Journal of the National Encampment*, 1888, p. 40; ibid., 1890, p. 190; ibid., 1899, p. 222. On Beath, see *Journal of the National Encampment*, 1884, p. 227.

84. Beath, *History of the GAR*, pp. 674–77; "Patriotic Societies of the Civil War"; *Veteran*, September 9, 1891, p. 12; *New York Times*, February 24, 1892.

85. *Grand Army Record*, November 1886, p. 1; ibid., May 1891, p. 7, letter from "Vet"; *New York Times*, August 30, 1890; *Philadelphia Record*, May 31, 1888, p. 1.

CHAPTER FIVE

1. *Rules and Regulations*, 1869, p. 24.

2. Comerford Post Minutes, Post 68, April 18, 1883, and March 5, 1884, Local Post Records Collection; *Rules and Regulations of Webster Post*, Art. 10, War Memorial Building Collection; Post 2 Minutes, January 25 and February 1, 1872, and November 22 and December 6, 1877 (the one-third provision was written into the 1883 bylaws, included in Orders Book, Post 2, November 30, 1883), Sons of Union Veterans Collection; Beath, *History of the GAR*, p. 652. The national total represents about 0.3 percent of what the federal government spent on pensions during the same year ($74 million).

3. Circular #1, Surgeon-General James L. Watson, August 15, 1876, and Post 2 Minutes, April 24, 1873, Sons of Union Veterans Collection; *Journal of the National Encampment*, 1888, p. 54.

4. Webster Post Minutes, May 19, 1886; Comerford Post Minutes, De-

cember 19, 1883; January 16, 1884; and September 2, 1885; Local Post Records Collection.

5. Post 2 Minutes, April 15, 1875, Sons of Union Veterans Collection; Webster Post Minutes, October 30, 1889; Comerford Post Minutes, March 5, 1884, and February 4 and September 2, 1885; Local Post Records Collection.

6. Beath, *History of the GAR*, pp. 379ff; General Order #19, Commander-in-Chief John Logan, December 30, 1868; letters, Post 2 Adjutant Charles Kennedy to Charles Weissert, July 23, 1887, and Kennedy to "Dear Comrade," October 17, 1887, in Adjutant's Letterpress Book, Sons of Union Veterans Collection.

7. Post 2 Minutes, November 30 and December 14, 1871, and December 3, 1881, Sons of Union Veterans Collection; Carnahan, *Decisions and Opinions*, p. 127; *Proceedings of the National Encampment*, 1869, pp. 57–63; [Faehtz], *The Grand Army's Bequest*; Meyer, "Fraternal Beneficiary Societies," p. 651.

8. Oliver M. Wilson, *The GAR under Its First Constitution*, p. 183.

9. Post 2 Minutes, September 19, 1872, and August 22, 1872, Sons of Union Veterans Collection; Webster Post Minutes, July 10, 1884 (the minutes, and the post adjutants' reports in the Massachusetts State House Collection, list Linehan's many suspensions for dues arrears and remissions of his dues by the post); Comerford Post Minutes, October 17, 1894, Local Post Records Collection.

10. Post 2 Minutes, November 20, 1873; March 8, April 19 and 26, May 10 and 24, and June 7, 1877; March 25, 1880; on the Von Nieda child abuse case, see January 18 and 25, July 12 and 19, and December 13, 1877; February 5, 1880; and circular inserted in the minutes of March 20, 1877; all in Sons of Union Veterans Collection.

11. Webster Post Minutes, December 26, 1878; April 28 and June 16, 1881, October 14, 1885; and March 13, 1889 (for a meeting given over almost entirely to charity cases, see ibid., March 7, 1888); Comerford Post Minutes, April 21, 1886; December 17, 1884; June 15 and July 20, 1892; November 2, 1887; Local Post Records Collection. Post 2 Minutes, July 20, 1871; December 19, 1872; June 19, 1873; March 2, 1876; February 4, 1867; Sons of Union Veterans Collection.

12. Letter, Post 2 adjutant Charles Kennedy to Mrs. James Dougherty, June 3, 1887, Adjutant's Letterpress Book, Sons of Union Veterans Collection. Comerford Post Minutes, November 15, 1893; June 6, 1894; and October 11, 1899; Local Post Records Collection. At one point, Post 2 was presented with a proposal that would have either barred post-funded funerals or provided them only if the family could not afford a funeral otherwise. The idea was tabled (Post 2 Minutes, October 14 and 25, November 22, and December 3, 1883).

13. "Burial of the Dead," in Lovering, *Services*, pp. 35–39; Post 2 Minutes, June 4, 1885; letter, Post 2 Adjutant Charles Kennedy to "Commander," November 25, 1887, Adjutant's Letterpress Book, Sons of Union Veterans Collection.

14. Post 2 Minutes, April 14, 1881, and September 26, 1889, Sons of Union Veterans Collection.

15. Ibid., March 31, 1881, August 12, 1885; and November 18, 1894. Webster Post Minutes, July 1, 1891, and November 16, 1892; Comerford Post Minutes, January 9, February 26, and May 11, 1885; December 11, 1890, Local Post Records Collection.

16. On rare occasions, charity funerals were also extended to indigent veterans who were not members. See, for example, the cases reported in Post 2 Minutes, August 23, 1883, Sons of Union Veterans Collection, and *National Tribune*, August 2, 1883, p. 6, and August 30, 1883, p. 5.

17. Comerford Post Minutes, December 11, 1890, Local Post Records Collection.

18. *Proceedings of the National Encampment*, 1872, p. 152. General Order #12, Commander-in-Chief Ambrose Burnside, October 28, 1871, National General Orders Book; General Order #13, Pennsylvania Department Commander Thomas Stewart, June 3, 1889, Pennsylvania Department General Orders Book; Post 2 Minutes, October 12 and November 16, 1871; June 6 and 20, 1889; all in Sons of Union Veterans Collection.

19. Beath, History of the GAR, p. 652; Lankevich, "The GAR in New York State," p. 88; *Proceedings of the National Encampment*, 1871, p. 154.

20. *National Tribune*, March 10, 1887, p. 4.

21. Reports of Webster Post relief committee, appended to Minutes of 1881 and 1882–84; report of Post 2 relief committee, included in Post 2 Minutes, December 28, 1876, Sons of Union Veterans Collection; *Proceedings of the Pennsylvania Department Encampment*, 1883–84, p. 181. Lankevich, "The GAR in New York State," estimates that one-third of all GAR charity went to nonmembers.

22. Beath, *History of the GAR*, p. 652; Webster Post relief committee report, appended to 1881 post Minutes. In 1888, the national average was $9.07 per case; in 1887, $9.54 per case; in 1886, $10.70 per case. In Brockton, the average donation in 1882 was $13.61; in 1883, it was $17.02.

23. Webster Post Minutes, April 28 and June 16, 1881; Comerford Post Minutes, March 19, July 2 and 16, August 6, October 15, and November 5, 1884; May 6 and November 5, 1885; January 6, 1886, Local Post Records Collection.

24. For bylaws limiting charity expenditures, see Webster Post *Rules and Regulations*, art. 14, War Memorial Building Collection; Comerford Post Minutes, April 18, 1883, Local Post Records Collection; Post 2 bylaws, art. 4, sec. 2, in Post 2 Orders, November 30, 1883, Post 2 Orders Book, Sons of Union Veterans Collection. Another austerity measure, often proposed but never implemented, was to discontinue aid to nonmembers. See, for example, Webster Post Minutes, March 13, 1889; *Proceedings of the National Encampment*, 1873, p. 247; ibid., 1875, p. 361; and *Grand Army Record*, January 1887, p. 4.

25. Scott, *Making the Invisible Woman Visible*, pp. 281–85.

26. Wiebe, *Search for Order*, pp. 149–50, 170–72. On the voluntary,

individual-centered charity movements of the Gilded Age and their difficulties in coping with the problems of the 1890s, see Boyer, *Urban Masses,*
pp. 143–87, and May, *Protestant Churches*; on the culture of self-reliance,
see Wyllie, *Self-Made Man in America.*

27. *New York Times,* January 19, 1879, p. 7; see also "The Causes of Our
Civil War," in *Soldier's Friend,* March 1865, p. 1, in which the author, Albert Mathews, argues that "in this great social element of *individual self-
respect* is centered, and upon it depends, the hope of the American Republic." On the Union soldier's fear of dependence, see Mitchell, *Civil War
Soldiers,* p. 13.

28. *Proceedings of the National Encampment,* 1868, p. 15; *Journal of the
National Encampment,* 1883, p. 199.

29. *Grand Army Record,* July 15, 1890, p. 7. Beath, *History of the GAR,*
pp. 379ff, notes the states that funded burials of indigent veterans (Maine,
Rhode Island, Connecticut, New York, New Jersey, Pennsylvania, Colorado,
Nebraska, Ohio, Wisconsin, Iowa, Minnesota, and Kansas) and those that
required localities to provide for poor veterans outside almshouses (New
Hampshire, Massachusetts, Wisconsin, and New York). For examples of
posts that buried veterans in post cemetery lots in order to keep them out
of potter's fields, see Webster Post Minutes, October 5, 1887, and Comerford Post Minutes, May 30, 1883, Local Post Records Collection. On
burials in national cemeteries, see David Charles Sloane, *Last Great Necessity,* pp. 232–33.

30. *New York Times,* August 13, 1883, p. 4; *Proceedings of the Pennsylvania Department Encampment,* 1883, pp. 192–93; *National Tribune,* January 25, 1883; Webster Post Minutes, March 9, 1892; *Proceedings of the
National Encampment,* 1893, p. 247.

31. *Proceedings of the National Encampment,* 1874, p. 293; Post 2 Min-
utes, January 18, March 5, April 5, and May 3, 1877; clip from *Philadelphia
Republic,* January 26, 1877, in Post 2 Scrapbooks, Sons of Union Veterans
Collection.

32. Letters, Post 2 Adjutant Charles Kennedy to James Lawry, September
24, 1887, and to H. E. Brown, October 3, 1887, Adjutant's Letterpress
Book, Sons of Union Veterans Collection.

33. Post 2 Employment Bureau Book and letter, George W. Cook to Post
2, March 26, 1897, inserted in ibid., both Sons of Union Veterans Collection.

34. General Order #15, Oregon Department Commander S. B. Ormsby,
April 2, 1895, Oregon Collection, GAR Papers.

35. Haskell, *Emergence of Professional Social Science,* pp. 39–42.

36. *National Tribune,* December 1877, p. 17.

37. Ibid., February 19, 1885, p. 4.

38. Post 2 Minutes, February 16, 1871, Sons of Union Veterans Collection. Webster Post Minutes, September 30 and October 7, 1880; June 8,
1882; April 3, 1883; February 10 and March 3, 10, and 31, 1886; and Fair
Book. *Proceedings of the National Encampment,* 1875, p. 321. For a study

of one of the largest wartime fairs, see Gallman, "Voluntarism in Wartime."

39. *Grand Army Record*, October 1890, p. 4.

40. Trattner, *From Poor Law to Welfare State*, pp. 68–71, 75–79. On the
Sanitary Commission, see also Fredrickson, *Inner Civil War*, pp. 98–112.

41. Brock, *Investigation and Responsibility*, p. 115; see also pp. 45–57
and 88–115.

42. Paul, *Pennsylvania's Soldiers' Orphan Schools*, pp. 150–51. On the
soldiers' orphans schools in Pennsylvania, see Beath, *History of the GAR*,
pp. 479–82; Wickersham, *History of Education in Pennsylvania*, pp. 586–
605; Alanko, "History of the Soldiers' Orphans Institutions in Pennsylvania," pp. 3–17; Post 2 Minutes, March 27 and November 20, 1873, Sons of
Union Veterans Collection; *Proceedings of the Pennsylvania Department
Encampment*, 1881, pp. 62, 130; ibid., 1883–84, pp. 73, 187, 191; and the
annual reports of the soldiers' orphans committees to the Pennsylvania department encampment.

43. *Proceedings of the Pennsylvania Department Encampment*, 1881, p.
40; ibid., 1883–84, pp. 216, 174; ibid., 1884–85, pp. 246, 247; ibid., 1885–
86, pp. 257–61. The relevant statute is Laws of Pennsylvania, 1885, PL
18-20.

44. *Proceedings of the Pennsylvania Department Encampment*, 1885–86,
p. 167; Beath, *History of the GAR*, p. 483. The relevant statute is Laws of
Pennsylvania, 1885, PL 62-64.

45. Beath, *History of the GAR*, pp. 379ff; *National Tribune*, January 3,
1889, gives the text of the New York statute. As of 1888, New Jersey was
still using a soldiers' home built in 1866, while Connecticut would pay for a
veteran's medical care in any general hospital instead.

46. The discussion that follows is based on Glasson, *Federal Military
Pensions*, pp. 123–47, 273.

47. Ibid., p. 155.

48. *National Tribune*, November 1877, p. 15, and April 1880, p. 1. See
also Dearing, *Veterans in Politics*, pp. 250, 264–66.

49. On land warrants, see the following *Proceedings* and *Journals of the
National Encampment*: 1870, p. 101; 1876, pp. 414–15; 1884, pp. 117–18,
124–26, 136; 1885, pp. 200–201. On the greenback compensation proposal, see Dearing, *Veterans in Politics*, p. 250; *Proceedings of the Pennsylvania Department Encampment*, 1884, p. 214; and the following *Journals
of the National Encampment*: 1884, p. 106; 1888, p. 193; 1890, p. 234. On
Grant's veto of bounty equalization, see Dearing, *Veterans in Politics*, pp.
219–20. On the other proposals, see *New York Times*, January 16, 1882, p.
4, and March 23, 1878, p. 4.

50. Glasson, *Federal Military Pensions*, pp. 164–66, 174–75.

51. Pension Commissioner John Bentley's report of 1879, cited in ibid.,
pp. 175–76.

52. Bacon, "A Raid upon the Treasury," p. 545.

53. Glasson, *Federal Military Pensions*, pp. 273, 177. This estimate of

Pension Commissioner J. C. Black does not include the cost of regular pensions to the thousands of veterans who successfully filed new claims and were added to the rolls.

54. Ibid., p. 160; *Proceedings of the National Encampment*, 1878, p. 160; Dearing, *Veterans in Politics*, p. 248. Lemon's fulminations in favor of the Arrears Act fill the *National Tribunes* of 1877 and 1878.

55. *National Tribune*, December 1877, p. 17; ibid., November 16, 1882, p. 4.

56. Ibid., December 27, 1883; circular of Commander-in-Chief Paul Vandervoort, April 18, 1883, and General Order #7 of Vandervoort, December 21, 1882, National General Orders Book, Sons of Union Veterans Collection; Dearing, *Veterans in Politics*, pp. 269–75; *Journal of the National Encampment*, 1884, p. 34.

57. *Journal of the National Encampment*, 1882, pp. 873–74; ibid., 1884, pp. 106–7.

58. Ibid., 1886, p. 222. Bennet was one of several Indiana politicians who made careers for themselves by advocating service pensions. See Dearing, *Veterans in Politics*, pp. 377–78, 398, and Glasson, *Federal Military Pensions*, p. 205.

59. Glasson, *Federal Military Pensions*, pp. 189–90, 192–93.

60. Ibid., pp. 207–17; Dearing, *Veterans in Politics*, pp. 333–37. Cleveland's veto message was printed and then denounced in *National Tribune*, February 17, 1887, p. 2.

61. Dearing, *Veterans in Politics*, p. 336; General Orders #12 and #13, Commander-in-Chief Lucius Fairchild, April 19 and 25, 1887, National General Orders Book, Sons of Union Veterans Collection; *National Tribune*, February 17, 1887, p. 2, and February 24, 1887, p. 4; Glasson, *Federal Military Pensions*, pp. 220–21.

62. Webster Post Minutes, March 16 and July 13, 1887; Comerford Post Minutes, December 5, 1883, and August 3, 1887, Local Post Records Collection. On the Service Pension Association, see Webster Post Minutes, December 2 and 9, 1880; August 3 and December 7, 1887; December 12, 1888; and July 16, 1890. Also see *Grand Army Record*, March 1894, p. 20.

63. Post 2 Minutes, June 5 and December 11, 1884; *New York Times*, October 5, 1889, p. 4.

64. *Journal of the National Encampment*, 1884, pp. 36–38, 115.

65. *Journal of the National Encampment*, 1888, pp. 190–91; ibid., 1890, p. 254; ibid., 1889, pp. 121–22; Glasson, *Federal Military Pensions*, pp. 231–32.

66. Glasson, *Federal Military Pensions*, p. 224; *Journal of the National Encampment*, 1890, p. 169.

67. Glasson, *Federal Military Pensions*, pp. 243, 246–50, 270, 273. Lankevich, "The GAR in New York State," p. 236, estimates the eventual cost of the act at $8 billion.

68. *Journal of the National Encampment*, 1884, p. 37; General Order

#12, Commander-in-Chief Robert Beath, May 6, 1884, National General Orders Book, Sons of Union Veterans Collection.

69. *Journal of the National Encampment*, 1886, p. 228.

70. Ibid., p. 232.

71. Ibid., 1890, p. 235; *Grand Army Record*, October 1890, p. 4. Farnham Post of New York put itself on record against extravagant pensions in 1893, a move that provoked much public comment and a reprimand from the New York department. See Lankevich, "The GAR in New York State," pp. 238–39; *Grand Army Record*, June 1893, p. 42; Foote, "Decisive Breach in the Grand Army"; and Finn, "Complete History of the Farnham Post Revolt."

72. *Journal of the National Encampment*, 1886, p. 221; *National Tribune*, December 24, 1885, p. 4; *Journal of the National Encampment*, 1890, p. 248.

73. *Journal of the National Encampment*, 1886, pp. 227, 219; *Grand Army Record*, January 1894, p. 1. The argument that liberal pension payments stimulated the economy also was made by Lemon (*National Tribune*, August 1, 1889, p. 4), by Vandervoort (*Journal of the National Encampment*, 1883, pp. 9–10), and by Commander-in-Chief Russell Alger (ibid., 1890, pp. 8–9).

74. *Grand Army Record*, March 1894, p. 20.

75. Ibid.; *Journal of the National Encampment*, 1886, p. 216; Lankevich, "The GAR in New York State," p. 196.

76. *Journal of the National Encampment*, 1883, p. 154; ibid., 1884, pp. 108–12; ibid., 1889, p. 170; ibid., 1890, p. 210.

77. On the Veterans' Rights Union, see *Journal of the National Encampment*, 1885, pp. 202–9; ibid., 1886, p. 198; Lankevich, "The GAR in New York State," pp. 163–68; Dearing, *Veterans in Politics*, pp. 310–11. Both Webster Post and Post 2 participated in the VRU.

78. *National Tribune*, December 17, 1885, p. 6. Similar comments were made in ibid., November 20, 1884, and in *Grand Army Record*, January 1888, p. 4.

79. Adams, "Pensions," pp. 386–90; *National Tribune*, May 8, 1890.

80. Dearing, *Veterans in Politics*, p. 470, refers briefly to "the fixed prejudice in the South" against pensions, and orators like Farnham asserted it, but to my knowledge Southern votes on pension bills have yet to be systematically studied.

81. *Nation*, May 8, 1890, p. 369.

82. Ibid., October 24, 1889, pp. 325–26. See also ibid., April 25, 1895, pp. 318–19, and May 15, 1890, p. 386.

83. Ibid., July 30, 1891, p. 81, and April 25, 1895, p. 319.

84. Waite, "Pensions," p. 236; Foote, "Degradation by Pensions," pp. 425, 430; Hale, "The Pension Carnival," pp. 13487–88; ibid., p. 13732; Hall, "Civil War Pensions," p. 129; and Foote, "Patriotism, Morality, and Pensions."

85. *Journal of the National Encampment*, 1883, p. 51; *Grand Army Rec-*

ord, March 1886, p. 3, and April 1890, p. 1; *National Tribune*, February 13, 1879, p. 13; *Journal of the National Encampment*, 1889, p. 47; *National Tribune*, April 8, 1886, p. 4; ibid., April 14, 1887, p. 4; ibid., February 23, 1888, p. 6; *Grand Army Record*, March 1891, p. 4, and April 1891, p. 8.

86. The ensuing argument is from William M. Sloane, "Pensions and Socialism." In addition to that of Miller, another reply to Sloane—and Sloane's rejoinder—may be found in the "Open Letters" column of *Century*, vol. 42, September 1891, pp. 790–92.

87. The rebuttal of C. W. Miller is summarized from the *National Tribune*, August 27, 1891, p. 4.

88. Veto message of Cleveland, reprinted in *National Tribune*, February 17, 1887, p. 2.

89. *Grand Army Record*, March 1894, p. 20.

90. Hale, "The Pension Carnival," pp. 13487–88, 13486.

91. *Nation*, May 2, 1895, p. 336; Leoser, "The Grand Army as a Pension Agency," p. 526; *New York Times*, August 9, 1887.

92. *Veteran*, February 1892, p. 12; Waite, "Pensions," p. 243; William M. Sloane, "Pensions and Socialism," p. 187; Hale, "The Pension Carnival," p. 13736; *New Haven Palladium*, cited in *New York Times*, July 30, 1890, p. 4.

93. Dearing, *Veterans in Politics*, pp. 352–401, esp. pp. 389–91.

94. *Proceedings of the Pennsylvania Department Encampment*, 1883, "unofficial proceedings."

95. Adams, "Pensions," pp. 329–31.

CHAPTER SIX

1. "What Monuments Teach," speech of James A. Garfield at Painesville, Ohio, July 3, 1880, in Edgar, *Gems of the Campaign of 1880*, pp. 85–86.

2. Linderman, *Embattled Courage*, p. 266.

3. Aaron, *Unwritten War*, p. 328; Moorhead, *American Apocalypse*, p. 218; and see Edmund Wilson, *Patriotic Gore*, pp. 131–218; Thomas Leonard, *Above the Battle*, pp. 9–39.

4. Edmund Wilson, *Patriotic Gore*, pp. 617–34 (Bierce), 669–742 (De Forest), 684, and 701 (Crane); Thomas Leonard, *Above the Battle*, pp. 20–24.

5. Tebbel, *History of Book Publishing*, 3:524–26; McFeely, *Grant*, p. 501; Edmund Wilson, *Patriotic Gore*, pp. 139–41.

6. Roy F. Nichols, Introduction to *Battles and Leaders of the Civil War*, New ed., (New York: Thomas Yosselef, 1956), 1:iv. The Sons of Union Veterans Collection houses the surviving volumes of the Post 2 library, as well as the Post 2 Business Directory, which includes a catalog of the library in 1886.

7. Grant, *Personal Memoirs*, 2:241; McFeely, *Grant*, pp. 510–11, and see also pp. 103, 145–46, 186–87; Edmund Wilson, *Patriotic Gore*, p. 152.

8. *Battles and Leaders*, 4:255 (Sherman), 3:406–19 (Meade and Sickles). Grant, *Personal Memoirs*, 2:387, 394.

9. See Linderman, *Embattled Courage*, and Mitchell, *Civil War Soldiers*, pp. 24–28, 76–77.

10. *National Tribune*, February 25, 1886, p. 4; Post 2 Minutes, 1871, Sons of Union Veterans Collection; Comerford Post Minutes, February 1, 1893, Local Post Records Collection; Webster Post Minutes, June 3, 1891; *GAR War Papers*.

11. Most of the twenty-six papers in the Fred Jones Post *GAR War Papers* collection, for example, are battle exegeses by former commissioned officers, though it also includes "The Signal Corps, U.S. Army," "The Army Mule," "Personal Reminiscences of the Assassination of President Lincoln," and "Experiences in Southern Military Prisons."

12. The Pennsylvania excerpts that follow are from the volume of personal war sketches of members of Simon Cameron Post 78, Middletown, Pa. (1896), MG-272, box 15, PHMC Archives, pp. 34 (John C. Miller), 46 (Phillip Snyder), 36 (Rudolph Pfanmiller), and 44 (George Blotcher). The Minnesota excerpt is from the personal war sketches of Charles Parker, a member of Acker Post 21, St. Paul, Minn., (n.d.), Department of Minnesota Papers, box 56, v. 182A.

13. Personal war sketch of David Higgins, Bryant Post 119, Minneapolis (1891), Minnesota GAR Records (43.D.1.4F ov). Of the fifty-eight members of Philadelphia's Post 2 who filled out personal sketches, only half a dozen provided anything more than a summary listing of ranks held and battles witnessed. In Post 8 of St. Paul, twenty-eight of seventy-seven gave details, while Post 119 of Minneapolis seems to have used personal sketches as obituaries—after the first year or so, they were filled out by the post "historian" after the member's death and thus rarely include more than the deceased's service record and some fraternal remarks about his good character in life. In St. Paul's Post 21, by contrast, sixty-one of a hundred members went beyond the listing of a service record.

14. General Order #6, Commander-in-Chief John A. Logan, November 14, 1869, National General Orders Book, Sons of Union Veterans Collection. Shaw, incidentally, was also one of the members who proposed the disastrous grade system.

15. At the Washington national encampment of 1892, the concept of the war as diorama was played out in the design of the tent city set up on the Ellipse, where the tents and stands were arranged to reproduce the positions of the Union armies in the closing campaign of the war; see *New York Times*, September 20, 1892, p. 2, and also the illustration in this chapter.

16. *Journal of the National Encampment*, 1885, p. 2; personal war sketch of Colonel David J. Higgins, Bryant Post 119, Minneapolis, Minnesota GAR Records (43.D.1.4F ov). See also Post 2 Minutes, May 15, 1890, Sons of Union Veterans Collection, in which the post endorses the publication of complete official records of the war so that "those who bore a part in the suppression of the Rebellion may have an opportunity to study the operations in which they were participants."

17. Post 2 Minutes, May 19, 1870; October 10, 17, and 31, 1878; October

23 and November 6, 1884; and March 23, 1893; Sons of Union Veterans Collection. Webster Post Minutes, October 19, 1887; March 28, 1888; March 6, 1891.

18. Post 2 Minutes, May 19, 1870, Sons of Union Veterans Collection. Webster Post Minutes, February 3, 1886; July 28, 1886; October 3 and December 3, 1888; March 19 and 26, 1890.

19. *National Tribune*, May 14, 1891, p. 3; November 4, 1888, pp. 8, 1; January 5, 1888, p. 8; *Field and Post Room*, January 1886, p. 6; Thomas Leonard, *Above the Battle*, p. 208, n. 9.

20. *New York Times*, December 14, 1880, p. 2; Webster Post Minutes, January 21 and 28, February 25, 1885; *National Tribune*, March 18, 1882, p. 8; Comerford Post Minutes, August 15 and September 19, 1883, Local Post Records Collection.

21. *Providence Morning Star*, June 27, 1877, in Post 2 Scrapbooks, Sons of Union Veterans Collection; *National Tribune*, April 3, 1881, p. 5, and August 9, 1888, p. 6; *Journal of the National Encampment*, 1883, "unofficial proceedings," p. 192; ibid., 1884, "unofficial proceedings," pp. 254–70.

22. Linderman, *Embattled Courage*, pp. 216–65; Sherwood Anderson, *Windy McPherson's Son* (1916), cited in Aaron, *Unwritten War*, p. 340; on prison narratives, see Mitchell, *Civil War Soldiers*, pp. 53–54.

23. *Letters of John Ruskin to Charles Eliot Norton* (1905), cited in Aaron, *Unwritten War*, p. 337.

24. *Philadelphia Sunday Republic*, January 29, 1879, in Post 2 Scrapbooks, Sons of Union Veterans Collection. Post 8 was largely German, a reference made slyly in another verse of the poem: "And you came straight from the post / And did not stop to see mine host / who keeps *potatoes* on the corner / Husband mine, husband mine."

25. Circular of Commander-in-Chief Paul Vandervoort, December 16, 1882, and General Order #15, Pennsylvania Department Commander F. H. Dyer, July 19, 1884, Pennsylvania Department General Orders Book, both in Sons of Union Veterans Collection; *Journal of the National Encampment*, 1881, p. 752; *Chester Evening News*, September 26, 1877, in Post 2 Scrapbooks, Sons of Union Veterans Collection.

26. For an interesting account of some of these *tableaux vivants*, see Glassberg, *American Historical Pageantry*, pp. 16–20.

27. *Grand Army Record*, April 1886, p. 5; June 1889, p. 8; January 1892, p. 8.

28. Webster Post Minutes, March 29, 1883; Post 2 Minutes, September 24, 1891, and October 29, 1896, Sons of Union Veterans Collection.

29. *Proceedings of the National Encampment*, 1871, p. 107.

30. *Journal of the National Encampment*, 1883, "unofficial proceedings," p. 196; ibid., 1881, "unofficial proceedings," pp. 845–46, 850, 849.

31. *Proceedings of the National Encampment*, 1879, pp. 645–46; *Journal of the National Encampment*, 1883, p. 4; *Grand Army Magazine*, April 4, 1883, p. 208 (the legislator making the comment, Aldridge Corder, was a Democrat and former Confederate); *Proceedings of the National Encamp-*

ment, 1869, p. 33 (Logan); *Journal of the National Encampment*, 1880, p. 663 (Wood); ibid., 1885, p. 234.

32. *Souvenir of the 24th National Encampment*, p. 212, Brockton Public Library; *Journal of the National Encampment*, 1882, "unofficial proceedings," pp. 964, 965–66; Grant, *Personal Memoirs*, 2:395.

33. For typical comments on "anarchy," see *Journal of the National Encampment*, 1892, pp. 67–68; on Mormons, see ibid., 1883, pp. 6–7; ibid., 1886, p. 214; and ibid., 1887, pp. 198–203.

34. General Order #11, Commander-in-Chief John Logan, May 5, 1868, National General Orders Book, Sons of Union Veterans Collection. Beath, *History of the GAR*, pp. 379ff, indicates states designating Memorial Day an official holiday as of 1888.

35. Comerford Post Minutes, June 6, 1894; *Journal of the National Encampment*, 1884, p. 234; *Grand Army Record*, April 1892, p. 25. On Cleveland fishing, see Dearing, *Veterans in Politics*, p. 350, and *National Tribune*, June 16, 1887.

36. Lovering, *Services*, pp. 11–21; Post 2 Minutes, January 24, 1884, Sons of Union Veterans Collection. On "ceremonial bereavement" in the United Confederate Veterans, see Foster, *Ghosts of the Confederacy*, pp. 36–46.

37. Comerford Post Minutes, May 18, 1887, Local Post Records Collection. Compare the quite similar Memorial Day service from the 1920s described by W. Lloyd Warner in *The Living and the Dead*, pp. 248–68.

38. *Philadelphia Press*, May 27, 1879, in Post 2 Scrapbooks; Post 2 Minutes, April 10 and May 1, 1879, both in Sons of Union Veterans Collection. It is unlikely that the ritual was actually performed on a public stage. More likely, either the reporter was a Grand Army member admitted to a closed service (the report does not say whether it was limited to GAR members) or he construed whatever action he saw on the stage as being the ritual.

39. *Journal of the National Encampment*, 1885, p. 120; Cunliffe, *Soldiers and Civilians*, p. 435.

40. Two essays that sum up the explosion of scholarship on republicanism are Shalhope, "Toward a Republican Synthesis," pp. 49–80; and Shalhope, "Republicanism and Early American Historiography," pp. 334–56. On antebellum republicanism, see Baker, "From Belief into Culture," and Oakes, "From Republicanism to Liberalism."

41. Ross, "Historical Consciousness," p. 924.

42. Among the many recent works that apply the idea of republicanism are McCoy, *Elusive Republic*; Kerber, *Women of the Republic*; Baker, *Affairs of Party*, esp. pp. 143–76; Faler, *Mechanics and Manufacturers*; Wilentz, *Chants Democratic*, pp. 172–254; and Oestreicher, *Solidarity and Fragmentation*, pp. 41–43. On the common republican and Revolutionary imagery of Union and Confederate soldiers, see Mitchell, *Civil War Soldiers*, pp. 1–3; Faust, *Creation of Confederate Nationalism*, pp. 30–32.

43. Moorhead, *American Apocalypse*, pp. 42–82; Baker, *Affairs of Party*, pp. 269–74; Faust, *Creation of Confederate Nationalism*, pp. 22–23, 29–30; Faust, "Christian Soldiers."

44. Ross, "Historical Consciousness," p. 925; *Proceedings of the National Encampment*, 1871, p. 126; Fredrickson, *Inner Civil War*, esp. pp. 183–238; Reformers such as Henry George, Edward Bellamy, and Henry Demarest Lloyd did apply the republican and evangelical traditions to new social problems, though it is perhaps significant that none of these men had taken an active part in the Civil War. See Thomas, *Alternative America*.

45. Shapiro, "Putting the Past under Glass"; Linden-Ward, "Putting the Past under Grass."

46. Personal war sketches of Corporal Charles Parker, Acker Post 21, St. Paul, Department of Minnesota Papers, box 56, v. 182A; and Chaplain Moses Jones Kelley, Bryant Post 119, Minneapolis, Minnesota GAR Records (43.D.1.4F ov).

47. Garfield, "What Monuments Teach," in Edgar, *Gems of the Campaign of 1880*, p. 86; Lovering, *Services*, p. 26. On the placement of Confederate monuments, see Foster, *Ghosts of the Confederacy*, pp. 40–41 and 128–30. Some of the battlefield monuments were intended not just as commemorations of the cause but also as markers of battle lines for use as "outdoor textbooks" by officer candidates in the army and the National Guard. Thus when a proposal was made in 1889 to move some of the monuments slightly in order to allow the construction of roads through the park, the *Grand Army Record* complained: "Those monuments were erected in the interests of history, not for the convenience of tourists" (January 1889, p. 4). My understanding of this issue has been greatly informed by a paper given by Jay Luvaas at a session on war memorials as historical and cultural symbols, part of the 1984 meeting of the Society of Historians of American Foreign Relations.

48. Webster Post Minutes, August 5 and 8, 1885; Post 2 Minutes, September 15, 1887; October 23 and November 6, 1890; Sons of Union Veterans Collection; *Journal of the National Encampment*, 1889, p. 178; Kilmer, "A Note of Peace"; Comerford Post Minutes, February 21, 1894, Local Post Records Collection.

49. On the development of Lost Cause mythology, see Foster, *Ghosts of the Confederacy*; Charles Reagan Wilson, *Baptized in Blood*; Connelly and Bellows, *God and General Longstreet*. On Gettysburg, see Kinsel, "From These Honored Dead"; on Blue-Gray reconciliation, see Foster, *Ghosts of the Confederacy*, pp. 67–70; on the 1902 encampment, see *Journal of the National Encampment*, 1902, pp. 140–42, 205; "unofficial proceedings," p. 300; and circular letter of Commander-in-Chief Ell Torrance, September 1, 1902, appended to ibid., pp. 375–77.

50. *Journal of the National Encampment*, 1884, "unofficial proceedings," p. 260.

51. *Proceedings of the National Encampment*, 1874, pp. 300–302; *National Tribune*, October 1, 1881, p. 3; General Order #4, Commander-in-Chief John Palmer, November 4, 1891, National General Orders Book, Sons of Union Veterans Collection.

52. Webster Post Minutes, February 20, 1889; *New York Times*, May 25,

1886, p. 5; *National Tribune,* January 28, 1891, p. 5; Post 2 Minutes, May 9, 1895; February 27, 1896; and August 19, 1897; Sons of Union Veterans Collection.

53. *Proceedings of the National Encampment,* 1869, p. 33; *Journal of the National Encampment,* 1880, p. 656.

54. The details of Logan's career follow the account given in James Pickett Jones's two-volume biography, *Black Jack* and *John A. Logan.* On the electioneering of Logan and other "political generals" during the war, see Dearing, *Veterans in Politics,* pp. 1–49.

55. Sherman, *Personal Memoirs,* 2:86; Jones, *John A. Logan,* p. 227. Although Logan voted for the Salary Grab of 1873 and was tangentially associated with the Credit Mobilier scandal, Jones finds his involvements in both affairs essentially innocent (*John A. Logan,* pp. 69–71).

56. Jones, *John A. Logan,* p. 227.

57. Ibid., pp. 171–97, 223–25; Webster Post Minutes, September 19, 1888; Post 2 Minutes, December 30, 1886, Sons of Union Veterans Collection. The subscription list for Mary Logan is printed in *National Tribune,* January 13, 1887, p. 4; it is headed by one George Lemon, with a donation of $1,000. On December 30, 1886, Lemon's paper also devoted its entire front page to the death of Logan.

58. When John A. Logan, Jr., was killed fighting in the Philippines in 1899, Post 2 commemorated the event by noting that the younger Logan was "the only son of the noble general and beloved Comrade whose hand placed the corner-stone of our great order." (Post 2 Minutes, November 16, 1899, Sons of Union Veterans Collection).

59. Grant, *Personal Memoirs,* 1:246. On the raising and early training of the Thirty-first Illinois, see Jones, *Black Jack,* pp. 104–9.

60. *Journal of the National Encampment,* 1883, "unofficial proceedings," pp. 201–2.

61. *Proceedings of the National Encampment,* 1877, p. 444. Baker, *Affairs of Party,* pp. 154–56, points out the affinity of antebellum Democrats (of whom Logan, recall, was one) for the militia idea and the ways in which they linked it to a "preservationist" rationale for fighting the war.

62. Jones, *John A. Logan,* pp. 35–36, 39–41, 54, 144–45, 161; Huntington, *The Soldier and the State,* pp. 222–69. On attitudes toward West Point during the Civil War, see Lisowski, "The Future of West Point," and Williams, "The Attack on West Point."

63. The following account is based on Logan, *Volunteer Soldier,* but see also his *Great Conspiracy,* which plays on the same themes but concentrates somewhat more closely (neither of these books really can be described as having a narrow focus) on the Civil War.

64. Logan, *Volunteer Soldier,* pp. 81, 83–84, 86.

65. Ibid., pp. 86–92.

66. Ibid., pp. 376–98, 555.

67. Ibid., pp. 423, 342–75, 440–58, 115–20, 434.

68. Ibid., pp. 598–607. In outlining his plan, Logan mentioned the military

systems of England, France, and Prussia but discarded them as inapplicable to a democracy—the British system because of its class bias, the Prussian system because of its universal-service requirement. He did, however, praise the French system's competitive examinations for officers' commissions.

69. Ibid., p. 424.

70. In Brockton, 90 percent of Webster Post's members had served in state volunteer regiments. In Comerford Post of Chippewa Falls, the figure was 97 percent; in Philadelphia's Post 2, 88 percent. See McConnell, "A Social History of the GAR," app. A, p. 570.

71. See *Journal of the National Encampment*, 1895, for references to the significance of this event. For the social side of the encampment, see Cummings, "Pomp, Pandemonium, and Paramours."

72. Jones, *John A. Logan*, p. 220.

73. Comerford Post Minutes, April 1 and June 17, 1891; July 27, 1892; December 22, 1897; February 9 and May 11, 1898; post resolutions of February 9 and May 11, 1898, ser. 1, box 12, folder 4; all in Local Post Records Collection.

74. Webster Post Minutes, June 8 and August 31, 1882; December 10, 1884; April 27, 1887; March 21, 1888. Kingman, *History of Brockton*, pp. 21, 746–49. *Brockton* (Mass.) *Enterprise*, October 21, 1890, p. 4, and October 23, 1890, p. 1.

75. Webster Post Minutes, March 30 and May 18 and 25, 1892; Kingman, *History of Brockton*, pp. 767–68. The decision of the court is *Kingman et al. vs. City of Brockton*, 153 Mass. R. 255–59. The Woman's Relief Corps of Brockton erected a small Union monument near the city hall in 1907, while the post was later successful in building a hall at another site.

76. After the consolidation of two rival branches in 1886, the Sons grew to a membership of 60,000 in 1888 (Beath, *History of the GAR*, pp. 669–74). On the boom in "militant orders," and their reflection of generational differences between older fraternalists and their sons, see Carnes, *Secret Ritual*, pp. 141–42.

77. *Journal of the National Encampment*, 1886, p. 45; *National Tribune*, September 9, 1886, p. 4; *Veteran*, December 1892, p. 3 (letter from "a Comrade in Washington, D.C."). See also General Order #14, Commander-in-Chief Lucius Fairchild, May 20, 1887, National General Orders Book, Sons of Union Veterans Collection; *National Tribune*, August 27, 1891, p. 4, and March 17, 1892, p. 6.

78. *Proceedings of the National Encampment*, 1878, p. 521; *Journal of the National Encampment*, 1891, pp. 283, 286.

79. See the following *Journals of the National Encampment*: 1881, pp. 808–9; 1883, p. 10; 1884, pp. 31, 138–39; 1885, p. 153; 1888, p. 191; 1889, pp. 171–72.

80. Post 2 Minutes, August 22 and September 5, 1889; January 23 and March 27, 1890; January 29, February 26, April 2, and May 7, 1891; June 11 and November 26, 1891; February 4 and 18, April 21, 1892; Sons of Union Veterans Collection. Comerford Post Minutes, April 21, 1886; June

15, 1887; April 14, 1888; Local Post Records Collection. Webster Post Minutes, January 18, February 1 and 8, March 15 and 29, April 19, August 2, and December 27, 1883; January 3, August 8, December 31, 1884; March 18, May 20, August 5, and November 4, 1885; January 13 and September 29, 1886; October 10 and December 19, 1888; December 11 and 26, 1889; July 9 and August 27, 1890; March 4 and 25, and October 21, 1891; April 20, all June meetings, and December 14, 1892; January 4, 1893.

81. *Journal of the National Encampment*, 1881, pp. 808–9; ibid., 1883, p. 10; ibid., 1884, p. 32; *Journal of the National Encampment*, 1883, p. 10; *National Tribune*, February 18, 1886, p. 6. At the local level, Webster Post told its Sons of Veterans camp to remove curtains with the inscription "Post 13 GAR" from its hall (Webster Post Minutes, December 14, 1887).

82. Comerford Post Minutes, February 4, 1885, Local Post Records Collection.

83 *Journal of the National Encampment*, 1886, pp. 31, 190–93; *Rules and Regulations*, 1896, chap. 2, art. 1; ibid., 1897, chap. 2, art. 2, sec. 11.

84. *Journal of the National Encampment*, 1885, p. 31; ibid., 1882, p. 869.

CHAPTER SEVEN

1. Mary Dearing makes the point that the decline in GAR membership after 1890 probably had less to do with deaths than it did with a general satisfaction regarding the Dependent Pension Act. Once the act was passed, she argues, many veterans who had joined the GAR because of its pension lobbying became indifferent and dropped out (Dearing, *Veterans in Politics*, pp. 445–46).

2. Eric Foner suggests such an ironic adjustment in *Free Soil, Free Labor, Free Men*, pp. 316–17; "The Causes of the American Civil War," pp. 213–14; and *Reconstruction*, pp. 478–88 and 514–18.

3. For a discussion of the concept of "public culture" and some of its limitations, see Bender, "Wholes and Parts," and Painter et al., "A Round Table."

4. Curti, *Roots of American Loyalty*, pp. 189, 191–93; Wallace E. Davies, *Patriotism on Parade*, pp. 44–73 and passim; Higham, *Strangers in the Land*, pp. 68–105; Swanberg, *Citizen Hearst*; Hofstadter, *Social Darwinism in American Thought*; Dumenil, *Freemasonry and American Culture*, pp. 115–26, 145–47.

5. *National Tribune*, June 4, 1885, p. 6; Post 2 Minutes, January 21, 1892, Sons of Union Veterans Collection; *Proceedings of the National Encampment*, 1869, pp. 70–71; *National Tribune*, September 1880, p. 6. In Post 2, 202 of the 219 members born outside the United States were from England, Scotland, Ireland, Wales, Canada, or Germany. In Brockton's Webster Post, 42 of 48 came from these countries; in Chippewa Falls's Comerford Post, 67 of 75.

6. *Ceremony of Flag Presentation to Columbia University*, pp. 110–11.

National Tribune, August 9, 1888, p. 1; August 16, 1888, p. 4; April 2, 1891, p. 4; October 24, 1889, p. 4; and April 23, 1891, p. 4. *Journal of the National Encampment,* 1892, p. 82. On the membership of the Sons, see *National Tribune,* November 26, 1891: of the 38,276 members returning the paper's questionnaire (roughly half the total in the organization), only 151 were foreign-born.

7. On Carey and producerism, see Unger, *The Greenback Era,* pp. 33–34, 50–60; on the relationship of producerism to reform, see Thomas, *Alternative America,* pp. 312–13, 336–37.

8. *Proceedings of the National Encampment,* 1878, p. 522 (emphasis added); Post 2 Minutes, July 23, 1877, Sons of Union Veterans Collection (and see also the minutes of July 26, August 2 and 23, October 4 and 25, 1877); *National Tribune,* June 3, 1886, p. 6; *Journal of the National Encampment,* 1889, p. 34; *The Volcano under the City,* pp. 331–32.

9. General Order #8, Pennsylvania Department Commander William Emsley, March 7, 1894, Pennsylvania Department General Orders Book, Sons of Union Veterans Collection; General Order #5, Oregon Department Commander S. B. Ormsby, July 21, 1894, Oregon Collection, GAR Papers; *National Tribune,* July 21, 1892, p. 6; *Journal of the National Encampment,* 1892, p. 67.

10. *National Tribune,* July 26, 1883, p. 4; April 9, 1885, p. 4; and July 14, 1892, p. 6. *Grand Army Record,* February 1887, p. 4.

11. On the growing disjunction between free-labor ideology and wage-work reality, in addition to the works of Foner cited above, see Paludan, *A People's Contest,* pp. 170–97; Montgomery, *Beyond Equality,* pp. 335–86; and Rodgers, *Work Ethic in Industrial America,* pp. 30–64, esp. pp. 31–32. A campaign lithograph of Grant the Tanner is conveniently reproduced in McFeely, *Grant,* p. 382.

12. Webster Post Minutes, December 30, 1885, and August 18, 1886.

13. On Douglass, see Blight, "For Something beyond the Battlefield," esp. pp. 1165–68; *Journal of the National Encampment,* 1882, "unofficial proceedings," pp. 965–66. On the Lost Cause, see Foster, *Ghosts of the Confederacy;* Charles Reagan Wilson, *Baptized in Blood;* Connelly and Bellows, *God and General Longstreet.*

14. Lester and Wilson, *Ku Klux Klan,* p. 171. The GAR was unusual among fraternal orders, however, in that it allowed black members at all, even in segregated posts; see Clawson, *Constructing Brotherhood,* pp. 132–35. The original GAR posts in the South were made up either of black veterans or of federal employees of the Reconstruction governments; the posts did not last much longer than did those governments. In most parts of the South the order languished until 1883, and even after that it was never strong in Alabama or South Carolina. See Beath, *History of the GAR,* pp. 379ff; and Primm, "The G.A.R. in Missouri." As for the "redeemed" Southern departments of the 1880s, Dearing notes that in 1885 the reconstituted Department of Tennessee and Georgia had 88 black and 1,145 white members, organized into separate posts (*Veterans in Politics,* p. 413).

15. *Proceedings of the National Encampment,* 1877, p. 446.

16. *Journal of the National Encampment,* 1887, pp. 250–55; Dearing, *Veterans in Politics,* pp. 413–14.

17. *New York Times,* January 5, 1890, p. 5; see also ibid., January 8, 1890, p. 1, and February 14, 1890, p. 3; *Journal of the National Encampment,* 1890, pp. 56–60, 258, 59.

18. *Journal of the National Encampment,* 1891, pp. 50–51; *National Tribune,* October 23, 1890, p. 6.

19. *Journal of the National Encampment,* 1891, p. 261.

20. Ibid., pp. 250, 254.

21. Ibid., p. 263; ibid., 1892, pp. 52–58. On white posts leaving the order, see also *New York Times,* May 19, 1892, p. 1.

22. See, for example, the reports of such rejections in *National Tribune,* November 12, 1885, p. 4, and December 31, 1885, p. 4; *Grand Army Record,* August 1892, p. 57; *New York Times,* October 22 and December 7, 1889, and March 10, 1890; and *Proceedings of the Pennsylvania Department Encampment,* 1885, pp. 260–61.

23. Dearing, *Veterans in Politics,* pp. 418–19; *Journal of the National Encampment,* 1898, p. 52; Wallace E. Davies, "The Problem of Race Segregation in the GAR."

24. *Proceedings of the National Encampment,* 1870, pp. 88, 102; ibid., 1871, p. 124; ibid., 1872, p. 190; ibid., 1875, pp. 351–52; *Journal of the National Encampment,* 1881, p. 793.

25. Webster Post Minutes, April 22, 1880; Comerford Post Minutes, May 4, 1887, Local Post Records Collection; Post 2 Minutes, February 20, 1890, Sons of Union Veterans Collection; *National Tribune,* October 29, 1885, p. 9; *Journal of the National Encampment,* 1892, p. 246. On the disbursement of charity funds, see the reminders of GAR commanders-in-chief (*Journal of the National Encampment,* 1886, p. 40, and ibid., 1888, p. 39) that the Woman's Relief Corps was still an independent organization and could not be ordered to turn over funds, as some posts apparently believed.

26. *National Tribune,* June 28, 1883, p. 2 (women's column); *Grand Army Magazine,* vol. 1, no. 4, April 1883, p. 268; *Journal of the National Encampment,* 1891, p. 281. On the Detroit banquet, see *Grand Army Record,* July 1891, p. 4, and August 1891, p. 5; and Wallace E. Davies, *Patriotism on Parade,* pp. 130–31.

27. Dumenil, *Freemasonry and American Culture,* pp. 25–26; Carnes, *Secret Ritual,* esp. pp. 79–89.

28. *Journal of the National Encampment,* 1884, p. 250; *Veteran,* April 1893, p. 4.

29. *Proceedings of the National Encampment,* 1869, p. 34.

30. Smith, *Nationalist Movements,* p. 2; Kedourie, *Nationalism,* pp. 73–74. The distinction made here between "patriotism" and "nationalism" is put in virtually the same terms by other writers on the subject; see Hayes, *Historical Evolution of Modern Nationalism,* pp. 1–12, and Gellner, *Nations and Nationalism,* pp. 137–38.

31. Hayes, *Historical Evolution of Modern Nationalism*, p. 292.

32. In addition to the works of Hayes, Smith, Kedourie, and Gellner cited above, useful analyses include Breuilly, *Nationalism and the State*; Benedict Anderson, *Imagined Communities*; Hobsbawm, *Nations and Nationalism since 1780*; and Segal, "Nationalism, Comparatively Speaking."

33. Compare, for example, Judson, " 'Whether Race or Conviction Should Be the Standard' "; Cohen, *Politics of Ethnic Survival*; Blackbourn, "The Discrete Charm of the Bourgeoisie," in Blackbourn and Eley, *Peculiarities of German History*, pp. 159–292; Elwitt, *The Making of the Third Republic*; and Verdery, *Transylvanian Villagers*.

34. Examples of the former include Nagel, *This Sacred Trust*, and Kohn, *American Nationalism*, esp. pp. 3–37. Breuilly takes the latter approach in *Nationalism and the State*, pp. 6–8.

35. Smith, "The Formation of Nationalist Movements," in Smith, *Nationalist Movements*, p. 3.

36. Breuilly, *Nationalism and the State*, pp. 11, 380. Peter Calvert addresses the issue of nationalism in new nation-states in "On Attaining Sovereignty," in Smith, *Nationalist Movements*, pp. 134–49.

37. Eley, *Reshaping the German Right*, pp. 176, 166–68, 125–33. V. G. Kiernan suggests that members of the petty bourgeoisie are drawn to nationalist movements largely because they have nowhere else to go ("Nationalist Movements and Social Classes," in Smith, *Nationalist Movements*, pp. 115–16). Breuilly also argues that this class is inclined toward nationalist movements (*Nationalism and the State*, pp. 316–18), as does Hobsbawm (*Nations and Nationalism since 1780*, pp. 117–22).

38. *Journal of the National Encampment*, 1888, p. 211.

39. Ibid., pp. 211–14, 215; ibid., 1891, pp. 275–77; ibid., 1892, pp. 80–83.

40. Comerford Post Minutes, May 6, 1891, and May 18, 1892, Local Post Records Collection; Post 2 Minutes, February 18, April 15 and 29, and November 18, 1897, Sons of Union Veterans Collection; Wallace E. Davies, *Patriotism on Parade*, pp. 240–41; Dearing, *Veterans in Politics*, pp. 483–84; *Journal of the National Encampment*, 1898, p. 192; ibid., 1900, p. 143.

41. Post 2 Minutes, February 8, 15, and 22, 1894, Sons of Union Veterans Collection; *Journal of the National Encampment*, 1894, p. 250.

42. *Journal of the National Encampment*, 1897, p. 232.

43. Ibid., 1894, p. 250.

44. General Order #11, Pennsylvania Department Commander John P. Taylor, August 9, 1892, Pennsylvania Department General Orders Book, Sons of Union Veterans Collection; also see Dearing, *Veterans in Politics*, pp. 407–8, and Comerford Post Minutes, October 19, 1892, Local Post Records Collection. On holiday flag presentations, see *Presentation of National Flags to the Public Schools of the City of Rochester on Washington's Birthday, 1889*. Several of the Lafayette Post flag presentations were on holidays unrelated to the Civil War: Columbus Day, Washington's Birthday, Boxing Day, Flag Day; see the presentations listed in *Ceremony of Flag Presentation to Columbia University*, p. 109.

45. *Journal of the National Encampment*, 1892, p. 81.

46. Ibid., 1891, pp. 275–77; ibid., 1892, pp. 80–83; Lankevich, "The GAR in New York State," p. 256; Dearing, *Veterans in Politics*, p. 405.

47. *Ceremony of Flag Presentation to Columbia University*, p. 40; similar scriptural references dot the 1898 address of Post Commander Daniel Butterfield, p. 76. On flag presentations to regiments of both armies during the war, see Mitchell, *Civil War Soldiers*, pp. 19–20.

48. *Journal of the National Encampment*, 1889, p. 41; Dearing, *Veterans in Politics*, p. 406; *Journal of the National Encampment*, 1897, p. 212.

49. Dearing, *Veterans in Politics*, pp. 405, 408, 472, 474–75; Curti, *Roots of American Loyalty*, pp. 190–91; *Journal of the National Encampment*, 1897, p. 237; ibid., 1898, pp. 192–93. The ban on the commercial use of the flag was ironic from the GAR standpoint, since it was prompted largely by the McKinley campaign's partisan use of the flag in the heated election campaign of 1896.

50. Lankevich, "The GAR in New York State," p. 260; General Order #6, Commander-in-Chief John Palmer, November 20, 1891, and General Order #4, Palmer, November 4, 1891, National General Orders Book, Sons of Union Veterans Collection; *Veteran*, December 1891, p. 4; Webster Post Minutes, November 2, 1892, and January 4, 1893. For resolutions from many other posts supporting Palmer's "flag order," see *National Tribune*, issues of November 1891.

51. On the battle-flag controversy, see Dearing, *Veterans in Politics*, pp. 342–51; Wallace E. Davies, *Patriotism on Parade*, pp. 257–60.

52. *Macmillan's Magazine*, vol. 65, November 1891–April 1892, p. 133. On the loaning of Post 2 colors, see the many loans recorded in the post minutes for 1882, Sons of Veterans Collection—for example, the meeting of October 19, 1882.

53. Dearing, *Veterans in Politics*, pp. 472–73; General Order #6, Commander-in-Chief John Palmer, November 20, 1891, National General Orders Book, Sons of Union Veterans Collection; Low to James Bach, April 20, 1898, in *Ceremony of Flag Presentation to Columbia University*, p. 71.

54. On the concept of "civil religion," see Bellah, "Civil Religion in America"; Richey and Jones, *American Civil Religion*; Albanese, *Sons of the Fathers*; and John F. Wilson, *Public Religion in American Culture*. On the flag as a ritual icon, see Kertzer, *Ritual, Politics, and Power*, pp. 9–12, 64–67, 90.

55. *Journal of the National Encampment*, 1898, p. 8.

56. On school drill, see Fowler, "Shall We Introduce the Military System in Schools?"; Cree, "Military Education in Colleges"; Bronson, "The Value of Military Training and Discipline in the Schools"; and "Our Schoolboy Soldiers," pp. 459–66.

57. *Proceedings of the National Encampment*, 1893, p. 242; *Journal of the National Encampment*, 1894, pp. 245–46; Dearing, *Veterans in Politics*, pp. 476–81; Lankevich, "The GAR in New York State," pp. 263–73.

58. "Military Instruction in Schools and Colleges," p. 469; "Our School-

boy Soldiers," p. 465; Love, "Military Instruction in Schools, Churches, and Colleges," p. 211. For objections in addition to those of Love, see Benjamin O. Flower, "Fostering the Savage in the Young," and "Playing with Fire."

59. *Grand Army Record*, September 1894, p. 65.

60. General Order #5, Oregon Department Commander S. B. Ormsby, July 21, 1894, Oregon Collection, GAR Papers.

61. *Journal of the National Encampment*, 1898, pp. 48–49.

62. Records of Webster Post relief committee, May 2 to June 17, 1898, appended to post Minutes; Comerford Post Minutes, April 23 and May 11, 1898, Local Post Records Collection; letter, Henry P. Marvin to Comerford Post, April 23, 1898, in ser. 1, box 12, folder 4, Local Post Records Collection; Post 2 Minutes, June 2 and December 8, 1898, Sons of Union Veterans Collection.

63. *History of the Gift of Six Hundred National Flags; Journal of the National Encampment*, 1898, pp. 8, 67.

64. *Journal of the National Encampment*, 1898, pp. 46, 48, 211–12.

65. Ibid. 1894, p. 250.

66. Linderman, *Mirror of War*, pp. 127–47.

67. *Journal of the National Encampment*, 1898, p. 49.

68. The following discussion is based on Linderman, *Mirror of War*, pp. 98–110, esp. pp. 107–10.

69. On the centrality of moral justification to the declaration of war, see ibid., pp. 37–59; on American images of the Spaniards and the Cubans, see ibid., pp. 127–47, and Thomas Leonard, *Above the Battle*, pp. 62–63.

70. *Journal of the National Encampment*, 1898, pp. 46, 8, 48, 211.

71. Ibid., 1902, pp. 125–27, 231–69, and 296 ("unofficial proceedings").

72. The language on women is from ibid., pp. 171, 173. On Du Bois, see, of course, Du Bois's *Black Reconstruction*. My understanding of Du Bois as a historian has been enriched by conversations with David W. Blight, who kindly shared some of his in-progress work on Du Bois with me; see Blight, "W. E. B. Du Bois and the Struggle for American Historical Memory" (forthcoming).

BIBLIOGRAPHY

Published Grand Army Materials

Beath, Robert B., comp. *The Grand Army Blue Book*. Philadelphia, 1884; revised intermittently thereafter.

Beath, Robert B., et al., comps. *Manual for the Guidance of the Grand Army of the Republic*. Philadelphia, 1881.

Carnahan, James R., comp. *Decisions and Opinions of the Commanders-in-Chief and Judge Advocates-General of the Grand Army of the Republic*. Indianapolis: Hasselman-Journal Co., 1884.

Lovering, Joseph F. *Services for the Use of the Grand Army of the Republic*. Boston: Grand Army Headquarters, 1881.

Proceedings of Enlistment and Muster of the Grand Army of the Republic. Springfield, Ill., 1866.

Proceedings of the Massachusetts Department Encampment, Grand Army of the Republic, 1866–1900. Place of publication varies.

Proceedings of the National Encampment, Grand Army of the Republic,
1866–1902. For 1881–92 and 1894–1902, title is *Journal of the National*
Encampment, Grand Army of the Republic. Place of publications varies.
Proceedings of the Pennsylvania Department Encampment, Grand Army of
the Republic, 1866–1900. Place of publication varies.
Proceedings of the Wisconsin Department Encampment, Grand Army of
the Republic, 1883–1900. Place of publication varies.
Ritual of the Grand Army of the Republic. Washington, D.C., 1869. Rev.
Philadelphia, 1883; Kansas City, 1889; Rutland, Vt., 1891; Rockford, Ill.,
1895; Philadelphia, 1898.
Rules and Regulations for the Government of the Grand Army of the Re-
public, 1869, 1870, 1872, 1874, 1879, 1884, 1887, 1890, 1896, 1897, 1898,
1899. Place of publication varies.
Rules and Regulations of Fletcher Webster Post 13, Grand Army of the Re-
public. N.p., 1871.

Unpublished Grand Army Materials

Boston, Massachusetts
  Massachusetts State House Collection, GAR Memorial Room
    Adjutants' Quarterly Reports, Fletcher Webster Post 13, 1873–1900
Brockton, Massachusetts
  War Memorial Building Collection
Harrisburg, Pennsylvania
  Pennsylvania Historical and Museum Commission Archives (PHMC)
    Descriptive Books, Pennsylvania Grand Army posts
    Memorial Record Books, Simon Cameron Post 78
Madison, Wisconsin
  GAR Memorial Hall, Local Post Records Collection
    Adjutants' Quarterly Reports, James Comerford Post 68, 1883–97
    Descriptive Books, Wisconsin Grand Army posts
    Membership Applications, James Comerford Post 68, 1883–1900
    Minutes, James Comerford Post 68, 1883–1900
    Miscellaneous Papers and Correspondence, James Comerford Post 68,
    1898–99
    Post Financial Record, James Comerford Post 68, 1883–1900
    Roster, 1890, James Comerford Post 68.
  State Historical Society of Wisconsin
    Manuscript State of Wisconsin Census, 1885 and 1895, special census
    of surviving Union soldiers and sailors
Philadelphia, Pennsylvania
  Sons of Union Veterans Collection, GAR Memorial Hall and Museum
    Adjutants' Letterpress Book, Post 2, 1887–88
    Black Book, Post 2, 1871–1910
    Business Directory, Post 2, 1886

Descriptive Books, Post 2, 1866–1900
Employment Bureau Book, Post 2, 1894
Memorial Record Books, Post 2, 1889
Minutes, Post 2, 1866–1900
National General Orders Book, 1866–1900
Orders Book, Post 2, 1866–1900
Pennsylvania Department General Orders Book, 1866–1900
Roster, Post 2, 1896
Scrapbooks, Post 2, 1877–80
Randolph, Massachusetts
  Private collection of Mr. Ken Oakley
    Fair Book, Fletcher Webster Post 13, 1886
    Minutes, Fletcher Webster Post 13, 1876–93
St. Paul, Minnesota
  Minnesota Historical Society
    Department of Minnesota Papers, 1866–1900
    Grand Army of the Republic Records
Salem, Oregon
  Oregon State Library
    Oregon Collection, GAR Papers
Washington, D.C.
  Martin Luther King, Jr., Public Library
    Washingtoniana Collection

Newspapers

Soldier Newspapers
  Field and Post Room. Harrisburg, Pa., 1886.
  Grand Army Magazine. Denver, 1883.
  Grand Army Record. Boston, 1885–1900.
  Great Republic. Washington, D.C., 1867.
  National Tribune. Washington, D.C., 1877–1900.
  Oregon Veteran. Portland, Oreg., 1886.
  Soldier's Friend. New York, 1864–70.
  Veteran. Worcester, Mass., 1891–94.

Other Newspapers
  Boston Post
  Brockton (Mass.) *Enterprise*
  Eau Claire (Wis.) *Free Press*
  New York Times
  New York Tribune
  Philadelphia Bulletin
  Philadelphia Inquirer

Philadelphia North American and U.S. Gazette
Philadelphia Public Ledger

Books, Articles, and Theses

Aaron, Daniel. *The Unwritten War: American Writers and the Civil War.*
New York: Alfred A. Knopf, 1973.

Adams, Charles Francis. "Pensions—Worse and More of Them." *World's
Work,* vol. 23, no. 2, December 1911, pp. 188–96; no. 3, January 1912,
pp. 327–34; no. 4, February 1912, pp. 385–98.

Alanko, Tyne. "History of the Soldiers' Orphans' Institutions in Pennsylvania." Master's thesis, University of Chicago, 1933.

Albanese, Catherine L. *Sons of the Fathers: The Civil Religion of the American Revolution.* Philadelphia: Temple University Press, 1976.

Alcorn, Richard S. "Leadership and Stability in Mid-Nineteenth Century
America: A Case Study." *Journal of American History* 61, no. 3 (December 1974): 685–702.

Anderson, Benedict. *Imagined Communities.* London: Verso Editions, 1983.

Anderson, Fred. *A People's Army: Massachusetts Soldiers and Society in
the Seven Years' War.* Chapel Hill: University of North Carolina Press,
1984.

Andreano, Ralph, ed. *The Economic Impact of the American Civil War.*
Cambridge, Mass.: Schenkman, 1967.

Andreski, Stanislav. *Military Organization and Society.* London: Routledge
and Kegan Paul, 1954.

Appleby, Joyce. "Republicanism and Ideology." *American Quarterly* 37,
no. 4 (Fall 1985): 461–73.

Bacon, Leonard Woolsey. "A Raid upon the Treasury." *Forum,* January
1889, pp. 540–49.

Baker, Jean H. *Affairs of Party: The Political Culture of Northern Democrats in the Mid-Nineteenth Century.* Ithaca, N.Y.: Cornell University
Press, 1983.

———. "From Belief into Culture: Republicanism in the Antebellum
North." *American Quarterly* 37, no. 4 (Fall 1985): 532–50.

Baltzell, E. Digby. *Philadelphia Gentlemen: The Making of a National Upper Class.* New York: Free Press, 1958.

Barron, Hal S. *Those Who Stayed Behind: Rural Society in Nineteenth-
Century New England.* New York: Cambridge University Press, 1984.

Baruch, Mildred C., and Ellen J. Beckman. *Civil War Monuments: A List of
Union Monuments, Markers and Memorials of the Civil War, 1861–1865.*
Washington, D.C.: Daughters of Union Veterans of the Civil War, 1978.

Battles and Leaders of the Civil War. 4 vols. New York: Century Company,
1884–87.

Beath, Robert B. *History of the Grand Army of the Republic.* New York:
Bryan, Taylor and Co., 1889.

Bedford, Henry F. *Socialism and the Workers in Massachusetts, 1886–1912*. Amherst: University of Massachusetts Press, 1966.

Bellah, Robert N. "Civil Religion in America." *Daedalus* 96 (Winter 1967): 1–21.

Bender, Thomas. *Community and Social Change in America*. New Brunswick, N.J.: Rutgers University Press, 1978.

———. "The Cultures of Intellectual Life: The City and the Professions." In *New Directions in Intellectual History*, edited by John Higham and Paul Conkin, pp. 181–95. Baltimore: Johns Hopkins University Press, 1979.

———. "Wholes and Parts: The Need For Synthesis in American History." *Journal of American History* 73, no. 1 (June 1986): 120–36.

Bierce, Ambrose. *Fantastic Fables*. New York: G. P. Putnam's Sons, 1899.

Blackbourn, David, and Geoff Eley. *The Peculiarities of German History*. New York: Oxford University Press, 1984.

Blight, David W. "For Something beyond the Battlefield: Frederick Douglass and the Struggle for the Memory of the Civil War." *Journal of American History* 75, no. 4 (March 1989): 1156–78.

Bloodgood, John D. *Personal Reminiscences of the War*. New York: Hunt and Eaton, 1893.

Boyer, Paul S. *Urban Masses and Moral Order in America, 1820–1920*. Cambridge: Harvard University Press, 1978.

Boynton, H. V. "Fraudulent Practices of the Pension-Sharks; Uselessness of Pension-Attorneys." *Harper's Weekly*, vol. 42, March 5, 1898, p. 230.

Breuilly, John. *Nationalism and the State*. New York: St. Martin's Press, 1982.

Brock, William R. *Investigation and Responsibility: Public Responsibility in the United States, 1865–1900*. New York: Cambridge University Press, 1984.

"Brockton, A City of Enterprise." *New England Magazine*, September 1911, pp. 67–80.

Brockton and Bridgewaters Directories. 1869–1900. Place of publication varies.

Brockton Board of Trade. *Manual*. Providence, R.I., 1899.

Bronson, T. B. "The Value of Military Training and Discipline in the Schools." *School Review* 2 (May 1894): 281–85.

Bull, Rice C. *Soldiering: The Civil War Diary of Rice C. Bull, 123rd New York Volunteer Infantry*. Edited by K. Jack Bauer. San Rafael, Calif.: Presidio Press, 1977.

Carnes, Mark C. *Secret Ritual and Manhood in Victorian America*. New Haven: Yale University Press, 1989.

Ceremony of Flag Presentation to Columbia University of the City of New York, May 2, 1896, and May 7, 1898, by Lafayette Post No. 140, Department of New York, Grand Army of the Republic. New York: Lafayette Post, 1899.

Chandler, Alfred D., Jr. "The Organization of Manufacturing and Transportation." In *Economic Change in the Civil War Era*, edited by David T.

Gilchrist and Walter D. Lewis, pp. 137–51. Greenville, Del.: Eleutherian Mills-Hagley Foundation, 1965.

——. *The Visible Hand: The Managerial Revolution in American Business*. Cambridge: Harvard University Press, 1977.

Childs, George William. *Recollections*. Philadelphia: J. B. Lippincott and Co., 1890.

Chippewa County, Past and Present. Chicago: S. J. Clarke, 1913.

Chippewa Falls City Directory. Chippewa Falls, Wis., 1907.

Clawson, Mary Ann. *Constructing Brotherhood: Class, Gender, and Fraternalism*. Princeton, N.J.: Princeton University Press, 1989.

——. "Fraternal Orders and Class Formation in the Nineteenth-Century United States." *Comparative Studies in Society and History* 27, no. 4 (October 1985): pp. 672–95.

Cochran, Thomas. "Did the Civil War Retard Industrialization?", *Mississippi Valley Historical Review* 48, no. 2 (September 1961): 197–210.

Cohen, Gary. *The Politics of Ethnic Survival: Germans in Prague, 1861–1914*. Princeton, N.J.: Princeton University Press, 1981.

"Commissioner Raum on Pensions and Patriotism." *Nation*, vol. 53, July 30, 1891, pp. 80–81.

Connelly, Thomas L., and Barbara L. Bellows. *God and General Longstreet: The Lost Cause and the Southern Mind*. Baton Rouge: Louisiana State University Press, 1982.

[Cook, Ezra Asher, comp.] *Five Standard Rituals. Odd-Fellowship illustrated, Knights of Pythias illustrated, Good Templarism illustrated, exposition of the Grange, ritual of the Grand Army of the Republic, and the Machinists and Blacksmiths Union*.Chicago: Ezra A. Cook, 1880.

Cooper, Jerry M. "The Wisconsin Militia, 1832–1900." Master's thesis, University of Wisconsin, 1968.

Crane, Stephen. *The Red Badge of Courage*. New York: New York Press, 1894. Reprint. New York: Norton, 1976.

Cree, John K. "Military Education in Colleges." *Education* 15 (April 1895): 473–79.

Cummings, William E. "Pomp, Pandemonium, and Paramours: The GAR Convention of 1895." *Register of the Kentucky Historical Society* 81, no. 3 (Summer 1983): 274–86.

Cunliffe, Marcus. *Soldiers and Civilians: The Martial Spirit in America, 1775–1865*. Boston: Little, Brown and Co., 1978.

Cunningham, Hugh. *The Volunteer Force: A Social and Political History*. Hamden, Conn.: Archon Books, 1975.

Curti, Merle. *The Making of an American Community: A Case Study of Democracy in a Frontier County*. Palo Alto: Stanford University Press, 1982.

——. *The Roots of American Loyalty*. New York: Columbia University Press, 1946.

Davies, Edward J. "Class and Power in the Anthracite Region: The Control of Political Leadership in Wilkes-Barre, Pa., 1845–1885." *Journal of Urban History* 9, no. 3 (May 1983): 291–334.

Davies, Wallace E. *Patriotism on Parade: The Story of Veterans' and Hereditary Organizations in America, 1783–1900*. Cambridge: Harvard University Press, 1957.

———. "The Problem of Race Segregation in the Grand Army of the Republic." *Journal of Southern History* 13 (August 1947): 354–72.

Davis, Susan G. *Parades and Power: Street Theatre in Nineteenth-Century Philadelphia*. Philadelphia: Temple University Press, 1986.

Dearing, Mary R. *Veterans in Politics: The Story of the GAR*. Baton Rouge: Louisiana State University Press, 1952.

"Defenders of the Union: Grand Army of the Republic on the Pacific Coast." *Overland Monthly* 27 (March 1896): 434–61.

Dennis, Thomas Fletcher. "Anomalies of Our Private Pension System." *Forum*, vol. 15, May 1893, pp. 377–86.

Diehl, James. *Paramilitary Politics in Weimar Germany*. Bloomington: Indiana University Press, 1977.

Donald, David H. "Died of Democracy." In *Why the North Won the Civil War*, edited by David H. Donald, pp. 77–90. Baton Rouge: Louisiana State University Press, 1960.

———. "A Generation of Defeat." In *From the Old South to the New: Essays on the Transitional South*, edited by Walter J. Fraser, Jr., and Winifred B. Moore, Jr., pp. 3–20. Westport, Conn.: Greenwood Press, 1981.

Doyle, Don Harrison. *The Social Order of a Frontier Community: Jacksonville, Illinois, 1825–1870*. Urbana: University of Illinois Press, 1984.

Du Bois, W. E. B. *Black Reconstruction*. New York: Harcourt, Brace and Company, 1935.

Dumenil, Lynn. *Freemasonry and American Culture, 1880–1930*. Princeton, N.J.: Princeton University Press, 1984.

Edgar, George P., comp. *Gems of the Campaign of 1880, By Generals Grant and Garfield*. Jersey City, N.J.: Lincoln Association, 1881.

Eley, Geoff. "Nationalism and Social History." *Social History* 6 (January 1981): 83–107.

———. *Reshaping the German Right: Radical Nationalism and Political Change After Bismarck*. New Haven: Yale University Press, 1980.

Elwitt, Sanford. *The Making of the Third Republic: Class and Politics in France, 1808–1884*. Baton Rouge: Louisiana State University Press, 1975.

[Faehtz, Ernest M.]. *The Grand Army's Bequest*. Washington, D.C., 1869.

Faler, Paul. *Mechanics and Manufacturers in the Early Industrial Revolution: Lynn, Massachusetts, 1780–1860*. Albany: State University of New York Press, 1981.

Fallows, Samuel, ed. *Grand Army Manual and Soldier-Citizen's Handbook*. Chicago, 1883.

Faust, Drew Gilpin. "Christian Soldiers: The Meaning of Revivalism in the Confederate Army." *Journal of Southern History* 53, no. 1 (February 1987): 63–90.

———. *The Creation of Confederate Nationalism: Ideology and Identity in* the Civil War South. Baton Rouge: Louisiana State University Press, 1988.

Finn, John J. "Complete History of the Farnham Post Revolt." *Forum*, vol. 15, July 1893, pp. 532–40.

Fish, Carl. "The Raising of a Wisconsin Regiment." *Military Historian and Economist* 1, no. 3 (July 1916): 258.

Flower, Benjamin O. "Fostering the Savage in the Young." *Arena* 10, no. 57, August 1894, pp. 422–32.

Flower, John Franklin. *Summary of Laws Relating to Soldiers' Claims*. Kittanning, Pa.: Reichert Bros., 1882.

Foner, Eric. "The Causes of the American Civil War: Recent Interpretations and New Directions." *Civil War History* 20, no. 3 (September 1974): 197–214.

———. *Free Soil, Free Labor, Free Men: The Ideology of the Republican Party before the Civil War*. New York: Oxford University Press, 1970.

———. *Reconstruction: America's Unfinished Revolution, 1863–1877*. New York: Harper and Row, 1988.

Foote, Allen Ripley. "The Decisive Breach in the Grand Army." *Forum*, vol. 15, June 1893, pp. 452–58.

———. "Degradation by Pensions—The Protest of the Loyal Volunteers." *Forum*, vol. 12, December 1891, pp. 423–32.

———. "Patriotism, Morality, and Pensions." *American Journal of Politics* 3 (June 1893): 638–43.

Forrester, George, ed. *History and Biographical Album of the Chippewa Valley*. Chicago, 1891–92.

Foster, Gaines M. *Ghosts of the Confederacy: Defeat, the Lost Cause, and the Emergence of the New South, 1865–1913*. New York: Oxford University Press, 1987.

Fowler, C. W. "Shall We Introduce the Military System in Schools?" *Educational Review* 11 (February 1896): 183–86.

Fredrickson, George M. *The Inner Civil War: Northern Intellectuals and the Crisis of the Union*. New York: Harper and Row, 1965.

French, Bella. *Chippewa Falls, Wisconsin*. La Crosse, Wis.: Sketch Book Co., 1874.

Fussell, Paul. *The Great War and Modern Memory*. New York: Oxford University Press, 1975.

Gallman, James Matthew. *Mastering Wartime: A Social History of Philadelphia during the Civil War*. New York: Cambridge University Press, 1990.

———. "Voluntarism in Wartime: Philadelphia's Great Central Fair." In *Toward a Social History of the American Civil War: Exploratory Essays*, edited by Maris A. Vinovskis, pp. 93–116. New York: Cambridge University Press, 1990.

"The GAR Encampment." *Public Opinion*, vol. 3, October 8, 1887, pp. 545–49.

GAR War Papers: Papers Read before Fred C. Jones Post #401, Department of Ohio. Cincinnati: Fred C. Jones Post, 1891.

Geer, Allen Morgan. *The Civil War Diary of Allen Morgan Geer*. Edited by
Mary Ann Anderson. New York: Cosmos Press, 1977.

Geer, Emily Apt. *First Lady: The Life of Lucy Webb Hayes*. Kent, Ohio: Kent
State University Press, Rutherford B. Hayes Presidential Center, 1984.

Gellner, Ernest. *Nations and Nationalism*. Ithaca, N.Y.: Cornell University
Press, 1983.

Gerrish, Theodore. *Army Life: A Private's Reminiscences of the Civil War*.
Portland, Maine: Hoyt, Fogg, and Donham, 1882.

Gerstle, Gary. *Working-Class Americanism: The Politics of Labor in a Tex-
tile City, 1914–1960*. New York: Cambridge University Press, 1989.

Gilkeson, John S., Jr. *Middle-Class Providence, 1820–1940*. Princeton,
N.J.: Princeton University Press, 1986.

Glassberg, David. *American Historical Pageantry: The Uses of Tradition in
the Twentieth Century*. Chapel Hill: University of North Carolina Press,
1990.

Glasson, William H. *Federal Military Pensions in the United States*. New
York: Oxford University Press, 1918.

"The Grand Army." *Nation*, vol. 49, October 24, 1889, pp. 325–26.

"The Grand Army Machine." *Nation*, vol. 45, July 14, 1887, p. 26.

"The Grand Army of the Republic." *Macmillan's Magazine*, vol. 65, December 1891, pp. 130–36.

"The Grand Army Reunion at Detroit." *Harper's Weekly*, vol. 35, August
15, 1891, pp. 619–20.

Grand Army Soldiers and Citizens Album. Chicago, 1890.

"The Grand Army in Washington." *Harper's Weekly*, vol. 36, October 1,
1892, pp. 944–46.

"The Grand Army's Progress." *Nation*, vol. 60, May 2, 1895, p. 336.

Grant, Ulysses S. *Personal Memoirs of U. S. Grant*. 2 vols. New York: Century Company, 1885–86.

Grodzins, Morton. *The Loyal and the Disloyal: Social Boundaries of Patriotism and Treason*. Chicago: University of Chicago Press, 1956.

Haber, Samuel. "The Professions and Higher Education in America." In
Higher Education and the Labor Market, edited by Margaret S. Gordon,
pp. 237–80. New York: McGraw Hill, 1974.

Hale, William Bayard. "The Pension Carnival." *World's Work*, October
1910, pp. 13485–504; November 1910, pp. 13611–26; December 1910,
pp. 13731–47; January 1911, pp. 13917–28; February 1911, pp. 13967–
77; and March 1911, pp. 14159–70.

Hall, E. H. "Civil War Pensions." *Proceedings of the Massachusetts Historical Society* 42 (February 1909): 113–33.

Harte, Bret. *Writings of Bret Harte*. New York: Houghton Mifflin Riverside
Edition, 1912.

Harwood, W. S. "Secret Societies in America," *North American Review*
164 (May 1897): 620.

Haskell, Thomas. *The Emergence of Professional Social Science*. Urbana:
University of Illinois Press, 1977.

Hayes, Carlton J. H. *Essays on Nationalism*. New York: Macmillan, 1926. Reprint. New York: Russell and Russell, 1966.

———. *The Historical Evolution of Modern Nationalism*. New York: R. R. Smith, 1931. Reprint. New York: Russell and Russell, 1966.

Heck, Frank H. *The Civil War Veteran in Minnesota Life and Politics*. Oxford, Ohio: Mississippi Valley Press, 1941.

Higham, John. *Strangers in the Land: Patterns of American Nativism, 1860–1925*. New Brunswick, N.J.: Rutgers University Press, 1955.

Hirshson, Stanley P. *Farewell to the Bloody Shirt: Northern Republicans and the Southern Negro, 1877–1893*. Bloomington: Indiana University Press, 1962.

History of Northern Wisconsin. Chicago: Western Historical Co., 1881.

History of the Gift of Six Hundred National Flags to the Schools of Porto Rico by Lafayette Post No. 140, 1898. New York: Lafayette Post, 1899.

Hitchcock, Henry. *Marching with Sherman: Passages from the Letters and Camp Diaries of Henry Hitchcock*. Edited by M. A. DeWolfe Howe. New Haven: Yale University Press, 1927.

Hobsbawm, E. J. *Nations and Nationalism since 1780: Programme, Myth, Reality*. New York: Cambridge University Press, 1990.

Hobsbawm, Eric, and Terence Ranger, eds. *The Invention of Tradition*. New York: Cambridge University Press, 1983.

Hofstadter, Richard. *Social Darwinism in American Thought*. New York: G. Braziller, 1959.

"How Shall the Pension List Be Revised?" *North American Review* 156 (April 1893): 416–31.

Howe, Daniel Walker, ed. *Victorian America*. Philadelphia: University of Pennsylvania Press, 1976.

Huntington, Samuel P. *The Soldier and the State: The Theory and Politics of Civil-Military Relations*. Cambridge: Harvard University Press, 1957.

Hyman, Harold M. *A More Perfect Union: The Impact of the Civil War and Reconstruction on the Constitution*. New York: Alfred A. Knopf, 1973.

Ingham, John. *The Iron Barons*. Westport, Conn.: Greenwood Press, 1978.

Jackson, Kenneth. *Crabgrass Frontier: The Suburbanization of the United States*. New York: Oxford University Press, 1985.

Jones, James Pickett. *Black Jack: John A. Logan and Southern Illinois in the Civil War Era*. Tallahassee: Florida State University Press, 1967.

———. *John A. Logan: Stalwart Republican from Illinois*. Tallahassee: Florida State University Press, 1982.

Judson, Pieter M. " 'Whether Race or Conviction Should Be the Standard': National Identity and Liberal Politics in Nineteenth-Century Austria." *Austrian History Yearbook* 22: 76–95.

Kammen, Michael. *A Season of Youth: The American Revolution and the Historical Imagination*. New York: Alfred A. Knopf, 1978.

Katz, Michael B., Michael J. Doucet, and Mark S. Stern. "Migration and the Social Order in Erie County, New York: 1885." *Journal of Interdisciplinary History* 8, no. 4 (Spring 1978): 669–701.

Kedourie, Elie. *Nationalism*. London: Hutchinson and Company, 1960.

Kemp, Thomas R. "Community and War: The Civil War Experience of Two New Hampshire Towns." In *Toward a Social History of the American Civil War: Exploratory Essays*, edited by Maris A. Vinovskis, pp. 31–77. New York: Cambridge University Press, 1990.

Kerber, Linda K. *Women of the Republic: Intellect and Ideology in Revolutionary America*. Chapel Hill: University of North Carolina Press, 1980.

Kertzer, David I. *Ritual, Politics, and Power*. New Haven: Yale University Press, 1988.

Kilmer, George. "The GAR As Seen from the Inside." *Century*, vol. 40, May 1890, pp. 154–56.

———. "A Note of Peace." *Century*, vol. 36, July 1888, pp. 440–42.

Kingman, Bradford. *History of Brockton*. Syracuse, N.Y.: D. Mason, 1895.

Kinsel, Amy J. "From These Honored Dead: Gettysburg in American History and Culture." Ph.D. dissertation, Cornell University, 1990.

Kohn, Hans. *American Nationalism*. New York: Macmillan, 1957.

———. *The Idea of Nationalism*. New York: Macmillan, 1945.

Lankevich, George J. "The Grand Army of the Republic in New York State, 1865–1898." Ph.D. dissertation, Columbia University, 1967.

Leech, Margaret. *Reveille in Washington, 1860–1865*. New York: Harper and Brothers, 1941.

Leed, Eric J. *No Man's Land: Combat and Identity in World War I*. New York: Cambridge University Press, 1979.

Leiby, James. *A History of Social Welfare and Social Work in the United States*. New York: Columbia University Press, 1978.

Leonard, Albert C., comp. *The GAR Handbook*. Lancaster, Pa.: A. C. Leonard, 1884.

Leonard, Thomas. *Above the Battle: War-Making in America from Appomattox to Versailles*. New York: Oxford University Press, 1978.

Leoser, Charles McK. "The Grand Army as a Pension Agency." *Forum*, vol. 15, July 1893, pp. 522–31.

Lester, John C., and D. L. Wilson. *Ku Klux Klan: Its Origin, Growth, and Disbandment*. New York and Washington: Neale Publishing Co., 1905.

Levine, Peter. "Draft Evasion in the North during the Civil War, 1863–1865." *Journal of American History* 67, no. 4 (March 1981): 816–34.

Linden-Ward, Blanche. "Putting the Past under Grass: History as Death and Cemetery Commemoration. *Prospects* 10 (1985): 279–314.

———. "Strange But Genteel Pleasure Grounds: Tourist and Leisure Uses of Nineteenth-Century Rural Cemeteries." In *Cemeteries and Gravemarkers: Voices in American Culture*, edited by Richard E. Meyer. Ann Arbor: University of Michigan Press, 1989.

Linderman, Gerald. *Embattled Courage: The Experience of Combat in the American Civil War*. New York: Free Press, 1987.

———. *The Mirror of War: American Society and the Spanish-American War*. Ann Arbor: University of Michigan Press, 1974.

Lisowski, Lori A. "The Future of West Point: Senate Debates on the Military Academy during the Civil War." *Civil War History* 34, no. 1 (March 1988): 5–21.

Livesay, Harold. *Andrew Carnegie and the Rise of Big Business*. Boston: Little, Brown, 1975.

Logan, John Alexander. *The Great Conspiracy: Its Origin and History*. New York: A. R. Hart and Co., 1886.

———. *The Volunteer Soldier of America*. New York and Chicago: R. S. Peale and Co., 1887.

Long, E. B., comp., with Barbara Long. *The Civil War Day by Day*. Garden City, N.Y.: Doubleday, 1971.

Lonn, Ella. *Desertion during the Civil War*. New York: Century Company, 1928.

———. *Foreigners in the Union Army and Navy*. Baton Rouge: Louisiana State University Press, 1952.

Love, Alfred H. "Military Instruction in Schools, Churches, and Colleges." *American Journal of Politics* 5 (August 1894): 205–11.

Lowenthal, David. *The Past is a Foreign Country*. New York: Cambridge University Press, 1985.

May, Henry. *Protestant Churches and Industrial America*. Cambridge: Harvard University Press, 1949.

McConnell, Stuart. "A Social History of the Grand Army of the Republic, 1867–1900." Ph.D. dissertation, Johns Hopkins University, 1987.

———. "Who Joined the Grand Army? Three Case Studies in the Construction of Union Veteranhood, 1866–1900." In *Toward a Social History of the American Civil War: Exploratory Essays*, edited by Maris A. Vinovskis, pp. 139–70. New York: Cambridge University Press, 1990.

McCoy, Drew R. *The Elusive Republic: Political Economy in Jeffersonian America*. Chapel Hill: University of North Carolina Press, 1980.

McFeely, William S. *Grant: A Biography*. New York: W. W. Norton, 1981.

McMurray, Donald L. "The Political Significance of the Pension Question, 1885–1897." *Mississippi Valley Historical Review* 9, no. 1 (June 1922): 20–36.

McPherson, James M. *Battle Cry of Freedom: The Civil War Era*. New York: Oxford University Press, 1988.

———. *Ordeal by Fire: The Civil War and Reconstruction*. New York: Alfred A. Knopf, 1982.

Merrill, George S. "The Grand Army of the Republic in Massachusetts." *New England Magazine*, vol. 4, no. 2 (o.s.), February 1886, pp. 113–21.

Meyer, Balthasar H. "Fraternal Beneficiary Societies in the United States." *American Journal of Sociology* 6, no. 5 (March 1901): 646–61.

"Military Instruction in Schools and Colleges: An Open Letter by Ex-President Harrison." *Century*, vol. 47, no. 3 (vol. 25, n.s.), January 1894, pp. 468–69.

"Military Morality." *Nation*, vol. 69, October 12, 1899, pp. 273–74.

"Military Training in Schools." *Harper's Weekly*, vol. 38, February 9, 1895, p. 127.

Minott, Rodney. *Peerless Patriots*. Washington, D.C.: Public Affairs Press, 1962.

Mitchell, Reid. *Civil War Soldiers: Their Expectations and Their Experiences*. New York: Viking Penguin, 1988.

———. "The Northern Soldier and His Community." In *Toward a Social History of the American Civil War: Exploratory Essays*, edited by Maris A. Vinovskis, pp. 78–92. New York: Cambridge University Press, 1990.

Montgomery, David. *Beyond Equality: Labor and the Radical Republicans, 1862–1872*. New York: Alfred A. Knopf, 1967.

Moorhead, James. *American Apocalypse: Yankee Protestants and the Civil War, 1860–1869*. New Haven: Yale University Press, 1978.

Mosse, George L. *The Nationalization of the Masses: Political Symbolism and Mass Movements in Germany from the Napoleonic Wars through the Third Reich*. New York: Howard Fertig, 1975.

Mottelay, Paul F., and T. C. Campbell. *The Soldier in Our Civil War*. New York: Stanley-Bradley Publishing Co., 1885.

Nagel, Paul C. *This Sacred Trust: American Nationality, 1798–1898*. New York: Oxford University Press, 1971.

"The New Pension Policy." *Nation*, vol. 49, May 30, 1889, pp. 438–39.

Noyes, Elmer Edward. "A History of the Grand Army of the Republic in Ohio from 1866 to 1900." Ph.D. dissertation, Ohio State University, 1945.

Oakes, James. "From Republicanism to Liberalism: Ideological Change in the Old South." *American Quarterly* 37, no. 4 (Fall 1985): 551–71.

Oestreicher, Richard Jules. *Solidarity and Fragmentation: Working People and Class Consciousness in Detroit, 1875–1900*. Urbana: University of Illinois Press, 1986.

———. "Urban Working-Class Political Behavior and Theories of American Electoral Politics." *Journal of American History* 74, no. 4 (March 1988): 1257–86.

"Our Schoolboy Soldiers." *Munsey's Magazine*, vol. 15, July 1896, pp. 459–66.

Painter, Nell Irvin. *Standing at Armageddon: The United States, 1877–1919*. New York: W. W. Norton, 1987.

Painter, Nell Irvin, Richard Wightman Fox, Roy Rosenzweig, and Thomas Bender. "A Round Table: Synthesis in American History." *Journal of American History* 74, no. 1 (June 1987): pp. 109–30.

Paludan, Phillip S. *A People's Contest: The Union and Civil War, 1861–1865*. New York: Harper and Row, 1988.

"Patriotic Societies of the Civil War," *Munsey's Magazine*, vol. 15, January 1896, pp. 322–31.

Paul, James Laughery. *Pennsylvania's Soldiers' Orphan Schools*. Harrisburg, Pa.: L. S. Hart, 1877.

"Pension Legislation." *Public Opinion*, vol. 2, February 12, 1887, p. 369.

"Pension Reform." *Harper's Weekly*, vol. 37, June 17, 1893, p. 566.

"The Pension Settlement." *Nation*, vol. 50, May 19, 1890, p. 482.

"The Pension Sharks." *Nation*, vol. 49, March 28, 1889, p. 255.

"Playing with Fire." *Dial* (Chicago), vol. 20, May 16, 1896, pp. 293– 95.

Post, Robert C., ed. *A Treatise Upon Selected Aspects of the Great Interna-
tional Exhibition Held in Philadelphia on the Occasion of our Nation's
One-Hundredth Birthday, with Some Reference to Another Exhibition
Held in Washington Commemorating that Epic Event and Called 1876, A
Centennial Exhibition.* Washington: National Museum of History and
Technology, Smithsonian Institution, 1976.

*The Presentation of Flags to the Schools of Portsmouth, New Hampshire,
October 9, 1890, by Storer Post #1, Grand Army of the Republic, Department of New Hampshire.* [Portsmouth, N.H., 1890].

*Presentation of National Flags to the Public Schools of the City of Roches-
ter on Washington's Birthday, 1889, in the City Hall, by George H.
Thomas Post #4, Department of New York, Grand Army of the Republic.*
Rochester, N.Y.: Democrat and Chronicle Printers, 1889.

"The President and the GAR." *Public Opinion*, vol. 3, September 10, 1887,
pp. 453–56.

"President Cleveland and the GAR." *Public Opinion*, vol. 3, June 18, 1887,
pp. 209–12.

"President Cleveland and the Soldiers." *Nation*, vol. 45, July 14, 1887, pp.
26–27.

Preuss, Arthur, comp. *Dictionary of Secret and Other Societies.* St. Louis:
B. Herder Book Co., 1924.

Primm, James N. "The G.A.R. in Missouri, 1866–1870." *Journal of Southern History* 20 (August 1954): pp. 356–75.

Randolph, Carmen. "Surplus Revenue." *Political Science Quarterly* 3, no. 2
(1888): 226–48.

Raum, Green B. "Pensions and Patriotism." *North American Review* 153
(August 1891): 205–14.

Reinders, Robert. "Militia and Public Order in Nineteenth-Century America." *Journal of American Studies* 11, no. 1 (April 1977): 81–101.

"The Reunion of the Grand Army of the Republic." *Harper's Weekly*, vol.
34, August 23, 1890, pp. 655–57.

Richey, Russell E., and Donald C. Jones, eds. *American Civil Religion.* New
York: Harper and Row, 1974.

Robbins, William G. "Opportunity and Persistence in the Pacific Northwest: A Quantitative Study of Early Roseburg, Oregon." *Pacific Historical
Review* 39, no. 3 (August 1970): 279–96.

Rodgers, Daniel T. *The Work Ethic in Industrial America, 1850–1920.* Chicago: University of Chicago Press, 1978.

Ronne, A. B. "The Spirit of Militarism." *Popular Science Monthly*, vol. 47,
June 1895, pp. 234–38.

Rorabaugh, W. J. "Who Fought for the North in the Civil War? Concord,
Massachusetts, Enlistments." *Journal of American History* 73, no. 3 (December 1986), pp. 695–701.

Rosenzweig, Roy. *Eight Hours for What We Will: Workers and Leisure in an
Industrial City, 1870–1920.* New York: Cambridge University Press, 1983.

Ross, Dorothy. "Historical Consciousness in Nineteenth-Century America." *American Historical Review* 89, no. 4 (October 1984): 909–28.

"The Sanctity of the Grand Army." *Nation*, vol. 60, April 25, 1895, pp. 318–19.

Schlesinger, Arthur M. "Biography of a Nation of Joiners." *American Historical Review* 50, no. 4 (October 1944): 1–25.

Scott, Anne Firor. *Making the Invisible Woman Visible*. Urbana: University of Illinois Press, 1984.

Segal, Daniel A. "Nationalism, Comparatively Speaking," *Journal of Historical Sociology* 1, no. 3 (September 1988): 301–21.

Semmel, Georg. "The Sociology of Secrecy and of Secret Societies." *American Journal of Sociology* 11, no. 4 (January 1906): 441–98.

"The Service Pension Bill." *Nation*, vol. 50, May 8, 1890, p. 369.

Severo, Richard. *The Wages of War: When America's Soldier's Came Home—from Valley Forge to Vietnam*. New York: Simon and Schuster, 1989.

Shannon, Fred A. *The Organization and Administration of the Union Army, 1861–1865*. 2 vols. Cleveland: Arthur H. Clark Company, 1928.

Shalhope, Robert. "Republicanism and Early American Historiography." *William and Mary Quarterly* 39, no. 2 (1982): 334–56.

———. "Toward a Republican Synthesis: The Emergence of an Understanding of Republicanism in American Historiography." *William and Mary Quarterly* 29, no. 2 (1972): 49–80.

Shapiro, Henry D. "Putting the Past under Glass: Preservation and the Idea of History in the Mid-Nineteenth Century." *Prospects* 10 (1985): 243–78.

Sherman, William T. "Camp-Fires of the GAR." *North American Review* 147 (November 1888): 497–502.

———. *Personal Memoirs of William T. Sherman*. 2 vols. New York: D. Appleton, 1875, 1886.

Shy, John. *A People Numerous and Armed: Reflections on the Military Struggle for American Independence*. New York: Oxford University Press, 1976.

Sloane, David Charles. *The Last Great Necessity: Cemeteries in American History*. Baltimore: Johns Hopkins University Press, 1991.

Sloane, William M. "Pensions and Socialism." *Century*, vol. 42, June 1891, pp. 179–88.

Slocum, Henry W. "Pensions—Time to Call a Halt." *Forum*, vol. 12, January 1892, pp. 646–51.

Smalley, Eugene. "The United States Pension Office." *Century*, vol. 28, July 1884, pp. 427–34.

Smith, Anthony D., ed. *Nationalist Movements*. New York: St. Martin's Press, 1976.

Souvenir of the 24th National Encampment (Boston, 1890).

"A Spot Cash Party." *Nation*, vol. 49, October 10, 1889, p. 286.

Stearns, Peter. *Be a Man! Males in Modern Society*. New York: Holmes and Meier, 1979.

Stephenson, Mary Harriet. *Dr. B. F. Stephenson, Founder of the G.A.R.: A Memoir.* Springfield, Ill.: H. W. Rokker, 1894.

Stevens, Albert C., comp. *The Cyclopaedia of Fraternities.* 2d ed. New York: E. B. Treat, 1907.

Susman, Warren I. "'Personality' and the Making of Twentieth-Century Culture." In *New Directions in American Intellectual History,* edited by John Higham and Paul Conkin, pp. 212–26. Baltimore: Johns Hopkins University Press, 1979.

Swanberg, W. A. *Citizen Hearst: A Biography of William Randolph Hearst.* New York: Scribner, 1961.

Tebbel, John. *A History of Book Publishing in America.* 3 vols. New York: R. R. Bowker, 1972–81.

Thernstrom, Stephen. *The Other Bostonians: Poverty and Progress in an American Metropolis, 1880–1970.* Cambridge: Harvard University Press, 1973.

———. *Poverty and Progress: Social Mobility in a Nineteenth-Century City.* Cambridge: Harvard University Press, 1964.

Thomas, John L. *Alternative America: Henry George, Edward Bellamy, Henry Demarest Lloyd, and the Adversary Tradition.* Cambridge: Harvard University Press, 1983.

Tilney, Robert. *My Life in the Army.* Philadelphia: Ferris and Leach, 1912.

Trachtenberg, Alan. *The Incorporation of America: Culture and Society in the Gilded Age.* New York: Hill and Wang, 1982.

Trattner, Walter I. *From Poor Law to Welfare State: A History of Social Welfare in America.* New York: Free Press, 1974.

Turner, Victor W. *The Ritual Process: Structure and Anti-Structure.* New York: Aldine, 1969.

Tuttle, William M., Jr. *Race Riot: Chicago in the Red Summer of 1919.* New York: Atheneum, 1970.

Underwood, Kathleen. *Town Building on the Colorado Frontier.* Albuquerque: University of New Mexico Press, 1987.

Unger, Irwin. *The Greenback Era: A Social and Political History of American Finance, 1865–1879.* Princeton, N.J.: Princeton University Press, 1964.

United States Bureau of the Census. *Compendium of the Eleventh Census, 1890.* Washington, D.C.: U.S. Government Printing Office, 1892.

———. *Historical Statistics of the United States, Colonial Times to 1970.* Washington, D.C.: U.S. Government Printing Office, 1976.

United States Centennial Commission. *Grounds and Buildings of the Centennial Exhibition, Philadelphia, 1876.* Washington, D.C.: U.S. Government Printing Office, 1880.

"An Unpleasant Contrast." *Nation,* vol. 50, May 15, 1890, p. 386.

Upson, Theodore F. *With Sherman to the Sea: The Civil War Diaries and Reminiscences of Theodore F. Upson.* Edited by Osburn Winther. Bloomington, Ind.: Indiana University Press, 1958.

Verdery, Katherine. *Transylvanian Villagers: Three Centuries of Political,*

Economic, and Ethnic Change. Berkeley: University of California Press, 1983.

Vinovskis, Maris A. "Have Social Historians Lost the Civil War? Some Preliminary Demographic Speculations." In *Toward a Social History of the American Civil War: Exploratory Essays*, edited by Maris A. Vinovskis, pp. 1– 30. New York: Cambridge University Press, 1990.

The Volcano Under the City, By a Volunteer Special. New York: Fords, Howard, and Hulbert, 1887.

Wainwright, Charles S. *A Diary of Battle: The Personal Journals of Colonel Charles S. Wainwright.* Edited by Allan Nevins. New York: Harcourt, Brace, and World, 1962.

Waite, Edward F. "Pensions: The Law and Its Administration." *Harper's Magazine*, vol. 86, January 1893, pp. 235–43.

Walkowitz, Daniel J. *Worker City, Company Town: Iron and Cotton-Worker Protest in Troy and Cohoes, New York, 1855–84.* Urbana: University of Illinois Press, 1978.

Walters, Ronald G. *American Reformers, 1815–1860.* New York: Hill and Wang, 1978.

Warner, John DeWitt. "Half a Million Dollars a Day for Pensions." *Forum*, vol. 15, June 1893, pp. 439–51.

Warner, Sam Bass. *Streetcar Suburbs: The Process of Growth in Boston, 1870–1900.* Cambridge: Harvard University Press, 1962.

Warner, W. Lloyd. *The Living and the Dead.* New Haven: Yale University Press, 1959.

Weber, Thomas. *The Northern Railroads in the Civil War, 1861–1865.* New York: King's Crown Press, 1952.

Weld, Stephen Minot. *War Diaries and Letters of Stephen Minot Weld, 1861–1865.* Boston: Massachusetts Historical Society, 1977.

Whalen, William J. *Handbook of Secret Organizations.* Milwaukee: Bruce Publishing Company, 1966.

"Who Are Excluded." *Nation*, vol. 60, May 2, 1895, pp. 336–37.

Wickersham, James Pyle. *A History of Education in Pennsylvania.* Lancaster, Pa.: Inquirer Publishing Company, 1886. Reprint. New York: Arno Press, 1969.

Wiebe, Robert H. *The Search for Order, 1877–1920.* New York: Hill and Wang, 1967.

———. *The Segmented Society: An Introduction to the Meaning of America.* New York: Oxford University Press, 1975.

Wilentz, Sean. *Chants Democratic: New York City and the Rise of the American Working Class, 1788–1850.* New York: Oxford University Press, 1984.

Wiley, Bell Irvin. *The Life of Billy Yank.* Indianapolis: Bobbs-Merrill, 1952.

———. *The Life of Johnny Reb.* Indianapolis: Bobbs-Merrill, 1943.

Williams, T. Harry. "The Attack on West Point during the Civil War." *Mississippi Valley Historical Review* 25, no. 4 (March 1939): 491–504.

Wilson, Charles Reagan. *Baptized in Blood: The Religion of the Lost Cause, 1865–1920*. Athens, Ga.: University of Georgia Press, 1980.

Wilson, Edmund. *Patriotic Gore: Studies in the Literature of the American Civil War*. New York: Farrar, Straus, and Giroux, 1962.

Wilson, John F. *Public Religion in American Culture*. Philadelphia: Temple University Press, 1979.

Wilson, Oliver M. *The Grand Army of the Republic under Its First Constitution and Ritual*. Kansas City, Mo.: Franklin Hudson Publishing Company, 1905.

Woods, Paul Joseph. "The GAR and Civil Service." Ph.D. dissertation, University of Illinois, 1941.

Wright, Chester. "The More Enduring Consequences of America's Wars." *Journal of Economic History*, supp. (December 1943): 9–26.

Wyllie, Irvin G. *The Self-Made Man in America: The Myth of Rags to Riches*. New York: Free Press, 1954.

Zelinsky, Wilbur. *Nation into State: The Shifting Symbolic Foundations of American Nationalism*. Chapel Hill: University of North Carolina Press, 1990.

INDEX

career of, 114; galvanizes GAR, 139–40, 145, 147–48; favors immigration restriction, 208, 210; on labor, 211–12

Leonard, Thomas, 21, 174

Leoser, Charles McKnight, 163

Liminality, veterans and, 22–23, 24

Lincoln, Abraham, xii, 28; assassins of, 2

Linderman, Gerald, xii, 167, 235

Linehan, John, 130

Lippert, E. G., 42

Localism: and veterans after Civil War, 10–13; in early GAR, 29–30

Logan, John Alexander, xiv, 6, 20, 30, 31, 36, 45, 83, 106, 107, 109, 112, 129, 182, 187, 193, 212, 213, 224, 225, 230; and GAR founding, 25; reorganizes GAR, 25–28; and war reminiscence, 181, 185–86; and Memorial Day, 183; career of, 193–96; monument to, 194; proposes militia reform, 196–97; attacks West Point, 197; writes *Volunteer Soldier of America*, 197–99; and spread-eagle oratory, 201

Loring, Edward, 155

Louisiana, GAR affairs in, 29, 216, 217

Lovering, Joseph, 107

Low, Seth, 230

Lynch, Frank, 61, 113

McAfee, John, 135

McCullough, Joseph, 131

McElroy, John, 106

McFeeley, William, 169

McKinley, William, 182, 236

McMaster, John Bach, 225

Maine (battleship), 233

Maine, GAR affairs in, 142

Manliness, 105–9; fraternal rituals and, 86; blackball undercuts, 112; and charity, 135–36; and pensions, 161–62; and Civil War service, 163

"Marching through Georgia," 180

March to the Sea, 5–6, 169, 171

Maryland, GAR affairs in, 32

Masonry, 38, 42, 79, 85–88, 93, 103, 104, 202, 208; grade system of, 31; segregation in, 213

Massachusetts, GAR affairs in, 142, 143, 180, 184. *See also* Andrew Post; Webster Post 13

Meade, George G., 2, 7, 12, 13, 122, 169, 195

Meade, Richard, 228

Meade Post 1, Philadelphia, 55, 56

Medical services, as charity, 128–29

Memorial Day, xiii, 16, 25, 115, 126, 180, 201, 203, 218; UVL and GAR dispute over, 121; as a funeral service, 183–87; and Confederate veterans, 184, 190–91; churches and, 254–55 (n. 66)

Merrill, George, 114, 151, 155, 204

Mexican War, veterans of, 12

Michigan, GAR affairs in, 32, 111, 143

Milford, Mass., 79

Militarism: wartime fear of, 7; and GAR, 28, 183

Military drill. *See* Drill, military, in schools

Militias, 122; antebellum, 46–47, 48; compared with GAR, 47–51, 247 (n. 85); in Civil War, 196–97; as alternatives to military academies, 199; during railroad strikes (1877), 246 (n. 84)

Miller, C. W., pro-pension argument of, 160–61

Miller, John C., 170

Miller, Roswell, 134

Minnesota, GAR affairs in, 32, 42, 44, 45, 143

Mississippi, GAR affairs in, 216, 217

Missouri, GAR affairs in, 29, 32

Mitchell, Reid, xii